The Longman Companion to
Russia since 1914

Longman Companions to History

General Editors: Chris Cook and John Stevenson

Now available

The Longman Companion to

Russia since 1914

Martin McCauley

Longman
London and New York

Addison Wesley Longman Limited
Edinburgh Gate,
Harlow, Essex CM20 2JE,
United Kingdom
and Associated Companies throughout the world

*Published in the United States of America
by Addison Wesley Longman Inc., New York*

DK266
.M353
1998x

© Addison Wesley Longman Limited 1998

First published 1998

ISBN 0 582 27640 3   CSD
      0 582 27639 X   PPR

British Library Cataloguing in Publication Data

A catalogue record for this book is available from the British Library

Library of Congress Cataloging-in-Publication Data

McCauley, Martin.
    The Longman companion to Russia since 1914 / Martin McCauley.
        p.   cm. — (Longman companions to history)
    Includes bibliographical references and index.
        ISBN 0–582–27640–3 (cloth). — ISBN 0–582–27639–X (pbk.)
        1. Soviet Union—History—Handbooks, manuals, etc.   2. Soviet
Union—History—Chronology.   3. Russia (Federation)—History—1991—
Handbooks, manuals, etc.   4. Russia (Federation)—History—1991—
Chronology.   I. Title.   II. Series.
DK266.M353   1997
947′.002′02—dc21   97–14166
                                                                                      CIP

Set in 35 by 9$\frac{1}{2}$/12pt New Baskerville
Produced by Longman Singapore Publishers (Pte) Ltd.
Printed in Singapore

Contents

Acknowledgements

The publishers would like to thank the following for permission to reproduce copyright material: Cambridge University Press for the tables: *Russian and Soviet gross national product (GNP), 1913–40* (p. 322); *Gross domestic product (GDP) per head of the USSR in international comparison, 1913–40 ($ and 1980 prices)* (p. 323); *Real GDP by sector of origin, 1937–44 (billion rubles and 1937 factor cost)* (p. 323); *Real burden of defence outlays, 1940–44 (billion rubles at 1937 factor cost)* (p. 324); *Labour productivity in large-scale industry, 1913–21* (p. 325); and *The main economic indicators* (p. 328); Macmillan Ltd for the table *Fulfilment of the principal goals of the Stalinist Five Year Plans 1928–50 (%)* (p. 326); and Europe-Asia Studies for the table *Performance 1928–90 according to G. I. Khanin*.

List of maps

List of abbreviations, acronyms and terms

APR	Agrarian Party of Russia
CC	Central Committee (of the Communist Party)
CCC	Central Control Commission
CFE	conventional forces in Europe (talks and treaty)
Cheka	Political or Secret Police (also known at various times as GPU, OGPU, NKVD, MVD, MGB and KGB)
CIS	Commonwealth of Independent States
CMEA	Council for Mutual Assistance (also known as Comecon)
Comecon	Council for Mutual Assistance
Cominform	Communist Information Bureau
Comintern	Communist International
CPRF	Communist Party of the Russian Federation
CPSU	Communist Party of the Soviet Union (formerly RSDRP, RCP(B) and CPSU(B))
CPSU(B)	Communist Party of the Soviet Union (Bolshevik) (becomes CPSU)
CSCE	European Conference of Security and Cooperation
dacha	country house
FRG	Federal Republic of Germany
FYP	Five Year Plan
GDR	German Democratic Republic
GKO	State Committee for Defence
Gosplan	State Planning Commission
GPU	Main Political Administration (see Cheka)
guberniya	province
gulag	forced labour camp
ICBM	intercontinental ballistic missile
INF	intermediate-range nuclear missiles
KGB	Committee of State Security (see Cheka)
kolkhoz	collective farm
krai	administrative-territorial division (usually contains an autonomous oblast within its boundaries)
kulak	better-off peasant
MRC	Military Revolutionary Committee (of the Petrograd soviet)
MVD	Ministry of Internal Affairs (see Cheka)
NATO	North Atlantic Treaty Organisation

NEP	New Economic Policy
NKVD	People's Commissariat of Internal Affairs (see Cheka)
oblast	administrative-territorial division
OGPU	see Cheka
okrug	region (subdivision of oblast)
Orgburo	Organisational Bureau of the CC
Politburo	Political Bureau of the CC
raion	administrative-territorial division
RCP(B)	Russian Communist Party (Bolshevik) (becomes CPSU(B) and CPSU)
RSDRP	Russian Social Democratic Labour (Workers') Party (becomes RCP(B), CPSU(B) and CPSU)
RSFSR	Russian Soviet Federated Socialist Republic
SALT	strategic arms limitation talks
SDI	Strategic Defence Initiative (also known as Star Wars)
SLBM	submarine-launched ballistic missile
sovkhoz	state farm
Sovnarkhoz	Council of the National Economy
Sovnarkom	Council of People's Commissars (the government, in 1946 becomes the USSR Council of Ministers
SRs	Socialist Revolutionaries
START	strategic arms reduction talks
TASS	Telegraphic Agency of the Soviet Union
TsIK	Central Executive Committee
uezd	administrative-territorial division
USSR	Union of Soviet Socialist Republics
volost	county
VSNKh	Supreme Council of the National Economy

SECTION ONE

Chronology

Chronology

Note: Until 1 February 1918 the Russians used the Julian (named after Julius Caesar) calendar. In the twentieth century it was 13 days behind the Gregorian (named after Pope Gregory) calendar used in the rest of Europe. All the dates until 1 February 1918 are given in the Julian calendar. If you want to express all these dates in the Gregorian calendar, just add 13 days. Thus 25 October becomes 7 November 1917, and so on. Hence the February Revolution took place in March according to the Gregorian calendar and the October Revolution happened in November, by the same token.

The First World War, 1914–17

1914
1 January: One of the results of a strike in the Putilov works in St Petersburg is the establishment of an enterprise health fund.
June–July: General strikes in Baku and St Petersburg.
12 July: Russia decides to support Serbia.
15 July: After the murder of the heir to the throne, Franz Ferdinand, and his wife, in Sarajevo, Austria-Hungary declares war on Serbia.
16 July: Partial Russian mobilisation, restricted to the Kiev, Kharkov, Moscow and Kazan military districts.
18 July: General mobilisation in Russia. Germany issues an ultimatum to Russia to stop preparing for war within 12 hours.
19 July: Germany declares war on Russia. Grand Duke Nikolai Nikolaevich is named Commander-in-Chief of all Russian forces.
24 July: Austria-Hungary declares war on Russia.
4 August: The Russian commander of the Vilno (now Vilnius) military district, General Paul Edler von Rennenkampff, and his troops cross the border into East Prussia and begin hostilities.
5 August–8 September: Russian forces drive Austro-Hungarian troops out of East Galicia and the Bukovina.
11–24 August: The Allies (France, Great Britain and Russia) agree not to sign a separate peace with the Central Powers. Japan joins this agreement on 27 August.

13–17 August: The battle of Tannenberg. The 2nd Russian army (Narev army) is surrounded and destroyed by the German 8th army under Hindenburg.

18 August: St Petersburg is renamed Petrograd.

24 August–2 September: The battle of the Mazurian lakes forces the 1st Russian army (Nemen army) to retreat from East Prussia back to Russia.

15 September–26 October: Russian and German armies fight to a standstill after great set-piece battles at Warsaw and Ivangorod. The war becomes a war of attrition.

5 November: The members of the Bolshevik faction in the Fourth Duma (see p. 152) are arrested in Petrograd and after a trial (10–13 February 1915) are exiled to Siberia.

1915

19 February: The claim by Russia to the Straits and Istanbul, contained in an official note by the Russian Foreign Minister, S. D. Sazonov, to the British and French ambassadors, is accepted by Great Britain (27 February) and by France (28 March).

9 March: The Austro-Hungarian fortress of Przemysl in Galicia falls to Russian troops after almost five months (since 26 October 1914).

14–26 April: A German offensive takes Lithuania and Courland from Russia.

28 June: A conference of Social Revolutionaries (SRs), Popular Socialists and Trudoviki passes a resolution on saving the motherland.

July: 1st Congress of the War Industries Committee is founded by resolution of the 9th Russian Congress of Trade and Industry, on 27–28 May 1915, to improve the collaboration of government, industry and workers in the defence industry, chaired by A. I. Guchkov. Soon 200 local committees are set up. They are dissolved by the Bolsheviks on 24 July 1918.

9 August: The bourgeois parties in the Fourth Duma (Kadets, Octobrists, Progressives, Centre faction, Progressive Nationalists, altogether about three-quarters of the deputies) form the Progressive Bloc. They demand a government of national confidence, domestic political concessions and reforms.

23 August: The Tsar personally takes over as Commander-in-Chief of Russian forces and relieves Grand Duke Nikolai Nikolaevich of his command.

23–26 August: The Zimmerwald conference of the Socialist International, attended by Lenin, whose slogan 'transform the imperialist war into a civil war' fails to obtain a majority. It adopts Kautsky's (German Social Democratic Party) position of no active revolutionary activity during wartime.

2–7 October: Bulgaria joins the Central Powers and declares war on Great Britain, Russia, France and Italy.

28 December–18 February: Successful offensive of the Russian Caucasian army under General Yudenich. Turkish troops retreat on 4 January. Russian troops occupy the Erzerum fortress and Bitlis (near Lake Van).

1916
January–June: Lenin works in Bern and Zürich on his book, *Imperialism, the Highest Stage of Capitalism.*
11–17 April: Socialist International conference in Kienthal. Lenin again fails to win a majority for his views. He begins to think of setting up a 3rd International.
26 April: Secret Russian–French agreement on the partition of Turkey.
22 May–31 July: A great Russian offensive, commanded by General Brusilov, in response to the request of the western Allies for help, achieves success in the first phase in Volhynia and Bukovina. These successes lead Romania to join the war on the Allied side.
17 October: Political strikes in Petrograd.
17 December: Rasputin is murdered by Prince F. F. Yusupov.

The 1917 Revolutions

1917
31 January: Strikes and unrest in many parts of Russia, especially Petrograd.
18 February: Strike begins in the Putilov works in Petrograd.
19 February: Bread shortages begin in Petrograd.
23 February: Demonstration by women marking the socialist women's congress, joined by locked-out workers of the Putilov works.
23–24 February: First worker demonstrations in the centre of Petrograd, which lead to armed confrontation with the police and army.
25 February: The strike in Petrograd becomes a general strike. The Tsar orders the demonstrations to be dispersed by any means necessary. The troops fire on the demonstrators, causing many casualties.
26 February: Duma members refuse to obey the Tsar's edict to disband.
26–27 February: The Petrograd garrison mutinies and joins the demonstrators. This results in the victory of the February Revolution.
27 February: The Duma elects a 12-member executive committee, with members from all the leading parties, chaired by M. V. Rodzyanko. The Petrograd soviet of workers' deputies convenes for the first time, in the Tauride Palace, Petrograd. It elects a shadow government, a provisional executive committee of the soviet of workers' deputies. It is led by Kerensky and Chkheidze.
28 February: The provisional Duma committee sets up a military commission and a food commission together with the Petrograd soviet. The

first number of *Izvestiya* (news in Russian), the organ of the Petrograd soviet, appears. Elections to the Moscow soviet of workers' deputies.

1 March: The British and French governments recognise *de facto* (as a fact but not in law, not *de jure*) the provisional Duma committee. The first meeting of the Moscow soviet of workers' deputies. The Petrograd soviet becomes the soviet of workers' and soldiers' deputies after some soldiers join. Order no. 1 of the Petrograd soviet is published and envisages the formation of soldiers' committees in all units to be responsible for the control of weapons.

2 March: The provisional Duma committee announces the formation of a Provisional Government, headed by Prince G. E. Lvov. All ministers are bourgeois (Milyukov as Foreign Minister, Guchkov as War Minister) except Kerensky (SR) as Minister for Justice. Nicholas II abdicates in favour of his son, Alexei, then in favour of his brother Mikhail, who declares he will only accept the crown if offered by the Constituent Assembly.

8 March: Nicholas II is arrested and with his family is taken to Tsarskoe Tselo.

10 March: The Petrograd soviet and the Petrograd Society of Entrepreneurs agree on an eight-hour day for workers, and factory committees are to be set up.

12 March: Stalin, Kamenev and other Bolsheviks, in exile in various parts of Russia, return to Petrograd. They immediately support the policy of the Petrograd soviet and Provisional Government.

25 March: State grain monopoly introduced along with strict price control of food because of the great shortage of food.

29 March–2 April: A Russian conference of soviets decides to support the Provisional Government to the extent that it implements a 'programme of revolutionary democracy'.

3 April: Lenin, his wife Krupskaya, and other Bolsheviks return to Petrograd from Zürich.

4 April: Lenin addresses Bolsheviks and members of the soviet on the tasks of the proletariat; his address is known as the April Theses.

20–21 April: Demonstrations in Petrograd against Milyukov's note to the Allies in which he confirms Russia will continue in the war and seek to obtain 'those guarantees and sanctions which are indispensable for the prevention of sanguinary conflicts in the future'. The soviet and demonstrators see this as seeking to obtain foreign territory and eventually force Milyukov to resign.

4 May: Trotsky arrives back in Russia from exile.

7–12 May: All-Russian conference of Mensheviks and united organisations of the Russian Social Democratic Labour Party (Bolsheviks) (RSDRP(B)) fails to agree.

3–24 June: The 1st Congress (see pp. 148–9) of the soviets of the workers' and soldiers' deputies takes place in Petrograd and is dominated by the SRs and Mensheviks, the moderate socialists. The Bolsheviks, the radical or left socialists, obtain only 35 of the 256 places on the executive committee.

18 June–1 July: The Russian army goes on the offensive (the Kerensky offensive) on the south-west front, commanded by General Brusilov. By mid-July it has come to a standstill and demonstrations against the Kerensky offensive in Petrograd reveal Bolshevik slogans in the majority for the first time.

2 July: Trotsky's party, the Mezhraiontsy, which was between the Mensheviks and the Bolsheviks, resolves to merge with the Bolsheviks and this adds, among others, A. A. Ioffe and A. V. Lunacharsky to the Bolshevik cause.

3–4 July: An armed demonstration of workers in Petrograd causes the Provisional Government to declare martial law, fearing a coup, and to arrest leading Bolsheviks.

7 July: The Provisional Government occupies the Bolshevik bureau and *Pravda* (see pp. 102–3). Trotsky and Kamenev are arrested and Lenin flees to Finland (11 July).

8 July: Prince Lvov resigns and Fedor Kerensky becomes Prime Minister.

19 July: After the débâcle on the south-west front, Brusilov is replaced by General Kornilov as Russian Commander-in-Chief.

26 July–3 August: The 6th Congress of the RSDRP(B) resolves to drop the slogan 'all power to the soviets' and strengthen the Party as the 'avant-garde in the struggle against counter-revolution'.

1 August: Nicholas II and his family are moved to Tobolsk.

25–30 August: Attempt by Kornilov to occupy Petrograd and dissolve the soviet; Kerensky and Kornilov had discussed this move but Kerensky pulls out and then declares Kornilov a rebel.

1 September: Russia becomes a republic and a five-member directory under Kerensky takes over.

8–9 September: The Bolsheviks obtain a majority in the presidium of the Petrograd soviet, chaired by Trotsky.

19 September: The Bolsheviks obtain a majority in the executive committee of the Moscow soviet.

25 September: Trotsky is elected chair of the Petrograd soviet.

10 October: The Bolsheviks achieve an absolute majority in the Petrograd and Moscow soviets. A secret meeting of the Central Committee of the RSDRP(B) resolves to launch an armed uprising. Only Kamenev and Zinoviev oppose this.

12 October: The Petrograd soviet sets up a Military Revolutionary Committee (MRC) to combat counter-revolution. This then permits the Bolsheviks to organise an uprising through the MRC.

The Bolsheviks in power, 1917–18

1917

24–25 October: The October Revolution (see pp. 167–8) takes place during the night when troops and sailors occupy important points in Petrograd.

25–26 October: During the night Bolshevik units take the Winter Palace and arrest 13 Provisional Government ministers, but Kerensky escapes dressed as a female nurse. The 2nd All-Russian Congress of Soviets convenes in Petrograd and confirms the seizure of power as Bolsheviks and left SRs are in the majority. Right SRs and Mensheviks leave the congress in protest. The congress then declares that power has passed to the soviets.

26–27 October: During an all-night sitting the Congress passes the decree on peace and the decree on land. A provisional Council (Soviet) of People's Commissars (Sovnarkom) (see p. 192) is confirmed, headed by Lenin, consisting only of Bolsheviks. It will be provisional until a Constituent Assembly convenes.

3 November: The Bolsheviks finally take the Kremlin and Moscow.

12 November: Elections to the Constituent Assembly begin; SRs and Mensheviks obtain 62 per cent of the votes, the Bolsheviks 25 per cent, the Kadets and other bourgeois parties 13 per cent. However, the Bolsheviks are in the majority in the garrisons and in Moscow and Petrograd.

2 December: Russia and Germany agree on a further armistice of 28 days. The Supreme Council of the National Economy (VSNKh) (see pp. 114–15) is set up to supervise the Russian economy and is subordinate to Sovnarkom.

9 December: The Bolsheviks and left SRs agree to form a coalition government.

9–15 December: The first round of peace talks between Russia and Germany and its allies at Brest-Litovsk.

1918

12 January: The 3rd Russian Congress of Soviets adopts the declaration on the rights of workers and the oppressed people, drafted by Lenin, containing much which is included in the Russian Socialist Federal Soviet Republic (RSFSR) constitution of 10 June 1918. Russia is declared a Soviet republic and a federation of national soviet republics is to be formed. All power rests with the workers and the previous ruling class may no longer participate in the running of the state.

19 January: The Polish Legion (25,000 men) declares war on the Bolsheviks and occupies Mogilev, headquarters of the Russian Supreme Command, on 20 January and Minsk on 22 January.

27 January: Germany and its allies conclude a separate peace with the Ukrainian Central Rada. 1 February becomes 14 February as the Gregorian calendar is introduced.

23 February: The Workers' and Peasants' Red Army is founded. Mass mobilisation to save the socialist motherland.

3 March: The Brest-Litovsk Peace is signed between Russia and Germany, Austria-Hungary, Bulgaria and Turkey. Russia recognises Poland, Finland, Ukraine and the Baltic region as independent. Russia loses 26 per cent of its population, 27 per cent of its arable land, 26 per cent of its railways, 33 per cent of its textile industry, 73 per cent of its iron industry and 75 per cent of its coal industry.

6–8 March: At the 7th Bolshevik Congress the name of the Party is changed from Russian Social Democratic Labour Party (Bolsheviks) to Russian Communist Party (Bolsheviks) (RCP(B)). The Congress confirms the Brest-Litovsk Peace, proposed by Lenin, by 30 votes to 12, with Trotsky and Bukharin voting against.

Intervention and Civil War, 1918–21

1918

9 March: British troops land in Murmansk and begin the Allied Intervention. Trotsky resigns as People's Commissar for Foreign Affairs and on 8 April takes over the military.

10–11 March: The Soviet government moves from Petrograd to Moscow and on 12 March Moscow is proclaimed the capital of the Soviet state.

15 March: The 4th Congress of Soviets ratifies the Brest-Litovsk Peace and in protest the left SRs leave Sovnarkom.

5 April: Japanese troops land in Vladivostok and begin their intervention in the Russian Civil War.

8 April: Trotsky is appointed People's Commissar for War. The Red Flag with the inscription RSFSR becomes the national flag.

13 April: General Denikin takes over command of the Volunteer Army (anti-Bolshevik) after General Kornilov is killed near Ekaterinodar (now Krasnodar).

11 June: Committees of the poor (kombedy) are set up and provided with grain and agricultural implements.

July–February 1919: The Reds (Bolsheviks) defend Tsaritsyn (later Stalingrad, now Volgograd) against the Don Cossacks under Krasnov and the Volunteer Army.

4–10 July: The 5th Congress of Soviets adopts the constitution of the RSFSR. Soviets are simultaneously ruling bodies and social mass organisations of the workers. Workers are given preference over peasants in elections to these soviets. Hostile social elements, the former ruling class, priests, etc. have no vote. There are soviets at all levels – village, city, oblast and at the republican level. The chair of the Central Executive Committee (see pp. 145–6) is head of state.

6–7 July: SR uprising against the Bolsheviks in Moscow and other cities leads to the murder of the German ambassador, von Mirbach, and the arrest of Dzerzhinsky, head of the Cheka (Secret Police, see pp. 208–9), but he is soon released. The Bolsheviks suppress the uprising ruthlessly.

16–17 July: Nicholas II and his family are murdered by the Bolsheviks in Ekaterinburg, on orders from Moscow.

15–16 August: US troops land in Vladivostok and begin their intervention in the Russian Civil War.

13 November: The Soviet government annuls the treaty of Brest-Litovsk and opens the way for Soviet troops to enter formerly German-occupied areas (the Reds fail to reoccupy the Baltic States).

30 November: The Council for Workers' and Peasants' Defence is set up to mobilise all resources for the defence of Soviet power. In April 1920 it is renamed the Council for Labour and Defence (STO) and is dissolved on 28 April 1937.

1919

2–6 March: The Communist International, the Comintern or 3rd International is founded in Moscow; Zinoviev is elected its President.

18–23 March: The 8th Congress of the RCP(B) adopts a new programme, the goal of which is socialism.

30 March: Mikhail Kalinin is elected chair of the Central Executive Committee of the soviets in place of Yakov Sverdlov, who died. Hence Kalinin becomes Soviet head of state.

21 June–7 January 1920: A great offensive of the Reds on the eastern front destroys the White armies of Admiral Kolchak. The Reds capture Perm on 1 July, Ekaterinburg on 20 July, Chelyabinsk on 24 July, Omsk on 14 November and Krasnoyarsk on 7 January 1920. Kolchak retreats to Irkutsk.

11 October: Red offensive against General Denikin stops him at Tula and then rapidly drives him southwards. Voronezh is recaptured on 24 October, Kharkov on 12 December, Tsaritsyn on 4 January 1920 and Rostov on Don on 8 January.

4–14 November: The Reds bring the resistance of Kolchak's armies on the eastern front to an end.

1920

7 February: Admiral Kolchak is executed in Irkutsk by the Reds.

29 March–5 April: The 9th Congress of the RCP(B) lays down the economic tasks of the state and adopts the plan for the electrification of Russia (GOELRO).

25 April: Polish offensive (led by Josef Pilsudski) against the Soviet government, together with the anti-Bolshevik Ukrainian government of Petlyura.

26 May–16 June: The Red counter-offensive against the Polish forces is successful; Zhitomir falls on 7 July and Kiev on 12 June.

19 July–7 August: The 2nd Congress of the Comintern in Petrograd and Moscow brings together 217 delegates from 37 countries. The Comintern adopts the 21 points, drafted by Lenin, for admission to it. The headquarters of the executive committee of the Comintern is to be Moscow. The language of the Comintern was German as it expected to move to Berlin after the successful socialist revolution there.

17 November: The Reds take Yalta and within 10 days the Crimea is in Bolshevik hands. The Whites flee abroad, mainly to Yugoslavia and France. The Reds have won the Civil War.

1921

January: Menshevik and SR leaders flee abroad and the Mensheviks set up their centre in Berlin and the SRs in Paris.

22 February: A state planning commission (Gosplan) (see pp. 89–90) is established as the supreme planning authority in the country.

2–18 March: The Kronstadt uprising against Bolshevik rule (see p. 219). The island base, in the Gulf of Finland, is of great strategic importance and the Bolsheviks suppress the uprising of the sailors with huge losses on both sides.

The New Economic Policy, 1921–28

1921

8–16 March: The 10th Congress of the RCP(B) is shocked by the Kronstadt uprising and under Lenin's leadership introduces the New Economic Policy (NEP) (see pp. 96–7) and bans factionalism (organised opposition) in the Party.

22 June–12 July: The 3rd Congress of the Comintern is held in Moscow with 608 delegates from 52 countries (including 48 communist parties) attending.

1922

27 March–2 April: The 11th Party Congress; despite his declining health, Lenin delivers the main speech, reports on the successes of NEP and announces more severe measures against capitalists in the country.

3 April: Stalin is elected General Secretary (Gensek) of the RCP(B).

10 April–19 May: The Genoa conference on economic affairs fails to resolve the problem of Soviet responsibility for Tsarist debts. It is the first time that a Soviet delegation participates in an international conference. Nearby at Rapallo, Rathenau, the German Foreign Minister, and Chicherin, the Commissar for Foreign Affairs, sign the Rapallo treaty, which establishes diplomatic and trade relations.

30 December: The 1st All-Union Congress of Soviets convenes with 2,215 delegates (1,727 from the RSFSR, 364 from the Ukrainian, 91 from the Transcaucasian and 33 from the Belorussian Soviet Socialist Republics). They adopt a state treaty to establish the Union of Soviet Socialist Republics (USSR). Kalinin chairs the new Soviet executive committee.

1923

4 January: Lenin, very ill, adds a postscript to his Testament (see pp. 159–60), advising that Stalin be removed from positions of power at the centre because of character defects.

20 April: At the 12th Congress of the RCP(B) Trotsky presents a gloomy economic picture and describes the scissors crisis, caused by rising industrial and sinking agricultural prices. (Lenin is absent through illness from the Congress, 17–25 April.)

15 October: The declaration of the 46, signed by left opposition groups (see pp. 158–9), including E. Preobrazhensky, protests against Stalin and calls for free discussion within the Party. It is distributed to members of the Politburo (see pp. 175–6).

15 December: Stalin opens a campaign against 'Trotskyism' in *Pravda* in response to Trotsky's attacks against bureaucratisation (too much bureaucracy) in the Party and the lack of inner Party democracy.

1924

21 January: Lenin dies in Gorky, near Moscow, and is succeeded by three men, the triumvirate – Stalin, Kamenev and Zinoviev.

26 January–2 February: At the 2nd All-Union Congress of Soviets Stalin swears to uphold Lenin's legacy and presents himself as the leading follower of the dead leader.

27 January: Lenin's embalmed body is placed in a specially built mausoleum in Red Square, Moscow. (It is still there.)

31 January: The plenum of the Central Committee of the RCP(B) resolves, after the great purge of the Party in 1923, to concentrate on the recruitment of workers. By 1 October 1924 it had recruited 241,600 new members.

2 February: Great Britain recognises diplomatically the Soviet Union. Many other European states follow.

23–31 May: At the 13th Congress of the RCP(B), Zinoviev and Kamenev attack Trotsky, with Stalin keeping his counsel. Lenin's Letter to the Congress, in which he comments on the qualities of the leading Bolsheviks, and his postscript, in which he speaks of Stalin's character defects, are read to the Congress but it is decided not to publish them (they were first published in the Soviet Union under Gorbachev).

1925

14 January: A free labour market is re-established; those wishing to hire labour no longer need to go to official employment bureaux.

20 January: Diplomatic relations are established between the USSR and Japan, and north Sakhalin is returned to the Soviet Union.

26 January: A Party Central Committee (CC) plenum dismisses Trotsky as chair of the Revolutionary War Council and as People's Commissar for War and appoints Frunze to succeed him.

10 April: Tsaritsyn is renamed Stalingrad.

27–29 April: At the 15th Conference of the RCP(B) Stalin's concept of socialism in one country (see pp. 186–7) is adopted against the opposition of Trotsky, Kamenev and Zinoviev.

10 July: TASS (the telegraphic agency of the Soviet Union) is set up as the official source of information.

12 October: A German–Soviet economic and trade treaty is signed, affording the USSR long-term credits.

18–31 December: The 14th Party Congress in Moscow adopts Stalin's views on industrialisation; a new Party statute (renaming the Party, the Communist Party of the Soviet Union (Bolsheviks) – CPSU(B)) condemns Kamenev and Zinoviev (New opposition) in their protest against Stalin's socialism in one country concept.

1926

1 January: The CPSU(B) has 1,078,185 members (638,355 full members and 439,830 candidate members), of which 750,000 are in the RSFSR, 167,000 in Ukraine and 16,000 in Belorussia.

4 January: Zinoviev is replaced by Sergei Kirov as Party leader in Leningrad.

14–23 July: At a joint plenum of the CC and the Central Control Commission (CCC) Trotsky presents the declaration of the 13, opposing the Stalin group in the leadership. The argument for more rapid industrialisation is rejected and Zinoviev is removed from the Politburo.

23 and 26 October: At a joint plenum of the CC and the CCC Trotsky is voted off the Politburo, Zinoviev ceases to be head of the Comintern and Kamenev is removed as a candidate member of the Politburo.

17–31 December: The first Soviet census reveals that the population is 147 million or 13 million more than in 1923: 18 per cent of the population is urban and 82 per cent rural. There are only 31 cities with a population of over 100,000, but the rapid growth of the urban population (it grew annually at 5 per cent over the years 1923–26) reveals the rapid economic changes underway.

1927

1 January: Russian industrial production is now 11 per cent and heavy industry 22 per cent above that of 1913. Privately owned factories only account for 24 per cent of the global output. Agriculture is still below the 1913 level despite the fact that the arable (cultivated) area is now 110.2 million hectares, compared with 105 million hectares in 1913. However, 28.3 per cent of the 25 million farms have no draught power (horses, oxen) and 31.6 per cent have no agricultural implements or equipment.

9 August: After 12 days of debate in a joint plenum of the CC and CCC, Trotsky, Kamenev and Zinoviev acknowledge their mistakes. The exclusion of Trotsky and Zinoviev from the CC is overturned but they receive a severe reprimand.

3 September: The leaders of the opposition again send a letter to the CC, signed by 13 of them, criticising the Party leadership and demanding a debate within the Party.

21–23 October: At a joint plenum of the CC and CCC Trotsky and Zinoviev are expelled from the CC because of their continuing opposition to Party policy.

12–14 November: A joint plenum of the CC and CCC expels Trotsky and Zinoviev from the Party and Kamenev and others from the CC and the CCC.

2–19 December: The 15th Party Congress confirms the expulsion of Trotsky and Zinoviev from the Party and Kamenev and another 74 opposition figures lose their Party membership. The same fate is meted out to 23 members of the 'anti-revolutionary' group lead by Sapronov. The Congress decides on the collectivisation of agriculture and the drafting of a Five Year Plan for the Soviet economy. The main victor is Stalin.

1928

16 January: Trotsky is told to leave Moscow and go to Verny (later Alma Ata, now Almaty), Kazakhstan, on the Soviet–Chinese frontier.

27 January: Kamenev and Zinoviev confess their errors in *Pravda* and declare they no longer belong to the opposition.

18 May–6 July: The Moscow trial of 53 engineers and technicians from the Donbass accused of anti-Soviet activities ends with five death sentences and long periods of imprisonment for others. The trial reveals the growing tension between the state and specialists.

Stalin defeats his rivals, 1929–41

1929

18 January: Stalin succeeds in the Politburo in forcing through the banishment of Trotsky from the Soviet Union, against the opposition of

Bukharin, Rykov and Tomsky. Trotsky leaves Alma Ata on 22 January and is to cross the Soviet–Turkish border to Constantinople. On 10 February he leaves Odessa for Turkey by boat, accompanied by his wife and his elder son.

23–29 April: The 16th Party Congress adopts the first Five Year Plan (FYP) (see pp. 87–8) for the development of the economy (eventually the first FYP ran from 1 October 1928 to 31 December 1932) and condemns the right deviation (Bukharin and Rykov) as a great danger to the Party.

1930

30 January: The CC passes a decree on the liquidation of kulak farms and the speeding up of collectivisation (see pp. 84–5). Kulaks are not allowed to join kolkhozes (collective farms) as they are regarded as hostile social elements and must leave areas which have been collectivised. All kulak property can be confiscated without compensation.

2 March: In an article in *Pravda*, 'Dizzy with Success', Stalin chastises those who have forced peasants into collectives and permits them to leave if they so desire. They rush out of the kolkhozes but Stalin's move is only tactical as his goal was to ensure that the spring sowing would not be interrupted. Later the peasants are recollectivised.

26 June–13 July: The 16th Party Congress confirms rapid collectivisation and measures against right deviationists.

25 November–7 December: Trial of 'Industrial Party' members who are accused of promoting armed foreign intervention (especially by France).

1931

1–9 March: The Moscow Menshevik trial involving former leaders of the right wing of the RSDRP (Sukhanov and Groman), accused of conspiring with émigré Mensheviks against the Soviet Union, results in long prison sentences.

15 June: A CC plenum decides on the construction of the Moscow underground, the Metro. Work begins in 1932 and the first stretch (11.6 km long with 13 stations) is opened on 15 May 1935.

1932

21 January–25 July: The Soviet Union seeks to establish friendly relations with all states along its borders and resolve all existing problems. This policy had already produced results with treaties of friendship and neutrality having been signed with Turkey (17 December 1925), Lithuania (28 September 1926), Iran (1 October 1927) and Afghanistan (24 June 1931). Further treaties are signed with Finland (21 January 1932), Latvia (5 February), Estonia (4 May) and Poland (25 July). The treaty with France (29 November) gives the Soviet Union indirect access to the

Little Entente in east-central Europe and the Balkan Pact in south-east Europe.

27 December: An internal passport system is introduced in cities so as to clear them of kulaks and speculators. The system is run by the GPU. Those in the countryside were not given internal passports until the 1960s. It was illegal to move to another place of residence in the Soviet Union without a passport (see pp. 97–8).

1933

19 April: British Metropolitan Vickers engineers are sentenced after a trial in which they were accused of industrial sabotage.

16–17 November: The US and the Soviet Union agree on the establishment of diplomatic relations after long negotiations between President Roosevelt and Chicherin, the Commissar for Foreign Affairs.

19 December: The Politburo decrees a reorientation of Soviet foreign policy because of the threatening situation in Europe and the Far East. It decides to join the League of Nations and join collective security pacts.

1934

1 January: The second FYP (1933–36) is published, which foresees the completion of socialist reconstruction.

12 January: The Party purge reveals that about 300,000 members in Siberia and the Soviet Far East (15.6 per cent of the total membership) have been expelled.

26 January–10 February: The 17th Party Congress (the Congress of the Victors) meets in Moscow and Stalin delivers the main speech and states that the Soviet Union has been transformed from an agrarian country into an industrial state.

18 September: The Soviet Union joins the League of Nations and is made a permanent member.

1 December: Sergei Kirov, Party leader in Leningrad, is murdered, and Stalin uses this act to begin a period of mass terror.

16 December: Kamenev and Zinoviev are arrested in the wake of Kirov's murder.

29 December: The murderer of Kirov and 13 others are sentenced to death and executed.

1935

15–17 January: Kamenev, Zinoviev and others are accused of treason but Kamenev gets only five years imprisonment and Zinoviev, 10 years; 76 supporters of Zinoviev are exiled to Siberia.

21 March: The NKVD states that 1,074 persons from Leningrad have been exiled for life to Siberia.

29 March: British Foreign Secretary Anthony Eden (later Lord Avon) arrives in Moscow to see Stalin, who attempts to convince him and the western powers to enter a collective security system against Hitler.

25 July–20 August: The 7th Comintern Congress meets in Moscow, attended by 510 delegates. The dangerous international situation leads to the adoption of a popular front strategy.

30 and 31 August: Aleksei Stakhanov, a miner, creates a new record by mining 102 tonnes of coal in one shift, equivalent to 13 norms (see p. 113).

22 September: Ranks are introduced in the Red Army (they were abolished on 16 December 1917).

1936

14 January: The exchange of Party books permits another purge of Party members.

18 June: Maxim Gorky, the writer, dies in Moscow and is buried in the Kremlin wall on 20 June.

27 June: Decree banning abortion and promoting the family. The family becomes again the basis of society.

19–24 August: First Moscow show trial (the trial of the 16) against the Terrorist Trotsky–Zinoviev Centre. The main defendants, Kamenev and Zinoviev, are sentenced to death and executed. Tomsky commits suicide on 23 August.

26 September: G. Yagoda is replaced by N. Ezhov as People's Commissar for Internal Affairs and this begins a purge in the police and security forces.

25 November: Germany and Japan sign the Anti-Comintern Pact in Berlin, which includes the agreement not to sign a treaty with the Soviet Union without the permission of the other country.

5 December: A new Soviet constitution is adopted at the 8th Congress of Soviets, which abolishes the three-class elector system (workers, peasants, intelligentsia) and introduces the general and equal right to vote and direct elections to all soviets. The USSR Supreme Soviet is to consist of two houses: Soviet of the Union and Soviet of Nationalities (see pp. 189–90). The number of Soviet republics increases from 7 to 11 with the dissolution of the Transcaucasian Federal Socialist Republic and the appearance of Azerbaijan, Armenia and Georgia as Soviet republics. Kazakhstan and Kirgizia are upgraded from autonomous republics to Union republics.

1937

23–30 January: Second Moscow show trial against 17 members of the 'anti-Soviet Trotskyist parallel centre': 13 are sentenced to death and shot (1 February) and the others to 10 years imprisonment.

11 June: The arrest of leading military officers (Marshal Tukhachevsky, deputy People's Commissar for Defence, and six generals) is announced. In a secret trial they are sentenced to death and executed. This begins a mass purge of the military.

Early September: Soviet troops move into the Mongolian People's Republic to protect it against a possible Japanese attack.

16 December: Eight Soviet officials, mainly leaders of national minorities (Jews, Armenians), are accused of spying and treason, sentenced to death and executed.

1938

12–19 January: First session of the newly elected USSR Supreme Soviet. M. I. Kalinin is elected chair of the Presidium of the Supreme Soviet (head of state). The Central Executive Committee of the USSR is then dissolved, having been the supreme state body between Soviet Congresses since 1922.

2–13 March: Third Moscow show trial against the 'anti-Soviet bloc of the right and the Trotskyists' involving 21 defendants, including Rykov and Bukharin. Eighteen are sentenced to death on 13 March and executed on 15 March.

29 July–11 August: A Japanese attack around Lake Khasan, near Vladivostok, is repulsed by the Red Army. (The Japanese attack was in response to the Soviet occupation of a part of Manchuria.)

1 December: After the appointment of Anastas Mikoyan as People's Commissar for Trade, the Soviet Union plans a rapid expansion of foreign trade with the Baltic States, Finland, Poland and Iran.

8 December: N. Ezhov, notorious for his role in the Moscow show trials, resigns as People's Commissar for Internal Affairs and is succeeded by Lavrentiya Beria.

29 December: A decree on raising labour discipline withdraws many of the social gains of the previous years (reduction of wages and holidays, including maternity leave, and the removal of benefits from those who change jobs twice). All workers and employees are to be given labour books (a record of their work performance).

1939

17–26 June: The second Soviet census reveals a population of 190,687,000 on 17 June.

10–21 March: The 18th Party Congress (the Party Congress of the completion of the victory of socialism) adopts the guidelines for the third FYP and a new Party statute. Stalin states that the goal is to catch up and surpass the developed capitalist countries and the construction of a classless socialist society.

11 May: Beginning of battle of Khalkin-Gol, on the Soviet–Mongolian border, against Japan. Moscow emerges the winner on 15 September.

11–23 August: British and French military officials negotiate in Moscow and they agree that in case of war the Soviet Union may occupy the Baltic States. No overall agreement is reached as Poland refuses to allow Soviet troops to cross its territory.

23 August: Molotov and von Ribbentrop, German Foreign Minister, sign in Moscow the German–Soviet Non-Aggression Pact, having already signed a trade and credit agreement (19 August). In a secret protocol the two sides divide up east-central Europe. The Soviet Union acquires Finland, the Baltic States (except Lithuania), eastern Poland and Bessarabia. (The existence of this secret protocol was denied by Moscow until the late Gorbachev era.)

1 September: Germany attacks Poland and penetrates up to the line agreed in the secret protocol and the Second World War begins.

3 September: Britain and France declare war on Germany.

17 September: Soviet troops begin their march into eastern Poland (as agreed by the secret protocol). Lvov falls to them on 21–22 September.

28 September: Molotov and von Ribbentrop sign in Moscow a new German–Soviet border and friendship treaty, which lays down a new demarcation line on Bug on the river Vistula. Lithuania becomes part of the Soviet zone of influence.

28 September–10 October: The Soviet Union signs agreements with Estonia (28 September), Latvia (5 October) and Lithuania (10 October) which permit Soviet bases on their territories. A similar agreement with Finland is not reached (11–12 October).

26–28 October: The Soviet-occupied west Ukraine, formerly in eastern Poland, votes to introduce Soviet power and to join the Ukrainian Soviet Socialist Republic. The Belorussian population of former eastern Poland do the same and become part of the Belorussian Soviet Socialist Republic on 28–30 October.

16 November: German–Soviet agreement on the return to Germany of Germans from former eastern Poland, now in the Soviet Union.

27 November: After the failure of Finnish–Soviet negotiations to establish a mutual assistance pact (Finland refused to permit Soviet bases on its territory), Moscow declares the non-aggression of 21 January 1932 null and void and breaks off diplomatic relations on 28 November.

30 November–12 March 1940: The Soviet–Finnish (or Winter) war begins with an air raid over Helsinki and the march of Soviet troops into Karelia. A Finnish People's Government, composed of Finnish émigré communists, headed by Otto Kuusinen, is announced by Molotov. Had Finland fallen, this government would have taken over the country.

14 December: The League of Nations rules that the Soviet Union was the aggressor in the war with Finland and excludes it from the League.

1940

11–12 March: Finland concedes Soviet demands at peace negotiations in Moscow. Finland gives up Vyborg and a part of Karelia. Hangö is rented as a military base to the Soviet Union for 30 years.

10 April: The Soviet Union judges the German occupation of Norway to be a defensive measure against Great Britain.

12–17 June: Soviet demands to Lithuania (12 June), Estonia and Latvia (16 June) to permit more Soviet bases and to elect governments according to Soviet wishes, lead to the transformation of the Baltic States into Soviet republics (21–22 July) which then join the Soviet Union (3–6 August).

22 June 1940: France agrees an armistice with Germany, after failing to stem German advances since May. Britain is now alone against Germany; Italy is allied to Germany.

26 June: The Soviet government demands that Romania secede Bessarabia and northern Bukovina to it. When Romania does not concur, Red Army units occupy both regions on 28 June.

21 July: Field Marshal von Brauchitsch, Commander-in-Chief of the German army, is ordered by Hitler to begin preparing for war against the Soviet Union. Hitler envisages a five-month campaign in the spring of 1941.

21 August: Trotsky dies in Mexico after an attempt on his life (20 August). It is widely assumed the killer was Stalin's agent.

12–13 November: Molotov arrives in Berlin for negotiations concerning the division of the world. Moscow wants Finland, Romania and Bulgaria.

18 December: Hitler signs instruction no. 21, Operation Barbarossa, which requires all preparations for an attack on the Soviet Union to be finished by 15 May 1941.

1941

11 March: USA begins Lend Lease economic and military aid to Britain (to USSR on 7 November).

13 April: The Japanese ambassador in Berlin, Matsuoka, returning to Tokyo, breaks his journey in Moscow (8 April) and signs a neutrality treaty with the Soviet Union: existing territory and borders are recognised, and in the case of war with third parties the signatories will remain neutral. Japan also recognises the independence of the Mongolian People's Republic.

30 April: Operation Barbarossa is postponed from 15 May to 22 June (the same date Napoleon launched his attack on Russia in 1812).

27 May: The General Staff orders the western border districts urgently to build up front command posts.

6 June: The German army provides instruction on how to deal with communist commissars (the commissar order). Captured Red Army commissars are to be executed.

12–15 June: Military districts are ordered to bring their divisions closer to the border.

19 June: Military districts are ordered to camouflage airfields, army units, transport, depots and other bases and disperse the planes on airfields.

The Great Patriotic War, 1941–45

1941

22 June: German units attack the Soviet Union across a broad front without a declaration of war. Over 3 million men are involved and behind the army come state security units whose task is to eliminate the Jewish population; 92 German divisions are using French or other captured vehicles. The Red Army has about 1 million soldiers in border areas, from the Arctic to the Black Sea. Churchill offers Stalin help, as does Roosevelt (23 June). Molotov, not Stalin, announces to the Soviet people that Germany has invaded.

22 June–20 July: The Soviet defenders of Brest capitulate after 20 days.

22 June–5 July: The Luftwaffe loses 807 planes.

23 June: Hungary breaks off diplomatic relations with the Soviet Union and Slovakia declares war on Moscow and provides Germany with two divisions.

26 June: Finland declares war on the Soviet Union.

27 June: Hungary declares war on the Soviet Union.

30 June: The State Committee for Defence (GKO) is set up and Stalin becomes its head (1 July).

3 July: Stalin, in a radio broadcast, proclaims the Great Patriotic (Fatherland) War and orders that no territory shall be conceded to the enemy.

12 July: Great Britain and the Soviet Union sign an agreement on mutual aid against Germany. Unilateral peace negotiations or armistices are ruled out.

18 July: Stalin, in a telegram, demands the establishment of a second front against Hitler. The Soviet Union and the Czechoslovak government in exile sign an agreement in London establishing diplomatic relations and mutual aid against Germany, including Czechoslovak units on Soviet territory. Similar agreements are signed with the governments in exile of Yugoslavia (22 July), Poland (30 July), Greece (5 August), Norway (5 August), Belgium (7 August) and France (20 September).

29 July–1 August: Roosevelt sends Harry Hopkins to Moscow to assess the political and military situation in the Soviet Union.

August–September: British and Soviet forces occupy Iran, required by the western allies as a supply route to the Soviet Union.

5 August: The Germans take Smolensk and 300,000 Soviet prisoners.

6 August: Polish prisoners of war in the Soviet Union form units, commanded by General Anders.

8 August: The Red Army loses Uman and 103,000 prisoners.

11 August: After meeting at sea off the coast off Newfoundland, President Roosevelt and Winston Churchill agree on the Atlantic Charter, promising the restoration of independence to occupied states.

28 August: Volga Germans are to be deported to Siberia because they are a security risk and the Volga German Autonomous Republic is dissolved.

8 September–20 January 1944: The 900-day siege of Leningrad.

26 September: The battle of Kiev ends with 665,000 Red Army prisoners.

30 September–20 April 1942: The battle for Moscow; Hitler calls it Operation Typhoon and it is code-named Moscow Cannae (the battle in 216 BC in south-eastern Italy where the Roman legions were destroyed by Hannibal). The German offensive comes to a stop in December and on 5 December a Soviet counter-offensive forces the Germans back.

16 October: The Soviet government and diplomatic corps move from Moscow to Kuibyshev (now Samara), but Stalin stays in Moscow.

4 December: Finnish units reoccupy Hangö after Soviet troops withdraw.

7 December: Japanese forces attack Pearl Harbor, Hawaii, thus bringing the USA into the war.

15–18 December: Anthony Eden (later Lord Avon) visits Moscow to meet Stalin and is informed that the Soviet Union wishes to retain its territorial gains of 1939–40.

1942

1 January: In Washington, 26 states, including the Soviet Union, sign the United Nations Pact (also called the Washington Pact), which recognises the Atlantic Charter as the joint programme of objectives and principles.

28 January: The Soviet Caucasian front is regrouped to form a Crimea front, but it is badly mauled by a German counter-offensive of 8 May. The Politburo resolves to set up a commission to study the post-war structure of the future states of Europe, Asia and other parts of the world, to be sent to foreign governments, political parties and interested individuals.

1 February–19 April: An offensive of the 33rd Russian army against Vyazma (1–2 February) is unsuccessful. A counter-offensive by the 4th German army encircles Soviet troops and wipes them out. General M. G. Efremov, their commander, commits suicide on 19 April.

11 April: President Roosevelt cables Stalin that the Americans are planning an offensive to relieve the Russians.

26 May: In London, Molotov signs an Anglo–Soviet alliance and friendship treaty for 20 years.

29 May–1 June: Molotov holds talks in Washington on a second front in western Europe (Britain had already agreed to this on 26 May) and economic aid.

11 June: The foreign ministers of the USSR and the USA sign, in Washington, a treaty on the principles of mutual aid in the struggle against German aggression and on cooperation in the post-war world.

28 June–8 July: First phase of the German summer offensive towards Kursk, aiming to take the Baku oil fields (Operation Blue). The 11th German army under General Field Marshal Manstein takes the Crimea after the fall of Sevastopol (1 July) and the Kerch peninsula (4 July).

17 July–2 February 1943: The battle of Stalingrad.

25 July–9 October 1943: The battle for the Caucasus.

12–15 August: Churchill and Averell Harriman, for Roosevelt, hold talks in Moscow with Stalin on measures against Germany and its allies.

19 August: German offensive against Stalingrad, commanded by General Paulus. By 3 September they are within 8 km of the centre of the city.

17 October–5 June 1946: The Brazilian uprising of November 1935 led to the ending of diplomatic relations between the Soviet Union and Latin America. Relations are revitalised by the German attack on the USSR and the dissolution of the Comintern on 15 May 1943. Diplomatic relations are established with Cuba on 17 October 1942, Mexico on 12 November 1942, Uruguay on 27 January 1943, Columbia on 3–4 February 1943, Chile on 11 December 1944, Venezuela on 14 March 1945, Brazil on 2 April 1945, Bolivia on 18 April 1945, Guatemala on 19 April 1945 and Argentina on 5 June 1946.

8 November: US and British forces land in north-west Africa; this is the first US involvement on land against German forces.

19–22 November: Great offensive of the south-west front (General Vatutin), the Don (General Rokossovsky) and Stalingrad (General Eremenko) against the German 6th army (General Paulus), which succeeds in encircling the German army.

12 December: A Soviet–Czechoslovak alliance is signed in Moscow, indicating the desire of the Czechoslovaks to collaborate with the Russians after the war.

1943

6 January: Decree of the USSR Supreme Soviet on the introduction of ranks in the Red Army (on 15 February for the navy).

12 January–16 February: The Soviet Volkhov front goes on the offensive against the German Don front, which collapses completely after the Red Army takes Voronezh on 5 February. Kursk is liberated on 8 February, Krasnodar on 12 February, Rostov on 14 February and Kharkov on 16 February.

31 January–2 February: The southern part of the German army at Stalingrad surrenders on 31 January (General Paulus) and the northern part on 2 February (General Strecker). The Russians lose 1.1 million men and the Germans 800,000 men – almost one-quarter of all German troops in Soviet Russia. The Wehrmacht also lose 3,000 tanks, 4,400 planes and over 12,000 artillery pieces. About 92,000 Germans and allies are taken prisoner, including 24 generals; it is the first time that a German Field Marshal (Paulus) is taken prisoner on the field of battle.

22 February–21 March: German offensive recovers much lost ground; recapture of Kharkov on 16 March and Belgorod on 21 March.

13 April: The mass graves of over 4,100 Polish officers are discovered at Katyn, near Smolensk. They had been murdered by the NKVD in 1940.

14 April: Stalin's son, Yakov, a prisoner of war in the German concentration camp, Sachsenhausen, deliberately seeks death by entering a prohibited zone and is shot dead. (The Germans apparently asked for Field Marshal Paulus in exchange but Stalin refused.)

25 April: The Soviet Union breaks diplomatic relations with the Polish government in exile over the latter's demand for an international inquiry into the Katyn affair.

6 May: The communist Union of Polish Patriots (a forerunner of the Lublin committee), set up on 1 March but only reported on 8 May, requests that Stalin permit the establishment of a Polish division in the Soviet Union to be called the Tadeusz Kosciusko division. Stalin grants permission on 9 May.

15 May: Stalin dissolves the Cominform to demonstrate that the Soviet Union has no expansionary aims; the functions of the Cominform are taken over by the Central Committee Secretariat and a department of international affairs is set up.

10 July: The Anglo–American invasion of Sicily and the liberation of western Europe begin.

12 July: Greatest tank battle of the Second World War at the Kursk salient involving over 1,200 tanks, 800 of them Soviet. The Germans break off the battle and retreat. Hitler loses over 500,000 men, 3,000 guns and almost all tanks; Soviet losses almost as heavy.

23 August: Red Army troops take Kharkov.

19–30 October: A Moscow conference of foreign ministers (Molotov, Eden and Cordell Hull (US)) agrees, *inter alia*, that Austria be reconstituted in its 1937 frontiers and that East Prussia be removed from Germany.

3–12 November: The 1st Ukrainian front breaks through the front of the 4th German tank army and liberates Kiev on 6 November.

28 November–1 December: Stalin, Churchill and Roosevelt agree, in principle, on the partition of Germany at Tehran. The Curzon Line is to be the Polish–Soviet frontier. Stalin requests Königsberg, the capital of East Prussia.

1944

14 January–18 February: Great offensive by Red Army troops against the German army group north. Novgorod is liberated on 20 January.

4 March–10 April: Spring offensive of the Red Army in the southern Ukraine along a 1,100 km front. Kherson is liberated on 13 March, Vinnitsa on 20 March and Nikolaev on 28 March.

26 March: Soviet troops reach the Romanian border on the river Pruth.

6 June: D-Day landing of Allied troops in Normandy, code-named Operation Overlord.

19–20 June: Soviet partisans interrupt railway communications of the German army group centre at 9,600 places in the greatest act of sabotage of the war.

22 June–1 August: Soviet summer offensive against the German army group centre.

1–22 July: Bretton Woods conference of 44 states on finance and economic affairs after the war. It agrees to establish the International Monetary Fund (IMF) to be concerned with macro-economic problems such as currency rates and fiscal and monetary policy, and to set up the World Bank to be concerned with micro-economic affairs such as funding of capital projects. The Soviet Union declines to join.

9 July: A new Soviet law on the family makes divorce more difficult and bans abortion. Awards for heroine mothers and taxes on families with up to two children attempt to increase the birth rate.

21 July: The Polish committee for national liberation is set up in Cholm after its liberation by Soviet troops. It then moves to Lublin on 25 July (the Lublin committee).

26 July: A treaty of friendship and alliance is signed by the Soviet government and the Lublin committee in Moscow. Diplomatic relations are established on 2 September.

1 August–10 October: Warsaw uprising, led by General Bor-Komorowski. Soviet troops refuse to come to their aid and the Poles surrender on 10 October.

20 August–1 September: Great offensive of the 2nd and 3rd Ukrainian front against the German 6th army.

23 August: Romania changes sides and declares war on Germany.

24 August–2 September: The German 6th army is encircled and annihilated near Kishenev.

4 September: Finnish troops cease hostilities and a Finnish delegation is sent on 6 September to Moscow to negotiate a peace treaty.

5 September: The Soviet Union declares war on Bulgaria and invades Bulgaria on 8 September.

8–9 September: Coup d'état in Bulgaria by the communists and officers to establish a democratic government of the patriotic front, led by Georgiev (pro-Soviet). Moscow declares the war over on 9 September.

12 September: London protocol, signed by the USA, the Soviet Union and Great Britain, on future occupation zones in Germany and the administration of Greater Berlin.

19 September: A cease-fire is agreed by the Soviet Union, Great Britain and Finland in Moscow. Finland is to withdraw to the 1940 frontiers. It concedes Petsamo to the Soviet Union and has to pay reparations.

7 October: At Dumbarton Oaks, the USA, Great Britain, the Soviet Union and China agree to establish the United Nations (and a draft UN charter) as the successor organisation to the League of Nations.

9–18 October: Stalin and Churchill meet in Moscow and negotiate a post-war settlement, especially on eastern and south-eastern Europe. Stalin agrees in principle to Churchill's 'percentages deal', apportioning zones of influence in the Balkans.

10 December: General de Gaulle signs a Soviet–French alliance treaty against Germany for 20 years. De Gaulle declines to recognise the Lublin committee and Stalin the separation of the Rhineland and Ruhr from Germany.

1945

1 January: The Lublin committee is renamed the Provisional Government of the Republic of Poland, and the Soviet government establishes diplomatic relations with it on 5 January. The USA and Britain refuse to recognise it.

20 January: Hungary, a German ally, signs an armistice with the Soviet Union.

4–11 February: Stalin, Churchill and Roosevelt discuss future military operations and the post-war world at Yalta.

3 March: Under Soviet pressure Finland declares war on Germany (effective from 19 September 1944).

6–9 April: Red Army troops (3rd Belorussian front) take Königsberg, capital of East Prussia.

11 April: Soviet–Yugoslav treaty of mutual assistance signed. Similar treaties are signed with the other east and south-east European states.

12 April: President Roosevelt dies and Vice-President Harry Truman becomes President.

16 April: Great offensive of the 1st Ukrainian and 1st Belorussian fronts towards Berlin, which is encircled on 25 April.

23 April: President Truman warns Molotov, the Soviet Foreign Minister, in a brusque fashion, that Moscow must keep to the Yalta agreements. Molotov ripostes that he has never been spoken to in this manner in his life.

25 April: Soviet and US troops meet on Torgau, on the Elbe.

2 May: Berlin capitulates to the Red Army.

7 May: The general capitulation of the German army (Wehrmacht) is signed by Colonel General Jodl in the headquarters of General Eisenhower in Reims, France. It is to be effective at 0.10 on 9 May.

8 May: General Field Marshal Keitel, Admiral von Friedeburg and Colonel General Stumpff sign the unconditional surrender of German forces at the Soviet headquarters at Berlin Karlshorst. The document is dated 8 May but it is signed at 0.16 on 9 May.

High Stalinism, 1945–53

1945

12 May: Churchill uses the term 'iron curtain' (see pp. 156–7) for the first time, in a telegram to President Truman.

24 May: At a victory reception in the Georgevsky Hall, in the Kremlin, for over a thousand officers, Stalin lauds the Russian nation and places it above all other nations in the Soviet Union.

26 June: In San Francisco, the charter of the United Nations is signed by 50 states.

4 July: An allied commission for Austria is agreed by the Soviet Union, the USA, Great Britain and France.

16 July: The USA tests successfully the first atomic bomb at Alamogordo, New Mexico.

17 July–2 August: The USA, the Soviet Union and Great Britain agree on the political and economic goals of their occupation policy in Germany at the Potsdam Conference.

6 August: The USA drops an atomic bomb on Hiroshima, Japan.

8 August: The Soviet Union declares war on Japan.

9 August: The USA drops an atomic bomb on Nagasaki, Japan.

14 August: The Soviet Union and China (Chiang Kai-shek) sign a treaty of friendship and alliance which confirms the Soviet use of Port Arthur and Dairen, the confirmation of the status quo in the Mongolian People's Republic and Soviet influence in northern Manchuria. The East Chinese railway, sold to the government of Manchukuo in 1935, reverts to joint Soviet–Chinese administration.

15 August: Japan surrenders on the understanding that Hirohito will remain emperor.

19 August: A Party and government decree on the fourth FYP (1946–50) envisages expansion of living space by 60 million square metres and huge power stations at Kuibyshev, Stalingrad and Kakhovka on the Dnieper, the Turkmen canal and the Volga–Don canal.

21 August: Japanese troops capitulate to the Red Army, including over 600,000 prisoners.

23 August: The USA ends the Lend Lease programme.

2 September: Japan surrenders to the Allies on board USS *Missouri* (V-J Day).

11 September–2 October: London conference of the foreign ministers of the Soviet Union, USA, Great Britain, France and China finds agreement difficult. Discussions on peace treaties for defeated states and reparations for the Soviet Union.

24 October: The Soviet Union, Belorussia and Ukraine join the UN as founding members.

16–26 December: A foreign ministers' conference in Moscow sets up a Far East Commission and Molotov and Byrnes (US) discuss the withdrawal of Soviet troops from China and non-intervention in the domestic affairs of China. On Korea Molotov proposes a Soviet–American commission to unite the two parts of Korea, politically and economically. The commission adjourns in May 1946 without achieving anything.

29 December: A Soviet–French trade treaty is signed but there is little agreement on compensation for French property in Soviet-occupied regions.

1946

22 January: Carpatho-Ukraine is separated from Czechoslovakia and becomes the Transcarpathian oblast, in the Ukrainian Soviet Socialist Republic.

9 February: Stalin launches a new Five Year Plan and celebrates the Great Patriotic War as a victory of 'our Soviet social system' and of 'our Soviet state'.

25 February: The Red Army is renamed the Soviet Army.

5 March: Churchill's speech at Fulton, Missouri, speaks of an 'iron curtain' descending in Europe from Stettin (Szczecin) in the north to Trieste in the south. He calls for an Anglo–American alliance. Stalin sharply criticises the speech on 13 March.

15 March: USSR Sovnarkom becomes the USSR Council of Ministers (see pp. 197–8). People's Commissariats are renamed Ministries.

25 April–15 May; 15 June–12 July: The 2nd conference of the four powers (the USSR, USA, Great Britain and France) discusses European security and Germany, the Trieste problem and a peace treaty with Austria.

14 August: A CC decree castigates the Leningrad journals, *Zvezda* and *Leningrad*, and introduces a period of cultural nationalism and xenophobia, known as the Zhdanovshchina, named after Andrei Zhdanov, which lasts until the death of Stalin in 1953. Cosmopolitanism and objectivism are pilloried and Anna Akhmatova and Mikhail Zoshchenko viciously attacked in Party and state publications.

26 August: A CC resolution on the theatre attacks the dominance of foreign, decadent-bourgeois plays in the repertoire of Soviet theatres and demands their replacement by relevant Soviet productions. There are similar resolutions on Soviet films (4 September) and opera and music (10 February 1948).

4 November–12 December: At the 3rd conference of foreign ministers, Molotov refuses to accept proposals on Germany and Austria.

1947

10 February: The foreign ministers of the victorious powers sign peace treaties with Italy, Romania, Bulgaria, Hungary and Finland.

10 March–24 April: Molotov, at the 4th foreign ministers' conference, in Moscow, rejects western proposals for a federal Germany and also the Marshall Plan. Reparations are agreed at US$20 billion, with the Soviet union receiving a half.

12 March: President Harry Truman proclaims the Truman doctrine, which promises US help to countries threatened by communism.

5 June: General George Marshall, US Secretary of State, announces the Marshall Plan, the European recovery programme.

27 June–1 July: At the foreign ministers' conference in Paris, Molotov rejects the supra-national organisation necessary to implement the Marshall Plan.

22–27 September: An information bureau of communist and workers' parties (Cominform) is set up in Szklarska Poreba, Poland, by communist and workers' parties from the Soviet Union, Hungary, Romania, Bulgaria, Poland, Czechoslovakia, France, Italy and Yugoslavia (until 1948). Its headquarters are in Belgrade, and then in Bucharest from mid-1948.

25 November–16 December: A council of foreign ministers meets in London but again fails to make progress on German and Austrian peace treaties. The USA, Britain and France begin considering the establishment of a west German state.

1948

19–25 February: The communists take power in Czechoslovakia.

23 February: The USA, Britain and France begin discussions in London to establish the future Federal Republic of Germany.

20 March: The Allied Control Commission in Berlin is paralysed by the withdrawal of Marshal Sokolovsky.

2 April: The US Congress approves Marshall Aid and an economic cooperation administration is set up to run it.

6 April: In Moscow, a treaty of friendship and mutual aid for 10 years is signed by Finland and the Soviet Union.

23 June: After the introduction of the Deutschmark in the western zones of Germany and West Berlin (20 June), a currency reform is also announced for the Soviet-occupied zone and all Berlin. The western Allies refuse to accept the Soviet reform and the Soviet military administration (SMAD) then blockades completely the three western sectors of Berlin (the Berlin Blockade).

24 June–12 May 1949: Berlin Blockade: all land and waterways to West Berlin and East Germany are blocked. Berlin is supplied by air lift from 26 June 1948 to 29 June 1949.

28 June: The Communist Party of Yugoslavia is expelled from Cominform at a conference in Bucharest and Cominform's headquarters are moved to Bucharest.

1949

25 January: The Council for Mutual Economic Assistance (Comecon or CMEA) is set up by the Soviet Union, Bulgaria, Hungary, Poland, Romania and Czechoslovakia.

4 April: The North Atlantic Treaty Organisation (NATO) is set up in Washington.

4 May: Four-power agreement in New York on the ending of the Berlin Blockade to be effective on 12 May.

23 May–20 June: A foreign ministers' conference in Paris fails to reach agreement as the Soviet Union rejects the Basic Law (Grundgesetz) announced for the three western zones on 23 May.

25 September: TASS reports on the explosion of the first Soviet atomic bomb.

1 October: Soviet note on the German question. The western powers are held solely responsible for the division of Germany after the formation of the Federal Republic of Germany (FRG) on 20 September 1949.

1–2 October: The Soviet Union is the first state to recognise the People's Republic of China.

7 October: The German Democratic Republic (GDR) is established.

1950

13 January: The Soviet Union ceases to participate in the UN Security Council and UN agencies (until 1 August 1950).

31 January: President Truman announces that the USA is to build a hydrogen bomb.

14 February: The Soviet Union and China conclude a treaty of friendship and mutual assistance for 30 years. Port Arthur and Dairen are to be returned to China by 1952 and a long-term credit is granted China. The Soviet Union is to give up its interest in the Chinese eastern railway (the transfer agreement was signed in Kharbin on 31 December 1952).

25 June: The Korean War begins.

27 June: The UN, with the USSR absent, approves the uniting for peace resolution to send troops to Korea.

27–29 June: Exchange of notes between the Soviet Union and the United States on Korea. Moscow protests against the intervention of US troops. On 7 July the UN Security Council, in the absence of the USSR, resolves to send a UN force under American command to Korea.

1951

10 March: The Soviet Union, in notes to the western powers, proposes a peace treaty with Germany.

25 May: British spies Guy Burgess and Donald Maclean flee to the Soviet Union.

23 June: The Soviet Union calls for a cease-fire in Korea; on 29 June the UN and on 1 July China agree to talks and these begin on 4 July.

4–8 September: In San Francisco a conference to agree a peace treaty with Japan meets but the Soviet Union, Poland and Czechoslovakia refuse to initial the agreement after the Soviet Union had failed to get its amendments accepted.

1952

September: Stalin's *Economic Problems of Socialism* is published.

10 March: Stalin proposes, in a note to the USA, Britain and France, a peace treaty which would result in a unified, neutral Germany; the west sends a non-committal reply on 25 March.

9 April: Another Soviet note on the proposed German peace treaty; the western powers do not reply until 13 May.

26 May: The Treaty of Bonn is signed by the USA, Britain, France and West Germany, ending the occupation and restoring sovereignty to the Federal Republic of Germany. (Four-power responsibility for Germany remained.) Its implementation depended on the treaty of Paris.

27 May: The Treaty of Paris is signed by France, West Germany, Italy, Belgium, the Netherlands and Luxembourg, establishing a European Defence Community, with German forces under federal control.

16 September: The Soviet Union agrees to restore Port Arthur and rights over railways to China.

3 October: Britain successfully explodes its first atomic bomb in the Montebello Islands.

5–14 October: The 19th Congress of the CPSU(B) adopts a new statute. The Politburo is replaced by a Presidium of the CC. The CC Secretariat, headed by Malenkov, is expanded to 10 members. The term Bolsheviks in the name of the Party is dropped. In future the Party will be called the CPSU.

1 November: The USA successfully explodes its first hydrogen bomb in the Marshall Islands.

1953

9 January: Nine Kremlin doctors are arrested and held responsible for the deaths of leading Soviet politicians. An anti-Semitic campaign begins with the announcement of the Doctors' Plot on 13 January.

5 March: Stalin dies from a heart attack suffered on 1 March.

The struggle for the succession, 1953–57

1953

7 March: It is announced that Georgy Malenkov has become chair of the USSR Council of Ministers with L. P. Beria and V. M. Molotov as first deputies and N. A. Bulganin and L. M. Kaganovich as deputies. Molotov becomes Foreign Minister, Beria becomes head of an amalgamated Ministry of Interior Affairs and State Security, Bulganin becomes Minister of War, and Mikoyan becomes Minister of Trade.

14 March: Malenkov chooses to give up leadership of the Communist Party and retain the position of Prime Minister. Khrushchev is the main beneficiary.

17 June: The raising of norms in East Berlin leads to the East Berlin uprising against the communist regime. It is suppressed by the intervention of Soviet forces.

10 July: The arrest of Beria on 26 June is made public. He is expelled from the Party, tried for treason and executed on 23 December 1953 (some sources state that he was dead long before his trial).

8 August: Malenkov launches his new course placing greater emphasis on consumer goods production. Compulsory deliveries from the private plots are reduced and prices paid for state deliveries from the farms are increased.

20 August: The Soviet Union announces the explosion of a hydrogen bomb (explosion was on 8 August).

13 September: Nikita Khrushchev is elected First Secretary of the CC, CPSU.

1954

25 January–18 February: Conference of the western powers and the Soviet Union in Berlin on Germany, the Austrian state treaty, and the problems in Korea and Indo-China. No agreement is reached.

19 February: The Crimea is transferred from the RSFSR to Ukraine.

1 March: The USA tests the first deliverable hydrogen bomb in the Marshall Islands.

21 April: The Soviet Union joins UNESCO, in London. Ukraine and Belorussia join on 12 May 1954.

26 April–21 July: The Indo-China conference in Geneva of the foreign ministers of the Soviet Union, France, Great Britain and the USA agree on the division of Vietnam along the 17th parallel.

7 May: Dienbienphu falls to the Viet-Minh, the day before the Geneva talks were to discuss Indo-China. This defeat heralds the end of French influence in Indo-China.

23 September: Ilya Ehrenburg's novel *Thaw*, which gave its name to the immediate post-Stalin period, is published.

29 September–12 October: Khrushchev's visit to Beijing. The Soviet Union transfers its interests in mixed Soviet-Chinese companies to China. A treaty is signed which recognises China as an equal partner and a key member of the communist movement.

1955

8 February: Georgy Malenkov resigns as Prime Minister and is succeeded by Nikolai Bulganin. Malenkov becomes responsible for energy. Marshal Zhukov becomes Defence Minister.

18–24 April: Bandung conference of Afro-Asian states in Indonesia; condemns racism and colonialism.

14 May: In Warsaw, the Soviet Union and Albania, Bulgaria, Hungary, the GDR, Poland, Romania and Czechoslovakia sign a treaty for the defence of peace and security in Europe for 20 years (known as the Warsaw Pact, see pp. 224–5). After ratification it becomes operative on 5 June 1955.

15 May: The four powers and Austria sign in Vienna the Austrian state treaty, which confirms the state frontiers of 1 January 1938, and Austria agrees not to conclude a political or economic union with Germany. Austria is to be a neutral country.

9–13 September: Konrad Adenauer, West German Chancellor, visits Moscow. Diplomatic relations are established and all remaining German prisoners of war and civil personnel will be repatriated (some choose to go to the GDR, e.g. General Paulus).

27 October–16 November: Geneva conference of the foreign ministers of the Soviet Union, the USA, Great Britain and France, which fails to achieve any progress on the German question.

18 November–19 December: Khrushchev and Bulganin visit India, Burma and Afghanistan.

1956

14–25 February: The 20th Party Congress in Moscow. Khrushchev, in a secret speech, pillories Stalin for misuse of power and the cult of personality (see pp. 149–50) and demands that the Party return to the principles enunciated by Lenin. The Party gains at the expense of the state and this is regarded as necessary in the transition from socialism to communism.

28 March: *Pravda* publishes an article condemning the Stalin personality cult and thereby reveals the main points of Khrushchev's secret speech at the 20th Party Congress.

17 April: The Cominform is dissolved and replaced by bilateral agreements between the Soviet Union and the individual states.

18–27 April: Khrushchev and Bulganin pay an official visit to London (the first visit by the Soviet leaders to a leading western state after the war) and meet Queen Elizabeth II and Winston Churchill. Agreement is reached only on cultural and trade ties.

30 May: Decentralisation of government in the Soviet Union with republics taking over the administration of many enterprises. The USSR Ministry of Justice is dissolved.

20 June: The first Yugoslav visit to the Soviet Union since 1948 (1–23 June) results in Tito and Bulganin signing a statement declaring that wide-ranging agreement has been reached between the two states.

30 June: Lenin's Testament of December 1922, criticising Stalin, is published for the first time, in *Kommunist*.

16 July: The Karelo-Finnish Soviet Socialist Republic becomes the Karelian Autonomous Soviet Socialist Republic and becomes part of the RSFSR.

19 October: Khrushchev, Molotov, Mikoyan and Kaganovich unexpectedly visit Warsaw in response to the rehabilitation of W. Gomulka (15 October). Discussions result in Marshal Rokossovsky being recalled (13 November) to Moscow and a treaty on the stationing of Soviet troops in Poland (17 December).

23 October–11 November: The Hungarian Revolution (see pp. 218–19) results in the appointment of Imre Nagy as Prime Minister (24 October), then the intervention of Soviet troops (26 October). Hungary leaves the Warsaw Pact on 1 November. A pro-Soviet Hungarian government under János Kádár is formed (4 November) and is the turning point, followed by the entry of a Soviet tank division (11 November).

31 October: After the attack by Israel against the Suez Canal (29 October) the Soviet Union issues a sharp warning to Israel, France and Great Britain.

5 November: The Soviet Union severs diplomatic relations with Israel and threatens France and Great Britain because of their troop landings in Suez (5 November), not excluding a rocket attack against London and Paris.

23 November: In *Pravda*, Tito is sharply attacked and suspected of sympathy for the anti-Soviet tendencies in Poland and Hungary. Albania begins the attacks on 8 November and they spread to all east European states by the beginning of 1957.

5–22 December: Anglo–French forces withdraw from Suez.

1957

5 January: President Eisenhower, in an address to Congress, commits the USA to oppose communism in the Middle East, called the Eisenhower Doctrine. Adopted on 9 March.

18 January: Zhou Enlai visits Moscow and objects to the leading role of the Soviet Union in its relations with the people's democracies of eastern Europe and supports their desire for more independence.

11 February: The USSR Supreme Soviet promulgates a law extending the rights of Union republics (more autonomy in developing their legal systems) and restoring the autonomous territories of the Balkars, Chechens, Ingushi, Kalmyks and Karachais (they had been deported to the east under Stalin in 1944 for allegedly collaborating with the Germans).

13–15 February: The CC plenum decides on a radical decentralisation of economic decision-making and the transition to regional economic management (105 councils of the national economy – sovnarkhozes – are set up).

10 May: The USSR Supreme Soviet promulgates decrees on the decentralisation of industry and construction. All but eight all-Union ministries (e.g. aviation, transport, power stations) are dissolved and enterprises subordinated to 105 sovnarkhozes, of which 70 are in the RSFSR, 11 in Ukraine, 9 in Kazakhstan, 4 in Uzbekistan and the other 11 Union republics having one each. Republican heads of government are to participate in the central government in Moscow. The reform was terminated on 2 October 1965.

19 June: The Presidium of the CC, CPSU, votes against Khrushchev by eight to three and demands his resignation. However, Khrushchev argues that the Presidium cannot dismiss him as he was appointed by the CC and demands a CC plenum. At the plenum Khrushchev defeats his opponents, partly due to the support of Marshal Zhukov, who placed military planes at the disposal of Khrushchev's supporters (4 July). Zhukov is elected a member of the Presidium but is dismissed as Minister of Defence and loses his Presidium seat on 26 October.

Khrushchev on top, 1957–62

1957

4 July: Malenkov, Molotov and Kaganovich lose their Presidium seats and their government posts (the defeated are called the Anti-Party Group because they opposed a greater role for the Party in running the country, see p. 142). Molotov become Soviet ambassador to Mongolia on 30 August.

26 August: The Soviet Union announces the testing of its first intercontinental ballistic missile.

19 September: The USA explodes its first nuclear device underground in Nevada.

4 October: The launch of Sputnik by the Soviet Union begins the era of space travel (see pp. 112–13).

15 October: A secret agreement between the Soviet Union and China provides Soviet help for the development of Chinese nuclear weapons. The agreement is cancelled by Moscow on 20 June 1959.

3 November: Launch of *Sputnik 2* with the dog Laika on board. It is the first time a living creature has been sent into space.

14–16 November: Conference of communist and workers' parties in Moscow on the occasion of the 40th anniversary of the October Revolution. Revisionism is stated to represent the 'chief ideological danger' and all parties are committed to defending the 'achievements of socialism' and 'mutual solidarity of workers as the principle of proletarian internationalism in its new form'. There is a clear desire by ruling Communist Party leaders for equality with the CPSU.

5 December: Launch of the first atomic-powered ice breaker, the *Lenin*.

1958

27 March: Bulganin resigns as Prime Minister and Khrushchev adds the post of Prime Minister to his leadership of the CPSU. This confirms Khrushchev as a strong, national leader.

6–7 May: The CC plenum decrees the rapid expansion of the chemical industry and the production of synthetic fibre and rubber during the next seven years.

23 October: The Soviet Union agrees to provide credits to build the Aswan Dam in Egypt (after the USA had declined). This is the first breakthrough for Soviet policy in Africa. Boris Pasternak is awarded the Nobel Prize for Literature and under pressure from the USSR Union of Writers he declines (29 October).

10 November: A new Berlin crisis begins with Khrushchev demanding that the Allies leave Berlin.

27 November: First Soviet ultimatum on Berlin. The Soviet Union withdraws from the agreement on the administration of Greater Berlin (12 September 1944), on the Control Council (1 May 1945) and its responsibilities under the 20 September 1955 treaty with the GDR. All the rights and duties in these agreements are transferred to the GDR government. West Berlin should become a demilitarised Free City. Khrushchev demands that the Berlin problem be resolved within six months.

1959

2 January: Launch of *Lunik*, the first Soviet two-stage rocket, which passes the moon on 4 January at a distance of 7,500 km and becomes the first satellite of the sun.

15–22 January: The third Soviet census (15 January) reveals a population of 208,827,000, of which 48 per cent are urban and 52 per cent rural dwellers.

27 January–5 February: The 21st Extraordinary Congress of the CPSU. Khrushchev announces that the Soviet Union has now achieved full socialism and that the phase of the construction of communism has now begun (classless society, elimination of the differences between urban and rural areas, etc.).

20 February–3 March: British Prime Minister Harold Macmillan, in Moscow, advises the Soviet government against being inflexible on the Berlin question.

11 May–5 August: The conference of foreign ministers from the Soviet Union, the USA, Great Britain and France fails to make any headway on Germany and the Berlin question.

14 September: The *Luna 2* space probe lands on the moon (launched on 12 September).

15–27 September: Khrushchev's first visit to the USA. He meets President Eisenhower at Camp David (26–27 September) and withdraws his Berlin ultimatum and this leads to the Camp David spirit emerging.

30 September–1 October: On his way home from the USA, Khrushchev visits Beijing and is given a frosty reception.

1 December: The Soviet Union and 11 other states sign the Antarctic Treaty, which bans atomic testing and rocket and military bases there.

1960

10 February–5 March: Khrushchev visits India, Burma and Indonesia.

4–13 February: Mikoyan visits Cuba and promises US$100 million credits and agrees to take 1 million tonnes of Cuban sugar annually for five years.

5 May: Moscow announces the shooting down of the US U2 spy plane, piloted by Gary Powers.

16–17 May: The U2 incident results in the Paris summit failing when Khrushchev demands that President Eisenhower apologise for the incident.

20–25 June: At the 3rd Congress of the Communist Party of Romania, Khrushchev openly attacks the Communist Party of China.

23 June: Chinese–Soviet polemics intensify as China rejects Khrushchev's view that 'peaceful co-existence with the capitalists' is possible and demands a policy of strength against the capitalist world.

17–19 August: Gary Powers, the American U2 pilot, is sentenced to 10 years imprisonment (he is exchanged for a Soviet spy in 1962).

18 August: The Soviet Union withdraws all its engineers and specialists from China.

19 September–30 October: Khrushchev attends the UN, addresses the General Assembly several times, thumps his desk during a speech by Macmillan (29 September) and bangs on his desk with a shoe during a speech by the Philippines delegate (12 October).

10 November–1 December: The conference of the 81 communist and workers' parties in Moscow supports the Soviet position adopted at the 21st Party Congress.

7–8 December: A Sino–Soviet meeting in Moscow fails to overcome the split between the two leading communist parties.

1961

20 January: During his inauguration, President Kennedy states that the USA will 'pay any price, bear any burden, meet any hardship, support any friend, oppose any foe, to ensure the survival and the success of liberty'.

12 April: Yury Gagarin, in *Vostok 1*, becomes the first person to circle the earth.

17–20 April: The Bay of Pigs invasion by Cuban exiles, backed by the CIA, is a disastrous failure.

27–29 May: Soviet advisers and specialists leave Albania and Soviet submarines quit Valona.

3–4 June: Khrushchev and President John F. Kennedy meet in Vienna. Khrushchev demands the demilitarisation of Berlin.

30 July: The draft of a new Party programme is published in *Pravda* (to replace the 1919 programme). The CPSU has moved from being the avant-garde of the working class (dictatorship of the proletariat) to being a 'people's party'. The programme asserts that war can be avoided and the transition from capitalism to socialism is inevitable.

6 August: German Titov, in *Vostok 2*, becomes the second person in space and returns the following day to earth.

13 August: The building of the Berlin Wall begins.

17–31 October: A 20-year plan is discussed at the 22nd Party Congress and lays down the transition to communism. It adopts a new programme and statue (Party rules) and removes Khrushchev's conservative opponents; Stalin's body is removed from the Lenin–Stalin mausoleum and buried nearby on 1 November; and the Chinese and Albanians are sharply criticised.

9–11 November: Stalingrad, Stalinsk, Stalino and Stalinabad (Tajikistan) are renamed, respectively, Volgograd, Novokuznetsk, Donetsk and Dushanbe.

10 November: The Soviet Union closes its embassy in Tirana, Albania.

1962

10 February: Moscow and Washington agree to exchange Gary Powers for the Soviet spy Rudolf Abel.

11–12–15 August: The Soviet cosmonauts Major Nikolaev and Colonel Popovich achieve the first joint space flight in *Vostok 3* and *Vostok 4*.

4 September: President Kennedy warns the Soviet Union not to deploy surface-to-air missiles in Cuba.

9 September: Professor Evsei Liberman of Kharkov publishes an article entitled 'Plan, Profit and Bonuses' in *Pravda*, which proposes a wide-ranging economic reform involving the decentralisation of planning and greater autonomy for the enterprises. The article begins a vigorous debate but the Party leadership signals its opposition on 19 November.

Khrushchev in decline, 1962–64

1962

25 September–7 January 1963: The Cuban Missile Crisis (see pp. 240–1) begins on 30 November 1961 when President Kennedy approves Operation Mongoose to 'help Cuba overthrow the communist regime'.

The Soviets place short-range nuclear rockets on Cuba and the Americans discover what is happening on 18 October. On 22 October Kennedy imposes a naval blockade of Cuba and between 23 and 28 October Kennedy and Khrushchev exchange letters. Khrushchev agrees to withdraw the missiles and the Americans agree not to invade Cuba and remove Jupiter missiles from Turkey. Khrushchev is humiliated but he saves the peace. The two sides inform U Thant, UN Secretary General, that they have arrived at a peaceful resolution of the conflict.

6 November: The USA states that Soviet nuclear bombers, together with the missiles, must also leave Cuba.

20 November: Khrushchev states bombers will leave Cuba but Castro will not permit US verification. The US pledge not to invade Cuba is therefore only formalised in 1970.

1963

27 April–24 May: First visit to the Soviet Union by Castro, who declares that Cuba now belongs to the socialist camp.

14 June–14 July: The Communist Party of China forwards an open letter to Moscow accusing the Russians of 'restoring capitalism' and betraying Marxism. The treaty on nuclear weapons of 15 October 1957 is annulled by the Russians and after unsuccessful discussions with the Chinese (5–20 June) Moscow refutes the Chinese accusations in an open letter (14 July).

16 June: Valentina Tereshkova becomes the first woman in space, aboard *Vostok 6*, and returns to earth on 19 June (there were no other women cosmonauts).

5 August: The foreign ministers of the Soviet Union, the USA and Great Britain, in Moscow, sign a treaty on the gradual ending of atomic tests in the atmosphere, in space and underwater. Many other states later join. It becomes binding on 10 October 1963. France and China refuse to sign.

22 October: The ruble bloc is created by Comecon members with a clearing bank, the International Bank for Economic Cooperation, becoming responsible, in Moscow. The currency unit is the transferable ruble, which has a fine gold content of 0.987412 gram or the same as a ruble. The transferable ruble never existed physically but was an accountancy device.

1964

9–25 May: Khrushchev visits the United Arab Republic to be present at the inauguration of the first part of the Aswan dam (work began on 9 January 1960). Khrushchev makes Nasser a Hero of the Soviet Union. However, towards the end of the year Nasser begins to play Moscow off against Beijing and China extends a loan of US$80 million on 21 December 1964.

12 October: Launch of the first spacecraft *Voskhod* with three cosmonauts. They return on 13 October.

14 October: Nikita Khrushchev is removed as First Secretary of the CC, CPSU, and as Prime Minister at a CC plenum which elects Leonid Brezhnev as First Secretary. Aleksei Kosygin becomes Prime Minister. It is agreed that in the future no person will simultaneously be able to be head of the Party and head of government.

Collective leadership, 1964–68

1964

16 November: The reform of the Party (19–23 November 1962) into industrial and non-industrial wings is declared to be over and Party secretaries are again responsible for all activities in their region.

1965

18 March: First walk in space by cosmonaut Aleksei Leonov.

1–5 May: The suggestion for a world communist conference by the Soviet Union on 10 February 1963 never comes about because of Chinese opposition. Instead a consultative meeting of only 18 parties (among those absent are China, North Vietnam, North Korea, Indonesia, Japan and Romania) undermines Moscow's continued attempts to dominate the world movement. It has to accept partnership relations between communist parties.

27–29 September: A CC plenum resolves to improve the management of industry, planning and increase incentives (Kosygin reform). The decentralisation of the economy, introduced in 1957, comes to an end and planning is again to be from the centre. The central ministries again come into being. However, enterprises receive some autonomy and the right to decide their suppliers.

1–2 October: The collective nature of the Soviet government is underlined. The USSR government is composed of the Prime Minister, his first deputy, 47 ministers, 15 chairs of state committees and the prime ministers of the 15 Union republics.

1966

10 January: Kosygin helps to bring the Indian–Pakistani conflict to an end and both sides sign an agreement in Tashkent. This is a coup for Soviet influence in Asia and helps to stem the increase in Chinese influence.

10–14 February: The Soviet writers, Andrei Sinyavsky and Yuli Daniel, are sentenced to five and seven years forced labour for anti-Soviet propaganda.

29 March–8 April: The 23rd Party Congress removes Khrushchev supporters and there is a partial rehabilitation of Stalin. Cultural policy becomes less liberal. The Politburo is reintroduced and Brezhnev becomes the General Secretary of the Party (the previous holder of the position was Stalin). The military budget is increased.

1967
27 January: A Soviet–US–British agreement on the peaceful use of space is signed simultaneously in Moscow, Washington and London and becomes effective on 10 October.
21 April: Stalin's daughter, Svetlana Alliluyeva, is granted political asylum in the United States.
28 April: The Crimean Tatars are rehabilitated but not permitted to return to their former homeland (now occupied by Russians and Ukrainians).
23–25 June: President Johnson and Aleksei Kosygin, the Soviet Prime Minister, meet in Glassboro', New Jersey, for a mini-summit.

1968
8 May: The Soviet Union, Poland, East Germany, Hungary and Bulgaria convene in Moscow to discuss the Prague Spring, launched by Dubcek.
1 July: Many states sign the nuclear non-proliferation treaty (54 in Washington, 36 in Moscow and 23 in London). The Soviet Union and the USA state they will begin strategic arms limitation talks (SALT).
14 July: At a Warsaw meeting the Soviet Union, Poland, East Germany, Hungary and Bulgaria discuss the situation in Czechoslovakia and demand a meeting with the Czechoslovaks.
29 July–1 August: Meeting of the Politburo of the CC, CPSU, and the Presidium of the CC, Communist Party of Czechoslovakia, in Cierna and Tisu to discuss the reforms in Czechoslovakia (Prague Spring and social-ism with a human face).
21 August: Invasion of Czechoslovakia by Warsaw Pact forces (see pp. 224–5), headed by the Soviet Union, with smaller contingents from the GDR, Poland, Hungary and Bulgaria. Romania, Yugoslavia, China and Albania protest against the invasion. The reform politicians are dragged off to Moscow but return on 27 August.
26 September: As the Warsaw Pact excludes intervention in the internal affairs of member states (article 8), the CPSU, in *Pravda,* advances the thesis of the 'limited sovereignty of socialist states in case of danger for the world socialist system'. Brezhnev advances the same concept on 6 November and it becomes known as the Brezhnev doctrine.
12 November: Leonid Brezhnev, in Warsaw, introduces the Brezhnev doctrine of limited sovereignty of communist pro-Moscow states.

Brezhnev emerges as *primus inter pares,* 1969–75
1969
2 March: Armed conflict between Chinese and Soviet forces on the islands in the Ussuri River. There is further fighting on 14–15 March (see pp. 222–3).

28–29 March: The defeat of the Soviet team by the Czechoslovaks in the ice hockey world championship in Stockholm leads to celebrations in Czechoslovakia and attacks on Soviet soldiers and buildings. On 30 March the deputy Soviet Foreign Minister Semenov is sent to Prague to force through changes in the Communist Party of Czechoslovakia (CPCz) leadership.

17 April: Alexander Dubcek and other reform communists are voted off the CC, Communist Party of Czechoslovakia, as a result of massive Soviet pressure. Gustav Husak becomes the new Party leader.

13 August: More Soviet–Chinese fighting along the Xinjiang border with Central Asia.

6 November: Alexander Solzhenitsyn is expelled from the USSR Union of Writers.

17 November–22 December: First rounds of talks on limiting atomic armaments between the Soviet Union and the USA in Helsinki (SALT). Further meetings rotate between Helsinki and Geneva.

1970

15–22 January: A census in the Soviet Union (15 January) reveals that the total population is 241,720,134, of which 111,399,377 are men and 130,320,757 are women; 135,991,514 live in cities and 105,728,620 in rural areas.

6 May: Soviet–Czechoslovak 'normalisation' treaty of friendship, cooperation and mutual assistance, in which the Brezhnev doctrine is included.

12 August: Aleksei Kosygin, Andrei Gromyko the Soviet Foreign Minister, Willy Brandt the West German Chancellor, and Walter Scheel the West German Foreign Minister, sign the Soviet–West German Moscow Treaty, which begins Bonn's Ostpolitik. This states that European frontiers can be changed only by negotiation. The treaty is followed by the Warsaw Treaty of 7 December 1970.

1 September: A USSR Ministry of Justice is re-established.

20 September: The space probe *Luna 16* lands on the moon, collects some stone fragments and returns to earth.

17 November: *Luna 17* places the first moon vehicle, *Lunokhod 1*, on the moon, and it can be guided from earth.

15 December: The space probe *Venus 7*, weighing 1.2 tonnes, lands after 120 days on Venus and transmits information for 25 minutes.

1971

11 February: The Soviet Union, the USA and Great Britain, in Moscow, Washington and London, sign the treaty banning nuclear weapons and other weapons of mass destruction in the sea, on the seabed and under water.

30 March–9 April: The 24th Party Congress discusses the ninth FYP (1971–75) which envisages living standards rising due to rising productivity and the acceleration of the scientific-technical revolution.

7 June: The space capsule *Soyuz 11* docks with the space station *Salyut 1*, launched on 19 April. Three cosmonauts transfer to the station and work there for 23 days and 18 hours.

3 September: Four-power Berlin treaty regulates the status of West Berlin (transit of civil goods and persons, expansion of links with West Germany, representation of West Berlin abroad). After GDR–FRG agreements, a final protocol is added on 3 June 1972. The treaty then becomes law.

2 December: The space probe *Mars 3* (launched 28 May) ejects a capsule which lands on Mars and sends back signals for a short time.

12 December: The hot line between the Kremlin and the White House is used for the first time under Nixon amid fears of Soviet (pro-Indian) or Chinese (pro-Pakistani) intervention in the war over Bangladesh; the US fleet is ordered to the Bay of Bengal.

1972

20 May: Petr Shelest resigns as First Secretary of the CC, Communist Party of Ukraine, and is replaced by Volodymyr Shcherbitsky (25 May).

22–30 May: Official state visit by President Richard Nixon to the Soviet Union, during which the SALT treaty is signed (26 May). Relations between the superpowers is to be based on peaceful coexistence and détente.

3 June: The USA, USSR, Britain and France sign an agreement on the future of Berlin.

5–10 June: During a visit to the Soviet Union Tito is showered with awards and honours, even though it is unclear whether the differences between the USSR and Yugoslavia have been resolved.

18 July: Differences between Cairo and Moscow result in 17,000 Soviet military and other advisers being expelled from Egypt.

3 October: President Nixon and Andrei Gromyko sign the Anti-Ballistic Missile (ABM) treaty.

18 October: US–Soviet trade agreement signed.

22 November–8 June 1973: Talks in Helsinki – with some breaks – on preparing a European conference on security and cooperation (CSCE). The Warsaw Pact states on 3 July 1966, in their Bucharest declaration, have already declared this to be a goal. The USA and Canada join 32 European states in discussions.

1973

1 March: The sixth exchange of Party books begins and for the first time is not aimed at purging the Party of undesirable elements. The goal is to attract skilled workers, engineers and managers. Party book no. 1 is in Lenin's name, no. 2 bears Brezhnev's name.

18–22 May: Leonid Brezhnev makes the first visit by a Soviet leader to West Germany and signs a 10-year agreement on economic cooperation.

18–25 June: During the visit of Leonid Brezhnev to the United States agreement is reached on the basic principles of talks cutting back further on strategic offensive weapons (21 June) and avoiding military confrontation and a missile war (22 June).

3 July: The conference on security and cooperation in Europe (CSCE) opens in Helsinki.

25–31 October: A conference on the peaceful use of atomic energy is attended by over 3,000 representatives from 143 countries. Brezhnev addresses it and presents Soviet foreign policy (26 October).

1974

27 June–3 July: During the visit of President Nixon to the Soviet Union several agreements on limiting strategic arms and cooperation between the two countries are signed.

4 July: Iraq expels 80 Soviet advisers (linked to the rapprochement with the USA and the desire for US weapons).

24 November: During a meeting between Leonid Brezhnev and President Gerald Ford in Vladivostok it is agreed to conclude a treaty on limiting strategic arms over the period October 1977–December 1985.

25 November: An agreement is signed by the Soviet Union, the USA and Japan on the exploitation of Siberian natural gas. It never takes effect because the USA refuses to grant the Soviet Union the necessary credits.

1975

3 January: President Ford signs the Trade Reform Act, which lays down the condition that trade between the Soviet Union and the USA can only expand (the Jackson–Vanik amendment) if Moscow permits greater Jewish emigration.

18 June: The Soviet Union warns China not to interfere in Soviet–Japanese relations (rejected by Japan on 19 June and China on 21 June).

17–19 July: Joint US–Soviet space mission, agreed in 1972, takes place.

29 July–1 August: Brezhnev attends the conclusion of the 3rd round of the CSCE negotiations and has meetings with leading politicians as well: Tito on 29 July, Pierre Trudeau (Canada) on 31 July, Demirel (Turkey) and chancellor Helmut Schmidt on 1 August, Moro (Italy) and Harold Wilson on 30 July, and President Gerald Ford on 2 August.

1 August: The Helsinki Final Act is signed by heads of states and governments.

20 October: US–Soviet agreement which obliges the USSR to import 30 million tonnes of grain over five years from the USA and the Soviet Union is to deliver at least 10 million tonnes of oil annually to the USA.

1–5 December: President Ford visits China and meets Mao Zedong, who criticises US–Soviet détente.

Brezhnev in physical decline, 1976–82

1976
24 February–5 March: The 25th Party Congress confirms the directives for the Soviet economy, 1976–80. In foreign policy Brezhnev declares that efforts will continue to reach agreement with the USA on limiting nuclear arms and ending the arms race between the two countries.
13 May: Nine Soviet dissidents announce the setting up of a group to monitor the implementation of the Helsinki agreement by the Soviet Union (Helsinki group), led by Academician Yury Orlov (other members include Elena Bonner (Sakharov's wife), Aleksandr Ginzburg and Petr Grigorenko).
28 May: The USA and the Soviet Union agree to limit the size of certain underground nuclear tests.
6–26 September: Arthur Schlesinger, a former US Secretary of State, visits China and offers Beijing an alliance against the Soviet Union and analyses the weaknesses of the Chinese air defence system.
18 December: The Soviet Union and Chile exchange the Soviet dissident Bukovsky for the General Secretary of the Communist Party of Chile, Corvalan.

1977
27–30 February: US Secretary of State Cyrus Vance visits Moscow but Andrei Gromyko, Soviet Foreign Minister, states that there can be no major revision of the agreement on SALT at Vladivostok in 1974; he also opposes US interference in domestic Soviet politics.
1 September: The Soviet Union adopts a new national anthem.
4–14 October: CSCE talks begin in Belgrade as a follow-up meeting to the Helsinki agreements of 1975. They continue until 9 March 1989.
7 October: The USSR Supreme Soviet adopts the new Soviet constitution unanimously. It replaces the 1936 Stalin constitution and introduces the concept of the Soviet Union as the state of all the people (article 1). The USSR is a 'unitary multi-national federal state' (article 2) and the CPSU is the 'leading and guiding force of Soviet society' and the 'core of its political system' (article 6). The Party is also the Party of the whole people.

1978
8 March: In Belgrade the final document of the CSCE follow-up meeting is signed. Talks are to continue in Madrid in November 1980.

14 April: Demonstrations in Armenia and Georgia against the omission of the statement in their constitutions that Armenian and Georgian are state languages. This article is then added.

26 April: Arkady Shevchenko, the top Soviet UN official, asks for political asylum in the USA.

13 July: Soviet dissidents Anatoly Sharansky and Aleksandr Ginsburg are sent to prison.

22 August: Crimean Tatars forward a request to the CC, CPSU, to permit them to return to their homeland (signed by over 5,000). They had been deported to Siberia and Central Asia in 1944, accused of collaborating with the Germans.

27 November: Mikhail Gorbachev is elected CC Secretary for Agriculture, succeeding Fedor Kulakov, his first patron.

1979

17–24 January: The Soviet census reveals a population of 262,442,000. Hence the population has increased by 8.6 per cent since the last census in 1970 but there has been only a small increase in European Russia and a huge increase in Central Asia – 20–31 per cent.

15–18 June: SALT 2 is signed at a Soviet–US summit in Vienna between President Carter and Leonid Brezhnev.

17 November: Mikhail Gorbachev is elected a candidate member of the Politburo.

12 December: In response to the stationing of SS20 medium-range missiles in the western regions of the Soviet Union, NATO announces, in Brussels, that it will station American Cruise and Pershing 2 missiles in western Europe from 1984. NATO adopts a double track policy: if negotiations with the Soviet Union are successful the missiles need not be put in place.

26–27 December: Soviet troops intervene in Afghanistan and Hafissulah Amin, Afghan leader, is overthrown and murdered with the aid of Soviet troops. The new pro-Soviet leader is Babrak Karmal.

1980

4 January: In response to the Soviet invasion of Afghanistan, President Jimmy Carter imposes a trade embargo for grain and advanced technology; he also suspends the ratification of the SALT II treaty and promises greater aid to Pakistan.

22 January: Academician Andrei Sakharov is arrested on a street in Moscow and exiled to Gorky (Nizhny Novgorod), which as a closed city is barred to foreigners.

19 July: The 22nd Olympic Games begin in Moscow with 81 nations participating. Over 40 states boycott the games.

11 October: The cosmonauts Leonid Popov and Valery Ryumin land in Kazakhstan after a record flight of 185 days in space. They took off from

Baikonur on 9 April 1980 aboard *Soyuz 35* and the following day transferred to the space station *Salyut 6*, which had been circling the earth for over 3 years.

21 October: Mikhail Gorbachev is elected a full member of the Politburo.

22–23 October: Aleksei Kosygin, head of government since 1964, resigns and also leaves the Politburo for health reasons. He is succeeded by Nikolai Tikhonov, first deputy chair of the USSR Council of Ministers and a member of the Politburo since 27 November 1979.

1981

23 February–3 March: The 26th Party Congress is a dull affair due to Brezhnev's physical frailty. However, he admits that there are still nationality problems which need addressing.

24 April: President Reagan lifts the grain embargo against the Soviet Union because it is not in the interests of American farmers.

6 August: President Reagan announces the stockpiling of neutron bombs by the USA.

23 September: Andrei Gromyko and General Alexander Haig, US Secretary of State, agree to begin talks on intermediate-range nuclear (INF) weapons.

16 October: President Reagan claims that Moscow plans to fight and win a nuclear war; Brezhnev denies this on 20 October.

18 November: President Reagan proposes a new disarmament agenda, including the complete elimination of INF weapons; this is the first time the 'zero option' is articulated.

1982

24 May: Yury Andropov is elected a CC secretary, filling the place vacated by Suslov, and ceases to be head of the KGB. This vital appointment prepares the way for his succeeding Brezhnev as it was virtually impossible for someone who was not in the Party Secretariat to take over as Party leader.

30 May: President Reagan promises that the USA will adhere to SALT II as long as the Soviet Union does.

29 June: The USSR and USA begin START talks in Geneva.

10 November: Leonid Brezhnev dies.

The interregnum: Andropov and Chernenko, 1982–85

1982

12 November: Yury Andropov is elected General Secretary of the CC, CPSU.

1983

9 March: President Reagan describes the Soviet Union as the 'evil empire'.

23 March: President Reagan announces the Strategic Defence Initiative (SDI), also called the Star Wars programme.

22 April: Mikhail Gorbachev, to mark the 113th anniversary of Lenin's birth, delivers the main speech in Moscow and stresses Lenin's definition of democratic socialism as a point of departure in the organisation of socialism. He calls for a free rein to be afforded creativity and initiative at the base in order to mobilise a maximum of initiative and display a maximum of independence.

1 September: South Korean airliner KAL007 is shot down after straying into Soviet air space.

9 September: Marshal Nikolai Ogarkov, Chief of the General Staff, appears at an international press conference to explain the shooting down of the Korean KAL007 airliner and expresses no regrets. Andropov is too ill to attend.

15 December: Mutually balanced force reduction (MBFR) talks, on conventional forces, end without agreement on further meetings.

1984

9 February: Yury Andropov dies.

13 February: Konstantin Chernenko is elected General Secretary of the CC, CPSU. Mikhail Gorbachev is regarded as his no. 2.

14 February: Andropov is buried and Chernenko fumbles his funeral speech, is short of breath, and quite obviously ill.

28 September: President Reagan meets Andrei Gromyko for the first time, in Washington, while the latter is attending the UN.

22 November: It is announced that Andrei Gromyko and George Shultz, the US Secretary of State, will meet in January 1985 to discuss disarmament.

15–21 December: Mikhail Gorbachev visits Great Britain and Mrs Margaret Thatcher, Prime Minister, regards him as a man with whom she can do business.

1985

7–8 January: Gromyko and Shultz agree in Geneva on three sets of talks: START, INF and defensive systems, including those based in space.

The Gorbachev era: in the ascendancy, 1985–89

1985

10 March: Konstantin Chernenko dies.

11 March: Mikhail Gorbachev is elected General Secretary of the CC, CPSU.

7 April: Gorbachev halts Soviet missile deployment but insists they will restart in November if NATO does not stop its deployment.

23 April: The April CC plenum accepts Gorbachev's vague reforms. Chebrikov, Ryzhkov and Ligachev become full members of the Politburo, and Minister of Defence Sergei Sokolov becomes a candidate member.

15 May: Gorbachev visits Leningrad and evokes much support for his policies and his frankness.

16 May: Aspects of the anti-alcohol campaign are announced, including reducing production of strong drink and increased penalties for drunken driving.

1 July: A CC plenum removes Grigory Romanov from the Politburo, Eduard Shevardnadze is elected a full member of the Politburo, and Boris Yeltsin and Lev Zaikov become CC secretaries.

2 July: Andrei Gromyko becomes chair of the Presidium of the USSR Supreme Soviet, head of state, and Shevardnadze succeeds him as Foreign Minister.

25–27 September: Eduard Shevardnadze visits the USA to prepare the ground for a Reagan–Gorbachev summit.

2–5 October: Gorbachev visits France, his first official visit to the west as leader. He uses the term 'reasonable sufficiency' for the first time, does not link INF negotiations to anything else and rejects ideology as the basis of foreign policy. He proposes that the superpowers reduce their strategic arsenals by a half.

19–21 November: Summit meeting in Geneva between Mikhail Gorbachev and President Ronald Reagan; they agree to meet in the future.

24 December: Boris Yeltsin replaces Viktor Grishin as First Secretary of the Moscow city Party committee.

1986

8 February: In an interview in *L'Humanité*, the French Communist Party newspaper, Gorbachev describes Stalinism as a 'concept thought up by opponents of communism and used on a large scale to smear the Soviet Union and socialism as a whole'.

18 February: A CC plenum discusses the 27th Party Congress and the economic plan for 1990–2000. Viktor Grishin leaves the Politburo and Boris Yeltsin is elected a candidate member.

25 February–6 March: The 27th Party Congress opens with a long keynote speech by Gorbachev in which he advocates the radical reform of the economic mechanism. He refers to the war in Afghanistan as a 'bleeding wound' and the Brezhnev era as 'years of stagnation'. On 6 March Lev Zaikov becomes a full member of the Politburo. Yeltsin addresses the Congress on the sensitive subject of Party privileges.

26 April: An explosion at the Chernobyl nuclear reactor, Ukraine, turns out to be the worst in Soviet history (see pp. 127–8). However, the initial response of the leadership is to play down its extent.

28 July: Gorbachev arrives in Vladivostok to tour the Soviet Far East and states that six regiments will be withdrawn from Afghanistan and that talks have begun with Mongolia on the withdrawal of Soviet troops.

10 October: Gorbachev arrives in Reykjavik for a two-day summit with President Reagan. They agree on most arms reduction issues. They almost agree on substantial cuts in offensive arms and even the elimination of nuclear weapons.

19 October: Five US diplomats are expelled from the Soviet Union in retaliation for the expulsion of Soviet UN officials.

21 October: The USA expels 55 Soviet diplomats from the Soviet Embassy in Washington and the Soviet Consulate General in San Francisco and establishes quotas for each.

22 October: The USSR expels five more US diplomats and withdraws Soviet employees from the US Embassy and Consulate General.

6 November: The USSR Ministry of Defence states that the withdrawal of six regiments (about 6,000 men) from Afghanistan has been completed and that they will not be replaced.

28 November: The US deploys the new B–52 bomber, which violates the START II treaty.

1987

28 March–1 April: British Prime Minister, Margaret Thatcher, visits the Soviet Union, where she stresses human rights and calls for the withdrawal of Soviet troops from Afghanistan.

28 May: Matthias Rust, a young West German, lands his Cessna light aircraft near Red Square, having penetrated Soviet air defences without being noticed.

30 May: Many top military changes are made in the light of Rust's achievement. General Dmitry Yazov replaces General Sergei Sokolov as USSR Minister of Defence.

28–30 June: The USSR Supreme Soviet session is devoted mainly to economic reform. Ryzhkov calls the central management of the economy 'obsolete' and advocates radical changes. A law on the state enterprise which affords enterprises autonomy over their budgets is adopted and is to be implemented on 1 January 1988.

24 September: A Politburo resolution permits small shops to be run by individuals and cooperatives, a very radical reform.

12 October: In Leningrad, Gorbachev champions perestroika and glasnost (see pp. 99–100 and 89) and warns that if the Party leadership does not support reform, the Party could lose its leading role.

21 October: At a CC plenum, Boris Yeltsin breaks a Party taboo that leaders do not criticise one another in public, and blames Gorbachev and Ligachev for the slow pace of reform. Gorbachev reacts very sharply. Yeltsin requests permission to resign as a Politburo member and as First Secretary of the Moscow city Party committee. Geidar Aliev is removed from the Politburo.

1 November: Gorbachev's book, *Perestroika and the New Political Thinking*, is published in Moscow. It is translated into many languages and is a huge best-seller.

11 November: Boris Yeltsin is attacked by Gorbachev and others at a meeting of the Moscow Party committee. Lev Zaikov takes over as First Secretary. On 18 November Yeltsin is made first deputy chair of the state committee on construction.

5 December: Gorbachev travels to London and meets Margaret Thatcher.

7–10 December: Gorbachev travels to Washington for meetings with President Ronald Reagan. In Washington he signs the treaty banning intermediate-range nuclear missiles (INF) (8 December). It is his first visit to the United States and becomes a huge personal triumph; Gorbymania has appeared.

1988

1 January: Law on the state enterprise becomes effective and affords factories considerable autonomy (this reform loosens central control of the economy and leads to increasing inflation and shortages).

28 February: Armenians and Jews are attacked in Sumgait, Azerbaijan, and several persons are killed.

13 March: *Sovetskaya Rossiya* publishes Nina Andreeva's letter attacking perestroika and those critical of Stalin.

14 April: Agreements on the ending of the Afghan war are signed in Geneva. The Soviet Union and the USA guarantee the agreements and promise not to interfere in the domestic affairs of Afghanistan and Pakistan.

29 May–2 June: President Reagan visits Moscow to meet Gorbachev for their fourth summit. Reagan also meets dissidents and praises freedom in an address to students at Moscow State University.

June–July: Continuing conflict in Nagorno-Karabakh. On 15 June the Armenian Supreme Soviet votes to incorporate Nagorno-Karabakh but the Azerbaijani Supreme Soviet rejects this on 17 June. On 20 July the USSR Supreme Soviet rules that the Armenian incorporation of Nagorno-Karabakh cannot be accepted.

28 June–1 July: The 19th Party Conference opens in Moscow and Gorbachev proposes a presidential system for the country, the removal of the Party from economic management and the convening of a USSR Congress of People's Deputies (see pp. 196–7) with contested elections.

25 July: Shevardnadze, addressing a conference in the USSR Ministry of Foreign Affairs, rejects the class struggle as the basis of Soviet foreign policy.

5 August: Egor Ligachev reiterates, during a speech in Gorky (Nizhny Novgorod), that class struggle is the basis of Soviet foreign policy.

12 August: Aleksandr Yakovlev, in a speech in Vilnius, Lithuania, espouses universal human values or the common interests of mankind.

19 August: The draft programme of the Estonian People's Front is published in an Estonian newspaper.

21 September: A state of emergency is declared in parts of Nagorno-Karabakh after disorders.

30 September: At a CC plenum a large number of members retire (having lost their posts, which afforded them CC status). Gromyko and Solomentsev retire from the Politburo. Ligachev is placed in charge of a CC commission on agriculture, a clear demotion. Aleksandr Yakovlev takes over the international department in the Party Secretariat.

1 October: Gorbachev is elected chair of the Presidium of the USSR Supreme Soviet, head of state, by the USSR Supreme Soviet.

16 November: The Estonian Supreme Soviet declares sovereignty and claims the right to give Estonian legislation precedence over Soviet legislation.

26 November: The USSR Supreme Soviet annuls the Estonian declaration of sovereignty and takes control of state property in the republic.

1 December: The USSR Supreme Soviet passes a new electoral law which provides for contested elections and secret ballots.

7 December: Gorbachev, at the UN, announces that the Soviet Union will reduce its armed forces by 500,000 within two years without requiring reciprocal moves by the USA or its allies. He also stresses that the common interests of mankind and freedom of choice are universal human principles. Later he meets Reagan and President-elect Bush on Governors Island. Marshal Sergei Akhromeev resigns as Chief of the General Staff and deputy Minister of Defence. Armenia is hit by a massive earthquake with over 50,000 dead. Gorbachev abandons his planned trip to Cuba and flies home.

1989

12 January: Nagorno-Karabakh comes under direct rule from Moscow by decree of the USSR Supreme Soviet. Arkady Volsky is appointed provisional administrator.

17–19 January: The CSCE Review Conference concludes in Vienna with agreement to begin negotiations on the reduction of conventional forces in Europe (CFE).

18 January: Estonia adopts a new language law which requires non-speakers of Estonian to learn the language within four years. On 26 January Lithuania does the same and on 1 February Latvia follows suit. Other republics adopt the same legislation: Tajikistan on 22 July, Kirgizia (Kyrgyzstan) on 24 August, Moldavia (Moldova) on 28 August, Uzbekistan on 21 October and Ukraine on 28 October.

15 February: The last Soviet troops leave Afghanistan; the Najibullah regime survives until 1992. Najibullah is killed by Taleban forces in September 1996.

26 March: Elections are held to the USSR Congress of People's Deputies. Many Party candidates lose and the pro-independence parties win in the Baltic States. Boris Yeltsin wins in Moscow.

9 April: The Soviet army attacks a peaceful demonstration in Tbilisi, killing 20 and injuring hundreds.

25 April: At a Party plenum, 74 members of the Central Committee resign. Soviet troops begin leaving Hungary.

15–19 May: Gorbachev visits China and announces the normalisation of relations between the two states.

25 May: The USSR Congress of People's Deputies opens in Moscow and is televised live. Gorbachev is elected chairman and on 26 May the members of the USSR Supreme Soviet, the new standing parliament, are elected from among the Congress's members. Yeltsin obtains a seat when Aleksei Kazannik stands down in his favour.

6 July: Gorbachev addresses the Council of Europe in Strasbourg and states that the Soviet Union will not stand in the way of reform in eastern Europe.

10 July: Coal miners in the Kuzbass, Siberia, go on strike, followed later by the Donbass, Ukraine.

29 July: The Inter-Regional Group is formed in the Congress of People's Deputies to promote reform. Among the leaders chosen by these 250-odd deputies are Boris Yeltsin, Gavriil Popov and Andrei Sakharov.

23 August: Over two million participate in a Baltic Way demonstration, forming a human chain across the three republics.

31 August: The Moldavian Supreme Soviet decrees that Moldavian (Moldovian or Romanian) is the state language and replaces the Cyrillic alphabet with the Roman.

22–23 September: James Baker, US Secretary of State, and Shevardnadze meet in Jackson Hole, Wyoming. Shevardnadze drops the Soviet demand which links reduction in strategic missiles to limits on the Strategic Defence Initiative (SDI) or Star Wars.

25–26 September: President Bush and Eduard Shevardnadze, at the UN, propose the elimination of chemical weapons.

7 October: Gorbachev, in East Berlin, tells the crowds that 'life punishes those who fall behind' and this further undermines the authority of Erich Honecker, the GDR leader. He is replaced by Egon Krenz on 18 October.

8 October: The Latvian Popular Front adopts independence as its goal.

9 November: The Berlin Wall comes down.

19 November: The Georgian Supreme Soviet declares sovereignty and decides that the Soviet occupation of Georgia in 1921 violated the 1920 treaty between Georgia and Russia.

28 November: The USSR Supreme Soviet ends direct rule over Nagorno-Karabakh despite objections by deputies from Armenia and Nagorno-Karabakh.

1 December: Gorbachev has an audience with Pope John Paul II in the Vatican and states that a law on freedom of conscience will be passed and that the Ukrainian (Greek) Catholic Church will be recognised again.

2–3 December: Gorbachev and Bush meet in Malta and Gorbachev states that force will not be used to ensure that east European communist regimes remain in power. Bush agrees to remove most controls on US–Soviet trade.

12 December: The second session of the USSR Congress of People's Deputies opens and Gorbachev refuses to consider amending or removing article 6 of the USSR constitution guaranteeing the Party a monopoly of political power.

20 December: The Communist Party of Lithuania declares itself independent of the Communist Party of the Soviet Union.

24 December: The USSR Supreme Soviet declares the secret protocol to the Nazi–Soviet Pact invalid but does not comment on the incorporation of the Baltic States and other territories acquired by the Soviet Union as part of this agreement.

Gorbachev in decline, 1990–91

1990

11–13 January: Gorbachev travels to Lithuania to discuss the republic's desire to break away from the Soviet Union. However, Lithuanians demonstrate for independence.

19–20 January: Clashes in Baku between Soviet forces and the local population leave many dead. The Azerbaijani National Front loses power.

February–March: Local elections are held throughout the Soviet Union with pro-independence candidates winning in the Baltic States; in Moscow and Leningrad the official Party candidates are rejected.

5 February: At a CC plenum Gorbachev proposes the Party abandon its leading role (article 6 of the USSR constitution), accept a multi-party system and adopt 'humane, democratic socialism'. These are accepted on 7 February after a stormy debate.

8 February: James Baker visits Moscow and proposes 2 (East and West Germany) + 4 (the USA, USSR, Britain and France) negotiations to discuss German unification.

10 February: Chancellor Kohl, in Moscow, gets an agreement in principle on German reunification.

12 February: The foreign ministers of the 2 + 4, meeting in Ottawa, agree to begin discussions on German unification.

11 March: Lithuania declares the restoration of independence and elects Vytautas Landsbergis Supreme Council chairman and President.

13 March: The USSR Congress of People's Deputies amends the USSR Constitution to create the office of President and revises article 6 to remove the Party monopoly of power.

14 March: Gorbachev is elected Soviet President by the Congress of People's Deputies.

25 March: The Communist Party of Estonia votes to be independent of the CPSU.

28 March: First free elections in Hungary since 1945.

1 May: The May Day parade in Red Square is disturbed by anti-Gorbachev protesters.

4 May: The Latvian Supreme Soviet endorses independence as a goal.

29 May: Boris Yeltsin is elected chairman (or President) of the Presidium of the RSFSR Supreme Soviet.

30 May–4 June: Gorbachev travels to Washington for his second summit with Bush, then visits Minneapolis-St Paul and San Francisco.

8 June: The RSFSR Supreme Soviet declares sovereignty and states its laws take precedence over Soviet laws.

19–23 June: The founding Congress of the Russian Communist Party convenes in Moscow.

22 June: Ivan Polozkov, a conservative, is elected leader of the Russian Communist Party.

30 June: Deliveries of oil and natural gas are resumed to Lithuania after the Lithuanian parliament temporarily suspends the implementation of its declaration of independence.

2–13 July: The 28th Party Congress convenes in Moscow. Gorbachev is re-elected General Secretary but with a significant number of votes against. The new Politburo contains only Party officials and will have no role in governing the country.

16 July: Ukraine declares sovereignty.

20 July: The 500-day programme of the Russian Republic is published. It envisages moving to a market economy in 500 days.

27 July: Belorussia declares sovereignty.

2 August: Iraq invades Kuwait.

3 August: Baker and Shevardnadze sign a joint statement in Moscow condemning the Iraqi invasion.

22 August: Turkmenistan and Armenia declare sovereignty.

25 August: Tajikistan declares sovereignty. The Abkhaz Autonomous Republic in Georgia declares independence from Georgia and requests Union republican status within the RSFSR.

9 September: Gorbachev and Bush meet for a one-day summit in Helsinki and agree to cooperate to end Iraqi aggression in Kuwait.

12 September: The 2 + 4 treaty is signed in Moscow ending four-power control over Germany.

24 September: The USSR Supreme Soviet grants Gorbachev special powers for 18 months to rule by decree during the transition to a market economy but cannot agree on an economic programme.

3 October: Germany is reunited.

20–21 October: The political movement, Democratic Russia, holds its first congress in Moscow.

25 October: Kazakhstan declares sovereignty.

28 October: The Kirgiz Supreme Soviet elects Askar Akaev President of Kirgizia. Pro-independence parties wins parliamentary elections in Georgia. The Rukh congress in Kiev accepts Ukrainian independence as a major goal.

30 October: Kirgizia declares sovereignty.

7 November: Shots are fired at Gorbachev during the revolution celebrations in Red Square.

17 November: The USSR Supreme Soviet accepts Gorbachev's proposal to set up a new Soviet government, consisting of representatives from all 15 Union republics, to be called the Soviet (Council) of the Federation.

19 November: The treaty on conventional forces in Europe (CFE) is signed in Paris.

23 November: The draft treaty of a new union is published, to be called the Union of Sovereign Soviet Republics. Most republican leaders criticise it.

1 December: Vadim Bakatin is removed as USSR Minister of Internal Affairs and replaced by Boris Pugo.

20 December: Eduard Shevardnadze, Minister of Foreign Affairs, resigns and warns of the threat of dictatorship.

25 December: Prime Minister Nikolai Ryzhkov suffers a heart attack.

26 December: Gorbachev chooses Gennady Yanaev as the new Vice-President of the Soviet Union but he is rejected on the first ballot by the Congress and accepted on the second the following day. Gorbachev is also afforded greater powers.

1991

11–13 January: Soviet black berets (Omon forces under the Ministry of the Interior) and the KGB Alpha division fire at the main printing press in Vilnius, Lithuania, and on 13 January attack and take the TV station there, killing 13 and one of their own dies also.

14 January: Valentin Pavlov is appointed Prime Minister of the USSR.

15 January: Operation Desert Storm, to remove Iraq from Kuwait, begins in the Persian Gulf.

20 January: Four die in clashes between Soviet forces and Latvian police.

9 February: Over 90 per cent of Lithuanian voters favour independence for Lithuania.

12 February: Valentin Pavlov, Soviet Prime Minister, claims there is a plot to undermine the Soviet economy and withdraws 100 ruble notes from circulation.

24 February: The US-led ground offensive begins against Iraq.

25 February: The Warsaw Pact agrees to annul all military agreements, effective as of 31 March, but to continue voluntary political links.

28 February: All military operations against Iraq are suspended.

1 March: Coal miners strike in the Donbass, Ukraine; the strike then spreads to other areas.

3 March: Referendums on independence are held in Estonia and Latvia with 78 per cent voting in favour in Estonia and 74 per cent in favour in Latvia.

14–16 March: Baker visits Moscow for discussions and meets Baltic leaders and other republican heads.

17 March: Referendum on the future of the USSR and (in the RSFSR) on the creation of a presidency and (in Moscow) a directly elected mayor. Large majority in favour of retaining the Union.

31 March: The Warsaw Pact is formally dissolved.

4 April: The RSFSR Supreme Soviet votes to give Yeltsin considerable power. Strikes begin in Minsk.

9 April: Georgia declares independence.

22 April: Prime Minister Pavlov presents an anti-crisis programme to the USSR Supreme Soviet.

23 April: In Novo-Ogarevo, the President's dacha outside Moscow, President Gorbachev and the heads of state of nine republics sign a joint statement on speeding up a new Union agreement (the 9 + 1 agreement).

24 April: The RSFSR Supreme Soviet passes a law providing for the election of a President of Russia.

12 June: Boris Yeltsin is elected President of the RSFSR in Russia's first democratic elections. He receives 57.3 per cent of the vote in a turnout of 74 per cent. Zhirinovsky polls 8 per cent. Gavriil Popov is elected mayor of Moscow with 65.3 per cent of the vote.

17 June: Prime Minister Pavlov requests the USSR Supreme Soviet to grant him special powers (without Gorbachev's approval) and is supported in camera (private meeting) by Marshal Yazov (Minister of Defence), Vladimir Kryuchkov (KGB) and Boris Pugo (Minister of Internal Affairs).

20 June: The US ambassador warns Gorbachev of a conspiracy to remove him.

30 June: The last Soviet soldier leaves Czechoslovakia (they had invaded on 21 August 1968).

4 July: Eduard Shevardnadze resigns from the CPSU to co-found an opposition group.

10 July: Boris Yeltsin is sworn in as President of the RSFSR and receives the blessing of the Russian Orthodox Church.

12 July: The USSR Supreme Soviet approves the Union treaty in principle, but suggests amendments.

17 July: Gorbachev meets G7 leaders in London but receives little support.

30–31 July: President Bush visits Moscow, meets Gorbachev and Nazarbaev, and pays a separate visit to Yeltsin.

1 August: President Bush visits Kiev and meets Leonid Kravchuk.

4 August: Gorbachev leaves for his vacation at Foros, Crimea.

The death throes of the Soviet Union, August–December 1991

1991

17 August: Kryuchkov, Pavlov and Yazov agree with several senior Party officials to demand that Gorbachev hand over power to them temporarily, and if he refuses, to detain him and take control.

18 August: Gorbachev rejects the demands of the delegation sent to persuade him at Foros to agree to the takeover. Shortly before midnight, Vice-President Gennady Yanaev agrees to support the takeover, and signs a decree assuming the powers of the President.

19 August: The Emergency Committee announces that it has assumed power and demands that all institutions obey its orders. Gorbachev is declared to be unfit to perform his duties for health reasons. A state of emergency is declared for six months. Yeltsin brands the takeover an illegal coup d'état and helps rally resistance at the White House.

20 August: Lack of military and state support gradually becomes clear. Estonia declares independence.

21 August: The attempted coup fails; Gorbachev returns to Moscow. The CPSU finally denounces the attempted coup. Yeltsin is given extra powers by the RSFSR Supreme Soviet and takes control of Soviet armed forces on Russian territory. He orders the CPSU to suspend its activities within the Russian Federation. Latvia declares independence.

24 August: Gorbachev suspends the activities of the CPSU and resigns as General Secretary. Ukraine declares independence subject to a referendum on 1 December 1991.

25 August: The Belorussian (Belarusian) Supreme Soviet declares political and economic independence.

27 August: Moldavia (Moldova) declares independence.

30 August: Azerbaijan declares independence.

31 August: Kirgizia (Kyrgyzstan) and Uzbekistan declare independence.

2–6 September: The 5th Extraordinary USSR Congress of People's Deputies calls for a new treaty for a Union of Sovereign States (see p. 196); it issues a declaration on human rights and freedoms; legislation to dissolve the Congress is presented.

6 September: Georgia announces the severing of all ties with the Soviet Union. The USSR State Council formally recognises the independence of Estonia, Latvia and Lithuania and supports their application for membership of the UN and CSCE. Leningrad votes to restore the city's original name, St Petersburg.

9 September: Tajikistan declares independence.

21 September: Armenia declares independence.

18 October: Treaty on the Economic Community of Sovereign States is signed by President Gorbachev and representatives of eight republics; Azerbaijan, Georgia, Moldavia (Moldova) and Ukraine decline to sign.

28 October: The RSFSR Congress of People's Deputies elects Ruslan Khasbulatov its chairman and speaker of the RSFSR Supreme Soviet. Yeltsin is granted power to implement economic reform by decree for one year.

4 November: Republican leaders meeting in the USSR State Council agree to abolish all USSR ministries except those for defence, foreign affairs, railways, electric power, and nuclear power. Yeltsin informs the meeting that Russia does not intend to set up its own armed forces.

6 November: President Yeltsin bans the activities of the CPSU and the Russian Communist Party on the territory of the Russian Federation.

15 November: Yeltsin signs 10 decrees taking control of almost all financial and economic activity in the Russian Federation.

25 November: Yeltsin and Shushkevich (Belarus) decline to initial the treaty on the confederation which had been negotiated.

1 December: In a referendum Ukrainian voters confirm Ukrainian independence.

5 December: The Ukrainian parliament formally revokes the accession of Ukraine to the 1922 treaty establishing the USSR.

8 December: In Belovezh forest, near Minsk, the presidents and prime ministers of Russia, Ukraine and Belarus declare the USSR dissolved and found a Commonwealth of Independent States (CIS) (see p. 239). Gorbachev describes the move as 'dangerous and illegal'.

12 December: Central Asian leaders, meeting in Ashkhabad (Ashghabat), request membership of the CIS as founding members.

17 December: Yeltsin and Gorbachev agree that by 1 January 1992 the Soviet Union will no longer exist.

21–22 December: Eleven former Soviet republics meet in Almaty and the CIS is extended (Estonia, Latvia, Lithuania and Georgia did not attend).

25 December: USSR President Gorbachev resigns and the Russian flag replaces the Soviet flag over the Kremlin.

The Yeltsin era: dual power, 1991–October 1993

1991
27 December: President Yeltsin takes over President Gorbachev's office in the Kremlin.
31 December: The Soviet Union ceases to exist in international law.

1992
2 January: Egor Gaidar launches his price liberalisation policy, also known as shock therapy.

1 February: Presidents Yeltsin and Bush meet at Camp David.

5 February: President Yeltsin visits France and Britain and receives promises of aid.

13–31 March: President Yeltsin and representatives of all territorial and national regions of the Russian Federation, except Tatarstan and Chechen-Ingushetia, sign the Federal Treaty on the delimitation of power between the centre and the regions; 18 of the 20 autonomous republics have signed.

16 March: Russian Ministry of Defence set up; President Yeltsin assumes defence portfolio temporarily.

6 April: The 6th RSFSR Congress of People's Deputies convenes.

17 April: The official name of the country becomes Russia – Russian Federation.

18 April: The RSFSR Congress of People's Deputies votes in favour of a draft Russian constitution which will form the basis of a new Russian constitution.

7 May: President Yeltsin signs a decree establishing the armed forces of the Russian Federation with himself as Commander-in-Chief.

31 May: Gaidar announces that monetary emission in June will be 142 billion rubles, a 250 per cent increase over May. Vladimir Shumeiko becomes first deputy Prime Minister; Viktor Chernomyrdin becomes deputy Prime Minister and Minister for Energy; Georgy Khizha becomes deputy Prime Minister and deputy Minister for Industry; Anatoly Chubais, chair of the state committee on property, also becomes a deputy Prime Minister; Aleksandr Shokhin, deputy Minister for Social Policy, becomes responsible for foreign economic relations; Gennady Burbulis becomes a state secretary under the President.

11 June: The RSFSR Supreme Soviet passes legislation on the privatisation law, which provides for every Russian citizen to be given a voucher; the enabling legislation is planned for 25 July.

14 June: The sale of land to private owners is now permitted, as is land for entrepreneurial activities (only reported on 18 June).

9 July: Democratic Choice, a new political bloc and pro-Yeltsin, is formed to counter the influential centrist opposition bloc, Civic Union.

26 August: An intergovernmental agreement between Russia, Armenia, Azerbaijan, Estonia, Kyrgyzstan, Lithuania, Moldova, Turkmenistan and Ukraine is signed in Moscow, covering economic, scientific, technological and cultural cooperation.

22 September: The RSFSR Supreme Soviet reconvenes after its summer break; Gaidar presents a report to it that the relaxation of the financial and credit policy since May has had to be reversed to prevent the collapse of the credit and monetary system; the Russian Central Bank suspends financial transactions with Ukraine, on the orders of the Russian government, until the two countries settle payments for goods already supplied.

24 September: The government agrees to introduce a unified wage structure by the end of the year for state employees, based on qualifications.

3–4 October: The 4th Congress of the Confederation of Mountain Peoples of the Caucasus in Grozny, Chechnya, increases tensions in Moscow as it calls for an independent Mountain Republic.

6 November: The Republic of Tatarstan adopts its own constitution.

9–10 November: President Yeltsin visits Britain and addresses both Houses of Parliament.

30 November: The Constitutional Courts end proceedings against the CPSU without any verdict.

14 December: President Yeltsin is forced by the Congress of People's Deputies to drop Gaidar as Prime Minister. He chooses Viktor Chernomyrdin as the new Prime Minister.

10 December: Ballot for candidates for post of Prime Minister: Yury Skokov 637 votes; Viktor Chernomyrdin 621 votes; Egor Gaidar 400 votes; Viktor Kadannikov 399 votes; Vladimir Shumeiko 283 votes. President Yeltsin proposes Chernomyrdin as Prime Minister; 721 votes in favour.

1993

20 March: On television, President Yeltsin announces the introduction of a 'special regime' and a referendum on 25 April.

24 March: President Yeltsin's decree of 20 March is published but 'special regime' has been removed.

28 March: Motion to impeach President Yeltsin at the 9th session of Congress of People's Deputies fails to achieve two-thirds majority of deputies (617 for and 268 against); motion to dismiss Khasbulatov fails (requires simple majority, but there are 339 for and 558 against).

26 March: The 9th Russian Congress of People's Deputies opens.

29 March: Congress approves four questions for the 25 April referendum; i) do you trust the President? ii) do you support his economic and social policy? iii) should early elections to the Congress of People's Deputies be held? iv) should early presidential elections be held?

25 April: In a nation-wide referendum voters (64.5 per cent turnout) express their confidence in the President (58.7 per cent); his economic and social reforms (53 per cent); early Congress elections (67.2 per cent); and early presidential elections (49.5 per cent).

18 May: Trial of coup plotters collapses as judge dismisses prosecution team.

12 July: Constitutional conference adopts the text of the draft constitution by 433 votes to 62 with 63 abstentions.

9 August: Mikhail Barsukov, chief of the main directorate for the protection of the Russian Federation and commandant of the Moscow Kremlin, declines to comment on the state of the President's liver.

10 August: Marshal Evgeny Shaposhnikov tenders his resignation as secretary of the Security Council; he is concerned about the legal status of the Council; his wife is Ossetian. The President denies he is ill and states that August is not a politically active month.

1 September: Vice-President Rutskoi and Vladimir Shumeiko, first deputy Prime Minister, are suspended by presidential decree; Oleg Soskovets will assume Shumeiko's duties. Shumeiko states that his suspension is at his own request; Khasbulatov claims it is a crude violation of the constitution.

10 September: It is confirmed that President Yeltsin is suffering from radiculitis but is recovering. A new, independent TV company, NTV, attracts journalists from Ostankino.

18 September: Last Russian soldiers leave Poland. Gaidar is appointed first deputy Prime Minister of the Russian Federation.

21 September: President Yeltsin signs a decree dissolving parliament and announcing the election of a State Duma on 11–12 December (see pp. 152–5). Parliament deposes the President and appoints Rutskoi to replace him. These are also new ministers of defence and security.

23 September: The Supreme Soviet appoints Rutskoi as acting President; Rutskoi calls for new elections for parliament and President soon; Valery Zorkin, chair of the Constitutional Court, tries to mediate. The Congress of People's Deputies convenes despite a presidential decree cancelling its mandate. The government suspends publication of *Sovetskaya Gazeta*, which had been founded by the Russian Supreme Soviet. The trial of the coup plotters is postponed again. The Presidium of the Russian Supreme Soviet meets in emergency session. President Yeltsin announces presidential elections for 12 June 1994.

29 September: President Yeltsin orders Khasbulatov and Rutskoi to leave the White House.

2 October: Khasbulatov and Rutskoi state they are willing to meet President Yeltsin. The Russian Orthodox Church continues its efforts to mediate; Patriarch Aleksi II suffers a heart attack.

The Yeltsin era: an authoritarian President, October 1993–1997

1933

3 October: President Yeltsin dismisses Rutskoi as Vice-President.

3–4 October: Conflict between forces supporting parliament and President Yeltsin results in bloodshed with Yeltsin's forces bombarding the White House.

9 October: President Yeltsin extends the state of emergency in Moscow until 18 October; Rutskoi's political party, the People's Party Free Russia, is suspended.

11 October: President Yeltsin decrees elections to the Council of the Federation (see pp. 152–5) for 12 December 1993.

15 October: President Yeltsin signs a decree for a referendum on the draft constitution on 12 December. Georgian President Shevardnadze signs a decree on Georgian entry to the CIS, which now consists of all ex-Soviet republics except Moldova and the Baltic States.

10 November: Eleven opposition newspapers are to be closed.

25 November: The trial of the August coup plotters resumes and a decision is taken to try them separately.

12 December: Elections to the State Duma reveal that the extreme right and left have done well. The draft constitution is confirmed, providing for a Federal Assembly, consisting of a lower house, the State Duma, with 450 deputies, and a Council of the Federation, with 178 deputies. Zhirinovsky's Liberal Democratic Party tops the poll with 24.6 per cent, with the pro-Yeltsin Russia's Choice securing 15.0 per cent and the Communist Party of the Russian Federation getting 11.6 per cent.

21 December: President Yeltsin abolishes the ex-KGB Ministry for Security Service and states that a new Federal Counter-Intelligence Service of the Russian Federation will be established in January.

22 December: The new constitution is officially in force.

1994

11 January: The inaugural session of the Federal Assembly; President Yeltsin assumes direct control of the power ministries – security, interior and defence.

13–14 January: President Clinton is in Moscow to discuss NATO's Partnership for Peace proposals with President Yeltsin.

14–15 February: John Major, the British Prime Minister, visits Moscow.

15 February: President Yeltsin makes a public appearance, the first since 3 January, and disappears from public view until 24 February.

26 February: The State Duma amnesties those involved in the October 1993 events; Rutskoi, Khasbulatov and three others are freed; also amnestied are the leaders of the attempted coup in August 1991.

9 March: Over 10,000 enterprises, involving 11 million employees, have been privatised through voucher auctions. About half of industrial workers are now employed in the private sector.

2 April: The Congress of the Liberal Democratic Party of Russia convenes in Moscow; Zhirinovsky is elected leader for 10 years with great powers; he criticises the legality of the CIS and suggests the borders of Russia should coincide with those of 1917.

28 April: President Boris Yeltsin signs the treaty on Civic Accord in the Kremlin, together with representatives of most of Russia's regions, republics, political parties and movements, trade unions and religious organisations. The document calls on everyone to refrain from the use of violence in pursuing political goals; the goals are to attain political stability in society, to overcome the socio-economic crisis, to consolidate the federal structure, and to foster morale, culture and ethnic relations.

10 May: The court case against the plotters of the attempted August 1991 coup is abandoned.

22 June: In Brussels, Andrei Kozyrev, Russian Foreign Minister, signs the NATO Partnership for Peace agreement and Russia thereby becomes the 21st state to join.

10 July: The Group of 7 (G7) leaders, meeting in Naples, welcome President Boris Yeltsin and Russia; Russia is participating for the first time in the political discussions and joins in the final communiqué. The second round of presidential elections take place in Ukraine and Belarus; Leonid Kuchma is elected President of Ukraine and Aleksandr Lukashenko is elected President of Belarus.

21 July: The law on the Constitutional Court, adopted by the Duma on 24 June and approved by the Council of the Federation on 12 July, comes into force. Judges may not engage in any political activity. President Yeltsin signs a decree giving impetus to the privatisation programme after the Duma rejects the second part of the privatisation programme. General Pavel Grachev, Minister of Defence, and his Kyrgyzstan counterpart sign agreements on cooperation between the Russian and Kyrgyz armed forces.

3 August: Presidents Yeltsin (Russia) and Rakhimov (Bashkortostan) sign a treaty, delimiting the competences between Russia and Bashkortostan and it reaffirms the sovereignty of Bashkortostan within the Russian Federation.

31 August: President Yeltsin and Chancellor Helmut Kohl take the salute in Berlin at the final parade of Russian armed forces before they leave Germany. The original agreement for their withdrawal was signed by President Gorbachev and Helmut Kohl in 1990. The Germans estimate that the bill for clearing up after 49 years of Soviet-Russian military occupation will reach DM25 billion (US$15 billion).

26 September: Addressing the UN, President Yeltsin appeals for a strategic partnership with the USA and proposes a nuclear security and strategic stability treaty with the nuclear powers. Presidents Yeltsin and Clinton meet for the fifth time in 18 months and claim that relations have never been better. Chechen opposition forces, supported by Moscow, prepare to attack Grozny; the Russian government warns Dudaev that it will 'do all it can to re-establish constitutional order and protect citizens'.

30 September: At a stopover at Shannon airport, President Yeltsin fails to appear to meet the Irish Prime Minister. It appears he had imbibed too much.

17–20 October: Queen Elizabeth II visits Russia and becomes the first British monarch since Edward VII in 1908 to visit the country.

27 October: In the Duma the government survives a vote of no confidence.

12 November: Gennady Zyuganov, leader of the Communist Party of the Russian Federation, states that the party now has 550,000 members and over 20,000 organisations.

14 November: A. Polevanov is appointed chair of the state committee on property.

11 December: Peace talks between Russia and Chechnya, which declared independence from Russia in 1991, end in deadlock in Vladikavkaz, north Ossetia. Russian troops enter Chechnya and the Chechen–Russian war begins (see p. 216). Washington states that it is an internal Russian matter but hopes that order will be restored without bloodshed; London calls for the respect of human rights.

17 December: Another Russian deadline, demanding that Chechens lay down their arms, passes and Moscow bombs Grozny; President Yeltsin confers full powers on Egorov in Chechnya.

18 December: 23,000 soldiers and 1,500 Omon men, with 300 armoured vehicles and helicopters, are pitted against about 3,000 Chechen rebels.

22 December: The Russians bomb Grozny and President Dudaev of Chechnya calls for a *jihad*, a Muslim holy war against Russia; General Vorobev resigns and other officers are dismissed.

27 December: President Yeltsin, on TV, defends the intervention in Chechnya and assures everyone that the political path to a resolution of the conflict is open; he assures the people of the Caucasus that Russia is not the 'enemy of Muslims' and states that 'peace and order will be re-established in Chechnya' and that Russia will 'use the appropriate means to ensure that this difficult problem does not last too long'.

1995

31 January: The deputy chair of the central electoral commission states that parliamentary and presidential elections will take place according to the constitution (December 1995 and 12 June 1996).

16 February: Presidential decrees appoint Oleg Soskovets, first deputy Prime Minister, as plenipotentiary representative of the President in Chechnya; and promise economic aid for the economy and infrastructure of Chechnya.

9 March: Russian sources state that Russian men now drink, on average, one litre of vodka every four days and their life expectancy has dropped to 59 years.

10 March: Sergei Kovalev, a fierce critic of the war in Chechnya, is sacked as Russia's human rights commissioner by the Duma.

18 April: Andrei Kozyrev, Foreign Minister, expresses concern at the plight of many ethnic Russians in the former Soviet republics and warns that Russia may have grounds for intervention. There are up to 25 million Russians in former Union republics.

25 April: Our Home is Russia, headed by Viktor Chernomyrdin, is set up to compete in the next parliamentary elections; it is supported by Stability, New Regional Policy, Party of Russian Unity and Accord, some members of Russia's Choice and the Democratic Party of Russia.

9 May: President Clinton arrives in Moscow for ceremonies marking the 50th anniversary of the end of the Second World War and a summit meeting with President Yeltsin.

12 May: The founding congress of Our Home is Russia, a new right-of-centre electoral bloc, headed by Viktor Chernomyrdin.

30 May: General Aleksandr Lebed resigns from the army in protest against cuts in the 14th Russian army in Transnistria.

19 June: Chechen gunmen free hostages in Budennovsk, thus ending a six-day siege of the town. Basaev agrees to the Russian terms for the recommencement of peace talks, which had ended on 1 January; 760 hostages are freed and 74 rebels board buses with 123 volunteers to act as a human shield. Basaev reveals that the Chechens got to Budennovsk by bribing border guards.

21 June: Vote of no confidence in the government in the Duma (241 votes to 72).

22 June: President Yeltsin reaffirms his confidence in the government of Viktor Chernomyrdin and warns the Duma he will dissolve it if it passes a second vote of no confidence in the government.

30 June: Presidential decree releasing Viktor Erin as Minister of Internal Affairs, Nikolai Egorov as Minister for Nationalities and Regional Policy, Sergei Stepashin, head of counter-intelligence, and E. Kuznetsov as governor of Stavropol krai; all had resigned the previous day; Oleg Lobov, secretary of the Security Council, and Pavel Grachev also resign but President Yeltsin declines to accept their resignations; law on elections to the Duma reveals that the number of deputies from Moscow and St Petersburg has been cut; US Vice-President Al Gore and Viktor Chernomyrdin sign 21 agreements in Moscow.

1 July: A motion of no confidence in the government in the Duma fails, 33 votes short of the 226 necessary.

11 July: President Yeltsin is taken to hospital suffering from heart trouble.

12 July: In the Duma, President Yeltsin survives a motion for his impeachment over the handling of the war with Chechnya and the Budennovsk crisis, proposed by the Communist Party. Russia's population fell by 1.7 million in 1993–94.

18 July: President Yeltsin appears on Russian TV and states he is working four hours a day.

30 July: Agreement signed on cease-fire in Chechnya; elections to the republic's legislature set for 5 November.

7 August: President Yeltsin returns to the Kremlin to begin work after suffering a heart attack on 10 July.

30 August: Bones found in Ekaterinburg in 1991 are confirmed as those of Tsar Nicholas II.

20 September: The central electoral commission states that all state-owned media must provide 30 minutes free air time to all registered political parties between 15 November and 15 December; parties may purchase additional air time; free newspaper space is to be granted ten days earlier.

25 September: The second stage of the privatisation programme is launched with a list of companies whose shares are to be offered for sale to the private sector.

17 October: Russia and China finish demarcating their 4,380 km border. An agreement is signed in Beijing on the final 54 km of disputed border and this concludes the work of the commission which began its task in 1991. Sovereignty over three islands in the Amur and Argun rivers has been left 'to future generations' to resolve.

23 October: Nikolai Ryabov, chair of the central electoral commission, confirms that 43 parties and blocs have submitted the required number of voters' signatures to register for the 17 December Duma elections. Each party has to submit at least 200,000 signatures, with not more than 7 per cent from any one region.

26 October: A helicopter rushes President Yeltsin to hospital with a recurrence of the myocardial ischaemia that forced him into hospital on 11 July.

10 November: The electoral commission draws lots for the order in which parties will appear on the ballot papers.

15 November: The Council of the Federation sets 16 June as the date for presidential elections; this is four days after President Yeltsin's term of office is due to expire; President Yeltsin says he is in favour of reforming the electoral law.

27 November: President Yeltsin leaves hospital and goes to a sanitorium.

28 November: 43 parties are registered for the elections with 5,675 candidates standing in 225 constituencies (the other 225 seats are awarded according to party lists, if parties cross the 5 per cent barrier).

14–17 December: Parliamentary elections: the turnout in Chechnya is 74.8 per cent and over half the votes cast in Chechnya are for Our Home is Russia; in simultaneous elections for the President of the Republic, Doku Zavgaev wins 93 per cent of the vote. Only four parties gain more than 5 per cent of the vote, thereby gaining a share of the 225 seats in the Duma. These parties are the Communist Party of the Russian Federation (22.3 per cent), the Liberal Democratic Party of Russia (11.2 per cent), Our Home is Russia (10.7 per cent) and Yabloko (6.9 per cent).

26 December: President Yeltsin leaves Barvikha sanatorium.

29 December: President Yeltsin returns to office.

1996

28–31 January: Viktor Chernomyrdin goes to the USA to meet Vice-President Al Gore for the sixth session of the US–Russian commission on economic and technical cooperation, during which a US$1 billion loan is agreed from the US government to Aeroflot for the building of airliners; in return the Russian government is to remove trade barriers for the sale or lease of US-built airliners.

18 February: Some 43 names are registered with the central electoral commission for the presidential elections; each candidate has to collect 1,000,000 signatures by 16 April as a pre-condition for formal registration; signatures could apparently by bought for $1–10 each.

1 March: Mikhail Gorbachev announces he will stand in the Russian presidential elections.

15 March: The Duma votes to uphold the legality of the results of the referendum on the USSR (taken on 17 March 1991) which voted in favour of the Union; the Duma votes for the resolutions of the Communist Party of the Russian Federation on 'deepening the integration of the peoples previously united in the Union of Soviet Socialist Republics'; this revokes the agreement to form the CIS.

29 March: Heads of state from Russia, Kazakhstan, Belarus and Kyrgyzstan sign a quadripartite integration treaty; President Yeltsin meets President Eduard Shevardnadze of Georgia.

2 April: Belarus and Russia sign a bilateral treaty on the formation of the Community of Sovereign Republics; monetary policies are to be united by the end of 1997.

16 April: Deadline for registration as a candidate for the presidential elections; 11 candidates register.

21 April: Dudaev is killed near the village of Gekhi-Chu, 30 km southwest of Grozny.

23–26 April: President Yeltsin visits China and signs 14 agreements.

25 April: Dudaev is succeeded by Zelimkhan Yandarbiev.

26 April: President Yeltsin and Chinese Prime Minister Jiang Zemin sign a multilateral non-aggression treaty with the leaders of Kazakhstan, Kyrgyzstan and Tajikistan, in Shanghai.

16 May: A decree is passed stating that conscripts are only to be sent to areas of conflict after they have given their consent and on a contractual basis; compulsory military service is to be phased out by 2000; the government announces a new exchange rate policy which will allow a gradual and controlled fall of the ruble.

17 May: Four British Embassy staff in Moscow are expelled from Russia; the UK responds in kind after a deal between the two governments.

3 June: Anatoly Sobchak is defeated by his deputy, Vladimir Yakovlev, in mayoral elections in St Petersburg.

16 June: First round of the presidential elections: President Yeltsin obtains 34.8 per cent, Zyuganov 32.1 per cent, Lebed 14.7 per cent; Yury Luzhkov is re-elected mayor of Moscow by an overwhelming majority. Valery Shortsev, his running mate, was seriously injured in a bomb attack on 7 June.

18 June: Lebed is appointed secretary of Russia's Security Council; General Pavel Grachev is dismissed and replaced on an acting basis by General Mikhail Kolesnikov, Chief of Staff; Lebed says on Russian TV that he prevented people close to Grachev organising a coup.

20 June: President Yeltsin dismisses Oleg Soskovets, first deputy Prime Minister, General Aleksandr Korzhakov, chief of the Presidential Guard and long-term (11 years) friend of the President, and Colonel General Mikhail Barsukov, director of the Federal Counter-Intelligence Service. It was alleged that this 'powerful and corrupt clique had dominated the Kremlin for the last four years, had backed the military invasion of Chechnya and had badly tarnished President Yeltsin's reputation'. The dismissals were welcomed by Anatoly Chubais (regarded by Korzhakov as the instigator) and Grigory Yavlinsky. Oleg Lobov, secretary of the Security Council, becomes deputy Prime Minister and Yury Krapivin replaces Korzhakov.

25 June: President Yeltsin dismisses seven generals, four of whom Lebed said were plotting against the President.

3 July: Second round of the presidential elections: President Yeltsin obtains 53.8 per cent and Gennady Zyuganov 40.3 per cent.

9 July: General Nikolai Kovalev is appointed director of the Federal Counter-Intelligence Service, replacing Barsukov. Various trolleybus bombs explode in Moscow and are blamed on Chechen separatists and organised crime. Chechen cease-fire (agreed in May) ends as fighting erupts near Grozny.

10 July: President Yeltsin addresses the people of Russia and admits that he and his government have made 'mistakes' and 'errors' and this is reflected in the wide support which Zyuganov received. Chernomyrdin is retained as Prime Minister. A decree expands the powers of the Security Council, whose secretary is Lebed.

11 July: Lebed states that the Security Council will concern itself with four main areas: defence security, public security, economic security, and information security; Lebed condones the actions of the Russian military in Chechnya.

15 July: Anatoly Chubais is appointed head of presidential administration (Chief of Staff) and chief presidential aide, replacing Egorov, appointed in January 1996. Chubais will help to set the political agenda and plan the implementation of president Yeltsin's goals. He was the chief architect of stabilisation and the most influential pro-reformist economist in the government.

17 July: Colonel General Igor Rodionov replaces Grachev as Minister of Defence. He is a close friend of Lebed and an Afghan war veteran. He is widely blamed for the 20 deaths of demonstrators in Tbilisi in April 1989. He intends to stamp out corruption, which was prevalent under Grachev.

19 July: The Central Bank of Russia announces the liberalisation of the bond market for foreign investors.

27 July: Russian and Chechen officials meet to discuss exchange of prisoners.

7 August: The Communist Party of the Russian Federation and the Agrarian Party of Russia (and other nationalist and left groups) form a Popular, Patriotic Union of Russia.

9 August: President Yeltsin's inauguration for his second term is overshadowed by fighting in Chechnya.

10 August: The Duma accepts Chernomyrdin's renomination as Prime Minister.

13 August: Rodionov delivers a pessimistic assessment of the armed forces; Lebed, the next day, criticises the state of armed units.

22 August: Lebed and Aslan Maskhadov, Chechen military leader, sign a fresh cease-fire agreement. President Yeltsin initially declines to receive Lebed but soon comes round and backs Lebed.

28 August: Withdrawal of Russian troops from Chechnya begins.

31 August: Lebed–Maskhadov peace agreement announced.

5 September: President Yeltsin announces that he is to undergo heart surgery after a prolonged absence since his re-election had fuelled fears about his health.

10 September: Vladimir Poltorin, first deputy Prime Minister, is also appointed chair of the government's operational commission for improving the system of payments and settlements.

19 September: Vladimir Polikov, ex-Minister of Finance, is removed from the Security Council and replaced by Aleksandr Livshits, deputy Prime Minister and Minister of Finance.

21 September: Heart surgeon Renat Akchurin tells French TV that Yeltsin had had a heart attack in June/July but this is refuted by the presidential administration. Chernomyrdin is to be the President's stand-in during his heart surgery.

11 October: The State Duma rejects the government's draft budget for 1997 by 280 votes to 33.

16 October: General Anatoly Kulikov, Minister of the Interior, launches a ferocious attack on Lebed. They are bitter rivals and in August Lebed had demanded Kulikov's resignation. Kulikov claims that Lebed is planning to form a 50,000-strong Russian legion, backed by the Chechens, to launch a coup in Russia.

17 October: President Yeltsin announces Lebed's dismissal on TV, saying he had disrupted the team. Lebed blames Chubais for his dismissal and claims that he is planning to establish a regency and seeking the presidency for himself. He also blames Boris Berezovsky, later deputy secretary of the Security Council, who had threatened Lebed after the Chechen peace agreement, claiming that it had ruined his business interests. Chernomyrdin and Luzhkov support the dismissal of Lebed.

19 October: Ivan Rybkin, speaker of the First Duma, is appointed secretary of the Security Council and as presidential envoy to Chechnya, replacing Lebed.

30 October: Boris Berezovsky is appointed deputy secretary of the Security Council on Chubais's recommendation.

2 November: Itar-Tass states that Russia's wage arrears now exceed 43 trillion rubles (about US$8 billion).

5 November: President Yeltsin successfully undergoes a quintuple heart bypass operation. Trade unions organise a Russia-wide day of action with rallies and strikes to protest against the government's failure to pay wage arrears. An estimated 15 million people take part.

23 November: Chernomyrdin and Maskhadov sign an agreement on the principles governing relations between the two sides.

25 November: The government extends its crawling corridor exchange rate policy introduced in May. Livshits states that the government will maintain its current tight fiscal and monetary policies.

30 November: General Vladimir Semenov, Commander-in-Chief of ground forces, is sacked for engaging in activities 'incompatible with his post'.

3 December: Some 400,000 of the 560,000 Russian miners go on indefinite strike, protesting against wage arrears of 1.5 trillion rubles (US$270 million). The strike is called off on 11 December.

5 December: The Council of the Federation votes 110 to 14 (with 7 abstentions) to reclaim Sevastopol as part of Russia. On 17 December the Russian Foreign Ministry rejects this, stating that Sevastopol is part of the Crimea and Ukraine.

8 December: President Boris Yeltsin, on the fifth anniversary of the founding of the CIS, states that it was the only way to 'save what could be saved' from the collapse of the USSR.

12 December: A spokesman for the Union of Muslims of Russia announces plans for the organisation of a Muslim deputies' group in the Russian Duma. Most of the 26 Muslim deputies support Our Home is Russia. However 35 deputies are needed to form a faction.

16 December: Six medical personnel, working for the International Committee of the Red Cross in a Norwegian-funded hospital in Novye Atagi, are shot dead. The Red Cross announces that it is withdrawing from Chechnya. Food imports in 1996 total US$13.5 billion, 35–37 per cent of domestic demand, the same as 1995. The grain harvest in 1996 is 68 million tonnes, or 6 per cent more than 1995. Russia is likely to export 7 million tonnes to the CIS and import 5 million tonnes for the Russian Far East.

17 December: The Duma passes the third and final reading of a bill regulating relations between krais, oblasts and autonomous okrugs, and the bill states that the latter cannot secede from the former. There are nine krais and oblasts in the Russian Federation which have autonomous okrugs on their territory. The bill's main aim is to preserve the territorial integrity of Tyumen oblast, where the Yamal-Nenets autonomous okrug, in the oil-rich north, had declared that it would not participate in the 2 December gubernatorial elections.

20 December: The government promises that the RTR state-run TV station will broadcast a regular parliamentary programme. *Rossiiskaya Gazeta* will become the joint government–parliamentary paper. The newspaper was the organ of parliament until October 1993. These are concessions made by the government to the Communist Party of the Russian Federation in the Duma to ensure the smooth passage of the 1997 budget.

23 December: President Yeltsin returns to the Kremlin, seven weeks after his 5 November operation. Lebed calls the President a 'sick man' who should resign his post.

25 December: The Council of the Federation approves the law passed by the Duma on 20 December increasing the minimum monthly wage by 10 per cent to 83,490 rubles (US$15), effective from 1 January 1997.

26 December: The government proposes to re-establish the alcohol monopoly. Alcohol contributed 3.5 per cent of budget revenue in 1996, compared with about a third before 1985.

27 December: Russia, China, Kazakhstan, Kyrgyzstan and Tajikistan announce an agreement on reducing troop levels and the number of weapons along the Chinese frontier. This covers a 100 km zone on both sides of the border.

29 December: The Last Russian combat troops leave Chechnya, ahead of the 27 January 1997 deadline.

30 December: According to the latest opinion poll of 1,600 respondents by VTsIOM, General Aleksandr Lebed leads with 29 per cent, President Yeltsin is second with 14 per cent, Gennady Zyuganov third with 10 per cent. Yury Luzhkov scores 6 per cent.

1997

8 January: The Moscow Arbitration Court rejects a move by the Russian Federal Bankruptcy Agency to declare AZLK, one of the capital's largest enterprises, bankrupt for non-payment of taxes. The verdict is seen as a victory for Yury Luzhkov, Moscow's mayor. The city government has promised 500 billion rubles (US$90 million) of subsidies for the plant. This and other verdicts against the Agency throughout Russia bring into question the ability of the Russian government to declare any enterprise bankrupt in its battle to increase tax receipts.

13 January: President Boris Yeltsin floats the idea of a referendum on a full merger between Russia and Belarus. In a letter to President Aleksandr Lukashenko, his Belarusian counterpart, Yeltsin proposes creating a single government controlling a joint budget with unified fuel and energy systems.

22 January: The State Statistical Committee (Goskomstat) announces that Russian GDP fell 6 per cent in 1996, the fifth consecutive year of economic contraction. Industrial output, which has halved since reforms began in

1992, fell by 5 per cent last year. However, these figures may not accurately reflect the growth of the services sector and the grey economy. Most Russian enterprises now tend to under-report output to reduce taxation. Unofficial measures of economic activity, such as electricity consumption, point to a much smaller drop of industrial output. Annual inflation fell from 230 per cent in 1995 to 22 per cent in 1996.

27 January: Aslan Maskhadov, the 45-year-old Chechen military commander, is the victor in the presidential elections in Chechnya, obtaining 65 per cent of the poll.

31 January: In an article in the *Financial Times* Grigory Yavlinsky claims that new menaces for Russia and the west are emerging: the loss of control over nuclear weapons, nuclear materials, and other weapons of mass destruction; the development of a breeding ground for terrorism and organised crime; the high probability of large-scale environmental disaster.

1 February: *The Times*, at the Davos summit, reports Russian government ministers as stating that their goal is to reduce government expenditure from the present 40 per cent of GDP to 25–30 per cent by 2000. This implies that Russia will be a low tax country (or perhaps a low tax collection country) and that the private sector will gradually become responsible for pensions, education, health, and other social services.

5 February: The International Labour Organisation, in Geneva, publishes a gloomy account of the Russian labour market. Goskomstat, in December 1996, reported 2.78 million or 3.4 per cent of the working population unemployed. The ILO calculates, in July 1996, that the unemployment rate is 9.5 per cent. The average life expectancy of males has dropped from 65 years in the late 1980s to 58 years in 1996. Alcohol-related deaths increased more than threefold over the years 1990–95. Goskomstat states that employment fell by 8.2 million in 1990–95, while the size of the working age population rose slightly.

7 February: A Russian delegation, headed by Viktor Chernomyrdin, signs 40 agreements with the USA in Washington. A summit between Presidents Yeltsin and Clinton is announced for 20 March in Helsinki. This indicates that President Yeltsin, whose turn it was to go to the USA, is unable to fly at present. The summit will be about NATO enlargement, arms and economic matters. One of the agreements signed envisages the USA providing US$2 billion over five years to help transform 7,000 nuclear warheads into electric power for the Russian economy.

7 February: General Igor Rodionov, Minister of Defence, and Yury Baturin, secretary of the Defence Council, present a gloomy picture of the Russian armed forces and plead for more resources. Rodionov claims that 'Russia might soon reach the threshold beyond which its rockets and nuclear systems cannot be controlled'. The military, at present 1.7 million strong, faces deep cuts in personnel.

10 February: Aleksandr Korzhakov, the former chief of the presidential guard, is elected to the Duma in a by-election in Tula, gaining 26 per cent of the poll. The election was called after Aleksandr Lebed resigned his seat last summer to bid for the presidency. Korzhakov was endorsed by Lebed. During the election campaign Korzhakov advocated a strong and nationally assertive Russian state.

13 February: A conference on money laundering is informed that an estimated US$50 billion had been transferred from Russia over the past five years and that outflows continue at about US$12 billion annually. The Swiss estimate that the Russian mafia has at least US$10 billion deposited in Swiss banks. About 41,000 companies, half of the commercial banks and 80 per cent of joint ventures involving foreign capital may be connected to criminal groups, of which there are around 5,000. The black economy is estimated to embrace 40 per cent of Russian economic activity.

19 February: Births have dropped from 17 per 1,000 people in 1985 to nine in 1996. Demographers estimate that in three decades the Russian population will decline from the present 147 million to 123 million. Car ownership in 1995 was 38 per cent higher than in 1992 and over 2.5 million Russians holidayed abroad in 1996.

20 February: The military celebrates the 50th anniversary of the invention of the Kalashnikov rifle. Some 70 million have been manufactured and it has been deployed in 55 countries. Over 40 different models were on display. The flag of Mozambique, which includes a drawing of the rifle, was also there. When Mikhail Kalashnikov, the 78-year-old inventor, first produced the design he was put in a Stalinist camp for his initiative.

10 March: President Boris Yeltsin delivers his annual state of the national speech to both houses of parliament. He appears to be in good health and speaks clearly. He promises swift action to reform the economy and to pay the arrears of wages and pension, estimated at US$10 billion.

11 March: Anatoly Chubais, presidential chief of staff, is appointed first deputy Prime Minister by the President. Prime Minister Viktor Chernomyrdin is given a week to name the new government team.

14 March: Aleksandr Lebed's new political party, the People's Republican Party of Russia, holds its inaugural congress.

17 March: Boris Nemtsov, 37 years old, governor of Nizhny Novgorod oblast, is named first deputy Prime Minister in the government reshuffle. He will be responsible for social welfare reform and regulation of the country's natural monopolies, such as gas, electricity, and railways. Chubais will take over the finance ministry from Aleksandr Livshits and be acting Prime Minister when Chernomyrdin is away. Yakov Urinson becomes the new Minister of Economics, replacing Evgeny Yasin, who remains in the government as a minister without portfolio in charge of long-term strategic economic planning. Alfred Kokh, head of Goskomimushchestvo, the state privatisation agency, is made a deputy Prime Minister, in charge of privatisation. Deputy Prime Minister Vladimir Bulgak is responsible for technology and science. Deputy Prime Minister Oleg Sysuev will supervise labour and social policy and deputy Prime Minister Valery Serov is responsible for centre–region relations, inter-ethnic relations, and CIS relations. Deputy Prime Minister Anatoly Kulikov remains Minister of the Interior and is the chief tax collector. Vladimir Potanin, first deputy Prime Minister, returns to his position with Oneximbank. Aleksandr Bolshakov also loses his post as deputy Prime Minister. None of the deputy Prime Ministers appointed bears responsibility for the defence sector. It appears that this sector will have few claims on the state budget.

21 March: the eleventh summit between Presidents Yeltsin and Clinton ends in Helsinki. No agreement is reached on NATO's plan to extend membership to Poland, the Czech Republic and Hungary. Yeltsin promises to push the ratification of START II through the Duma. Then the two sides will begin with START III, which envisages reducing nuclear warheads to 20 per cent of their existing levels by 2007. Russia is to attend the next G7 summit in Denver, when it will be called the summit of the eight.

22 March: During a meeting with the President of Finland, in Helsinki, President Yeltsin says that Russia might eventually apply to join the EU. This takes Brussels by surprise.

2 April: Presidents Yeltsin and Lukashenko sign an outline union treaty in Moscow. The treaty commits both countries to closer cooperation in the military, social and economic fields and to 'strengthen brotherhood'. The agreement will not restrict each country's sovereignty or their constitutions. A full monetary union is not envisaged in the near future. Russian liberals are alarmed at the prospect of 10 million Belarusians joining Russia, especially since the regime in Belarus is authoritarian and little progress towards a market economy has been made. In Minsk, 4,000 demonstrated against the treaty.

23 April: Presidents Yeltsin and Jiang Zemin sign, in Moscow, a joint Russian–Chinese declaration which rejects the 'attempt to enlarge and strengthen military blocs' [opposing NATO expansion] and calling for a 'multipolar rather than a bipolar world'.

24 April: Russia, China, Kazakhstan, Kyrgyzstan and Tajikistan sign, in Moscow, an agreement to limit troop levels in their border regions. It sets strict limits on the number of ground troops, tactical air force and anti-aircraft personnel deployed by all the countries concerned in a 100 km zone each side of China's frontier. It does not cover strategic air defence and rocket forces. Russia and the Central Asian states may keep 3,900 tanks in the border zone, all but 100 of these being provided by Russia. China may have the same number. President Yeltsin appoints Boris Nemtsov, first deputy Prime Minister, Minister of Fuel and Energy. He thereby strengthens his position vis-à-vis Viktor Chernomyrdin, the Prime Minister. The President also chided Chernomyrdin for not promoting enough young people.

12 May: President Boris Yeltsin of Russia and President Aslan Maskhadov of Chechnya sign a treaty setting out the principles for peaceful relations, thereby ending 400 years of enmity between the two peoples. Yeltsin states that it is 'our firm intention never to use force or threaten to use it in relations between the Russian Federation and the Republic of Ichkeria' [the name preferred by Chechens].

14 May: NATO and Russia agree in Moscow to sign an agreement establishing a NATO–Russia Joint Consultative Council, in Paris, on 27 May. Russia will have an ambassador in Brussels and there will be a secretariat. Javier Solana, NATO secretary general, and Evgeny Primakov, Russian foreign minister, reached agreement during the six rounds of negotiations. NATO states that it has no intention of stationing nuclear weapons on the territory of new members. The agreement clears the way for invitations to be extended to Poland, the Czech Republic and Hungary to join NATO.

22 May: President Yeltsin sacks General Igor Rodionov, Minister of Defence, and Viktor Samsonov, Chief of the General Staff, during a televised meeting of the Defence Council. He expressed his anger at the lack of progress in reforming the military and fumed that the 'soldier is getting thin while the general is getting fat'. General Igor Sergeev, head of the strategic rocket forces, is made acting Minister of Defence.

23 May: President Yeltsin appoints General Igor Sergeev Minister of Defence, and General Anatoly Kvasnin Chief of the General Staff. President Yeltsin of Russia and President Lukashenko of Belarus sign a union treaty in the Kremlin. It provides for greater co-operation between the two Slavic neighbours, but does not envisage the integration of the two states.

27 May: President Yeltsin, in Paris, signs the founding act on mutual relations, co-operation and security between NATO and the Russian Federation, which provides Russia with a consultative voice in NATO affairs. The accord establishes a NATO–Russia permanent joint council at NATO headquarters in Brussels. A Russian ambassador will be appointed and there will be Russian military officers stationed there. After signing the document, which was also signed by Javier Solana, NATO secretary general, and the 16 NATO members, President Yeltsin announced that all missiles targeted on NATO countries would have their nuclear warheads removed.

31 May: In Kiev, President Boris Yeltsin and President Leonid Kuchma sign a Russian–Ukrainian friendship treaty. On six previous occasions President Yeltsin had cancelled his planned visit to conclude an agreement. The treaty includes a 20-year lease of part of the naval base of Sevastopol, in the Crimea, by Russia, at an annual rent of US$100 million. Both the Russian and Ukrainian navies will use the base. Russia also agrees to pay Ukraine US$ 526 million for the lion's share of the fleet stationed there. Russia also writes off Ukraine's outstanding energy debts. The treaty is a breakthrough for Ukraine as Russia, for the first time, acknowledges its neighbour's independence and territorial integrity. Hence the Crimea is acknowledged as part of Ukraine.

SECTION TWO

Glossary

As with all the books in the Companions to History series, this volume is made up of chronologies, mini-biographies, notes on wars, treaties and summits, maps, bibliographical information and so on. This section, the Glossary, provides a range of short essays on key topics which are mentioned elsewhere in the book. A diverse range of subjects are included, and so that readers may locate what they need quickly and easily the section has been divided into four parts: the economy, society, religion and culuture; nationalities and territories; politics; and the law. If readers are in any doubt which category a particular subject falls into, they should consult the index, where the main entry appears in bold and other references in normal type.

Economy, society, religion and culture

Agriculture

Only about 10 per cent of the land mass of the Soviet Union could be classified as agricultural land. About 75 per cent of the country had less than 120 frost-free days a year and this meant the growing season was usually short. About 80 per cent of the USSR was subject to drought. About 75 per cent of the country was covered in forests or was waste-land. Lenin, in the April Theses, proposed that landlord estates, after nationalisation, should become model farms. The reality was that the peasants seized the land and distributed it among themselves. If they lived near a large estate, they got more; in other areas very little was available for redistribution. In 1922 peasant land use had increased by 8.3 per cent in the north, 15 per cent in the centre and 16.3 per cent in the lower Volga. Overall this meant that the average peasant house-hold in Russia was fortunate if it acquired an extra hectare of land. Hence the agrarian revolution after 1917 was very modest. The chief result of this agrarian revolution was the elimination of large estates, which had supplied most of the marketable produce before 1914. Mid-dle (serednyaki) peasants dominated the village commune but the Civil War and requisitions led many to divide up their property further among their sons so that by 1921 there were 25 million peasant households. The vast majority of these were subsistence economies (only producing for their own needs). NEP was the golden era of the Russian peasant and by 1925 output had reached the level of 1914. Only 1.7 per cent of the sown area in 1927 was in kolkhozes and sovkhozes (collective and state farms), the rest was on peasant farms. Despite the fact that grain output was above the level of 1914, the quantity of grain marketed was lower and this was an important reason why forced collectivisation was adopted. This led to the famine of 1932–34 in the Ukraine and the excellent Soviet harvest of 1933 saved many lives. The main problem of Soviet agriculture was motivation. The labour force had little interest in raising labour productivity. Under Gorbachev there were debates about reverting to NEP but private agriculture was no longer an option as very few peasants had the skill or the desire to become private farmers. In order to expand production, Khrushchev launched the virgin and idle lands programme in 1954 and by 1960 an additional 41.8 million hectares had been put under the plough. The failure of the 1963 harvest led to the import of grain from North America for the first time and this became a normal phenomenon under Brezhnev. Demand for food and other agricultural products was never satisfied. International health norms in annual per capita consumption in 1985 were only reached in grain and were not attained in meat, fish, milk, vegetables, fruit and eggs. The parlous state of Russian agriculture in 1991 was underlined by the danger of hunger in certain areas. Privatisation since 1991 has only affected less than 10 per cent of the arable (crop-producing) land and an agrarian revolution is needed if Russia is going to feed its own population (about 35 per cent of Russian food was imported in 1995).

Agrogorod

Literally, an agricultural town or a town in the countryside with urban amenities. Nikita Khrushchev, as First Secretary of the Moscow Party organisation, began amalgamating kolkhozes (collective farms) in Moscow oblast. The peasants objected to this and began to slaughter cattle during the summer of 1950. The Party discussed setting up kolkhoz settlements with urban conveniences – schools, clubs, bath houses, palaces of culture, kindergartens, water and electricity. Blocks of flats for peasants were to be built. The whole concept was described as a 'mistake' by Georgy Malenkov at the 19th Party Congress in 1952. (The main reason appears to have been the huge cost such an initiative would have entailed.)

Anti-Semitism

The Bolsheviks campaigned against anti-Semitism until the early 1930s. There were anti-Jewish pogroms during the October Revolution and the Civil War, especially in Ukraine. All anti-Jewish legislation was annulled and this led in the 1920s and 1930s to a flood of Jews from the traditional areas to Russian cities, especially Moscow and Leningrad. They prospered and by the 1930s Jews were over-represented in almost all elite groups. In the 1930s they made up 2 per cent of the population but 16 per cent of doctors and teachers and 4 per cent of Party members. This led to growing anti-Semitism and by the end of the 1930s most Jewish schools, theatres, publications and other cultural manifestations had been shut down. After the signing of the Hitler–Stalin Pact of August 1939, the anti-Semitism inherent in national socialism was not mentioned. It is estimated that 2 million of the 5 million Jews in the Soviet Union perished during the Great Patriotic War. The wartime anti-fascist Jewish committee was dissolved in 1948 and most members arrested. The years 1948–52 were black ones for Jews in the Soviet Union, when anti-Semitism reached a crescendo. In the 1960s anti-Semitism was disguised as anti-Zionism and a virulent anti-Israel policy was conducted. However, between 1971 and 1984 about 260,000 Jews emigrated officially from the Soviet Union, most of them to the USA. This led to Jews being eliminated from some Soviet elite groups; for example, Jews were removed from the diplomatic service. The existence of anti-Semitism was conceded under Gorbachev's glasnost and a rapprochement with Israel was achieved.

Atheism

Atheism was one of the cornerstones of Bolshevik ideology and was regarded as an integral part of Marxism–Leninism until the late 1980s. Lenin was a God hater and like Marx saw religion as false consciousness which would die out under socialism. The reason for its prevalence was the skill of the exploiting classes in deploying religion as the 'opium of the people' (Marx) to mask the reality of exploitation. To Lenin the struggle with religion was the ABC of materialism and indeed of Marxism. Tactically Lenin expressly welcomed the cooperation of religious workers and also collaboration with religious organisations at home and abroad if their goals coincided with those of Soviet power. Party members had to be atheists from the 1920s onwards. Lenin engaged in refined double talk. Whereas the Party was expressly called on to combat religion, Lenin insisted that the Soviet state be neutral towards religious organisations. This was a fiction as the Union of the Fighting Godless, between 1925 and 1941, were presented with the task of destroying the Russian Orthodox Church. In 1947 the All-Union Association for Spreading Scientific and Political Knowledge came into being and in 1963 it was renamed the All-Union Society of Knowledge. Both these institutions were charged with spreading scientific atheist propaganda. Atheism was part of the school curriculum and from the early 1960s scientific atheism was a compulsory subject in universities, and medical, technical and agricultural colleges. This led to discrimination against religious believers and it was difficult for believers to obtain further education. This changed under Gorbachev when he attempted to harness the potential of the churches and believers for perestroika.

Censorship

The Bolsheviks, by a decree on 27 October 1917, closed down the bourgeois press and publishing houses and described it as an exceptional measure until the new order was in place. However, in a resolution of the Central Executive Committee (TsIK) on 4 November 1917 the restoration of the 'so-called press freedom' was dismissed as an undoubtedly 'counter-revolutionary démarche'. In December 1917 the People's Commissariat for Justice issued a decree on the establishment of a special revolutionary tribunal for the press, which was to function as the main censorship agency. This was confirmed in a Sovnarkom decree of 28 January 1918. By mid-1918 the whole opposition press was banned. In June 1922 a new body, the main administration concerning literature and publishing (glavnoe upravlenie literatury i izdatelstva or Glavlit) took over and was subordinate to the People's Commissariat for Enlightenment. Anatoly Lunacharsky regarded Glavlit as a temporary phenomenon but it remained almost to the end of the Soviet Union. It changed its name several times and was finally called the main administration for the protection of military and state secrets in printed matter and was subordinate to the state committee for publishing of the USSR Council of Ministers. The Soviet constitutions of 1936 and 1977 underlined the need to strengthen the socialist system and defend the interests of the workers. Censorship was to ensure that these objectives were placed first in all publishing. Just as important as censorship was self-censorship. Authors were aware where the limits were and kept to them. The xenophobic Zhdanovshchina imposed strict censorship and it was only under Khrushchev that a mild thaw appeared. This ended in the mid-1960s but gave rise to samizdat (self-publishing). A vigorous counter-culture began to develop and it found full expression only under Gorbachev when he opened the floodgates with glasnost. Since he courted the cultural intelligentsia in order to secure support for perestroika, a war developed between those whose views were culturally conservative, such as Ligachev, and those who were liberal, such as Aleksandr Yakovlev. Gorbachev supported the latter and this meant that censorship gradually became a dead letter.

City

The city was defined in Soviet literature as a large settlement whose inhabitants were mainly engaged in industry and trade, in services, administration, science and culture. The decisive factor in naming a settlement a city was population. In the RSFSR a city (gorod) had over 12,000 residents and an urban settlement (poselok gorodskogo tipa) of over 2,000, and was involved in industrial production, administration, culture, spas, leisure, etc. Cities were characterised by high residential densities and compactness. The number of cities expanded rapidly during the industrialisation of the first and second FYPs and the forced collectivisation which resulted in many peasants abandoning the countryside. Whereas there were 709 cities in 1926 there were 1,190 in 1939 (1,935 in 1970). In 1926 only 18 per cent of the population was urban but this grew to 56 per cent in 1970. The major cities expanded very rapidly: Petrograd in 1923 had 1.044 million residents but in 1939 there were 3.385 million in Leningrad. The fastest growth was, not surprisingly, in Moscow, where the population grew from 1.49 million in 1923 to 4.13 million in 1939. The rapid growth of the cities resulted in huge problems as living norms could not be attained. The construction industry concentrated on meeting the needs of industry and the administration. City plans were drawn up, first for Moscow and the capitals of the Union republics, then for other cities. Moscow levelled most of its old buildings and a new city came into being. The construction of the underground (Metro) also led to many fine, old buildings being demolished. The Great Patriotic War was very destructive as the retreating Germans attempted to blow up anything of value. About half of the 2.57 million dwellings in the occupied territories were destroyed as well as 82,000 schools. Kiev and many other cities were devastated and this provided the opportunity to rebuild according to an urban plan. As elsewhere, dormitory towns grew up near large cities and large conurbations developed.

Under Khrushchev a great effort was made to satisfy the tremendous demand for housing but much of the construction was sloppy. It was normal for construction companies to fail to complete a block of flats (individual houses were never built) and pay the imposed fine. The new residents had to make the block habitable. Citizens could form a group, borrow money and hire a contractor to build a block of flats for them. All cities with a population of 1 million or more qualified for an underground system. The emerging middle class built dachas (weekend, normally wooden, one-storey chalets) around the cities and moved there at the weekends whenever possible. The older generation normally lived there during the summer and tended the vegetable garden. Housing was apportioned by the city soviet and depended on one's status. However, only about one-third of dwellings in Moscow belonged to the Moscow soviet in the 1980s. The others were owned by enterprises, institutions and privately. A common complaint about Soviet cities and housing was that they all looked the same. The same design and building techniques were applied everywhere. However, this was not true of Armenia and Georgia, where local architecture was retained.

Classes

Lenin defined classes as groups of persons involved in social production, their relations to the means of production and their role in the social division of labour. Under capitalism antagonistic contradictions developed over the unequal distribution of wealth. According to Stalin these antagonistic contradictions were overcome in the Soviet Union after 1936 but classes continued to exist. They would last until the distinction between mental and manual labour and the contradictions between city and countryside had been overcome. Then a classless society would come into being. After the October Revolution the working class assumed the leading role, eliminated the exploiting capitalist class and ruled in association with the working peasantry and segments of the intelligentsia. During the 1930s this was developed further and the working class was joined by another class, the collective farm peasantry (kolkhozniki) and the stratum of working intelligentsia. Stalin developed the theory that class conflict increased as the Soviet Union moved towards socialism, but this was rejected after Stalin's death. The intelligentsia was not classified as a class since it had no direct control over the means of production. Employees caused a problem because they did not engage in manual work (workers) nor were they highly qualified mental workers (intelligentsia). They were gradually classified as a stratum. However, it remained unclear where the boundaries between employees and intelligentsia and employees and working class were. Gradually it emerged that employees were those who did not engage in physical labour and performed jobs requiring modest qualifications. Kolkhoz employees were a lower group within employees, as was the kolkhoz intelligentsia within the intelligentsia.

Collectivisation

The process of combining peasant private farms into kolkhozes (collective farms), which began voluntarily in 1917 but was enforced after 1929. Collectivisation totally altered economic and social relations in the countryside and ended the NEP period of mixed economy. Three forms of collective agricultural economy emerged after 1917. First, there were communes – at the end of 1920 there were 2,117 in the RSFSR – in which everything, except personal belongings, became the property of all. Then there was the agricultural artel – at the end of 1921 there were 8,581 in the RSFSR – in which implements, animals and land became common property and the land was worked in common but peasants lived on their own farms and looked after their own animals. Peasants were rewarded according to their labour input. Then there were the cooperatives (TOZ) – at the end of 1921 there were 946 in the RSFSR – in which peasants worked their own land but helped one another when needed. Lenin was very enthusiastic about developing cooperatives as a way of drawing peasants into socialist construction but entry had to be voluntary. The demonstration effect was to attract peasants into large-scale socialist farms. However, collectives during NEP were of marginal importance and not attractive to industrious peasants.

The grain crisis of 1927 and 1928, when the state had great difficulty in buying sufficient grain for the cities from the peasants, convinced the Bolsheviks that a solution to the agrarian problem was necessary if industrialisation was not to be put at risk. On 5 December 1929 a Politburo commission on collectivisation was set up and Stalin declared on 27 December 1929 that the time had come to 'liquidate the kulaks' as a class (the kulaks were the most successful private farmers). On 5 January 1930 the Central Committee passed a decree aiming to complete collectivisation in the main by 1931–32. On 20 January 1930 21.6 per cent of peasant households had been collectivised (there were about 25 million peasant households) and by 1 March 1930 65 per cent had been collectivised. In order to ensure that the spring sowing was completed Stalin published an article in *Pravda* on 2 March 1930 criticising the dragooning of peasants into kolkhozes. If they wanted to leave they could. They left in droves and in August 1930 only 21.4 per cent of households were in collectives. However, they were recollectivised during the autumn. Peasants reacted by slaughtering their animals and between 1928 and 1934 the number of cattle in the country dropped by 45.5 per cent, horses by 54.6 per cent, sheep by 66.1 per cent and pigs by 55.7 per cent. In summer 1931 the number of collectivised peasant households had risen to 52.7 per cent and the resistance of the rest was broken by imposing prohibitive taxes and using OGPU troops and volunteer brigades. The authorities set up Machine Tractor Stations to provide the draught power. There was famine in certain areas. In 1934 71.4 per cent of peasant households had been collectivised, and in 1940 96.9 per cent. The territories acquired by the Soviet Union after 1940 were collectivised over the years 1949–53. Collectivisation was predominantly a political move but it was an economic disaster. All ambitious rural dwellers sought to leave the countryside and the Soviet Union was never able to produce enough marketable food to satisfy its population.

Cooperatives

Cooperatives were highly developed in Russia in 1917, when consumer cooperatives counted 11.5 million members and 35 per cent of the retail trade turnover. The Bolsheviks advocated that the whole population should belong to consumer communes, which were to supervise consumption and ensure equal distribution of consumer goods. A decree of 12 April 1918 required the cooperatives to provision the whole population and on 27 May they were subordinated to the People's Commissariat for Supply. There was considerable tension between the cooperatives and the Bolsheviks because the executive committee of the cooperatives was dominated by Socialist Revolutionaries (SRs) and Mensheviks. But the breakthrough for the Bolsheviks came in July 1919. Agricultural and artisan cooperatives were linked up with local cooperatives in January 1920. Cooperatives were forced to participate in state requisitioning and this damaged the movement fatally. Cooperatives reappeared during

NEP on a voluntary basis and were mainly concentrated in the villages. In 1929 80 per cent of peasant households belonged to consumer co-operatives. Agricultural cooperatives expanded once again. There were credit, processing and marketing cooperatives and they played a role in the economy alongside the socialist sector. Forced collectivisation and industrialisation completely changed the cooperative movement. Tsentrosoyuz, the central union of the cooperatives, was transformed into a planning and distribution agency and when in 1935 state trade took over all cooperatives in the cities, it concentrated its activities in the village. In 1958 consumer cooperatives had 37.4 million members and about 30 per cent of the retail trade turnover. In 1974 there were 9,500 cooperatives with 62 million members, accounting for 30 per cent of the retail trade turnover. Besides consumer cooperatives there were also construction and fishing cooperatives. Perestroika revitalised the cooperatives. The law on cooperatives of 26 May 1988 permitted the setting up of independent cooperatives and in March 1991 8.2 million persons were employed in the new cooperative sector. This created the conditions for the privatisation of state property, which got under way in Russia in 1992.

Cultural revolution

The taking over by the proletariat of education, art, music, literature and other arts after October 1917. The supporters of Proletkult (proletarian culture) regarded the cultural revolution as being as necessary as the political, economic and social revolutions and it was their responsibility. They set out to establish a new culture in workers' clubs which excluded peasant and bourgeois culture. Lenin had different views. He regarded Russia's first priority to raise itself from its 'half-Asiatic culturelessness' to the level of European bourgeois states. The elimination of illiteracy was only possible if bourgeois specialists were used and the raising of cultural levels in the village had to involve the peasants. Bourgeois culture could not be overcome by simply writing it off but by learning from it and developing it further. Only the Communist Party could ensure that the cultural revolution could lead to the victory of socialism. Lenin's views did not find universal acceptance within the Party, with Lunacharsky and Trotsky advocating a position somewhere between the Proletkult and Lenin. Another use of the term is by Sheila Fitzpatrick, who uses it to describe the mobilisation of society at the end of the 1920s and the early 1930s by which unskilled workers became skilled and skilled workers became employees. A new technical intelligentsia of worker and peasant origin gradually replaced the old bourgeois specialists. In China the term designates the violent attempt by Mao Zedong (mid-1960s to 1975) to replace conservative elites with new cadres.

Family

After the October Revolution the Bolsheviks issued, in December 1917, a flood of decrees on civil marriage, on children and divorce. These decrees and the rights of guardians were included in the first marriage law book in April 1918. The goal of this legislation was to break the influence of the Russian Orthodox Church and to make women equal to men. Marriage was voluntary and divorce possible. A new marriage law book was issued on 1 January 1927 and it placed unregistered and registered marriages on a common basis. The law on the family changed during the 1930s. The existing law was revised on 27 June 1936 and attempted to strengthen the family as the foundation of the socialist state. Divorce became more difficult and abortion banned. A revised family law of 9 July 1944 placed greater emphasis on the family. There were to be awards for mothers of large families and a single person tax was introduced. In 1955 abortion was again made legal. In the 1950s the traditional role of the woman continued to dominate despite the increased involvement of women in the work process from the 1930s onwards. Women therefore had a double burden. They were expected to work but be a traditional wife at home. The proportion of women in the workforce was 25 per cent in 1922 and reached 51 per cent in 1970 but never rose above this figure.

Famines

Famine before 1917 was a normal phenomenon because some of the most populous areas were subject to drought. There were two main famines in the Soviet Union, 1921 and 1932–34. The 1921 famine followed the end of war communism and the Civil War. Peasants, as a result of requisitions, planted less, but there was also drought and this led to a catastrophe, especially in south Russia. Officially the number of deaths was put at 4– 5 million. The famine of 1932–34 resulted from the resistance to forced collectivisation and was especially severe in Ukraine. Stalin would not permit food to be transported to the worst affected areas. Western specialists estimate that about 5.5 million died.

Five Year Plans (FYPs)

The most salient factor in socialist planning from 1928 to 1990. Originally FYPs were conceived as part of a general plan spanning 10–15 years but these quickly declined in significance and the FYPs came to dominate Soviet economic development. They were law and had to be implemented. The FYPs were drawn up by Gosplan and approved by the Politburo. As they replaced the market, all the market's function of allocation and distribution had to be taken over by the planners. There was a Gosplan (see p. 89) in each Union republic to help draft the plans and the ministries and branch ministries 1925–26 with control figures for the economy and in March 1926 the first draft plan by Gosplan appeared. There were variants of the plan with different growth rates and the variant with the largest growth rates in April 1929 was chosen as the first FYP (October 1928–December 1932). Hence the first FYP spanned only four years and three months. The growth rates to be achieved were astronomical: industrial production was to rise by 230 per cent over 1927–28 and producer goods were to grow by 264 per cent. Consumer goods, on the other hand, were only to grow by 106 per cent. This underlines one of the cardinal principles of Soviet planning: the preference for producer goods (machinery and other equipment) over consumption. Economic growth was demanded but the necessary skilled workers and engineers had not been trained, so crash programmes were necessary. The second FYP embraced the years 1933–37, the third 1938–June 1941, the fourth 1946–50 and the fifth 1951–55. The sixth FYP, 1956–60, was interrupted in 1959 and a Seven Year Plan, 1959–65, introduced. In 1966 the Brezhnev–Kosygin leadership reverted to the FYP. The final FYP was the twelfth, 1985–90, under Gorbachev, and was characterised by the collapse of the Soviet economy.

Foreign trade

Foreign trade was of no importance immediately after the October Revolution since the Civil War and the Allied blockade made it virtually impossible. Foreign trade was also nationalised on 22 April 1918 along with large-scale industry, land, transport and the banks. This meant that a foreign trade monopoly came into being. Negotiations with foreign companies and governments could only be carried out through such organisations. A People's Commissariat for Foreign Trade was set up in 1920 and a decree of the Soviet Central Executive Committee, on 13 March 1922, reconfirmed the foreign trade monopoly, stating that this was to protect the Soviet economy from predatory capitalists and to ensure political control over trade turnover. During NEP foreign trade turnover grew but by 1929 it was still less than two-thirds that of 1913. The structure of foreign trade was that of an underdeveloped state, raw materials and agricultural products were exported and machinery and industrial goods imported. During the 1930s trade turnover declined and in 1940 was a third that of 1929. The German attack of June 1941 brought help through the Lend Lease Act. After the onset of the Cold War in 1947, foreign trade turnover expanded fast with socialist countries in eastern Europe, mediated through Comecon after 1949. Trade with capitalist countries averaged 19–26 per cent between 1950 and 1989, with the exception of 1980, when it attained the remarkable figure of 33.5 per cent, but this was due to the rapid rise of oil prices. Trade with the socialist world gradually became a liability for the Soviet Union and by 1989 almost every state had a large balance of payments deficit with Moscow. Trade was also used to prop up communist regimes in the Third World, such as Vietnam and Cuba.

Glasnost

Perestroika, glasnost and democratisation made up the trinity of the Gorbachev era. Gorbachev's aim was to overcome the political, economic, social and moral decline of the Soviet Union, suffered during the period of stagnation under Brezhnev. The word Glasnost can be translated as openness or transparency. It was conceived as a weapon against those in the leadership who were resisting perestroika. It was to provide information against existing cadres and to involve the population in policy formation. It was used against bureaucratism, administrative arrogance, corruption and the abuse of power. As censorship became looser, banned authors were published, banned films and plays presented, and taboo subjects discussed (criminality, drug abuse, accidents, demonstrations). This spilled over into discussing consumer goods shortages, the goals of Soviet foreign policy, the legal system, ecology and the Stalinist past. Multi-candidate elections were introduced for elections to the USSR Congress of People's Deputies in March 1989 and this permitted new parties and movements to challenge the monopoly of the Communist Party. Glasnost radicalised the population and Gorbachev believed that this would promote perestroika. At the 19th Party Conference in June 1988 a separate resolution was devoted to glasnost, defining it and stressing the need for it. Glasnost was used by nationalists in the Baltic republics to promote autonomy and then independence.

Gosplan

Gosplan was founded on 22 February 1921 and charged with drafting an economic plan for the whole country. In the first half of the 1920s Gosplan had little influence as the people's commissariats went their own way. During the second half of the 1920s Gosplan presented various draft FYPs, which competed for influence with those of the Supreme Council of the National Economy (VSNKh). Gosplan's draft was adopted as the first FYP and its role expanded (it had 34 staff in 1921, 615 in October 1930 and 2,570 in October 1931). It was divided into nine sections, which concerned themselves with: industry and transport, energy, construction, labour, state defence, statistics, etc. It was reorganised on 15 December 1947, when a state committee for material technical supply

(Gossnab) and one for the introduction of new technology (Gostekhnika) were set up and added to Gosplan. In 1955 Gosplan was divided in two: a state committee for perspective planning, concerned with long-term plans, and a state committee for current planning. The sovnarkhoz reform of 1957 ended the functions of these two committees but the first carried on as Gosplan, without any executive authority. In 1959 a state scientific economic council of the USSR Council of Ministers was set up and made responsible for perspective planning. In 1962 a new Gosplan appeared and the state council became part of the Supreme Economic Council. In 1965 this body was abolished and Gosplan expanded its role until the Gorbachev era, when less and less stress was placed on central planning. Gosplan became the USSR Ministry of Economics and Forecasting in 1991 as part of the economic reform of the Cabinet of Ministers.

Health

Health was one of the most important sectors for the Soviet government to demonstrate that under socialism the whole population could be provided with a level of care unknown under capitalism. The People's Commissariat of Health was set up on 11 July 1918 to cater for the population, taking over from the zemstvos (local government bodies) and private medicine. The commissariat made little headway during the Civil War, when the health of the population declined and epidemics were common. Some died of starvation. Under NEP the situation improved and the number suffering from contagious diseases declined. This tendency was reversed during the 1930s (there was a famine between 1932 and 1934, mainly in Ukraine), when the declining living standards reduced immunity. This occurred despite a rise in the number of doctors and the number of beds available in towns and villages. The war was another blow and afterwards there were few resources available as reconstruction took precedence. The health of the population improved during the 1950s and 1960s but this was reversed in the 1970s, when child mortality rose from 22.9 per 1,000 live births in 1971 to 35.6 in 1976. Alcoholism was a scourge. In 1980 17 per cent of the population was dependent on alcohol, or 40 million persons, of whom 17 million were classified as alcoholics.

As the health of the population declined, so the number of doctors and dentists increased, so that in 1983 there were 1.1 million doctors, or 40 doctors per 10,000 persons, the highest proportion in the world. However, the standard of medical training (except in military establishments) was low and medicines were in very short supply. Doctors were trained in 83 institutions and they spent six years studying. Some republics were better served than others, with Georgia having 51.2 doctors per 10,000 citizens. During the 1970s and 1980s the health budget was repeatedly cut (along with education) as the budget increased. Besides the polyclinics, hospitals and centres for the population, there existed a parallel system for the nomenklatura, many of whose clinics corresponded to western standards. Under Gorbachev the health service was severely criticised and in 1990 statistics comparing the USSR (1987) and the USA (1984) were published. They make dismal reading. The first figure is for the Soviet Union, the second for the USA: life expectancy, 70 and 75 years; mortality of mothers (per 100,000 births), 47.7 and 8.0; child mortality (per 1,000 births), 24.7 and 10.0; number of doctors (per 10,000 citizens), 43.3 and 25.7; number of beds (per 10,000 citizens), 130.6 and 54.5; expenditure per citizen per year, 80 rubles and $1,772. As regards diseases, the numbers per 100,000 citizens were: dysentery, 197.4 and 73.5; viral hepatitis, 304.6 and 133.2; measles, 67.4 and 1.1; tuberculosis, 44.0 and 9.4; gonorrhea, 59.8 and 372.0; syphilis, 5.6 and 12.2.

Housing

One of the most pressing problems for the Soviet government was to construct sufficient dwellings to provide the population with the statutory minimum living space. It never achieved this objective. Industrialisation and urbanisation had created a shortage of housing in Russia before 1917, but the Civil War saw the urban population decline and this made the problem less pressing. However, under NEP many citizens moved back into towns and the shortage was compounded by the rapid industrialisation and urbanisation of the Five Year Plans. In 1923 there was 6.45 square metres of living space per person on average in the Soviet Union but in 1932 this had dropped to 4.66. Much housing was destroyed during the Great Patriotic War and after 1945 the reconstruction of industry took first place. Nevertheless some accommodation was built after 1950. This, however, was quite incapable of coping with the rapid rise in the urban population, which alone between 1950 and 1956 grew by 18.8 million. More rapid building techniques were developed (pre-fabricated panels which could be slotted into place) and the 20th Party Congress in 1956 resolved to speed up the construction of dwellings. Whereas between 1950 and 1955 240.5 million square metres (6.1 million dwellings, average size 39.7 square metres) were constructed, this increased to 474.1 million square metres (11.3 million dwellings, average size 42 square metres) in 1956–60 and to 490.6 million square metres (11.6 million dwellings, average size 42.5 square metres) in 1961–65. Living space during the 1980s in the Soviet Union increased by about 30 per cent, so that in 1989 there was 15.3 square metres of living space per person. The countryside was always better served and in 1989 there was on average per person 16.8 square metres.

In the 1970s citizens could form housing associations, borrow the money from the bank and have their own flats built. Those who took advantage were mainly from the intelligentsia and in cities. It was very rare for a detached house to be built in a city; they were to be found only in rural areas. Large five-storey blocks, without lifts, were the norm in the 1960s and 1970s. Many dwellings had communal kitchens with several families on a level sharing facilities. In 1989 about one-third of housing was owned by municipalities, one-third by enterprises and the rest by other institutions and privately. Rents were very low and gas, heating and water were not metered and hence included in the rent.

Illiteracy

Lenin recognised illiteracy as a major problem but the Civil War made it impossible to tackle it. The breakthrough was achieved during the 1930s. Decrees in 1931 and 1932 introduced compulsory education and this eliminated illiteracy among the younger generation, but it still remained a problem for the older generation. Special classes were arranged for them. By 1939 93.5 per cent of men and 81.6 per cent of women declared themselves literate. By 1970 only 0.3 per cent of the population was illiterate. The campaign for mass literacy was an important propaganda tool for the Party, especially in the non-Russian republics.

Industrialisation

All Bolsheviks agreed that industrialisation was the main goal of Soviet power but they could not agree on how it should be effected. During NEP the Soviet Union was an agrarian society and it was only in 1926–27 that industrial production attained the pre-war level. There were two main schools of thought as the industrialisation debate got under way in 1924 (intertwined with the struggle to succeed Lenin). Evgeny Preobrazhensky proposed that the capital needed to fund industrialisation should come from the peasantry through low prices for food and high prices for industrial inputs (called primitive socialist accumulation). Nikolai Bukharin regarded such a policy as doomed to failure and proposed that capital should come from an expanding, prosperous agriculture. This would increase demand for industrial goods and provide more tax revenue for the state. The first FYP (October 1928–December 1932) rapidly increased industrial output at the expense of restricting the consumption of the whole population, but mainly the rural population. Defence and heavy industry were given preference and consumption neglected. This played an important role during the war and made it possible for the Soviet Union to defeat Germany. The industrial model of the 1930s was inefficient and wasteful and efforts to reform it began under Khrushchev.

Intelligentsia

A social stratum whose activity – highly qualified mental work – differentiates it from the working class, the collective farm peasantry (kolkhozniks) and employees. Members of the intelligentsia are graduates of higher schools and technical colleges and those who carry out their jobs without special education (called practitioners or praktiki). Before the revolution the intelligentsia was viewed as a critically thinking educated elite. After the October Revolution the Bolsheviks had to cooperate with the available qualified personnel as few Bolsheviks had received further education. The specialists had little respect for Soviet power and the Bolsheviks mistrusted the bourgeois specialists. During NEP, many bourgeois specialists were employed and their numbers were swelled by returning emigrants. The situation changed dramatically during industrialisation, when bourgeois specialists were treated as scapegoats for the shortcomings of the FYPs. The Soviet state began training its own specialists, and through promoting shop floor workers to senior positions and the rapid expansion of higher education, the Party attempted to produce its own specialists who would implement the goals of the FYPs and be loyal to the Party. In 1940 the size of the intelligentsia was estimated to be 2.4 million, in 1950 3.2 million, in 1955 5.1 million, in 1960 8.8 million, in 1965 12 million and in 1970 16.8 million. Soviet writers referred to the technical intelligentsia (managers, engineers, agronomists, zoologists, etc.), those involved in science, art, education and medicine (further education teachers, journalists, actors, painters, doctors, etc.), and those in the state apparatus and the management of social organisations (judges, lawyers, Party, state, trade union officials).

Islam

Islam was the second largest religious group, after the Orthodox Church, in the Soviet Union. By the mid-1980s there were about 50 million Muslims or 18 per cent of the population in the Soviet Union, concentrated predominantly in Central Asia, the Volga–Urals region, the north Caucasus, Dagestan and Azerbaijan. Due to the struggle against the Bashmachi in Central Asia immediately after the revolution, the Soviets were very restrained in their policy towards Islam, not desiring to provoke Muslims into opposition. It was only in 1925 that they moved against the Waqf land, which supported the religious schools, and nationalised it and closed down the schools. They closed the sharia (religious) courts, deported mullahs, closed down mosques and campaigned against the veil. In 1941 there were only 1,300 mosques still open, compared with 26,000 in 1913. The religious persecution in 1960 saw many of these closed. In 1986 there were 751. In 1943–44 four spiritual leaderships for Muslims were set up: in Tashkent for Central Asia and Kazakhstan; in Ufa for the

European part of the Soviet Union and Siberia; in Baku for Transcaucasia and for all Shiites in the USSR; and in Makhachkala, Dagestan, for the north Caucasus. The Mufti in Tashkent spoke politically for Muslims. A religious education could only be obtained at two medrese (Islamic academies) in Bukhara and Tashkent. Officially Islam appeared almost moribund but unofficially it was vibrant with several thousand unregistered mullahs active. Most boys in Central Asia, Azerbaijan and the north Caucasus were circumcised and almost all funerals were performed according to Muslim rites. Few could go on the pilgrimage to Mecca so many holy places sprang up in the Soviet Union and pilgrims visited them. Some clerics were trained in Saudi Arabia during the communist era. After the collapse of the Soviet Union, Turkey, Iran, Saudi Arabia and other Muslim states sought to increase their influence: money was provided to build many thousands of new mosques and hundreds of young Muslims went to Egypt, Saudi Arabia and other states to be trained.

Kolkhoz (collective farm)

Ostensibly a voluntary union of peasants to work land together and share the results, but in reality from 1929 individual peasants had no choice but to join. The kolkhoz was distinct from a sovkhoz (state farm) in that it was viewed as a cooperative. The kolkhoz received land from the state rent-free in perpetuity and had control over buildings, machines, animals and money. Management was elected by the kolkhoz assembly. Work was carried out in brigades, based on a system of norms and rewarded by earning labour days. Kolkhoz members were permitted to work their own private holdings around their cottages and sell the produce in kolkhoz markets. However kolkhozes were required to carry out plans handed down to them, and to deliver certain quantities of produce to the state (compulsory deliveries) at prices fixed by the state (procurement prices), which were often lower than those in the kolkhoz markets. Kolkhozes existed from 1917 but in 1929 they became the norm for the inhabited countryside. Various model statutes regulated their activities (1930, amended in 1935, 1938 and 1965). In the early 1950s many kolkhozes were amalgamated and the total number declined. There were 121,400 in 1940 and 26,000 in 1979. On the other hand the number of sovkhozes constantly increased. Originally sovkhozes were set up in uninhabited areas but under Khrushchev many kolkhozes were transformed into sovkhozes. Whereas there were 5,000 sovkhozes in 1950 there were 20,800 in 1979.

Kolkhoz (collective farm) market

The only free legal market in the Soviet Union after 1932, when kolkhozes were given permission to sell grain left over after state procurements had been met. In the model kolkhoz charter of 17 February 1935 kolkhozniki (collective farm peasants) were also permitted to sell their surplus products in kolkhoz markets. The local soviet supervised the kolkhoz market and prices were not supposed to be excessive. In 1940 kolkhoz markets accounted for 19 per cent of the retail trade turnover but in 1961 it was only 6 per cent. In the mid-1980s, even though the private plots accounted for only about 4 per cent of the arable land in the Soviet Union, they produced about one-third of marketed food.

Kulak (in Russian, fist)

Term used in the 1920s and 1930s to describe better-off peasants. It was a term of abuse and implied that all such peasants were class enemies. A kulak was a peasant who had working animals and could hire labour. He could also own a mill, and earn income from renting out machinery and working animals and trading in agricultural produce. About 4 per cent of the 25 million peasant households in the 1920s were classified as kulak. They were not permitted to join kolkhozes as they were regarded as saboteurs. Many families were deported to the east and others fled. Economically the Soviet Union turned its back on all its most able farmers. Not only the kulaks were wiped out, the middle peasants (serednyaki), those who had enough land to live on, were also targeted and dragooned into collective farms.

Labour day (Trudoden)

(i) The measurement of labour in kolkhozes (collective farms), where a peasant could achieve several labour days by working machinery for a day.

(ii) one of the first measures of the Soviet government was to introduce the eight-hour day (29 October 1917). On the tenth anniversary of the revolution, in 1927, the Soviet Central Executive Committee announced the planned introduction of the seven-hour day. This had been achieved by 1934. The average day in industry in 1926–27 was 7.45 hours, in 1928–29 7.37 hours and in 1934 6.98 hours. Reducing the working day was one of the measures adopted to overcome unemployment. In 1940 the eight-hour day was again introduced and being late for work severely punished. During the Great Patriotic War the 10 or 11-hour day became the norm but in 1945 the eight-hour day again became usual. Khrushchev attempted several times to go over to the seven-hour day but all his efforts remained mere promises.

Machine tractor stations (MTS)

The first MTS was set up in Ukraine in 1929 as a cooperative and in 1930 they were nationalised and established throughout the Soviet Union as part of enforced collectivisation. They were to play a key role in managing and supervising kolkhozes where there were few Party organisations. Given the limited amount of machinery, they had to service several kolkhozes and were paid in kind. However, they were only capable of providing a small part of the technology needs of the kolkhozes. There were 66,000 tractors in 1930 and 531,000 in 1940 to meet demand from 242,500 kolkhozes working 116 million hectares of arable (crop-bearing) land. There was also a shortage of spare parts so that one-quarter or more of machines were in need of repair. In 1940 there were 7,069 MTS. During the Great Patriotic War tractors were needed for the war effort and enterprises had to produce tanks and not tractors. There were 8,985 MTS by 1953 and 7,903 in 1957 after a reform disposing of over 1,044,000 tractors. In 1958 Khrushchev judged that the time had come for the kolkhozes to own their own machinery and dissolved the MTS. However, farms did not want all of the MTS machinery but were informed that unless they took some of the less desirable machinery they would not acquire the much-desired tractors. Hence they had to pay for equipment they did not need or want. Altogether the kolkhozes paid 32 billion rubles. The mechanics went with the equipment so that farms could repair their own machinery. The shortage of mechanics resulted in the setting up of Repair Tractor Stations (RTS) but broken-down machinery had to be transported there before it could be repaired. In 1961 Khrushchev created the All-Union Selkhoztekhnika organisation to provide agriculture with technical equipment. This proved less than satisfactory and even Gorbachev tried, in vain, to make it more efficient.

New Economic Policy (NEP)

The policy adopted by the Communist Party at its 10th Congress in March 1921, which represented a retreat from the policies of war communism. The Party was forced to rethink war communism after peasant revolts on the Volga, the Kronstadt uprising, strikes by workers and the Makhno movement. The Party conceded that the transition to communism was not feasible and decided to place the interests of retaining power ahead of ideological considerations. Lenin forced NEP on the Party and also introduced the fateful resolution on Party unity through the Congress, realising that, in a free vote, comrades would not vote for the return of the market. The essence of NEP was a reconciliation with the peasants, the ending of forced requisitioning and its replacement by a tax in kind (later in money). Artisans and craftsmen, from May 1921, were again permitted to work and sell their products. Moscow attempted to attract foreign capital and expertise by offering concessions for sale. The commanding heights of the economy (energy, heavy industry, transport, communications, banking, foreign trade) remained in state hands, but light industry and agriculture were predominantly in private hands. The special organs, committees and commissions, created during the Civil War, were dissolved. The famine of 1921 cost many lives and industrial prices rose faster than agrarian prices (scisssors' crisis), which reduced the incentive of peasants to market their produce. Industrial production rose until in 1925–26 it was back to the level of 1914 and agriculture followed soon after. The debate about NEP then took off in earnest. Had NEP almost reached its full potential or was it capable of further development? There was a danger that capitalism would take over the countryside and the kulaks would rule the roost. The petty bourgeois traders were becoming more influential in the cities. The left, Trotsky, Preobrazhensky, Zinoviev and Kamenev, wanted rapid industrialisation at the expense of the peasantry, but the right, Bukharin, Stalin, Rykov and Tomsky, demurred and warned that the peasants could not be forced into socialism. The left lost their Party and government posts in 1926–27 but the advent of forced industrialisation and collectivisation took over most of their demands and, indeed, made them more extreme. The first FYP (October 1928–December 1932) buried NEP. The Bolsheviks had reverted to their belief under war communism that the solution to all problems was a central plan with everyone fulfilling it in the interests of the state.

Norms

Laid down by the centre for individual enterprises or the whole economy for the use of inputs or for the length or results of activities by workers. Hence it was similar to piecework. Soviet labour economists were greatly attracted to the concepts of the scientific organisation as developed by Ford and Taylor. Norms changed with the introduction of new technology and new labour processes, in other words they were always being increased. The state used various techniques to increase labour, for example the Stakhanovite movement. Afterwards norms were raised. Stakhanovites and other super-performers were understandably unpopular at the workplace. A major task of the 1930s was to discover what reserves there were in the enterprise and labour had an interest in ensuring that their norms and targets were not too demanding. The resistance of Soviet industry to innovation was partly due to labour's lack of commitment.

Passport

The internal passport, which had existed until the February Revolution, then discontinued, was reintroduced by the Soviet authorities on 27

December 1932. According to this decree, every citizen over 16 years old in cities and workers' settlements, in transport, sovkhozes and building projects had to acquire and carry a passport. The goal of the new regulation was to slow down the migration of the population from one part of the country to another in search of better working and living conditions. Kolkhoz members were not provided with passports and this signified that it was illegal for them to move without permission. Employers when recruiting labour had to enter the place of employment on the passports. It was hoped that the very high labour turnover would thereby be slowed down. The passport also included information on the bearer's nationality, social status, military duty and family details. The passport was registered at the person's permanent place of residence and changes of residence were to be entered. In this way the authorities had a useful instrument to control the migration and movement of the population. However, it could be circumvented. Kolkhoz members could get round the regulation before the mid-1960s when they acquired passports by going to work on building sites or other places where labour was scarce. The major cities, especially Moscow and Leningrad, were the targets for ambitious, upwardly mobile citizens. These cities made it very difficult for newcomers to settle legally there. Moscow introduced a system of issuing passports for a limited period (the holders were known as limitchiki) to overcome its labour shortage. Such was the attractiveness of Moscow for country girls that Muscovites could acquire them as home helps and concubines. The passport system remained until the collapse of the Soviet Union in 1991. It did not permit the bearer to travel abroad. A separate passport had to be acquired for that.

Peasants

Individual and collective farm (kolkhozniki) peasants comprised the largest social group in the USSR until the Great Patriotic War. In 1927 individual peasants accounted for 74.9 per cent and kolkhozniki 0.8 per cent of the population; in 1928 it was 73.7 per cent and 1.7 per cent; in 1939 it was 0.3 per cent and 44.9 per cent; in 1959 it was 0 per cent and 31.4 per cent; in 1970 0 per cent and 20.5 per cent; and in 1980 0 per cent and 14.9 per cent. These data reveal the transformation of the countryside through urbanisation, forced collectivisation and the gradual growth of state farms, where labourers were classified as workers (sovkhozniki). There was clear evidence of this in the proportion of the population which was rural (kolkhozniki, sovkhozniki, rural employees). In 1960 51.2 per cent of the Soviet population lived in rural areas, in 1970 43.7 per cent, in 1980 37.2 per cent and in 1989 36.3 per cent. Before collectivisation peasants were divided into bednyaki (poor), serednyaki (middle) and kulaks (rich). The composition of the peasant population before the

February Revolution was 65 per cent bednyaki, 20 per cent serednyaki and 15 per cent kulaks. In 1928 the situation had changed as a result of the Civil War, when many households were divided so as to avoid being classified as kulaks, and the levelling process which was under way under NEP: 35 per cent were classified as bednyaki, 60 per cent as serednyaki and 4–5 per cent as kulaks. There were significant social differences within the village and in 1927 28.3 per cent of the farms had no working animals, while about 20 per cent of agricultural implements and working animals were concentrated in about 5 per cent of the farms.

Perestroika

The word can be translated as reform, reformation and reconstruction, and was used at various times by the Party to describe fundamental changes in Party structure. For instance, Stalin used it to describe the changes in the Party in 1929–30 and in 1934. Gorbachev, however, gave the term new content after he became General Secretary of the Party in March 1985. He was aware that the Soviet system had to be reformed and began in 1985 with economic reform. The term uskorenie (acceleration) was used to signify a rapid expansion of the machine tool industry so as, among other things, to provide the capital goods to expand consumer goods output. Since this policy brought little success, Gorbachev replaced it with perestroika during the summer of 1986. This was to embrace all aspects of life and activity. Gradually it began to add up to a systemic reform, which involved greater openness (glasnost) and a reform of industrial relations (democratisation), and the latter spilled into other aspects of life.

Gorbachev advocated a radical reform of the economic mechanism, in other words stimulating enterprises to expand production, cut costs and increase labour productivity. There was talk of a socialist market economy. Law was upgraded and the goal was a socialist *Rechtsstaat*, where the rule of law would prevail. Social justice had to become prevalent in society. This brought into question the Party's behaviour in the past, especially the role of Stalin. The term Stalinism was used for the first time in the Soviet Union in the western sense. The new thinking in domestic and foreign policy abandoned class interests as the basis of decision-making and universal human values were adopted. The 27th Party Congress did not change much – Gorbachev was mostly concerned about effecting personnel changes – but the CC plenums in 1987 and the 19th Party Conference, in June 1988, did. At the latter the Party was removed from supervision of the economy. The law on the state enterprise, in effect from 1 January 1988, gave management control over enterprise budgets, and signalled the loss of control of the centre over the economy. The sensitive problem of price reform was shied away from until 1990 and then it was, to all intents, neutered. The law on the cooperatives made private business activity legal in industry, agriculture and services. It was also legal to own private property. Commercial banks could be founded from 1988. An unexpected by-product of this legislation was that it allowed the mafia in the shadow economy to go legal – they could now set up their own businesses and invest their dirty money in them.

Constitutional reform led to the election of a USSR Congress of People's Deputies in March 1989. Two-thirds of the deputies were directly elected and many radicals became deputies. A standing parliament, the USSR Supreme Soviet, was elected by these deputies. In 1990 the RSFSR elected a Congress of People's Deputies but all other republics elected only Supreme Soviets. In the Baltic republics and Georgia nationalist separatists were in the majority.

Perestroika was a catch-all concept, understood quite differently by segments of the population. To many it meant an economic and social revolution, while to others, especially in the Party apparatus, it signified a reform of the economy but excluding the market. The latter expected the Party to become stronger as a result. A conflict developed between those who believed that the planned economy should give way to a market economy and those, especially Ligachev, who rejected such a proposition as heresy. Ligachev would not tolerate private ownership of any means of production, including land. Gorbachev went along with the pro-market enthusiasts and a 500-day programme to move to a market economy was drafted, but conservatives put so much pressure on him that he backed away during the autumn of 1990. There was an attempt at stabilisation under the new Prime Minister Valentin Pavlov and blood was shed in Vilnius in January 1991. The reaction of the population to these events was such that a return to the old days was no longer possible for the apparatus. Gorbachev again changed tack and several republics were on the point of signing a draft document establishing a Union of Sovereign States to supersede the Soviet Union. This would have been a genuine federation, unlike the sham the USSR had been. The attempted coup in August 1991 was timed to prevent this signing ceremony taking place. The attempted coup ended perestroika and power then passed to the republics, first and foremost Russia.

Planned economy (also known as command economy)

The planned economy was viewed as the most effective way of implementing the economic policy of the Party. It embraced all aspects of economic life, from the drafting of the plan, to production, investment, innovation, distribution, domestic and foreign trade, and all the results of these activities. The primary task of the plan was to permit productive forces to flourish and to bring about a secular rise in living standards. Eventually the plan was to satisfy all the material and social needs of the population. The planned economy consciously eliminated the market and consequently the planners had to provide all the signals which the market provides. Prices were to be for accounting purposes only and not to reflect relative scarcities. The Party believed that the most effective way of running an economy was to concentrate its management at the centre. Priorities and targets would be set by the Party and not by the consumers. The Supreme Council of the National Economy (VSNKh) was the first attempt to run all industry from the centre and under the conditions of war communism this was merely a pipe dream. The first attempt at putting together a nation-wide plan was the Goelro plan of 1920, which envisaged the electrification of the country. In the mid-1920s Gosplan and VSNKh began to publish control figures and draft FYPs. Annual plans were then to be elaborated.

Various attempts were made to find an optimal central planning organ: Gosplan, Council of the National Economy, VSNKh and economic councils. The economic targets were set by the Politburo, Central Committee and Sovnarkom. A conflict developed between the People's Commissariat for Finance, responsible for the day-to-day running of financial life, and Gosplan, which concentrated mainly on long-range planning and was not responsible for finding the capital to fund them. Eventually sound finance (balanced budget) gave way to ambitious industrial targets which many Bolshevik economists did not believe should be held back by lack of cash. Their thinking was that if the Soviet state needed something, it had to be achieved, irrespective of the cost. Hence combating inflation came very low on their list of priorities. When the first FYP got under way in 1929 (it dated from October 1928) the planners set enterprises targets which had to be met. The intermediate layer, between the planners and the enterprises, was filled by the ministries and their branches (glavki), state committees for science and technology, material supply, prices, standardisation, etc. Khrushchev departed radically from the central model of planning by introducing 105 councils of the national economy (sovnarkhozes), most of them covering an oblast, as a radical way of improving performance. At the same time most industrial and agricultural ministries were abolished. This reform was reversed in 1965 and it was only under Gorbachev that radical changes were again attempted. The planned economy was successful in building up heavy industry, especially for military purposes. However, as the economy grew it became more and more difficult to manage it from the centre. Enterprises and labour attempted to acquire 'soft' plans, easy to achieve, by hoarding and not revealing their potential. There were various economic slowdowns in the 1930s and there was an economic crisis looming in 1939 which was circumvented by war in 1941.

A major problem for the planners was objective, accurate data from the enterprises. It was finally conceded in the 1960s that enterprises had no interest in providing objective information. The party leadership was perpetually attempting to find ways of increasing efficiency and labour productivity. Some economists advocated greater emphasis on commodity–money relations (prices) as an indicator. These debates occurred from the 1920s to the 1970s. Prices were always rejected as guides to action because the planners (and the Party) wished to have overall control. The question of ownership (public versus cooperative) was raised in the 1930s and 1940s but afterwards was too sensitive to be aired publicly. The Kosygin reforms of 1965 were the most radical and promised much but were torpedoed by the events in Czechoslovakia in 1968. From the 1970s to the mid-1980s economists concentrated on refining the 'economic mechanism'. The search was on to find a method of stimulating enterprises to raise efficiency and output and also increase labour productivity.

When Gorbachev took over in 1985 he was aware that the economy was under-performing and launched his uskorenie (acceleration) policy. Perestroika attempted to reform all aspects of the economy and social life but it did not address the most important question: that of ownership. The law on the state enterprise, commencing on 1 January 1988, and conferring wide budgetary powers on management, was a disaster from the central planner's point of view. Gosplan began to lose control of the economy and this was compounded by the decision, taken at the 19th Party Conference in June 1988, to remove the Party from the management of the economy. What the reformers had failed to understand was that the Party was the glue which kept the Soviet system together. Enterprises henceforth concentrated on consumption and paid little attention to accumulation and investment. As the dislocations increased, regions sought to retain their output for their own consumers and to barter with other regions for other goods. The Pavlov cabinet attempted to restore central control but it was too late. The planned economy had collapsed under its own contradictions. Gosplan became a Ministry of Economics and Forecasting in 1991.

Pravda (Truth)

The most famous Soviet newspaper, published by the Central Committee of the CPSU. It was founded in 1912 as a legal organ of Russian social democracy. Conflict with the authorities led to numerous name changes (*Rabochaya pravda, Severnaya pravda, Pravda truda*, etc.) and in July 1914 it had to cease publication. It reappeared after the February Revolution but was again banned after the July Days. After the October Revolution it became the official organ of the Bolshevik Party. The date of the first number in 1912, 5 May, was celebrated as press day in the Soviet Union.

The newspaper was awarded two Orders of Lenin (1945 and 1962) and one Order of the October Revolution (1972). It was a mass newspaper with a print-run of 10.7 million copies in 1983. *Pravda* was also translated into western languages and was distributed widely in the mid-1980s. The attempted coup of August 1991, the banning of the CPSU, and the disappearance of its subsidies brought the paper to the point of closure. It re-emerged in March 1992 with only four sides and three times weekly.

Press

The press in the Soviet Union had always to perform a political function: to contribute to the building of socialism and later communism, and to inspire and educate the new Soviet man and woman. The guiding principle until the 1980s was partiinost (party-mindedness) and the papers set the tone for Soviet life. This was serious and little frivolity graced their pages. The western concept of press freedom, giving the readers what they wanted, was rejected. The Bolsheviks moved quickly to close down their rivals' newspapers and publications after the October Revolution. They did this by seizing the publishing houses, the printing presses and paper. The decree on the press of 27 October 1917 claimed that the banning of these organs was temporary, but on 4 November the Central Executive Committee of the Soviets declined to restore freedom of the press and claimed that doing so would be to connive at the 'poisoning of the masses' and to agree to a counter-revolutionary measure. *Pravda* took over the printing presses of the conservative newspaper *Novoe vremya* (New Times). The publishing house of the liberal daily *Rech* (Speech) passed into the hands of *Soldatskaya pravda* (Soldier's Truth). The *Den* (Day) printing press went over to printing *Derevenskaya bednota* (Village Poverty). For the Party, the press was an instrument of propaganda, agitation and organisation. The first Soviet Russian constitution, July 1918, confiscated the bourgeois printing presses and transferred them to the proletariat and the poorest strata of the peasantry. This, it was claimed, would guarantee real press freedom instead of the previous bourgeois pseudo-freedom. The 8th Party Congress in March 1919 confirmed this view and called on *Pravda* to educate the masses in their rights and freedoms. The 1936 constitution dropped the class nature of civil rights and guaranteed freedom of opinion and the press for everyone. However, these rights and freedoms were to be exercised only if they coincided with the interests of the workers and served to strengthen the socialist order. Access to printing presses and paper was limited to those who met the above criteria. In 1986 over 8,500 daily newspapers were being published with a print-run of over 198 million copies. The largest print-run was by the trade union organ *Trud* (Labour) with 13.5 million copies and *Pravda* printed 10.7 million copies. *Selskaya zhizn* (Country

Life) printed 9 million copies, *Komsomol* (Young Communist League) printed 10 million copies and the government newspaper *Izvestiya* (News) printed 8.6 million copies (all these print-runs refer to 1983). Newspapers appeared in 57 languages of the USSR and 10 foreign languages. There were also over 5,000 journals and magazines, some of which printed over a million copies. The arrival of glasnost under Gorbachev and later the law on the press saw a mushrooming of publications and print-runs so that *Pravda,* always regarded as conservative, was overtaken by the more radical *Komsomolskaya pravda* and *Izvestiya.*

Proletkult

An abbreviation for proletarskaya kultura (proletarian culture), which was a cultural revolutionary movement that came into being just before the October Revolution and then developed into a mass organisation. Its goal was to establish a new proletarian culture which would be independent of the intelligentsia and peasantry. It also desired to be independent of the Communist Party. Proletkult regarded the Party's task to be the political revolution, that of the trade unions the economic revolution and its task the cultural revolution. It set up Proletkult clubs and circles, literary studios and workers' universities. It contributed to the overcoming of illiteracy, promoted folklore and experimented with street theatre as a means of influencing consciousness and encouraging creativity. In 1920 Proletkult had 400,000 members and 80,000 activists and published 20 journals. Its most influential thinker was A. A. Bogdanov (1873–1928) who had been expelled from the Bolshevik Party in 1909 for his 'heretical' views. Anatoly Lunacharsky, the People's Commissar for Education, was well disposed to Proletkult but Lenin would not tolerate an organisation which wished to distance itself from the Party. He also did not share its view that proletarian culture must be based on bourgeois culture. In December 1920 the Central Committee of the Party resolved to submerge Proletkult in the People's Commissariat for Education, where it became a department, subject to the guidance of the Party.

Prostitution

Prostitution was not a criminal offence in the Soviet Union. The problem was resolved administratively in Russia from 1843 onwards and this legislation was removed from the statute book after the October Revolution. It was assumed that the reasons for prostitution would be removed by building socialism. After the 1936 constitution was adopted, the state argued that prostitution no longer existed and it was claimed that it was the only country in the world in which this was true. Not only was prostitution absent but the social and economic grounds for its existence had been eliminated. Hence there was no legal regulation of the phenomenon. This relieved the police of the task of registering prostitutes, and hospitals of the need to keep a medical check on the health of prostitutes. However, it was illegal to entice under-age persons into prostitution, to run bordellos, to procure and to spread contagious diseases. Discussion of prostitution disappeared from newspapers and journals in the mid-1930s. The subject again appeared under perestroika and the widespread nature of the phenomenon led some conservative newspapers and journals to advocate making it illegal, but the RSFSR Supreme Soviet decree of 29 May 1987 only levied a fine of 100 rubles for it. If the person offended again within a year, the fine rose to 200 rubles. Prostitution became a rapidly growing business in the Gorbachev era and in 1987 special police units were set up in Moscow and other cities to deal with the problem.

RAPP

The rossiiskaya assotsiatsiya proletarskikh pisatelei (Russian Association of Proletarian Writers) was the largest group within VOAPP (All-Union Union of Associations of Proletarian Writers, known as VAPP until 1928) and exerted decisive influence over Russian literary policy between 1928 and 1931. After the 15th Party Congress had resolved in December 1927 to accelerate the industrialisation of the country, the Party Central Committee convened a meeting in May–June 1928 and instructed culture and propaganda to participate in the re-education of the masses to achieve socialist construction, to heighten the class struggle against non-proletarian, bourgeois influence in all areas of life, to strengthen the participation of the proletariat in science, technology and art and to develop a proletarian art. VOAPP and RAPP were designated the 'elite troops of the cultural revolution . . . which were to implement all tasks set by the party in literature'. RAPP used its dominant position to force all other proletarian writers' associations into subordination, many to disband and then join RAPP. Under L. L. Averbakh, RAPP did not tolerate any fellow-travellers: one was either fully committed or was an enemy. In the early 1930s conflict prevailed but the Party changed tack and sought to consolidate forces. It accused RAPP of impatience and vulgar socialism. On 23 April 1932 the Party Central Committee passed a decree dissolving RAPP and VOAPP. The successor organisation was to be the USSR Union of Writers.

Russian Orthodox Church

Until 1917 the Orthodox Church was a constituent part of the Russian state and was headed by the Tsar. It was also the bearer of the national culture, as to be a Russian meant being a member of the Orthodox Church. In August 1917 the church began its first council in Moscow for over 200 years. In October it elected Tikhon Patriarch and thereby reinstated the form of leadership which Peter the Great had suspended. Lenin, a militant atheist, regarded the church as a bulwark of reaction which had to be swept away. Lenin drafted the decree on the separation of the church from the state and education of 23 January 1918 which excluded the church from all educational activity. The decree also denied church congregations the status of a legal entity (juridical person) and their right to own property. At least 28 bishops and thousands of priests were murdered during the Civil War. The secret police (GPU) promoted the formation of a supreme church administration, consisting of 'renewers'. The latter introduced reform of the liturgy – Russian replaced Old Church Slavonic – and married bishops. They proclaimed the Bolsheviks as the builders of a new, more just and socialist future. Most of the hierarchy acknowledged the renewers as leaders of the church but they found little support among the faithful. When Patriarch Tikhon was released from detention in June 1923 he declared himself loyal to the new Soviet government. Many bishops and priests left the renewers and came back to Tikhon.

The church came under greater pressure during the 1920s (117 out of 160 bishops were arrested between 1925 and 1927) and in 1927 Metropolitan Sergei signed another declaration of loyalty to the regime which went much further than the previous one. The Bolsheviks concentrated their attention on the hierarchy and their cathedrals, buildings and seminaries, and the most active priests and lay persons in the cities. The church in the countryside was not molested to anything like the degree suffered in the cities. In 1930 the Moscow patriarchate still claimed 30,000 congregations. Stalin's campaign against the church began with the RSFSR decree on religious communities, of 8 April 1929. All social, charitable and teaching activities of church communities were now banned. The mass collectivisation of 1929 was accompanied by a mass closing of churches and deportation of priests. By the end of the 1930s the church was on its knees with only seven bishops active and a few hundred churches open.

The war transformed the situation for the church. Also the incorporation of eastern Poland in 1939 led to many Belorussian and Ukrainian orthodox believers joining the fold. The church called on the faithful to do their patriotic duty from the first day of the war, organised collections, and glorified Stalin. On 4 September 1943 Stalin met Metropolitan Sergei and four days later he was elected Patriarch. When he died in 1945 Aleksei was elected Patriarch. The church recovered after the war and by the end of the 1950s there were about 25,000 congregations, eight seminaries and two academies. Most of these communities were in the western part of the country, which had not suffered the persecution of the rest of Russia. Stalin also obliged the Ukrainian Catholic (Greek Orthodox) Church to merge with the Orthodox Church in 1946. However, many of these faithful organised their own underground church. The autonomous Orthodox Church and the autocephalous Orthodox Church, established under German rule in Ukraine, were also merged with the Orthodox Church. The latter had emerged in the 1920s and 1930s as a Ukrainian national church (it again became significant after 1991).

In 1959 Khrushchev descended on the church like a wolf on the fold and by 1964 about two-thirds of churches had been closed down or demolished. Five of the eight seminaries were shut. By the mid-1980s there were about 7,000 congregations. Under Gorbachev the situation radically changed as he espoused universal human values, one of which was freedom of conscience and worship. During his travels he was particularly interested in the social role played by churches and the faithful. After 1991 the Orthodox Church was again proclaimed the national church of Russia and many favours were extended it. The Patriarch blessed Boris Yeltsin during his inauguration as Russian President on 10 July 1991.

Samizdat

Literally self-publishing, which, of course, was illegal in the Soviet Union. All printing presses and paper were under the control of the state, and intellectuals and dissidents who wished to spread their ideas found that there were few opportunities to break through censorship and be published officially. The texts and manuscripts were typed in as many copies as possible (there was little chance of using a Xerox machine) and then distributed to friends and acquaintances. Sometimes they typed the manuscript again and passed it on to more readers. It began in the late 1950s and flowered in the 1960s, warning against re-Stalinisation, which appeared to be on the agenda after the trials of the poet Joseph Brodsky in 1964 and the writers Andrei Sinyavsky and Yuly Daniel in 1966. The first number of the Chronicle of Current Events appeared in samizdat on 30 April 1968, attempting to provide information on informal movements and initiatives and breaches of civil and human rights and to campaign for them. Over 60 issues of the Chronicle appeared. Religious groups, national, civil and human rights committees reported on their activities as well as 'true' communists and 'true' Marxist–Leninists. As well as the above, there were reports on national discrimination, reports of trials of dissidents, religious and political tracts, literature no longer published officially and foreign material. There was also the phenomenon of magizdat (tape recorder publishing), where the songs and ballads of Bulat Okudzhava, Aleksandr Galich and Vladimir Vysotsky circulated and were hugely successful (Yury Andropov, head of the KGB, listened to and enjoyed them too). Some authors dared give their work to foreign publishers to bring out (tamizdat – over there publishing). The KGB became much less accommodating towards the end of the 1970s and proceeded to use articles 90 and 190–1 of the Soviet criminal code (anti-Soviet propaganda and defamation of the Soviet Union) against dissidents and human rights activists. By the early 1980s they had effectively silenced them. Under glasnost there was a flowering of such publishing but it was now legal.

Schools

Tsarist Russia made considerable strides towards increasing literacy but never achieved universal compulsory primary education. After October 1917 there were many other problems which took priority, but efforts were made through literacy trains and other campaigns to reduce illiteracy, the goal being to increase support of the Soviet regime. It was only in the early 1930s that the legislation introducing universal education entered the statute book. A. S. Bubnov, the successor to Lunacharsky as People's Commissar for Enlightenment, was enthusiastic and energetic in devising programmes to reduce illiteracy and provide all schoolchildren with a place. It was normal in the 1930s for most children to spend only four years at school; later this was extended to seven, eight and even ten years of compulsory education. Eleven years at school became the Soviet goal. Primary and secondary education took place in general schools, and vocational schools such as the middle schools (tekhnikums) became common. There were medical, agricultural, pedagogical and other tekhnikums. These schools produced graduates whose knowledge was well below those from the university sector. In 1985 there were 4,495 secondary schools with 4.5 million pupils taking technical subjects but 1.7 million of these were studying by correspondence. Those who graduated from the technical schools and the 10-year schools qualified for university admission if they passed their final examinations. Khrushchev was disturbed to discover that students at Moscow State University were overwhelmingly from the intelligentsia and introduced reforms in 1958–59 to oblige every secondary school pupil to spend a year in industry or agriculture and thereby increase their respect for manual labour. The reform failed because it was implemented by the intelligentsia and they ensured that the much-sought-after university place was not denied their offspring. In order to increase the possibility of regional or rural children passing the university entrance examination, special courses were put on for them in the cities. The last Soviet educational reform was passed in 1983 and envisaged most children studying at vocational secondary schools until they were qualified to study at university. General secondary education faded into the background as the interests of the economy received greater recognition.

Seven Year Plan (1959–65)

As the sixth FYP (1956–60) was proving disappointing, Khrushchev launched the even more ambitious Seven Year Plan to supersede it. The main reasons given for introducing a new plan were the discovery of new raw materials and the dislocations caused by the setting up of 105 councils of the national economy (sovnarkhozes), which were responsible for economic activity on their territory. Khrushchev was seeking methods to accelerate economic growth, to expand rapidly the chemical industry and the use of oil and natural gas. According to official Soviet statistics much of the plan had been realised by 1965 but it failed miserably in agriculture. Oil and electricity output, for example, exceeded the plan.

Shock workers (Udarniki)

They were workers during war communism who were used to carry out urgent tasks. The term was used again during rapid industrialisation but for workers who were distinguished by high labour productivity or those who promised to achieve high goals. The first shock worker brigades were formed probably at the local level in 1926–28, and after socialist competition was proclaimed in 1929 the shock worker movement then became part and parcel of it. By the beginning of 1931 an estimated 60 per cent of workers were in shock worker brigades. Given this level of participation, it is unlikely that the term meant very much or exactly what a shock worker achieved above the norm. They were also unpopular as their achievements led to the norms for other workers being raised. The fact that the Stakhanovite movement replaced the shock worker movement in 1935 revealed that the latter had run its course. The term was resurrected under Khrushchev but did not enthuse workers. The movement again reveals that the communists regarded higher labour productivity as the key to industrial expansion. They, arguably, should have concentrated much more on cutting costs, innovation and upgrading the product.

Socialist competition

In an article penned by Lenin in January 1918 but only published in 1929, entitled 'How Should One Organise Competition?', the Soviet leader argued that competition is not something which exists solely under capitalism but can only be fully developed under socialism. It permits the worker to develop his full potential, to display his initiative and inspire his

colleagues. Socialist competition only became a reality when rapid industrialisation got under way. Lenin's article was published in *Komsomolskaya
pravda* on 26 January 1929 and the newspaper called on all Komsomol
members to organise country-wide competitions. The 16th Party Conference in April–May 1929 added to the momentum. In 1934 73.4 per cent
of industrial workers, 54.5 per cent of construction workers and 40 per
cent of sovkhoz workers were involved in it. It took various forms such
as the Stakhanovite and the shock worker movements. In 1931 material
rewards were introduced such as bonuses and special goods. The 21st
Party Congress in 1959 gave new impetus to the concept and in 1975
it was claimed that 91 per cent of all Soviet citizens were involved in
it. This figure reveals the weakness of the concept since if everyone is
involved what is distinct about it? Under glasnost it was conceded that
most of the claims made about socialist competition had been false and
that it did not motivate workers. It is significant that Lenin introduced
the concept as he was much taken by Taylorism, which regarded labour
productivity as the most important part of production. Stalin continued
this way of thinking in Stakhanovism, shock working and so on. This
led to a neglect of technology and innovation in Soviet industry as the
emphasis was always placed on cheap machines and cheap labour. Soviet
engineers gradually came to perform different functions from those in
the western world: they concentrated on output and not on product
design, quality control and innovation. Cutting costs was not important,
producing quantity was.

Socialist realism

An important aspect of the Stalinist revolution from above in the 1930s.
Its goal was to express culture in socialist garb as a contribution to the
building of socialism and the strengthening of the Soviet Union. Socialist realism applied to all cultural expression but literature was the main
art form. It was preceded by the reorganisation of all writers' groups in
1932 and the emergence of the USSR Union of Writers in 1934. Stalin
and Zhdanov were intimately involved and on 26 October 1932 Stalin
stated that writers were to become the 'engineers of human souls'. Socialist realism was declared to be the guiding principle of Soviet literature
at the 1st Congress of the USSR Union of Writers in August 1934. The
first objective for a writer was to ensure that his output was imbued with
partiinost (party-mindedness), in other words he was in tune with the
latest Party line. Next he had to express himself in language which was
easily accessible to the average worker. This eliminated experimental
and formalist styles. His heroes had to be persons who were dedicated to
building socialism and could serve as role models for workers and others.
Thus the positive hero is fundamental to the Soviet novel and poetry.

The positive hero is to be someone who is attractive, friendly, hard-working, unselfindulgent, devoted to the family and prepared to make any sacrifice in the interests of building socialism. His hero is Stalin. In contrast to the anti-hero, the superfluous person, who inhabits the Russian novels of the nineteenth century, he is always beaming optimism and *joie de vivre*. Classic socialist realist novels are always about industrial output: for example, Ostrovsky's *How the Steel Was Tempered*. Predecessors of socialist realist novels are strewn throughout the nineteenth century, with Chernyshevksy's *What is to be Done* (1863) being very influential. Gorky's *Mother* (1906) and Gladkov's *Cement* (1925) are also important signposts on the way to the new novel. Mikhail Sholokhov's *Quietly Flows the Don* and *Virgin Land Upturned*, published during the 1930s, are among the most successful of this genre. The coming of glasnost undermined socialist realism as greater objectivity was demanded and the blank spots of history examined.

Sovkhozes (state farms)

Literally sovetskoe khozyaistvo (Soviet economy), they were also known as state farms. They were different from kolkhozes (collective farms) in that the latter were cooperatives but state farms were state property and operatives were classified as workers and enjoyed their social benefits. They also received a monthly wage whereas kolkhozniks were paid out of the surplus generated by their farm. The first sovkhozes appeared in 1917–18 and corresponded to Lenin's proposals in his April Theses, which advocated the retention of landed estates, after nationalisation, as model farms. This had little impact on the peasants, who were land-hungry and divided up all available land among themselves. In 1922 there were 4,316 sovkhozes in Soviet Russia but they farmed only 2 per cent of the agricultural land. The others forms of collective ownership also fared poorly. This underlined the desire of the Russian peasant to have control over his own land. Sovkhozes were to provision the Red Army with food and raw materials and to achieve a demonstration effect among peasants by revealing the superiority of this form of production. This was never the case during NEP and when collectivisation got under way sovkhozes were set up on land which had previously not been farmed. Kolkhozes were formed by merging the peasant farms in one or several villages. The motto 'the bigger the better' prevailed. The Gigant sovkhoz covered 127,000 hectares in 1928 and 239,000 hectares in 1931. International experience has demonstrated that such a large farm cannot be farmed efficiently. The sovkhozes were more expensive for the state than kolkhozes and this slowed down their expansion until the 1950s, when Khrushchev began amalgamating kolkhozes and transforming them into sovkhozes. This trend continued until the end of the Soviet era. By the 1980s they accounted for about half of the arable land.

Sovnarkhoz

These appeared in the early years of the revolution but here are defined as the councils which were set up by Khrushchev in 1957 when he decentralised Soviet industry. In this struggle with his Presidium opponents whose power base was the industrial ministries, Khrushchev hit on the idea of devolving economic decision-making from the centre to the regions. He had come to the conclusion that the central ministries were too powerful and were holding back local initiative. The central industrial ministries (except for defence industries) were abolished and 105 sovnarkhozy were set up. They followed the existing territorial-administrative divisions of the country. The sovnarkhozy began acting as mini-states and attempted to expand their industrial base. It soon became clear that economic coordination was lacking. In 1960 sovnarkhozy were set up for the RSFSR, Ukraine and Kazakhstan and made subordinate to the republican Council of Ministers to integrate the economic activity of the respective republics. A Central Committee plenum of the Party in 1962 resolved to create a sovnarkhoz for the whole of the Soviet Union. It was to take over the previous responsibilities of Gosplan and be responsible for the day-to-day running of the economy. On 13 March 1963 the USSR sovnarkhoz became the USSR Supreme Economic Council. After Khrushchev's removal in 1964 the new leadership soon resolved to abolish the whole sovnarkhoz edifice and revert to the central industrial ministries and this took effect in 1965. Khrushchev correctly identified some of the problems of Soviet industry – the over-centralisation of decision-making, the lacking of innovation and initiative at the enterprise level – but his solution to decentralise merely created 105 (later 103 and finally 47) centres. Since he would not countenance any aspects of a market economy, such as the question of ownership, his reform was doomed. However, it did contribute to the growing strength of regionalism in the Soviet Union, an unexpected by-product he would not have desired.

Sputnik

Literally fellow-traveller, it was the first artificial earth satellite to be launched by the Soviet Union on 4 October 1957 and was an overnight sensation throughout the world. It was round, 60 cm long, had four antennae and weighed 80 kg, circled the world in 96.2 minutes and sent a 1 watt strong signal to earth (for 3 months). The launch was an enormous prestige coup for the Soviet Union and was an unpleasant surprise for the west, especially the USA (Richard Nixon assured Americans there was nothing up there, it was a Soviet trick!) and revealed that the USSR was ahead in developing intercontinental ballistic missiles. The Americans could have been the first to launch a satellite but development was held back by President Eisenhower, who was uncertain about the legality of sending a space vehicle over enemy territory. He favoured the Russians taking the lead as this would permit the USA to follow. Khrushchev attempted to use the rocket superiority of the Soviet Union to force the west into serious disarmament talks but without success. Instead the American Security Council resolved to speed up production of middle-range missiles, to accelerate development of intercontinental ballistic missiles and to prepare the way for the second generation of long-range missiles. On 3 November 1957 the USSR launched a second Sputnik and on 15 May 1958 another Sputnik with the dog Laika on board and weighing 500kg. The earth stood and wondered. Hence an unexpected consequence of the Sputniks was to speed up the arms race, which was eventually to prove too burdensome for the Soviet Union.

Stakhanovite movement

One of the many state initiatives to increase labour productivity and improve the deployment of labour. It began in 1935 and continued until 1941. It was named after the miner, Aleksei Stakhanov, who on 31 August 1935, in one shift, mined 102 tonnes of coal. The standard norm was 7 tonnes. Under glasnost it was revealed that the whole exercise had been a fraud. Stakhanov had been helped by many auxiliaries and the machinery and equipment was ready and kept running. Stakhanov was held up as a hero and his record was used as an example to increase labour mobilisation. Stakhanovism can be regarded as a tactic to undermine the authority of management at a time when the planner's goal was to raise output at any price. It was counter-productive in that it concentrated on quantity and ignored quality and nurtured the belief that any economic problem could be solved by campaigns and the mobilisation of workers. It is also testimony to the mistaken Soviet belief that labour productivity was the key problem in industry. Managers and engineers should have been concentrating on improving the product through greater quality control, innovation and more advanced technology. Instead output at any cost was the norm.

State capitalism

Before 1917 the term in Marxist literature refers to capitalist states in which government has become subordinate to large industrial enterprises and banks. When Lenin coined the expression to describe a certain stage of the construction of socialism in Soviet Russia, he gave it a new meaning. Two phases can be identified. In May 1918 in his pamphlet 'On left wing infantilism and on petty-bourgeois tendencies', he claimed that state capitalism was not a bad objective in a country where small-scale private production was the predominant form of economic activity. He conceded that the argument that workers and peasants held power in Russia was false but was an article of faith for Bolsheviks. The supposed reality of a government based on popular consent would ensure that state capitalism would not involve the abandonment of the commitment to socialism. Nationalisation of enterprises and land, workers' control, the requirement to work and the state distribution of goods would be employed for the good of the people and would be quite unlike state capitalism under capitalism. Since most economic activities were in small units it would be difficult to control them without using force. State capitalism would gradually take over as it become more competitive. Socialism, however, could not be built with large-scale enterprises and state of the art technology. He came back to state capitalism after war communism had run its course and NEP was being implemented in 1921. In his pamphlet 'On the tax in kind', he analysed the practicalities of state capitalism in Soviet Russia. It consisted of concessions granted to foreign entrepreneurs to attract investment and know-how, cooperatives, free trade and the leasing of enterprises to entrepreneurs. Lenin regarded this capitalist phase as inevitable and the problem was how to ensure that its development could be guided in the direction of the construction of socialism. State capitalism would eventually be subsumed under socialism. He conceived of the Bolsheviks retaining control of the commanding heights of the economy (large-scale industry, banks, public utilities, foreign trade monopoly, and so on) and the enhancement of proletarian political power in the Soviet state (banning of bourgeois parties, the Menshevik party).

Supreme Council of the National Economy (VSNKh)

The name of the main management agency of the Soviet economy between 1917 and 1932 and between 1963 and 1965. The VSNKh was set up on 2 December 1917 and was responsible for managing Soviet industry until the end of the first FYP. It underwent many changes. Lenin originally expected workers' control (through factory committees, trade unions, soviets, etc.) to run industry under Bolshevik guidance, but this soon collapsed as labour sought to manage in its own interests. VSNKh was to run industry along the lines of German wartime industry. This led to rapid nationalisation in the spring of 1918. Under war communism, high inflation led to the glavki (main administrations) physically allocating raw materials, fuel and distributing the finished goods. Under NEP VSNKh went over to khozraschet (economic accountability). Industry was divided up into trusts and to manage them a central administration for industry was set up. A main economic administration was established to engage in planning. From the mid-1920s VSNKh and Gosplan put forward draft FYPs and competed for prominence. At the end of the first FYP, 1932, VSNK's functions were transferred to newly founded people's commissariats for heavy, light and the timber industry. Under Khrushchev's sovnarkhoz reforms, a Supreme Council of the National Economy, as part of the USSR Council of Ministers, was set up on 13 March 1963 and headed by Dmitry Ustinov, who later became USSR Minister of Defence. He had the task of coordinating the activities of Gosplan (perspective or long-term planning), the Supreme Council (engaged in current planning), and the state committee for construction (Gosstroi). The Supreme Council was dissolved by a Central Committee plenum in September 1965 with Gosplan taking over all planning.

TASS (Telegraphic Agency of the Soviet Union)

The official Soviet news agency was set up in July 1925 by a decree of the Central Executive Committee of the USSR and was to cover the whole of the USSR. It replaced the Russian telegraphic agency (known as ROSTA), which had been in existence since September 1918. In September 1971 TASS became a state committee of the USSR Council of Ministers. TASS collected general and specialised information and illustrative material and passed them on to the Soviet print media, radio and television, to other Soviet organisations and to foreign subscribers. TASS had its own correspondents and bureaux in over 100 countries and over 500 correspondents in the Soviet Union. It was always accepted that a proportion of TASS staff were KGB and GRU officers whose main task was the collection of special information. TASS disappeared with the dissolution of the Soviet Union but became a limited company and part of the media in post-communist Russia.

Thaw

The limited cultural relaxation in the Soviet Union which followed Stalin's death and lasted until the mid-1960s. The name derives from the novel *Ottepel* (The Thaw) by Ilya Ehrenburg, published in 1954. There was a flood of literature about the dreadful conditions and suffering in the labour camps (gulag). Khrushchev was quite content to allow this literature to be published as it served a political purpose, the blackening of the reputations of those of his opponents who had been among

Stalin's elite. He enjoyed listening to criticisms of Stalin's Russia as the decision to publish them was sometimes taken in the Party Presidium. However, writers and artists were more concerned about reflecting reality and objectivity in their work rather than promoting the new Party line. This led to continual tension between many cultural figures and the Party as it was quite clear that they were flouting socialist realism and partiinost (party-mindedness). When Boris Pasternak's *Dr Zhivago* was published abroad, Khrushchev hounded him on the advice of the cultural bureaucrats. In retirement he admitted that he should have read the novel rather than judge it by the out-of-context extracts he had been fed by officials. He also remarked that he could not understand the fuss that was made over the novel. The Thaw ended with the trials of Sinyavsky and Daniel in February 1966, with the former being sentenced to five years and the latter seven years in a labour camp.

Trade unions

Trade unions began organising during the 1905–7 revolution and by 1917 there were several hundred thousand members, with Mensheviks dominating craft unions. Bolsheviks and SRs also competed for influence. The Bolsheviks regarded trade unions as part of workers' control, but factory committees and soviets also competed for influence. At the 1st Trades Union Congress in 1918 the trade unions declared they would support Soviet power and were willing to manage production. They preferred to maintain a level of independence towards the state but during the Civil War they became more and more involved in state functions. A conflict developed within the Bolshevik Party on the role of trade unions. Trotsky and Bukharin wanted the trade unions to be taken over by the state but the Workers' Opposition advocated that economic management should be entrusted to the trade unions. Lenin compromised and proposed that trade unions should be subordinate to the state but should represent workers' interests. During NEP the trade unions held positions in the factories and in the People's Commissariat for Labour, which permitted them to mediate in disputes between the enterprise director and the Party secretary. Rapid industrialisation transformed the role of trade unions and they now had the task of mobilising the labour force. Trade unions ceased to participate in decisions about wage levels. During the 1950s and 1960s trade unions took over many social functions, the drafting of social plans and socialist competition. They were involved in deciding bonuses and hygiene, arranged leisure activities and distributed accommodation and kindergarten places. In 1980 about 98 per cent of all workers and employees were trade union members. Under perestroika they were pushed aside as new independent unions appeared. The mass strikes of the late Gorbachev era found them on the sidelines.

Trudoden   *see* Labour day

USSR Academy of Sciences

The Academy was a successor institution of the Imperial Academy of Sciences, founded in 1725. The USSR Academy of Sciences was renamed in 1925 and its personnel was extensively changed in 1929 as part of the Stalinist revolution from above. The Academy was to serve the Five Year Plans and was subordinated to the Council of People's Commissars (Sovnarkom), the Soviet government, in 1933, and most of it moved from Leningrad to Moscow in 1934. It received a new statute in 1935 which declared that the Academy was to help in building the classless society. The Academy was regarded as the general staff of science and technology in the Soviet Union. Academicians enjoyed great privileges and prestige, and could either be corresponding members or full members. The Academy integrated many research institutes and was conentrated almost entirely in the RSFSR. A Siberian branch was set up in Akademgorodok, near Novosibirsk. Each Union republic, except the RSFSR, had its own Academy of Sciences. The Academy was expanded by the addition of the Academy of Agricultural Sciences, the Academy of Medical Sciences and the Academy of Pedagogical Sciences. The USSR Academy had about 250 research institutes and 50,000 research scientists, and as such was the largest scientific institution in the world. It had 274 full members, 542 corresponding members and 70 foreign members. In 1991 the Academy became the Russian Academy of Sciences.

USSR Union of Writers

The Party Central Committee decreed on 23 April 1932 that 'all writers who support Soviet power and who wish to participate in the construction of socialism are to be united in a single Union of Soviet Writers'. This took place in 1934 at the 1st All-Union Congress of Soviet Writers and became known as the USSR Union of Writers. A statute was passed which regulated local groups of writers, right up to the republican organisations, all subordinate and part of the USSR Union of Writers. Socialist realism was declared to be the guiding principle of Soviet literature and criticism. Entry to the Union was voluntary but the most important task of the writer was to 'participate actively in socialist construction' and educate the working masses in the spirit of socialism. Those who transgressed could be expelled from the republican-level organisations. The Union was part of the trend to centralise all activities in one organisation and was paralleled in other areas of endeavour. Publishing was taken over wholly by the state at the end of the 1920s with the elimination of the independent houses. Hence the only way to be published was through the Union. This provided the state and the Party with a powerful weapon to ensure uniformity and support for present policy. It was only possible to give well-paid lectures and sign translation contracts if one was a member of the Union. Expulsion from the Union deprived a writer of access to leisure facilities, spas, medical treatment in special clinics, foreign travel and other privileges. Hence besides the prevailing censorship (exercised by Glavlit) there was also self-censorship. Stalin succeeded in attracting Maxim Gorky back to the Soviet Union and he played an important role in the organisation of the Union and literary life, and as head of the Union.

The Union became the handmaiden of the Stalinist dictatorship and glorified the leader. The purges hit writers especially hard, especially after the death of Gorky. State control was loosened during the Great Patriotic War but became almost suffocating under Zhdanov. Writers and poets such as Zoshchenko and Akhmatova were expelled and vilified. The same treatment was meted out to other art forms, such as music. The 2nd Congress of the Union took place in 1954, although there should have been a Congress every three years according to the statutes. Khrushchev's denunciation of Stalin at the 20th Party Congress in 1956 threw Aleksandr Fadeev, the first secretary of the Union, into a fit of despair and he hanged himself – a tragic end to a tragic career. Aleksandr Tvardovsky, as editor of *Novy Mir*, presided over a liberal phase, but this came to an end under Brezhnev with the trial of Sinyavsky and Daniel in 1966. Alexander Solzhenitsyn was expelled from the Union in 1969 and deported to West Germany. Tvardovsky was forced out of the editorial chair at *Novy Mir* in 1970. This is the period when samizdat made its appearance in protest against the creeping Stalinisation of culture. However, the brutal methods of Stalin's time were not deployed. The arrival of Gorbachev transformed the situation and there was a flowering of literature under glasnost, with many previously banned works being reprinted or published for the first time in the Soviet Union. The Union, at its 8th Congress, discussed its problems frankly. The espousal by Gorbachev of universal human values which led to legislation on the freedom of conscience, religion and the press transformed the literary and cultural scene in the USSR. Socialist realism passed into history.

Virgin and idle lands programme

A grandiose scheme, drafted by Nikita Khrushchev, to solve the eternal Soviet problem of food shortages. The object was to plough up new and idle (out of current use for several years) land in west Siberia, northern Kazakhstan, the Volga, the Urals and the north Caucasus. West Siberia and northern Kazakhstan came to dominate the programme. A Party Central Committee plenum in February–March 1954 gave the go ahead and hundreds of thousands of young enthusiasts (most of them Komsomol members) headed to the east and the harsh realities of the steppe. Since many new areas were uninhabited, vast sovkhozes were set up, from 20,000 to 40,000 hectares in extent (too large to be managed efficiently). A staggering total of 41.8 million hectares was added to the arable area in the Soviet Union (about the arable area of Canada) and grain (predominantly spring wheat) production from the new lands rose almost 30 million tonnes annually between 1954 and 1963. Practically all the land was marginal and hence the risk of harvest failure was great. On average every other year was a disappointment as lack of precipitation (the regions were almost all in dry farming zones), wind erosion, weed infestation and poor management took their toll. After Khrushchev some of the land was allowed to pass out of cultivation. The virgin and idle lands programme had resulted in higher grain production but at a very high cost. The harvest failure of 1963 led to imports of grain from North America and this became the pattern under Brezhnev and his successors. Soviet agriculture could not feed its population.

War communism

The strictly centrally directed wartime German economy fascinated the Bolsheviks. They were the most anti-market political party in 1917 and the organisation of the economy without the market was conceived of as a technical–economic task which consisted of deciding the best use of productive capacity and not linked to the interests of the various economic actors (managers, workers). They thought of the Soviet economy as a single factory and hence all these conflicts would disappear. If the Bolsheviks could lay their hands on political power they could solve all macro-economic tasks. The concept of efficiency was disregarded as Bolshevik economists tended to the view that national needs took precedence over calculations of cost. Under war communism the Bolsheviks rejected self-interest, which they dismissed as petit bourgeois. The worker's role in the industrial process was likened to that of a bolt or a nut in a machine. Hence the concept of freedom or democracy was ignored. How were the Bolsheviks to organise central management? They tried to construct a whole edifice of workers' control, such as factory committees, trade unions and soviets, as institutions of central management. The organs of workers' control soon disappointed the Bolsheviks as self-interest took precedence over accumulation, growth and efficiency. The Bolsheviks then sought to create a single planning and management organ, the Supreme Council of the National Economy (VSNKh), which sought to direct the activities of all enterprises throughout the country as if they were one large factory. Soon problems of supply and distribution appeared and the Bolsheviks concluded they needed a powerful central organ to decide distribution. Attention was concentrated on this rather than on problems of production. Shortages were perceived as a problem of distribution. They debated how best to construct a single plan for the Soviet economy. Only the threat of total economic collapse in early 1921 forced them to admit elements of the market again when NEP was launched in March 1921. Politically war communism meant the elimination of democracy and private interests subordinated to state interests. Peasants had to deliver their produce to the state at fixed prices and due to the rapid inflation were often given vouchers to be redeemed later. Money disappeared and the economy went over to barter. Workers were paid in shoes or bolts. Those who demurred were dealt with by the Cheka. Lenin described the policies of the years 1918–20 as communism forced on the Bolsheviks by the war. Nevertheless the skeleton of Soviet central planning became visible and the thinking behind it formed, and this was to inform the FYPs. It is tempting to see all the faults of central planning already visible in 1918–20.

Worker faculties (Rabfak)

The Sovnarkom decree of 2 August 1918 opened higher learning to all citizens without reference to their previous education. It quickly transpired that most applicants did not possess basic education and to overcome this the RSFSR People's Commissariat for Education, on 11 September 1919, introduced the first Rabfaks at universities. Another decree of the Commissariat of 19 September 1920 made it compulsory for all technical colleges to introduce Rabfaks. They lasted three years and four years by correspondence. Hundreds of thousands of young workers went through the Rabfaks but by the end of the 1930s they had been phased out.

Workers

According to the Marxist definition, workers are those under capitalism who do not own the means of production (factories, land) but receive wages for their work. They produce surplus value, which is appropriated by the capitalists. Collectively they constitute the working class (worker class is a more correct translation of Marx's *Arbeiterklasse*) or the proletariat and are opposed to the bourgeoisie, the class of owners of the means of production. Under socialism workers become the owners of the means of production and instead of surplus value they produce surplus product. During the October Revolution the number of industrial workers was about 3 million, but this dropped to about 1.2 million in 1922. In 1928 there were 2.69 million and in 1932 5.15 million. The number of transport workers and construction workers also expanded rapidly. Gradually workers became the numerically dominant group in Soviet society and in the 1959 census 49.5 per cent of the population were classified as workers. By 1980 this had risen to 60 per cent.

Workers' control

Before and after the October Revolution, workers' control was a major instrument for establishing control over enterprises. The movement arose spontaneously in large enterprises in Moscow, Petrograd, the Urals and also the railways. After the February Revolution, as well as the soviets, there were trade unions and factory committees, which all represented workers' interests. The increasing conflict and tension led to these bodies becoming more and more involved in production and management. Workers' control was institutionalised on 14 November 1917 by a decree of the Soviet Central Executive Committee, which stated that factory committees were to act as control organs in all enterprises and their decisions were to be binding on the owners. The factory committees were brought together in a Russian Council (Soviet) of Workers' Control. They quickly came into conflict with employers, trade unions and soviets. After the nationalisation of industry in June 1918 the factory committees, and thereby workers' control, lost their significance.

Zhdanovshchina (Zhdanov era)

Although Zhdanov died in 1948 the term refers to the nationalistic, xenophobic, conservative Soviet cultural policy of the late 1940s and early 1950s. Stalin apparently believed that increasing contact with the west could only undermine his dictatorship and the beginning of the Cold War increased hostility to the outside world. The west was written off as bourgeois and decadent compared to the optimistic, vibrant Soviet culture. The cultural intelligentsia were required to contribute to the development of Soviet patriotism. Instead of rootless cosmopolitanism, fighting Bolshevik partiinost was to take over, and instead of bourgeois objectivism and abstract formalism, socialism realism was to inform creative endeavour. Those who declined to follow these directives were putting their careers, if not their lives, at stake. Andrei Zhdanov was the moving force behind this policy and he had exercised great influence over cultural policy in the 1930s. Hence the separation of the Soviet Union culturally from the west preceded the political demarcation which found expression in the formation of the Cominform in 1947. Here again Zhdanov was a leading Soviet figure. The more relaxed cultural world of the war and post-war eras ended abruptly on 14 August 1946 when two journals, *Zvezda* and *Leningrad*, were accused of publishing works of the satirist Mikhail Zoshchenko and the writer Anna Akhmatova, which were judged slanderous, anti-Soviet, decadent and pessimistic. Zoshchenko and Akhmatova were expelled from the USSR Union of Writers (which meant they could not publish legally), *Leningrad* was closed down and the editor of *Zvezda* dismissed. This was the first move in a campaign to reorganise Soviet culture. On 26 August there was a Central Committee decree on the theatre which criticised the predominance of non-Soviet bourgeois plays and demanded changes. On 4 September the Central Committee turned its attention to the film world and decrees on opera, music and the arts followed. The campaign against rootless cosmopolitans penetrated the academies and universities, where there were many Jewish specialists, and they became special targets. Stalin became involved in the polemics on linguistics, and Marr. T. D. Lysenko seized the opportunity to promote his views on agrobiology and denigrated genetics as a bourgeois pseudo-science. Stalin also participated actively in this conflict. At the same time it was claimed that Russians had invented everything that was worth inventing. Science in the outside world was bourgeois, only socialist science in the Soviet Union could solve problems. This scientific xenophobia cost the Soviet Union dear but there were many brave Russian scientists who ignored instructions and carried on their research in secret. For instance, Russian geneticists trained a few trusted students secretly so that when genetics was rehabilitated in the 1960s they could provide leadership. Among the musicians pilloried was Dmitry Shostakovich, who found ways to continue his composing while appearing to obey Party instructions.

Nationalities and territories

Armenia

The smallest of the Union republics but also the republic with the greatest ethnic homogeneity. Of its 3.4 million inhabitants in 1991 93 per cent were Armenian, only 2.3 per cent were Russian, and the rest were ethnic minorities, of whom the Azeris were the largest. The proportion of Azeris was much higher before the Nagorno-Karabakh conflict which began in 1988. Many fled to Azerbaijan but some Armenians from Azerbaijan returned to Armenia. Armenia was declared a Soviet republic in 1920 and was part of the Transcaucasian Socialist Federal Soviet Republic from 1922 to 1936. It then became a Union republic when the federation was dissolved. The capital is Erevan. Over time Armenia has lost much of its territory and the present republic is about one-tenth of historical Armenia. About 45 per cent of the 6 million Armenians throughout the world live there and about 80 per cent of the 4 million Armenians who lived in the Soviet Union. Armenia, like Georgia, has a history older than that of the Russians and Ukrainians, and east Armenian territory, then under Persian rule, passed under Russian control between 1805 and 1828. The Armenians have their own Orthodox Church (headed by a Catholicos), their own language and alphabet. Russian attempts at integrating the two churches produced rising Armenian nationalism, headed by the Dashnaks, which was more directed at the Azeris, a Turkic-speaking Islamic people to the east of Armenia. Survivors from the Turkish massacre of Armenians in Anatolia increased inter-ethnic tension. After the October Revolution of 1917 Armenia, Azerbaijan and Georgia formed a union but it soon fell apart because of ethnic tensions. Armenia declared itself an independent republic on 28 May 1918 but was beset with ethnic and other problems, especially conflict with Azerbaijan over territory – Nagorno-Karabakh, for example. In late 1920 the Red Army took over and declared Armenia a Soviet republic. Armenia then became part of a Transcaucasian Federation. Armenia lost territory to Azerbaijan, Georgia and Turkey. For example, Nagorno-Karabakh was transferred to Azerbaijan. The Armenians quickly joined the Communist Party and in 1922 89.5 per cent of communists were Armenian. Armenia suffered during the 1930s as Stalin set about wiping out national elites (he accused them of being bourgeois nationalists). Stalin's chief butcher was Lavrenty

Beria, a Georgian. Opposition to collectivisation resulted in famine and guerrilla warfare. Industrial growth was marked but the republic was poor in raw materials. Under Khrushchev and after, Armenian living standards rose above the Union average, helped by the black economy. Armenians dominated the Communist Party and government and Moscow used Armenia to attract the Armenian diaspora. Before Gorbachev there were two themes which were taboo: the Turkish massacre of 1915 and the regaining of Nagorno-Karabakh. On 24 April 1965, the anniversary of the massacre, there was a large demonstration in Erevan. Glasnost opened the floodgates and in 1988 the conflict over Nagorno-Karabakh flared up, with the earthquake of December 1988 adding to the travails of the republic. Armenia declared sovereignty on 23 August 1990 but was mindful of the fact that it had few friends in Transcaucasia. It declared independence in September 1991 after the failed coup. It needed an understanding with Russia for security reasons and Azeris have always complained that Russia supported Armenia during the Nagorno-Karabakh conflict. Armenia's population grew from 3 million in 1979 to 3.3 million in 1989, when 93.3 per cent of the inhabitants were Armenian and 1.6 per cent Russian.

Autonomous Soviet Socialist Republic

In the USSR constitution of 30 December 1922 those peoples which possessed all four criteria of Stalin's definition of a nation (a common language, a common territory, a common economic life, and a common psychological make-up) became Union republics (100,000 people or more) or autonomous republics (less than 100,000). Those peoples which possessed less than the four criteria were classified as nationalities (narodnosti) and were divided into autonomous regions (oblasts) and autonomous territories (okrugs).

Azerbaijan

The largest of the Transcaucasian republics with a population of about 7 million in 1991, of whom 81 per cent were Azeris, 8 per cent Armenian and 8 per cent Russian. The Nagorno-Karabakh conflict resulted in over half a million Azeri refugees coming to the republic. Many Armenians also left Azerbaijan for Armenia and Russia. In April 1920 Azerbaijan was proclaimed a Soviet republic and between 1922 and 1936 was part of the Transcaucasian Socialist Federal Soviet Republic, together with Armenia and Georgia. In December 1936 Azerbaijan became a Union republic and its capital was Baku. There are sizeable Azeri minorities in Armenia, Georgia, and Russia, and in Iran they constitute the largest minority, about 10 million. The Azeris speak a Turkic language (at present

Turkish is the first foreign language) and are Muslim. Russian–Persian wars led to the division of Azerbaijan in 1828 between the two states. In the 1870s foreign capital began to develop the oil industry in Baku and the city attracted immigrants, especially Armenians. There was some tension between these two ethnic groups. Baku was the centre of Bolshevik influence in Transcaucasia. After the October Revolution Azerbaijan declared its independence but then entered a union with Armenia and Georgia which quickly fell victim to ethnic rivalry. In May 1918 Azerbaijan again declared itself an independent republic. There was armed conflict with Armenia over Nagorno-Karabakh. The republic was never able to defend its independence and the British and the Turks occupied it for short spells before the Red Army took Baku in April 1920. The economy was back to its pre-1914 level by 1927. Besides the oil industry, the machine-building and chemical industries were developed. Collectivisation was as unpopular in Azerbaijan as elsewhere and during the 1930s the old Azeri nationalists were liquidated, as was much of the intelligentsia. Islam was targeted by Moscow as a threat to communism and hopes for union with Azeris in Persia were suppressed. After Stalin's death Azerbaijan developed but there were always anti-corruption campaigns, providing evidence of the strength of the black market and the involvement of Party officials in it. The first Azeri to rise to Soviet prominence was Heidar Aliev, who headed the Party between 1969 and 1982. The Nagorno-Karabakh conflict became violent in 1988 and proved insoluble under Soviet rule. A popular front gradually emerged and the Azeri Supreme Soviet declared sovereignty in September 1989. There were pogroms against Armenians in Sumgait in February 1989 and in Baku in January 1990. The Communist Party of Azerbaijan could not cope – Nagorno-Karabakh was put under special rule from January–December 1989 and then Soviet forces intervened in Baku in January 1990, killing many. Moscow argued it was defending the Union against attempts to break away by nationalists. The National Popular Front took power in August 1991 but the Nagorno-Karabakh conflict destroyed it. It had to cede power to Gaidar Aliev in June 1993. The population grew from 6 million in 1979 to 7 million in 1989, when 82.7 per cent of the inhabitants were Azeris and 5.5 per cent were Russian.

Belarus

Belarus has changed its boundaries at least three times this century. This flat, featureless land between Poland and Russia has been invaded, conquered and ruled in turn by all the present neighbours of Belarus. It was reluctant to declare independence when communism collapsed as it had little historical tradition and the Belarusian language was little spoken. Russian was the dominant language of communication and culture.

The republic has the bloodiest history of the region. Russia's Jews were confined here in the Pale of Settlement after the partitions of Poland in the late eighteenth century. Some of the worst pogroms in the 1890s took place here and led to the emigration of many Jews to America and Britain. The name Minsky (a man from Minsk) became common in New York. On 25 March 1918 the Belarus Rada proclaimed the Belarus People's Republic during the German occupation. However, when the Germans withdrew in late 1918 the Bolsheviks took over and established the Belorussian (in Russian or Belarusian in Belarusian) Soviet Socialist Republic. It merged with the Lithuanian Soviet Republic, as the Lithuanian–Belorusian Soviet Republic, and signed a treaty with the RSFSR. The treaty of Riga divided Belarus. The Belarusian Soviet Republic, re-established on 31 July 1920, acquired Mogilev and Vitebsk oblasts in 1924 and Gomel (Homel) and Rechitsa oblasts in 1926. The other part, embracing about 5 million persons, of whom only 1.6 million regarded themselves as Belarusians, went to Poland. The republic developed agriculturally and industrially and it was only in 1938 that Russification of the educational system set in. The Polish regions of Belarus became part of the republic again on 2 November 1939. During the Second World War Belarus lost about a quarter of its population, a higher percentage than any other Soviet republic. On 16 August 1945 a Polish–Belarusian treaty agreed on frontiers very little different from the Curzon Line. Belarus became a founding member of the UN in 1945. The machine-building industries developed fast in the 1960s, as did the chemical and mineral fertiliser enterprises. A devastating blow struck Belarus in April 1986 when the nuclear reactor at Chernobyl, in nearby Ukraine, exploded. The wind blew the radioactive fall-out north and Belarus was heavily contaminated. Large tracts of land were contaminated (about one-third of the republic) and many thousands of people suffered dangerously high doses. During the 1990s hundreds, including children, have contracted cancer. Belarus declared independence on 26 August 1991. However, under President Lukashenko, Belarus moved back towards a Soviet dictatorship. His openly expressed desire was to see the Soviet Union re-established. An economic union between Belarus and Russia was signed in 1995 but remained largely on paper. The population of the republic rose from 9.5 million in 1979 to 10.2 million in 1989, when 77.9 per cent of the inhabitants were Belorusians, 13.2 per cent were Russian and 2.9 per cent Ukrainian.

Belorussia   *see* Belarus

Central Asia

Consists of the independent republics of Kazakhstan, Kyrgyzstan, Uzbek-istan, Tajikistan and Turkmenistan and covers an area of over 4 million square km south of Siberia to the Afghan border and in the west to the Caspian Sea. In the east it borders on China. Originally it was West Turkestan, with East Turkestan now in China. The region fell under Russian control in the second half of the nineteenth century but by then the Kazakhs had already been ruled by Russians for a hundred years. The Generalgouvernement of Turkestan was established in 1867 with its capital at Tashkent. However, the emirate of Bukhara and the khanate of Khiva (Khorezm), dominated by Uzbeks, remained to a large extent autonomous of Russian control until 1920. Kazakhstan was ruled by the Generalgouvernement of the Steppe. Europeans began moving into the region (the population of Turkestan in 1906 was 6.24 million) and by 1911 6 per cent of the population was European. Land was confiscated and passed into European hands and this contributed to the uprising of 1916 against Russian power. The region was developed by the Russians by expanding the railway system, irrigation and the introduction of small enterprises. The small, local Muslim elites responded by forming groups to oppose Russian colonialism and a Muslim national movement emerged during the 1905 Revolution and was influenced by the Young Turk movement. Educational reform was an important element. When Soviet power was declared at the end of 1917 the local Russian Bolsheviks refused to permit Muslims to participate in soviet institutions. In April 1918 the Autonomous Republic of Turkestan was founded and until 1924 was mainly concerned with combating the Bashmaki guerrillas. The complex nationality mix led to the establishment of the Turkkommissiya under Frunze. Its goal was to attract more native cadres to help administer the region. It had to combat Muslim national communism, which propagated the unity of Turkestan and demanded a Communist Party of the Turkic Peoples. Conflict between religious and secular currents in Bukhara and Khiva led to soviet intervention and in 1923–24 they were annexed. The Fergana valley, the most fertile area in Central Asia, was divided among various Union republics when these were set up. Russian nationality policy during the 1920s favoured the emergence of nations, national cultures and native cadres (korenizatsiya) but this was reversed in the late 1930s, when native elites were decimated. Khrushchev began again to promote native cadres in the 1950s, but again the policy was reversed by Brezhnev, who became aware of local self-consciousness, based on belonging to a common Islamic culture. Soviet nationality policy created the modern nations and states of Central Asia and since 1991 they have been discussing, periodically, political and economic union.

Chernobyl

A town about 100 km north of Kiev, capital of Ukraine, which in late April 1986 suffered the worst nuclear disaster in the history of the civil use of nuclear energy. Block 4 of the nuclear power station exploded and blew about 5 tonnes of radioactive substances up to 1,000 metres high. Winds transported the material northwards and then throughout Europe. The Soviet leadership tried to present the catastrophe as something minor which was under control, but was gradually forced to reveal the truth. This was an important step for glasnost under Gorbachev. Over 100,000 people were evacuated and an area 30 km in diameter around the reactor was placed out of bounds. The death toll was given as 31 but since 1986 many more have died. Large areas of Ukraine, Belarus and the RSFSR were contaminated and the economic losses were massive.

Cossacks

Boisterous, half-autonomous mercenaries and soldiers who originally protected the Russian and Polish frontiers between the Dnieper and the Urals. They had certain privileges and developed their own language, slightly different from Russian and Ukrainian. From the end of the eighteenth century they were divided into 11 hordes or military colonies (Don, Kuban, Terek, Astrakhan, Orenburg, Urals, Siberian, Semireche, Transbaikal, Amur and Ussuri). They were the best horsemen in the Imperial army and also acted as bodyguards of the Tsar. They were feared for their long curved swords. Most Cossacks supported the Provisional Government and the Whites during the Civil War. Short-lived Cossack republics were set up under various atamans (from the German *hauptmann*, or captain), such as Kaledin and Krasnov on the Don, and Dutov in Orenburg. Budenny led the Red Cavalry army, formed from Don and Kuban Cossacks, against the Whites and the Volunteer army, which included many Cossacks. About 50,000 Cossacks were evacuated from the Crimea after Wrangel's defeat and sought refuge in many countries of the world. Resistance to forced collectivisation led to uprisings in 1931 and 1932 and they were put down savagely. In his memoirs Gorbachev mentions a Red general in the 1950s who still feared to go to a Cossack village where his troops had massacred everyone. Cossack cavalry served during the Great Patriotic War but were an anachronism. Not many Cossacks went over to the Germans in the Don and Terek, but Cossack units were formed under German officers, though they did not distinguish themselves. They were taken prisoner by the British and handed over, with their families, to Stalin. He had all the leaders executed and the rest put in labour camps until released by Khrushchev in 1956. Nikolai Tolstoy became their champion in Britain and published several books accusing the British authorities of committing a crime by returning the Cossacks to Stalin, where certain death awaited many of them.

Donbass

An abbreviation for the Don coal basin, it became the most important coal producer in the European part of the Soviet Union. It embraces parts of the oblasts of Lugansk (Voroshilovgrad until 1990), Donets and Rostov-on-Don. The reserves of coal were put at 128 billion tonnes in 1968 (600 million tonnes of lignite; 1,800 million tonnes of hard coal). The first mines were sunk in 1795–97, and in the second half of the nineteenth century the Donbass became the centre of Russian coal mining and industry in Ukraine. The discovery of iron ore at Krivoi Rog led to the region developing into a centre of heavy industry. In the 1990s it became clear that many of the mines are not cost-effective as coal has to be mined deeper and deeper. This is the Russian-speaking region in Ukraine.

Estonia (Eesti in Estonian)

Peter the Great's defeat of the Swedes in 1721 led to Estonia becoming part of the Russian Empire. On 30 March 1917 Estonian representatives succeeded in gaining from the Provisional Government in Petrograd the right to administer all the Estonian inhabited areas and a certain level of autonomy. A national parliament was elected on 1 July 1917 and Bolshevik members increased their influence. On 24 February 1918 the parliament proclaimed Estonia an independent republic but the Treaty of Brest-Litovsk placed Estonia under provisional German administration. After the withdrawal of German troops in November 1918 civil war broke out between bourgeois and Soviet forces. The latter were driven out of Estonia in late January 1919, with the aid of the British fleet and 4,000 volunteers from Finland and Scandinavia, and the independent Estonian Republic was proclaimed. On 2 February 1920 the Tartu Peace Treaty was concluded and the RSFSR recognised the Republic of Estonia. The Nazi–Soviet Non-Aggression Pact of August 1939 placed Estonia in the Soviet sphere of influence and on 17 June 1940 the Red Army occupied the republic. On 14–15 July rigged elections were held to a parliament and it proclaimed a Soviet Republic on 21 July, and on 6 August 1940 Estonia became part of the Soviet Union. Over 10,000 persons were deported to Siberia. When the Wehrmacht invaded the following year, many Estonians joined them and took revenge on Russians. When the Red Army reoccupied Estonia, at least 20,700 were deported, mainly to Siberia. In January 1945 some territory was conceded to the RSFSR. As Estonia was developed industrially, many Russians moved to the republic so that by 1989 only 61.5 per cent of the population of 1.6 million were Estonian, with Russians making up 30.3 per cent of the population. Estonian agriculture was per capita the most productive in the Soviet Union and living standards were also the highest. On 16 November 1988 the Estonian Supreme Soviet passed a declaration of sovereignty which placed Estonian legislation above that of the Soviet Union. On 23 August 1989 the popular fronts of Estonia, Latvia and Lithuania organised a 600 km long human chain from Vilnius to Tallinn, demanding 'freedom for the Baltic States'. The popular front in Estonia became dominant in 1989 and on 30 March 1990 it proclaimed Soviet power in Estonia to be illegal and a transition period for the restoration of the Republic of Estonia. Moscow countered by declaring this illegal and a war of laws emerged. On 8 May 1990 the flag and symbols of the Estonian Soviet Republic were abolished and the official name of the country became the Republic of Estonia. Estonia achieved its independence on 20 August 1991 and the USSR State Council recognised this on 6 September 1991. Since then it has developed faster than Latvia and Lithuania.

Georgia (Sakartvelo in Georgian)

An ancient kingdom, wedged between the Ottoman and Persian empires, Georgia sought protection from Russia in the late eighteenth century and was then annexed in 1801. The Mensheviks were particularly influential in Georgia before and after the February Revolution and Nikolai Chkheidze and Irakli Tsereteli were prominent in Petrograd, with the latter becoming a minister in the Provisional Government. After the October Revolution Azerbaijan, Armenia and Georgia formed a federation but it quickly fell apart. On 26 May 1918 Georgia proclaimed itself an independent republic and placed itself under German protection. The Menshevik government, under Noi Zhordaniya, implemented social reforms and in May 1920 Georgia signed a treaty with the RSFSR with the latter recognising the sovereignty of the republic. However, in February 1921 the Red Army under Ordzhonikidze took Tbilisi and with the help of the local Bolsheviks overthrew the Menshevik government. The Georgian Soviet Republic was proclaimed on 25 February 1921. In 1922 Georgia was made part of the Transcaucasian Federation. The Georgians wished to join the Soviet Union as a Union republic but Stalin and other Bolsheviks opposed this due to the very developed national consciousness of the Georgians. Had Lenin lived he might have sided with the Georgians against Stalin, whom he accused of Great Russian chauvinism. Such was the opposition that it led to an uprising in August 1924 which cost over 4,000 lives. NEP and a more relaxed nationality policy defused tension during the 1920s but collectivisation again led to a peasant revolt in February 1931. Georgia became a Union republic on 5 December 1936. Stalin's butcher in Transcaucasia turned out to be Lavrenty Beria, a fellow Georgian, during the 1930s. The intelligentsia was one of his special targets. Georgians did not take kindly to de-Stalinisation. The black economy developed rapidly in Georgia, aided and abetted by Vasily Mzhavanadze, First Secretary of the Communist Party of Georgia, 1953–72. Eduard Shevardnadze replaced Mzhavanadze and began a clean-up. In 1985 Shevardnadze became Gorbachev's Foreign Minister. Georgia had the highest number of graduates per head of the population of any Union republic and a thriving culture. Georgians played a leading role in Soviet cinema, opera and theatre. Under Gorbachev Abkhazia sought greater autonomy but Georgian nationalists would not countenance this. This led to the tragedy of 9 April 1989 in Tbilisi when Soviet troops attacked unarmed demonstrators, killing several. Afterwards many Georgians favoured leaving the Soviet Union; Zviad Gamsakhurdia was elected President in May 1991 and Georgia proclaimed its independence on 9 April 1991. However, Gamsakhurdia's confrontational, nationalist style of politics led to armed conflict in south Ossetia, Abkhazia, and the rest of Georgia. He was forced out of office and Eduard Shevardnadze became head of state, later President, in 1992. The population of Georgia increased from 5 million in 1979 to 5.4 million in 1989, when 70.1 per cent of the inhabitants were Georgian, 6.3 per cent were Russian, 8.1 per cent were Armenian, 5.7 per cent were Azeris, and 1 per cent were Ukrainian.

Kazakhstan

The second largest republic of the Soviet Union (after the RSFSR), it covers a vast territory, much of it desert and semi-desert. After the October Revolution an Alash Orda government took power and remained until 1919, fighting on the White side during the Civil War. Kazakhstan became an autonomous republic within the RSFSR in 1920 – first as the Kirgiz Autonomous Republic and then, in 1925, as the Kazakh Autonomous Republic – and became a Union republic in 1936. The Arabic script (Kazakhs are Muslims) was replaced by the Latin script in 1929 and this in turn was superseded in 1940 by a Cyrillic script, which is still in use. In 1996 the Kazakhstan President announced that the Latin script will again take over in future. The population was 16.7 million in 1994, making it one of the most sparsely populated countries in the world (6.2 persons per square kilometre compared with 12 for Russia and 143 for western Europe). In 1993 Kazakhs made up 43 per cent and Russians 36 per cent of the population. At the same time Ukrainians made up 5.2 per cent, Germans 4.1 per cent and Tatars 2 per cent of the population. Northern Kazakhstan is highly developed with much heavy industry and in the 1990s the oil and gas industries began to expand. This region is predominantly inhabited by Russians and Ukrainians. Kazakhs became subordinate to Russia in the eighteenth century and were mainly nomadic.

In 1916 the Kazakh population was 5,065,000 but resistance to Tsarist conscription in 1916 led to an uprising which continued until 1922. Between 1916 and 1922 over 950,000 Kazakhs perished and another 400,000 moved or were deported to Xinjiang, China, Mongolia, Afghanistan, Turkey and Iran. The ethnic Kazakh population declined by another 2.3 million between 1926 and 1939 because of disease, famine, executions and deportation. In 1959 ethnic Kazakhs made up only 29 per cent of the republic's population. Alma Ata, the capital, was mainly Russian, as was the Communist Party of Kazakhstan. Khrushchev's virgin lands campaign brought many Russians and Ukrainians to northern Kazakhstan in the 1950s. Dinmukhamed Kunaev, First Party Secretary from 1964 to 1986, was the first Kazakh to become a member of the Politburo. Gorbachev removed him, allegedly for corruption, and Gennady Kolbin, a Russian, took over. This led to anti-Russian riots in Alma Ata and other centres, and Kolbin soon gave way to Nursultan Nazarbaev. The latter was elected President of Kazakhstan in April 1990 and on 16 December 1991 he proclaimed Kazakhstan an independent republic. Industrial production declined after 1991 due to the close links between Kazakhstan industry and that of southern Russia. When Russia suffered so did Kazakhstan. The republic is an active member of the CIS and has signed an economic union with Russia, Belarus and Kyrgyzstan, which appears to exist mainly on paper. Western companies flocked to Kazakhstan after 1991 but in 1996 it was clear that Uzbekistan had become the leader in Central Asia.

Kirgizia   *see* Kyrgyzstan
Kuzbass

The Kuznetsk coal basin in west Siberia, east of Novosibirsk, was one of the largest coal-mining areas of the Soviet Union. It was producing 110 million tonnes of coal in 1978 and at that rate had reserves for at least 400 years. The mountainous area of the Kuzbass also has silver, lead, zinc and iron ore. Coal mining began in the eighteenth century but the decision of the Bolsheviks in 1930 to establish a coal and metallurgical centre there (the Urals–Kuznetsk combine) transformed it. There were 90 deep and open mines there in the 1970s. The coal is much superior to that of the Donbass. Under Gorbachev the Kuzbass miners became militant and launched their first major strike during the summer of 1989. They forced Nikolai Ryzhkov, the Prime Minister, to sign an agreement live on TV since they did not trust the Soviet government to honour its word, given in private. The radicalism continued after 1991 when Yeltsin, who had championed the miners under Gorbachev, found himself at the receiving end of their anger. A common complaint was that they were not paid their wages for months on end.

Kyrgyzstan (Kirgizia)

Kyrgyzstan formed in the nineteenth century as part of the khanate of Kokand, but there were Kyrgyz in the khanate of Khiva and the emirate of Bukhara. They became Muslim in the seventeenth and eighteenth centuries. When the Russians conquered Kokand in 1876 the Kyrgyz became subordinate to Russia and Russian farmers came to claim the pastures there. The Kyrgyz, like the Kazakhs, rebelled in 1916, and about 150,000 nomads moved to China. In early 1918 Kyrgyzstan fell under Bolshevik control and became a part of the Soviet Republic of Turkestan. In 1924 it became the Karakirgiz autonomous oblast and in 1936 the Kirgiz Soviet Socialist Republic. Russians dominated and in the 1920s Kyrgyz communists wanted land occupied by Russian farmers to revert to the Kyrgyz. Forced collectivisation and the demand that the nomads settle down led to Basmachi Muslim guerrillas operating in the republic. The mountainous nature of the republic made industrialisation difficult and most were peasants. In 1990, of the population of 4.4 million, 52.4 per cent were Kyrgyz, 21.5 per cent were Russian and 12.9 per cent were Uzbeks. Political reform was more far-reaching than in other Central Asian republics under Gorbachev and in 1990 Askar Akaev, a physicist, was elected President of the republic. He had worked in the Kyrgyz Academy of Sciences. Akaev was one of the few Soviet leaders to come out strongly against the attempted coup of August 1991. The republic declared itself independent on 31 August 1919 and became officially known as Kyrgyzstan.

Latvia (Latvija in Latvian)

Latvia consisted of much of the guberniyas Livland and Courland, and Russian territory east and south of the Riga bay which came under Russian control in 1710. Latvian national consciousness developed during the conflicts in the late nineteenth century with the German landowners and merchants who controlled much of the wealth of the republic. Latvians fought against the Germans in 1915 (the Latvian riflemen). After the February Revolution there were calls for Latvian autonomy to embrace all Latvian-inhabited areas. The Germans occupied Riga in September 1917 and middle-class Latvian politicians, led by K. Ulmanis, formed a democratic bloc. The Treaty of Brest-Litovsk resulted in the whole of Latvia being occupied by the Germans, and after the Germans left on 18 November 1918 the Republic of Latvia was proclaimed and a national government, headed by Ulmanis, took office. However, the communists proclaimed a Latvian Soviet Republic on 17 December 1918 and a government, headed by P. Stucka. With the help of Germans, Estonians and the Allies, Ulmanis was able to overcome the Reds and in late 1919 the Whites were also driven out. With Polish help the Ulmanis government took Lettgallia, in the south, and on 11 August 1920 peace was made with Moscow. On 22 September 1921 Latvia was admitted to the League of Nations. The world depression led to conflict in Latvia and Ulmanis ruled as a dictator, without parliament, between 1934 and 1940. Latvia fell within the Soviet sphere of influence in the Nazi–Soviet Non-Aggression Pact and on 5 October 1939 Latvia had to concede Soviet bases on its territory. On 16 June 1940 it had to permit the military occupation of the republic and, after rigged elections, a Latvian Soviet Republic was proclaimed on 21 July, which requested and was granted entry to the Soviet Union on 5 August 1940. In June 1941 about 15,000 Latvians were deported to Siberia. The Wehrmacht occupied Latvia from June 1941 to 1944 and eliminated most Jews. In January 1945 Latvia conceded some territory to the RSFSR and the Soviets began deporting the intelligentsia and property owners – in March 1949 over 42,000 persons were deported. Latvia developed industrially under the communists and many Russians and Ukrainians moved into the republic. This resulted in 1989 in only 52 per cent of the 2.7 million population being Latvian with Russians accounting for 34 per cent. Russian was the language of communication in Riga, the capital. The Latvian Popular Front grew in influence in 1989 and won the republican elections to the Supreme Soviet in 1990. The Communist Party of Latvia contained many Latvians devoted to the Soviet Union and considerable tension existed. In January 1991 some Latvians were killed in Riga when pro-Soviet elements attempted to provoke a conflict. Latvia declared on 4 May 1990 the restoration of its independence and on 28 August 1991 this became reality. On 3 March 1991 73.7 per cent of voters supported the renewal of independence of the Republic of Latvia. Latvia, after independence, linked up with the other Baltic states, in security and economic affairs.

Lithuania (Lietuva in Lithuanian)

In the Middle Ages, a territory which stretched from the Baltic into Ukraine, it merged with Poland and after the partitions of Poland became part of the Russian Empire. Roman Catholic priests represented Lithuanian national consciousness in the nineteenth century and became active after the February Revolution. In Vilna (Vilnius), in German-occupied Lithuania, a Lithuanian Council (taryba) issued a decree on the restoration of independence on 16 February 1918, but it was only in November 1918 that this became reality. In early January 1919 the new Lithuanian government had to move to Kaunas because of approaching Polish and then Soviet troops. On 6 January 1919 the communists proclaimed the Lithuanian Soviet Republic and on 27 February the union with Belorussia to form the Lithuanian–Belorussian Soviet Republic. The Polish occupation of Vilna put an end to this in April 1919. With the help of German troops, the newly formed Lithuanian army drove the Reds out of the republic. Lithuania and the RSFSR signed a peace treaty on 12 July 1920 and Russia acknowledged the Lithuanian claim to Vilna. Memelland was taken over by Lithuania in January 1923 and the Allies accepted this on 16 February 1923. Lithuania fell into the Soviet sphere of influence in the Nazi–Soviet Non-Aggression Pact and had to make concessions to the Soviet Union in a treaty on 10 October 1939 by which Lithuania was given Vilna and part of the Vilna region. On 14 June 1940 Moscow demanded the formation of a new Lithuanian government and permission to station more Soviet troops in the country. Over 100,000 Red Army soldiers moved into Lithuania the following day. On 17 June the People's Government was formed; on 14–15 July rigged elections were held to the People's Sejm; on 21 July it declared Lithuania a Soviet Socialist Republic and requested admission to the Soviet Union; and on 3 August 1940 Lithuania was accepted as a Union republic. Before the German occupation in June 1941, about 50,000 Germans had returned to Germany and about 12,600 Lithuanians were deported to Siberia. The German occupation wiped out about 200,000 Lithuanian Jews and when the Wehrmacht withdrew in 1944 some Lithuanians left with them. The Soviets then began more deportations. The number deported in 1941 and 1944–52 is estimated at 120,000 (if political prisoners are added the figure is about 300,000). Vilna returned officially to Lithuania and some Belorussian raions were added. The fact that 79.6 per cent of the 3.7 million inhabitants (1989) were ethnic Lithuanian helped to preserve Lithuanian national identity. Russians accounted for only 9.4 per cent. This indicates that Lithuania was less industrialised than the other two Baltic republics. Numerically the largest of the Baltic republics, it was the poorest in per capita national income. In mid-1988 Sajudis (movement) became active, headed by members of the intelligentsia. Members of the Communist Party of Lithuania also supported the national, democratic goals of Sajudis, and in December 1989 this party, led by Algirdas Brazauskas, declared itself independent of the CPSU and in 1990 renamed itself the Lithuanian Democratic Labour Party. In 1990 Sajudis-backed candidates won a majority in the elections to the Supreme Soviet and on 11 March 1990 the speaker of parliament, Vytautas Landsbergis, proclaimed the restoration of the independence of Lithuania. Moscow demanded that the declaration be rescinded and some concessions were made by Landsbergis. Pro-Soviet Lithuanian communists and Soviet troops attempted to take over the Vilnius TV station on 11–13 January 1991 and 13 persons were killed and 165 injured. A national referendum on 9 February 1991 resulted in 90.5 per cent of those voting supporting independence for Lithuania. Lithuania's independence was acknowledged by the USSR State Council after the failure of the August

1991 coup. Landsbergis was elected the President of Lithuania but in February 1993 he was defeated by Algirdas Brazauskas. He, in turn, gave way to Landsbergis in presidential elections in September 1996.

Moldavia   *see* Moldova

Moldova (in Russian Moldavia)

A region lying between the east Carpathians and the middle and lower Dniester and the mouth of the Danube. Until 1812 it was in Romania and then a part of it, called Bessarabia, passed to Russia. In December 1917 local socialists proclaimed the democratic Moldavian Republic and it sought to become part of the Russian Federation. After Ukraine declared its independence in February 1918, Moldova was cut off from Russia and it again proclaimed its independence. However, on 8 April 1918 it became part of Romania and the Ukrainian People's Republic *de facto* accepted this in early 1919. In October 1924 parts of the Balta, Tulchin and Odessa oblasts, on the left bank of the Dniester, forming part of the Ukrainian Soviet Socialist Republic, became the Moldovan Autonomous Soviet Socialist Republic, in Ukraine. The capital was Balta, which was renamed Tiraspol in 1929. The new territory had a population of about 550,000, only about a third of whom were Moldovans. Bessarabia was acknowledged as coming within the Soviet sphere of influence in the secret protocol to the Hitler–Stalin Non-Aggression Pact of August 1939. On 26 June 1940 the Soviet Union issued an ultimatum to Romania to clear the region between the Dniester, Pruth and the mouth of the Danube and to hand it over to Moscow. On 2 August 1940 the USSR Supreme Soviet established the Moldovan Soviet Socialist Republic, consisting of the Moldovan Autonomous Republic and the Kamenka, Rybnica, Dubossary, Grigoriopol, Tiraspol and Slobseya raions, on the left bank of the Dniester. The capital was Kishinev (now Chisinau). The remaining eight raions of the Moldovan Autonomous Republic remained in Ukraine. The south Bessarabian district of Cetatea Alba (after 1944 Belgorod Dnestrovsky) and most of Ishmail were also added to Ukraine. A Soviet objective was to ensure that Moldova did not have a Black Sea coastline. By the Soviet–German treaty of 5 September 1940, the 90,000 Bessarabian Germans were resettled in German-occupied Poland. A land reform in Moldova confiscated all private property and the formation of about 170 kolkhozes and sovkhozes. In June 1941 the invading Romanian forces, Hitler's allies, took over the territory until 1944. The Romanian–Soviet cease-fire of 12 September 1944 transferred Moldova again to the Soviet Union. The peace treaty with Romania of 10 February 1947 acknowledged this transfer. Moldova was the second smallest (after Armenia) Soviet republic and its population increased from 3.9 million in 1979 to 4.3 million in 1989. The number of Moldovans in the Soviet Union in 1989 was 3.4 million, of whom 91.6 per cent gave Moldovan as their mother tongue. The population of Kishinev in 1989 was 722,000. Besides Moldovans, Ukrainians, Russians, Gagauz (Christian and Turkish speaking), Jews and Bulgarians live in the republic. In 1989 53 per cent of the population lived in rural areas and this testifies to the importance of agriculture in the republic's economy. Wine was one of its well-known products. The republic declared itself sovereign on 23 June 1990 and independent on 27 August 1991. The new republic became known as Moldova, which is the Romanian word for the Russian Moldavia. Fears of incorporation into Romania led to civil war in the breakaway Transdniester republic between Ukrainians, Russians and Moldovans. General Aleksandr Lebed, commander of the 14th army in Moldova, brokered a cease-fire in 1994.

Siberia

One of the treasure troves of the world, it stretches from the Urals to the Pacific and is thus entirely in Asia, covering 12.5 million square km, or just over twice the area of the European part of the Soviet Union (5.57 million square km). Russian Siberia does not reach to the Pacific: it is divided into west and east Siberia and the territory between east Siberia and the Pacific is known as the Far East. Soviet power in Siberia was replaced in the spring of 1918 by a provisional Siberian government of SRs and Siberian regionalists and in November 1918 Admiral Kolchak declared himself supreme regent of Russia there. However, the Red Army reasserted itself in early 1920. The Far East Republic was a buffer between Russia and Japan between April 1920 and October 1922. In 1922 the Yakut Autonomous Republic was established, in 1923 the Buryat-Mongolian (renamed the Buryat in 1958) Autonomous Republic, in 1930 the east Siberian, west Siberian and Far East krais were established, as were national okrugs for the small nations of the north. The population of Siberia grew from 12.3 million in 1926 to 32.1 million in 1989. Over 90 per cent of the population was Russian. Its geographical location ensured that Siberia received large military industrial investments and these began in the 1930s with the construction of the Urals–Kuznets Combine, which was second only to the Donets Basin in the Soviet Union. Many enterprises were transferred to Siberia from the west after the German invasion of June 1941. Industrial production tripled during the war. Huge hydroelectric power stations were built, making use of the abundant rivers of the region. Oil production took off in the 1960s and also natural gas (especially in Tyumen oblast). By 1980 Siberia was producing over 300 million tonnes of oil. Under Brezhnev the Baikal Amur Magistral was built. The Siberian branch of the USSR Academy of Sciences in Novosibirsk enjoyed a formidable reputation. There were plans to divert the northern rivers to Central Asia under Brezhnev, in an attempt to overcome its shortage of water, but opposition from the Siberian and Russian intelligentsia eventually managed to kill the project. The novelist Valentin Rasputin became the voice of those who regarded industrialisation and collectivisation as a disaster for Siberia. After 1991 the various parts of Siberia (excluding the Far East) came together in the Siberian Accord so as collectively to represent their region in Moscow. Many regarded the centre as treating Siberia as a raw material and energy appendage of Russia and wanted to call a halt to the ruthless exploitation of its resources. The future of Siberia is uncertain as its economic future may lie with the countries of the Pacific Rim. Few desire at present to break away from Russia as the region is unable to defend itself militarily.

Tajikistan

Tajikistan, in Central Asia, borders on Afghanistan and China and is the only republic in the former Soviet Union in which a civil war is being fought between secular and Islamic forces. In 1924 Tajikistan became an autonomous republic in Uzbekistan and in 1929 it became a Soviet Socialist Republic. Its capital is Dushanbe (called Stalinabad until 1961). The Gorno-Badakhshan autonomous oblast, home to Iranian Pamir peoples, occupies the eastern part of the republic. The population of Tajikistan in 1989 was 5.1 million, of whom 33 per cent lived in urban areas. In 1979 35 per cent of the population lived in cities, revealing that most of the population increase had been in the countryside. In 1989 62.3 per cent of the population were Tajik, 23.5 per cent Uzbek and 7.6 per cent Russian. However, the civil war has led to many Russians leaving. Over 800,000 Tajiks live in Uzbekistan and there are also many in Afghanistan. Unlike the Turkic peoples of the other Central Asian republics, the Tajiks are an Iranian people and Sunni Muslims. Cotton is important and there are important deposits of bauxite (the aluminium industry is developed), silver and other minerals. The republic had the highest birth rate in the Soviet Union but also the highest infant mortality rate. Health care was quite inadequate. Under Gorbachev informal groups formed and stressed the role of Tajik as the state language, the return of Khiva and Bukhara from Uzbekistan and even the reintroduction of the Arabic script. After independence the civil war, which can be viewed as between the old and new elites, or between secular and Islamic forces, has devastated the country.

Turkmenistan

The Soviet Republic of Turkmenistan was established on 27 October 1924 from parts of Turkestan, Bukhara and Khorezm, with Ashkhabad (now Ashghabat), and was known previously as Transcaspia. Over 80 per cent of its territory is desert (Kara Kum) and it was one of the least developed of the Soviet republics. The population grew from 855,000 in 1924 to 3.53 million in 1989, of whom 45 per cent were in urban areas. Some 72 per cent of the population in 1989 were Turkmen, 9.5 per cent Russian and 9 per cent Uzbek. Turkmen are to be found in Uzbekistan, Tajikistan, Afghanistan, Iran and Turkey. They are a Turkic people, closer to the Azeris, the Crimean Tatars and the Turks than the other Turkic peoples of Central Asia. They are Sunni Muslims. They were predominantly nomadic before collectivisation during the 1930s. Stalin liquidated many of the Party and government elites in the 1930s, accusing them of bourgeois nationalism. The economy was dominated by cotton, oil and natural gas. Cotton monoculture was destructive of the environment and led to salinisation of the soil. Since independence in 1991 the republic has been ruled autocratically by President Niyazov (the former Party leader) but it has developed good relations with Iran. Its natural gas resources make Turkmenistan an increasingly rich state.

Ukraine

Ukraine is the second largest Slav republic after Russia and is regarded by many Russians as part of their state. On 25 January 1918 the Rada (see p. 177) proclaimed the Ukrainian People's Republic and sought to remain separate from Russia. The small Bolshevik group in Ukraine had declared a Soviet republic in Kharkov (Kharkiv in Ukrainian) on 26 December 1917. Sovnarkom troops, under Antonov-Ovseenko, drove the Rada out of Kiev (Kiiv in Ukrainian) in late January 1918 but had to retreat in the face of German and Austrian troops, who took over after the Treaty of Brest-Litovsk. In April General Skoropadsky was elected hetman by the occupying forces. In November 1918 the Bolsheviks, led by Pyatakov and Rakovsky, again set up a Ukrainian Soviet government. In January 1919 the battle for power in Ukraine recommenced after the withdrawal of the Central Powers. The Ukrainian Directory overthrew Skoropadsky and re-established the People's Republic. The People's Republic, led by Petlyura, succumbed to the Reds in the Civil War but west Ukraine, which had declared itself an autonomous part of the People's Republic in January 1919, was occupied by Polish troops in June 1919 and became part of Poland in the Treaty of Riga in 1921. Bukovina and Bessarabia became part of Romania in April 1918. Ukraine was of great importance to Russia as Lenin did not believe that Soviet power could be sustained in Moscow if Ukraine became independent. Agriculturally and industrially it was vital. Ukraine became a founding republic of the Soviet Union and had considerable autonomy, which fostered nationalism and regionalism, until the first Five Year Plan. The capital only moved from Kharkov to Kiev in 1934. Opposition to collectivisation was broken by force and famine haunted the land in 1932–33. East Galicia became part of Ukraine, as did Volhynia, on 1 November 1939, and north Bukovina and part of south Bessarabia joined Ukraine from Romania on 2 August 1940. The war devastated the republic and cost over 5 million lives. The national Ukrainian partisans, led by Bandera, resisted the reimposition of Soviet power until the late 1950s. Ukraine became a founder member of the UN and on 29 June 1945 Czechoslovakia presented Ukraine with Sub-Carpathian Ukraine. On 19 February 1954, Khrushchev awarded Ukraine the Crimea to mark the 300th anniversary of Ukraine joining Russia. The population grew from 49.6 million in 1979 to 51.5 million in 1989, when 72.7 per cent were Ukrainian and 22.1 per cent were Russian. Ukraine was a major centre of the metallurgical industry (about 40 per cent of production) in the Soviet Union and about one-third of the coal was mined there. The chernozem (black earth) turned Ukraine into the bread basket of the Soviet Union but its performances rarely came up to the expectations of the plan. The explosion of the Chernobyl nuclear power station in April 1986 was a terrible disaster and fuelled the nationalist movement. Ukraine declared its independence on 24 August 1991 and on 1 December 1991 there was an overwhelming vote in favour by the population. Ukraine, Russia and Belarus proclaimed the Commonwealth of Independent States (CIS) on 8 December 1991, although since then Ukraine has been unwilling to commit itself to political or economic integration with Russia.

Uzbekistan

It has now established itself as the leading republic in Central Asia and was created out of parts of the People's Republics of Bukhara and Khorezm (Khiva) and the Turkestan Autonomous Republic on 27 October 1924, becoming part of the USSR in 1925. The capital was Samarkand but in 1930 Tashkent took over. There was rapid population growth after 1945 and in 1979 it was 15.4 million and in 1989 19.8 million. The growth of 28.7 per cent over the decade was the second largest in the Soviet Union, only exceeded by Tajikistan. In 1989 71.4 per cent of the inhabitants were Uzbek, 8.3 per cent Russian and 4.1 per cent Kazakh. Under communism Uzbekistan had the third largest population, after the RSFSR and Ukraine. There are over 1.5 million Uzbeks in other Central Asian republics and about 1.6 million in Afghanistan. Soviet nationality policy produced an Uzbek language and nation as Moscow sought to break up Turkestan. Unlike many of their neighbours Uzbeks are a sedentary people. The Russians conquered Tashkent in 1865 and established the Turkestan Generalgouvernement in 1867. When established in 1924 Uzbekistan was the most favoured economically and the most densely populated new republic in Central Asia. In 1929 it lost Tajikistan but in 1935 gained the Karakalpak Autonomous Republic. In 1963 it acquired part of the Golodnaya Steppe from Kazakhstan. Samarkand and Bukhara, as centres of Sunni Islam, were not put under pressure until 1927. Most mosques in the republic had been closed by 1936. Irrigation expanded in the 1920s and under collectivisation cotton became king. Uzbek protests went unheeded and the Prime Minister, Faizullah Khodzhaev, was included in the last great Moscow show trial in March 1938. He was found guilty and executed. In the late 1980s cotton accounted for 65 per cent of Uzbek republican output and 40 per cent of the labour force. Ecologically this was disastrous. The Uzbek leadership under First Party Secretary Rashidov sought to redress the balance by falsifying output figures and this became known as the Uzbek cotton scandal with Moscow paying for mythical Uzbek cotton. Ethnic conflict flared up involving the Meshetian Turks and the Kyrgyz. Uzbekistan declared its independence on 31 August 1991. The Communist Party became the Democratic People's Party; Islam Karimov, the First Party Secretary, became President; and the old nomenklatura became the new nomenklatura. Karimov was careful to take the oath of office with one hand on the Koran and the other on the Uzbek constitution. His authoritarian rule has suppressed Islamic dissent but has attracted much foreign direct investment. Uzbekistan can produce over 60 tonnes of gold a year and has huge hydrocarbon and mineral reserves.

Politics

Activist

A member of a Party, trade union, Komsomol or other social mass organisation's aktiv. The latter consisted of the full-time officials and voluntary workers, who provided the driving force of the institution. The Party aktiv were mostly concerned with agitation and propaganda.

Anti-Party Group

The name applied afterwards to the opposition in the summer of 1957 in the Party Presidium (Politburo) to the domestic and foreign policy of the First Secretary, Nikita Khrushchev. Its members were Georgy Malenkov, Lazar Kaganovich, Vyacheslav Molotov, Kliment Voroshilov, Nikolai Bulganin, Mikhail Pervukhin, Mikhail Saburov and the Presidium candidate member, Dmitry Shepilov. They obtained a majority in the Presidium to remove Khrushchev, but the latter argued that, as the Party Central Committee had elected him, it was the only institution which could dismiss him. This led to the conflict moving to the CC, where Khrushchev carried the day. A reason for this was that Marshal Georgy Zhukov provided military aircraft to bring Khrushchev's supporters to Moscow. This CC plenum took place between 22 and 29 June 1957. Malenkov, Kaganovich, Molotov and Shepilov were removed from the Presidium and CC, Bulganin was removed from the Presidium and was given a severe warning (he lost his post as Prime Minister the following year), Saburov lost his Presidium seat and Pervukhin was demoted to candidate member of the Presidium. The Anti-Party Group resisted Khrushchev's desire for the Party to play an increasing role in government and the economy. Khrushchev's success ensured the Party the leading position in the state until the 19th Party Conference in 1988, when Gorbachev ended it.

Anti-Soviet Bloc of the Right and Trotskyites

An inner Party conspiratorial group which allegedly came into existence in 1932–33 and was accused of engaging in espionage in the Soviet Union on behalf of foreign spy networks. Its task was to undermine the security of the country and provoke an attack on the USSR, its defeat and territorial dismemberment, and eventually the defeat of socialism and the return of capitalism. Members of the bloc who stood trial in March 1938, in the last great show trial, were Nikolai Bukharin, Aleksei Rykov, G. G. Yagoda, N. N. Krestinsky and 17 other defendants. In reality no such bloc existed and the trial was a pretext for Stalin to dispose of real or potential opponents. Of the 21 defendants, 18 were executed. The first great show trial took place in 1936 and involved the Trotsky–Zinoviev terror centre, and the second was against the Anti-Soviet Trotskyite Centre in 1937.

Anti-Soviet Trotskyite Centre

This show trial involved Yu. L. Pyatakov, Karl Radek, G. Ya. Sokolnikov, L. P. Serebryakov, N. I. Muralov and 12 other prominent Party officials, who stood trial in January 1937. The defendants confessed to treason, espionage, diversionary activities and the preparation of terroristic acts. Their criminal organisation allegedly came into being in 1933 on the instructions of Lev Trotsky with the task of undermining the military and economic potential of the Soviet Union before an invasion of the USSR, the abolition of the Soviet Republic and the restoration of capitalism. All 17 were found guilty and 13 were executed.

Apparatchik

A full-time official of the Party and state bureaucracy.

Attempted coup of 18–21 August 1991

On 17 August 1991 Vladimir Kryuchkov the head of the KGB, Valentin Pavlov the Prime Minister, Marshal Dmitry Yazov and several senior Party officials decided to force Gorbachev to give up power to them temporarily and if he refused, to isolate him and take over. An Emergency Committee consisting of eight members was formed. On 18 August Gorbachev rejected the demands of the delegation presented to him at his holiday dacha at Foros, in the Crimea. Shortly before midnight, Vice-President Gennady Yanaev agreed to support the takeover and signed a decree assuming the powers of the President. On 19 August a state of emergency was declared and all institutions were ordered to carry out the orders of the Emergency Committee. Tanks were sent into Moscow and other cities. It was claimed that perestroika was in a cul de sac, the country was ungovernable and in deadly danger. Law and order had to be re-established, crime mercilessly fought and the Union treaty to be discussed throughout the country. Yeltsin was not arrested when he returned from Alma Ata (Almaty) on 18 August – the units were merely instructed to keep him under observation – and he immediately made for the White House, the seat of the Russian government, and, standing on a military vehicle, declared the attempted coup illegal and called for the release of Gorbachev and the re-establishment of constitutional order. The new Union treaty, affording much greater decision-making powers to the republics, was to be formally signed on 20 August. Hence the attempted coup was timed to prevent this occurring. The Union treaty was perceived as undermining the control of Moscow and with it the power of the Party, the military, the KGB, the centrally planned economy, Marxism–Leninism as a state ideology and the superpower status of the Soviet Union. This was reflected in the composition of the Emergency Committee: the Vice-President, the Prime Minister, the ministers of defence, and internal affairs (Pugo), Gorbachev's deputy chairman of the defence council (Baklanov), the head of the KGB, and the chairmen of the union of kolkhozes (Starodubtsev) and the union of state enterprises (Tizyakov). The attempted coup failed after three days and the major reason was that Soviet politics had changed so rapidly in the previous few years that the old-style *putsch*, with the population acquiescing, was no longer possible. Another reason was that the US ambassador warned Gorbachev of an attempt to remove him on 20 June and this meant that the plotters had to restrict discussion of the coup to a limited number of confidantes. Hence most military officers were surprised by orders to act against Gorbachev. Many of them prevaricated or refused, first and foremost Marshal Evgeny Shaposhnikov. The attempted coup accelerated the processes which the plotters had sought to slow down or reverse: the advance of the reformers, the weakening of the Party, the loss of power of the centre and the transformation of the Soviet Union into a federation or confederation. All the plotters were arrested except Pugo, who had committed suicide with his wife (another suicide was Marshal Sergei Akhromeev who, on hearing of the attempted coup, hurried back from his holiday in the Crimea and offered his services), and many others fell with them. One of these was the USSR Minister of Foreign Affairs, Aleksandr Bessmertnykh, who had been unable to make up his mind which side to support. Yeltsin ordered the CPSU to suspend its activities on the territory of the Russian Federation on 23 August. The building of the Central Committee on Staray Ploshchad had been sealed on 22 August. Gorbachev resigned as General Secretary of the Party on 24 August and advised Central Committee members to do the same on 24 August. Only Yeltsin and Akaev (Kirgizia) condemned the attempted coup from the very beginning, but the other republican leaders were swift to change sides and banned the activities of the CPSU on their territory. The CPSU as a party ceased to exist. A USSR Congress of People's Deputies was convened immediately after the failure of the coup and it resolved to speed up the transition of the Soviet Union to a Union of Sovereign States. The new Union was to be based on the principles of independence and territorial integrity, human and civil rights, social justice and democracy. The desire of the states to be recognised in international law and to join the UN was to be supported. The Baltic states were recognised as having left the Soviet Union on 6 September (see also Chronology pp. 57–8).

Bureaucracy

The term has been used in various ways but there has been constant criticism of bureaucracy, often bureaucratism. Lenin, Stalin and other Bolshevik leaders attacked bureaucratism, regarding it as maladministration, sloppiness and lack of culture. Trotsky criticised mainly the ever-expanding state apparatus and the branch ministries (glavki). Trotsky developed the concept of bureaucracy as a new ruling stratum which had emerged because of the deformation of the Party. An Italian, B. Rizzi, developed this perception further and referred to bureaucracy as bureaucratic collectivism which had risen to become the ruling class. The elimination of the market in the 1930s ensured that the state bureaucracy expanded to perform its functions. The desire by Stalin to have total control over society led to more and more officials supervising others. Khrushchev's victory over the Anti-Party Group in 1957 increased the Party's involvement in the economy. Collectively the Party and state bureaucrats (officials) made up the nomenklatura.

Cadres

Signifies the officials of an organisation, an enterprise, the Party or a mass organisation, and in a wider sense all permanent employees. In the military all permanent staff were classified as cadres. The Communist Party referred to itself as a cadre party, a party of professional revolutionaries, in contrast to mass parties. All key positions in the Communist Party were held by full-time, professional revolutionaries.

Central Executive Committee (TsIK)

The committee (its full title was the All-Russian Central Executive Committee) was elected at the 1st Congress of Workers' and Soldiers' Deputies in Petrograd in June 1917 and consisted of about 250 members, who were responsible for acting in the name of the Congress between Congresses. The first RSFSR constitution of July 1918 stated that the Congress of Soviets was the 'supreme organ' and the TsIK, elected by it, was the 'supreme legislative and supervisory organ' of the RSFSR. The TsIK formed the government (Sovnarkom) and supervised its activities. When the USSR came into being the TsIK remained for the RSFSR but a new TsIK of the USSR was set up in 1923–24 to embrace the whole country. It had over 700 full and candidate members and was bicameral, consisting of the Soviet of the Union and the Soviet of Nationalities. The Soviet of the Union was elected by the USSR Congress of Soviets and the Soviet of Nationalities was elected by the Congresses of Soviets of the Union republics. The constitution also provided for a Presidium of the TsIK, which was to act on behalf of the TsIK between sittings. The 1936 constitution abolished the TsIK and the Congress of Soviets at union, republican and autonomous republican levels. In their place came a USSR Supreme Soviet, which was bicameral, again consisting of a Soviet of the Union and a Soviet of Nationalities. The USSR Supreme Soviet elected its own Presidium. The chair of the Presidium functioned as head of the Soviet state.

Collective leadership

The name given to those politicians who took over the leading positions in the Party and state after the death of Stalin in March 1953. They were Kliment Voroshilov, Georgy Malenkov, Lavrenty Beria, Vyacheslav Molotov and Nikita Khrushchev. At the 20th Party Congress in February 1956 Khrushchev described this démarche as a return to the basic principle of Leninist policy and of primary importance. The new Party statute of 1961 described collective leadership as the 'main leadership principle of the Party'. It was the necessary precondition for the normal development of Party organisations and the correct training of cadres. The cult of the personality was condemned as being irreconcilable with Leninist principles. Despite formal recognition of this principle, Brezhnev added the title of head of state in 1977 to his leadership of the Party. Andropov, Chernenko and Gorbachev all followed suit.

Communism

According to Karl Marx, communism is a socio-economic form of society which inevitably emerges after a socialist revolution when the private ownership of the means of production has been abolished, the economy has been nationalised and goods are distributed according to the principle of need. When a society has reached communism there is an abundance of goods, which smoothes the way to social equality, permits the rational planning of social development and frees everyone from political and economic constraints. Socialism is regarded as the lower stage, when everyone is rewarded according to the contribution he or she makes to society. Hence there is inequality under socialism but this will disappear under the higher stage of communism. After the October Revolution

Lenin conceived of communism as the transformation of society into workers and employees, who would be part of a massive social organisation to which they would be answerable and which would distribute goods according to achievement. Lenin coined the expression: communism is Soviet power plus electrification of the whole country. He resisted all attempts to declare that the higher stage of communism was being reached and reacted fiercely to, attempts by the left to do so. This brings into doubt his belief that the higher stage could be reached. However, the advent of communism was proclaimed several times during the history of the Soviet Union. The first time was during war communism (1918–20), when money ceased to be the main legal tender, the economy reverted to barter and it was believed for a short time that communism was feasible. The 3rd Party programme in 1961 proclaimed a massive 20-year plan and expected communism to be reached by 1980. Khrushchev came up with the slogan: the present generation will live under communism. As it became clear during the 1970s that the goals of communism were unachievable, the Party had to reformulate its concept of socialism: socialism was going to last longer than envisaged. This found expression in the concept of developed socialism. Soviet society was not near communism but was completing socialism. The 4th and last Party programme, adopted at the 27th Party Congress in February–March 1986, no longer spoke of developed socialism but referred to the 'planned and all-round development of socialism'. Indeed the expression developing socialism was also used.

Communist Party of the Soviet Union (CPSU)

The Party was founded in 1898 as the Russian Social Democratic Labour or Workers' Party (RSDRP) but in 1903 it split into Bolshevik (majoritarian) and Menshevik (minoritarian) factions. From 1903 to 1918 the Party was known as the Russian Social Democratic Labour or Workers' Party of the Bolsheviks (RSDRP(B)). From 1918 to 1925 it was the Russian Communist Party of the Bolsheviks (RCP(B)). From 1925 to 1952 it was the All-Union Communist Party of the Bolsheviks (VKP(B)). The Party was also referred to as the Communist Party of the Soviet Union of the Bolsheviks (CPSU(B)). From 1952 to 1991 it was the Communist Party of the Soviet Union (CPSU). It was the only legal party and the ruling party in the Soviet Union from 1921. It shared power with the left Socialist Revolutionaries from December 1917 to March 1918 but did not entrust any important ministry to them. The Party legitimised its rule through its ideology (Marxism–Leninism), which claimed to possess special knowledge about social processes and hence was qualified to lead society to socialism and then communism. The Party was a mass party with a party base which comprised the vast majority of members (referred to as communists) and a superstructure consisting of paid officials (appar-atchiks who formed the nomenklatura) and the top leadership, found in the Politburo.

There was always tension between the Party and the state apparatus. This was only resolved in 1988 when Gorbachev, at the 19th Party Con-ference, removed the Party from the management of the economy and the state. Lenin was uncertain about the role of the Party after October 1917 and it is instructive that he chose to be head of Sovnarkom or Prime Minister until his death and never occupied any formal position in the Party. The Civil War destroyed any democracy which existed in the country and by 1921 the Politburo was the main decision-making body. Stalin's dictatorship from 1936 to 1953 reduced the party to being a mere instru-ment of his rule. After his death it was unclear which was the leading institution, the Party or the government. Khrushchev's defeat of the Anti-Party Group in June 1957 established the Party as the dominant institu-tion and it gradually acquired more and more influence over the economy and state. In January 1917 the Party counted only 23,600 members and this rose to 732,521 in 1921 and to 3,872,465 in 1941. There was a very rapid expansion of the Party after 1953 and by 1964 it had 11,022,369 members. It reached its apogee in 1987 with over 19 million members.

Throughout Party history there were purges to cleanse it of undesir-able elements. By the 1980s it was necessary to be a Party member in order to rise to the top in Soviet society. Gorbachev discovered that the nomenklatura were more interested in retaining their power and privil-eges than in reforming the country. Remarkably, the Party did not see the gathering clouds and attempted to respond to the aspirations of the population in order to stay in power. The USSR Congress of People's Deputies, elected in March 1989, undermined Party authority and became the main legislative body. The repeal of article 6 of the 1977 constitu-tion, which stated that the Party was the ruling and guiding force of Soviet society, ended its monopoly on power. Gorbachev believed that the Party could compete successfully with the emerging parties and movements. He was wrong. The involvement of the Party in the attempted coup against Gorbachev on 18–21 August 1991 sealed its fate. Immediately after the return of Gorbachev to Moscow President Boris Yeltsin of Russia banned the CPSU. It was legalised later at local level but was quickly replaced by the Communist Party of the Russian Federation.

Congress of Soviets

The RSFSR constitution of July 1918 prescribed congresses of soviets at volost, uezd, guberniya, oblast and national level and these were to be the supreme institution in their territory. Elections to congresses was indir-ect, the subordinate bodies electing the superior, except local soviets, village and city soviets, which were to be directly elected. Delegates were sent by soviets to the congress and the countryside was under-represented and the cities over-represented. The congress elected an executive committee, which acted in its name between congresses. The highest congress was the All-Russian Congress of Soviets and it elected an All-Russian Central Executive Committee (TsIK). It elected the government (Sovnarkom) and was to supervise its activities. The 1918 constitution declared the All-Russian Congress of Soviets to be the supreme power in the country. Before the constitution of 1918 it was to meet three times a year, but the constitution laid down that it was to meet twice annually; however from 1919 it met only annually. The 1936 USSR constitution abolished the congresses and established a USSR Supreme Soviet, which was bicameral, consisting of the Soviet of the Union and the Soviet of Nationalities. The constitution abolished congresses at the national, republican and autonomous republican levels and established a directly elected all-Union Supreme Soviet.

Criticism and self-criticism

Introduced at the end of the 1920s as a form of social control to overcome the gulf which had developed between state and society. A CC decree of 2 June 1929 called on all workers to criticise the shortcomings of Soviet policies without respect for any person (except Stalin, of course). The worker was also invited to criticise his own behaviour. The goal of this policy was to draw everyone into the process of building a new society. It was lauded for decades as one of the driving forces of socialist society. Politically, however, it soon lost its shine as it was transformed by the Party into a weapon for disciplining the population. Gorbachev attempted to reinvigorate the concept and to use it to further democratisation.

Council of the Federation   *see* Duma (post-1991)

Cult of the personality

The term used by Khrushchev to denigrate Stalin during his secret speech to the 20th Party Congress in 1956. The western term was Stalinism and this was adopted in the Soviet Union under Gorbachev. It epitomised all the negative aspects of Stalin's personality and rule. Khrushchev was careful in his speech only to criticise Stalin's record after 1934. This signified that industrialisation and collectivisation were not being criticised. Khrushchev's demolition of the infallibility of the Party weakened the east European parties, and in 1956 the Hungarian Revolution and the unrest in Poland were direct results. This led to the attacks on the cult being muted, but Khrushchev resumed the attacks at the 22nd Party

Congress in October 1961. He condemned the cult of the personality as alien to Marxism–Leninism and violating the principle of the collective leadership of the Party. The explanation for the emergence of the cult were the deformed aspects of Stalin's personality and the incredible difficulties encountered during the building of socialism, which had necessitated limitations being set on the exercise of socialist democracy. The fact that the hero worship of the leader was a concomitant part of communist regimes can be illustrated by the fact that Khrushchev developed his own personality cult, as did Brezhnev after him.

Democratic centralism

A concept which was at the heart of the Marxist–Leninist Party and its main administrative principle. It is to be found in the Party statutes of 1906 and 1919, where the autonomy of local basic organisations is referred to. It was defined in detail for the first time in the 1934 Party statutes. It signifies: the election of all leading Party organs, from top to bottom; the regular presentation of overviews by Party organs to their Party organisations; strict Party discipline and the subordination of the minority to the majority; and decisions of higher organs must be implemented by lower level organs and all Party members. The Party statutes of 1961 reproduce these definitions almost word for word. The principle of democratic centralism was transferred by the Party to the soviets and the government apparatus. The 1977 constitution defines it as the basic principle of the organisation and functioning of the socialist state. The concept attempted to combine democracy and centralism – opposites in reality – but centralism always won the day. The left opposition in the 1920s referred to themselves as democratic centrists, placing stress on the democratic aspect.

De-Stalinisation

The move after Stalin's death by the Party leadership away from the terror and brutality of the Stalin period and also the moves deemed necessary to rectify the distortions of Stalinist development in state and society. It began on 28 March 1953 with a general amnesty for criminals. On 3 April 1953 those involved in the Doctors' Plot were rehabilitated. The all-pervasive power of the secret police was broken with the arrest of Lavrenty Beria in June 1953. The gulags were wound up and millions released and some rehabilitated. Consumer goods production increased (Malenkov's New Course) and culture became more liberal. De-Stalinisation reached its peak in February 1956, when Khrushchev delivered his secret speech at the 20th Party Congress. It demolished

Stalin's reputation and found him guilty of mass terror and the deportation of many peoples. The term Stalinism was avoided and the euphem-
ism cult of the personality was used instead. The Party attempted to jus-
tify the emergence of the cult by the difficult security situation in the
1930s. De-Stalinisation ceased with the removal of Khrushchev in October
1964 and under Brezhnev criticism of Stalin was toned down. Elements
of de-Stalinisation which survived were the reform of the civil and criminal
code and legal system, which contributed to the development of socialist
legality. Stalin's perception that class struggle intensifies as socialism is
approached, which served as a justification for the terror, was abandoned.
The attack on Stalin's cult of the personality made it unlikely that such
a cult could be developed by a successor. The liberalisation of cultural
policy and the weakening of censorship engendered permanent tension
between writers and the Party leadership.

Dictatorship of the proletariat

Marx conceived of the transition phase to socialism, after the successful
overthrow of the bourgeoisie, as constituting the dictatorship of the proletariat, during which the remnants of the former ruling class would be
mopped up. This would involve taking all capital from them and transferring all means of production to the state, dominated by the organised
proletariat. Lenin was confronted with a situation where the proletariat
was small and weak and the industrial economy was underdeveloped.
Initially the state became the Soviet state, ruled by the urban and rural
proletariat and the poor peasantry. In the 1918 Soviet Russian constitution Lenin does not expect that there will be classes under socialism or
any state administration. In the 1930s Stalin stated that socialism had
almost been built and that there were no more antagonistic classes in the
Soviet Union. The franchise was extended to all citizens. However, the
term dictatorship of the proletariat was retained (also in the Party statutes of 1936), but it disappeared in Khrushchev's new Party programme
as the Soviet Union is described as a state of the whole people. This means
that the CPSU, founded as a class party, had become a party of the
whole people. These concepts were included in the 1977 constitution.

Duma (pre-1917)

The October Manifesto of 1905 established a Duma or representative
assembly, which had only consultative powers. The government, as before,
was appointed by and responsible to the Tsar. There were four Dumas
before the February Revolution (all dates Old Style, add 13 days for New
Style):

First Duma   27 April 1906–8 July 1906
Second Duma   20 February 1907–2 June 1907
Third Duma   1 November 1907–9 June 1912
Fourth Duma   15 November 1912–25 February 1917

Duma (post-1991)

The First Duma (11 January 1994–22 December 1995)

On 21 September 1991 President Boris Yeltsin issued decree no. 1400 on constitutional reform in the Russian Federation, which dissolved the RSFSR Congress of People's Deputies and the RSFSR Supreme Soviet. A Federal Assembly was to be constituted consisting of a lower house, the State Duma, and an upper house, the Council of the Federation. There were to be 450 deputies in the Duma, 225 elected in first-past-the-post contests and 225 by proportional representation, on the basis of party lists. Only those parties which achieved 5 per cent or more of the proportional representation vote qualified for seats. In order to qualify for registration, candidates for the single constituencies had to collect the signatures of not less than 1 per cent of the voters, by 15 November 1993. Those on party lists had to collect, by 7 November 1993, at least 100,000 signatures, of which not more than 15 per cent were to be from any one subject of the Russian Federation. A presidential decree of 11 October 1993 fixed elections to the State Duma for 12 December 1993 and elections to the Council of the Federation. A central electoral commission was set up for the Duma elections and one for elections to the Council of the Federation. Two deputies from each of the 89 newly created subjects of the Russian Federation were to be elected, making 178 in all. On 6 November 1993 only 21 parties and movements were admitted to the elections. The Agrarian Party of Russia (APR) had collected 500,000 signatures, the Communist Party of the Russian Federation (CPRF), 438,000 signatures, the Democratic Party of Russia, 142,000 signatures, the Party of Russian Unity and Accord, and the Russia's Choice bloc, about 200,000 each, and Civic Union, 150,000 signatures. Eight of the original 21 were disqualified because they had not met all the requirements of the commission. A presidential decree of 19 October 1993 disqualified some social organisations from participating in the elections to both chambers. Some 3,797 were registered to participate in elections to both houses, of which 494 stood for the Council of the Federation and 1,586 for the Duma and a further 1,717 on party lists.

On 12 December 1993 56 million of the 105.3 million registered voters took part. According to the provisional figures of the central electoral commission, the Liberal Democratic Party of Russia received 24.58 per cent of the votes on the party lists; the Russia's Choice bloc, 15.03 per cent; the Communist Party of the Russian Federation, 11.16 per cent; the Agrarian Party of Russia, 8.02 per cent; the Yabloko bloc, 7.71 per cent; the Democratic Party of Russia, 5.64 per cent; the Party of Russian Unity and Accord, 5.76 per cent; the Women of Russia political movement, 8.72 per cent. Those electoral associations which did not cross the 5 per cent barrier (5 per cent of the total valid votes cast) were: the Future of Russia–New Names, 1.61 per cent; the Civic Union for Stability, Justice and Progress, 1.61 per cent; the Dignity and Charity political movement, 0.68 per cent; Kedr ecological movement, 0.81 per cent; and the Russian movement for democratic reform, 4.01 per cent.

Some 444 deputies were elected to the Duma, of whom 219 were elected in single constituencies and 225 by party list. In Tatarstan there was a very low turnout in five electoral districts and in constituency no. 32 in Chechnya. On 13 March 1994 there were new elections in five constituencies and five deputies were elected. According to the party lists, the Agrarian Party of Russia received 21 seats; the Yabloko bloc, 20; Russia's Choice, 40; the Democratic Party of Russia, 14; the Communist Party of the Russian Federation, 32; the Liberal Democratic Party of Russia, 58; the Party of Russian Unity and Accord, 17; Women of Russia, 21. According to the constitution, each of the 89 subjects of the Russian Federation was entitled to send two deputies to the upper house.

Some 171 deputies were elected to the Council of the Federation. On 13 March 1994 new elections were held in Tatarstan and on 15 May 1994 in Chelyabinsk oblast, which resulted in four more deputies being elected. The total number of deputies elected was thus 175 (there were three vacant places, two in Chechnya and one in the Yamal-Nenets autonomous okrug). Of the deputies 11 were from the Communist Party of the Russian Federation; six from Russia's Choice; and nine other parties had a deputy each; 80 per cent of the deputies were independents. The executive was well represented among them. There were five presidents of republics, 11 prime ministers, 43 krai and oblast governors (gubernatory) and three federal ministers. About 15 per cent of the deputies were chairs of soviets, about 5 per cent were former members of the Russian Supreme Soviet, over 10 per cent were heads of state enterprises, and there were also academics, businessmen, journalists and lawyers. Over 40 per cent of the deputies of the Council of the Federation had been USSR and RSFSR people's deputies (before 1991) and 35 per cent had been Russian people's deputies (1991–93). According to the central electoral commission, 58.2 million voters or 54.8 per cent of all registered voters took part in the constitutional referendum: 32.9 million voted for (58.4 per cent of those voting), and 23.4 million voted against (41.6 per cent). This meant that less than one-third of all voters had voted in favour of the constitution. On 20 December 1993 the central electoral commission declared the constitution adopted.

The Federal Assembly convened on 11 January 1994 and was opened by President Yeltsin. Until speakers had been elected to the two chambers it was decided that the three oldest members would preside. There were 17 nominations for speaker of the Council of the Federation but 13 of them withdrew. On the following day in the third round of voting V. Shumeiko obtained 98 votes (or 12 votes more than the minimum of 86 votes). On 14 January 1994 R. G. Abdulatipov was elected deputy speaker for links with the territories and V. N. Viktorov was elected deputy speaker for industry and agriculture. The third deputy speaker was not elected.

The first session of the State Duma took place on 11 January 1994 and was opened by the oldest deputy, G. G. Lukav, a professor at the Moscow Aviation Academy (LDPR). After the formal opening and a message from President Yeltsin and a speech by Viktor Chernomyrdin, the Prime Minister, the Duma adjourned for a day and a half to permit the parties to form parliamentary factions and to advance candidates for the various Duma offices. On 13 January 1994 Sergei Stankevich, the chair of the provisional secretariat, announced the formation and registration of parliamentary factions and groups of deputies. Each electoral group which had received over 5 per cent of the total vote at the election formed its own parliamentary faction. Among these were (leader given in brackets): Russia's Choice, with 76 members (E. Gaidar); the LDPR, 63 members (V. Zhirinovsky); the APR, 55 members (M. Lapshin); Women of Russia, 23 members (E. Lakhova); Yabloko, 25 members (G. Yavlinsky); the Party of Russian Unity and Accord, 30 members (S. Shakhrai); CPRF, 45 members (G. Zyuganov); the Democratic Party of Russia, 15 members (N. Travkin), and a new group of deputies, New Regional Policy, 65 members (V. Medvedev). It was agreed that a group needed to have at least 35 members before it could be registered. Later other groups of deputies were formed: the Union of 12 December, 35 independent deputies as members (B. Fedorov); and the Russian Way (Yu. Vlasov), but it was not registered. Each party put forward its nominee for speaker. Ivan Rybkin (APR) was elected speaker on 14 January 1994. On 17 January M. A. Mityukov (Russia's Choice) was elected first deputy speaker, and V. A. Kovalev (CPRF), A. V. Fedulova (Women of Russia) and A. D. Vengerovsky (LDPR) were elected deputy speakers. One position remained vacant and on 10 June 1994 A. N. Chilingarov (New Regional Policy) was elected the fifth deputy speaker. On 17 January 23 Duma committees were set up. The system chosen was quite similar to the German electoral system, a mixture of first-past-the-post and proportional representation. The aim of having party lists was to develop pan-Russian parties. Russia's Choice had confidently expected up to a third of the vote but the surprise winner was the LDPR. Most analysts put this down as a protest vote. The Duma deputies could be divided into 179 conservaties, 103 centrists, 100 radicals and 57 rapid transitionists. Hence those opposed to the government could almost muster a two-thirds majority, if all deputies were present. The balance of the new parliament was quite similar to that of the Russian Congress of People's Deputies but there were slightly more conservatives in the new Duma. The President was quite conciliatory towards the new parliament and it in turn did not seek confrontation with the President or the Prime Minister. One reason for this was that the Duma did not wish to be blamed by the public for the deteriorating economic situation – as the old Congress had been. The Duma preferred the population to blame the President and his government for their problems and this was achieved in the new Duma elections in December 1995.

The Second Duma (16 January 1996–)

The tension between President Yeltsin and Russia's Choice, led by Egor Gaidar, led to a new pro-President party being formed: Our Home is Russia, headed by Viktor Chernomyrdin. It was modelled on the Republican Party in the USA and it was intended that a party resembling the Democratic Party, headed by Ivan Rybkin, would form, but this never came about. By 21 September 1995 over 50 parties and movements had been registered for the Duma elections. They had to provide 200,000 signatures to register. On 23 October Nikolai Ryabov, chair of the central electoral commission, confirmed that 43 parties and blocs would participate in the elections. The elections were held on 17 December 1995 and only four parties crossed the 5 per cent barrier in the party lists: the CPRF, 22.3 per cent; the LDPR, 11.2 per cent; Our Home is Russia, 10.7 per cent; and Yabloko, 6.9 per cent. These four parties, however, obtained only 50 per cent of the vote. The combined vote for the communists and the liberal democrats in 1995 was only 2.2 per cent less than their 35.7 per cent in 1993. The combined vote of Our Home is Russia, Yabloko and Gaidar's Russia's Democratic Choice was 2.5 per cent less than their total vote in 1993. This pointed to continuity in Russian politics. However, overall, the composition of the second Duma reflected a shift in favour of those opposed to rapid market reforms and this was a major shift in public opinion. When the Duma factions were formed the largest group were the communists, people's power and agrarians with a total of 221 deputies. The liberal democrats, the nationalists, counted 51 deputies. There were 152 pro-reform deputies and 26 independents. Hence communists and nationalists were clearly in the majority, about 60 per cent of deputies. The new Duma convened on 16 January 1996 and elected Gennady Seleznev (CPRF) speaker. On 22 January the Council of the Federation elected Egor Stroev speaker.

General Secretary

The official title of the leader of the CPSU. He (no woman ever occupied the position) heads the Secretariat of the Central Committee (CC) and since the late 1920s dominated decision-making in the Party. The post was created at the 8th Party Congress in 1919 but referred to as Responsible Secretary. The post was renamed General Secretary at the 11th Party Congress in 1922 and Stalin got the job. At the 17th Party Congress in 1934 the title was dropped and Stalin was referred to as Secretary until his death in March 1953. Nikita Khrushchev was elected First Secretary of the CC, CPSU, in September 1953 and he remained head of the Party until he was removed in October 1964. Leonid Brezhnev began as First Secretary but reverted to General Secretary in 1966. This title was retained by Yury Andropov (1982–84), Konstantin Chernenko (1984–85) and Mikhail Gorbachev (1985–91).

Internationalism

Internationalism was a fundamental tenet of Marxism–Leninism since 1917. Lenin regarded it as one of the commandments of revolution, which had to oppose the international nature of capitalism. As the Bolsheviks expected the world-wide socialist revolution to be victorious, their foreign policy (decree on peace) was couched in the interests of the world proletariat and the Soviet state acted in the interests of all workers. Gradually the interests of the international proletariat were subordinated to the interests of the Soviet state. This is clearly perceptible in Stalin's concept of socialism in one country. The Soviet intervention in the Spanish Civil War was presented as a contribution to internationalism but the Comintern was dissolved in 1943. Since the Cold War got under way in 1947 the USSR used the term internationalism as an instrument for the closer association of the socialist camp. Khrushchev's Third World policy and the invasion of Czechoslovakia were represented as examples of internationalism. The Soviet Union's claim to represent the interests of the world proletariat was disputed by China in the 1960s as the communist world split into camps.

Iron Curtain

Winston Churchill, the wartime British Prime Minister, used the expression in a speech at Fulton, Missouri, on 5 March 1946. He declared that an iron curtain had descended from Stettin (Szczecin) on the Baltic to Trieste on the Adriatic. Behind this curtain Soviet influence was dominant. The Soviet zone of influence was actually wider than this and was to include East Germany so that the Iron Curtain ran from the Elbe. In the south Yugoslavia was expelled in 1948. The metaphor describes the mutual suspicion between east and west which fuelled the arms race and almost resulted in nuclear war during the Cuban Missile Crisis of October 1962. Détente in the 1970s led to the Helsinki Final Act in 1975, which recognised post-war frontiers. However, the Soviet invasion of Afghanistan rekindled the conflict and it was only with the arrival of Gorbachev that the curtain began to become porous. One can say that the Iron Curtain was taken down in the late Gorbachev era.

Komsomol (All-Union Leninist Union of Youth)

Komsomol served to prepare members for the CPSU and played a very important ideological role. The first groups of communist youth came together at a congress from 29 October to 4 November 1917 in Moscow and formed the Communist Union of Youth of Russia. They fought on various fronts during the Civil War and in 1920 there were over 400,000 members. They were given the name Komsomol in 1926. The organisation was organisationally based on the CPSU. Those between 14 and 28 years old could join and those that proved themselves were often recruited as CPSU cadres. The Pioneer youth organisation, for those under 14, was supervised by the Komsomol. Komsomol members distinguished themselves during the 1930s by providing volunteers for some of the largest projects, in the Donbass and Magnitogorsk, and they also contributed much to the building of the Moscow metro. There were 2.3 million members in 1929 and 10.2 million in 1940. The east Siberian city, Komsomolsk-on-Amur, was named after the Komsomol builders. They provided much labour for the virgin lands scheme and also the construction of BAM (Baikal–Amur Magistral). By 1982 there were over 40 million members. In the universities the Komsomol played an important role (Gorbachev became an official at Moscow State University) and also required students to volunteer for unpaid labour. Officials of the Komsomol could be older than 28 years. During the 1950s many Komsomol members were recruited into the KGB. The Komsomol did not distinguish itself under Gorbachev and became known for corruption and nepotism. It was dissolved in 1991. Its newspaper, *Komsomolskaya Pravda*, survived and is today one of the most informative Russian newspapers.

Left communists

A group of leading Bolsheviks who during the spring and summer of 1918 opposed Lenin's domestic and foreign policy. They were centred in the Moscow Party organisation and included Nikolai Bukharin, A. S. Bubnov, V. V. Obolensky-Osinsky, G. I. Lomov-Oppokov and Karl Radek. The group also published its own journal, *Kommunist*, for a short period.

The group formed during the controversies around the signing of the Treaty of Brest-Litovsk, which they strongly opposed. They advocated transforming the war into a civil war against international capital and this would promote world revolution. They also supported wildcat national-isation of enterprises at a time when Lenin and Trotsky advocated state capitalism (leaving factories in capitalist ownership but supervised by workers' control). They wanted the social revolution to be speeded up and not run from the centre. It should be spontaneous and develop at the local level. Bukharin changed sides later and supported Lenin's New Economic Policy. The criticisms of the left communists were articulated during the 1920s by other groups.

Left opposition (also left deviation)

From October 1917 there were Bolsheviks who believed that the Party leadership was not revolutionary enough and had abandoned certain tenets of the socialist revolution. The first confrontation came during the debate on the Treaty of Brest-Litovsk, which led to the formation of the left communist group, but it died away during the Civil War. In 1919–20 two other left groups emerged: the democratic centralists and the workers' opposition. The democratic centralists were unhappy with the increas-ing 'centralisation, militarisation and bureaucratisation' of the state and economy, which threatened to deprive workers of their rights. The leading democratic centralists were T. V. Sapronov, V. N. Maksimovsky and V. V. Obolensky-Ossinsky. The other group was the workers' opposition, which was against the central management of the economy. They demanded, from autumn 1920, the ending of one-man management (edinonachalie) in enterprises and the reintroduction of collective management based on soviets with decision-making from the bottom upwards. The leading members were Aleksandr Shlyapnikov and Aleksandra Kollontai. They had considerable support in factories but at the 10th Party Congress in March 1921 (meeting in the shadow of the Kronstadt uprising) they were defeated and labelled an 'anarcho-syndicalist deviation'. The demo-cratic centralists and workers' opposition, however, continued to exist and formed two new groups, Workers' Group and Workers' Truth. The left opposition played a major role in the debates in the USSR between 1925 and 1927 on the future direction of Soviet power. They were against the decline in inner-Party democracy, the resurrection of capitalist forms during NEP and Stalin's concept of socialism in one country. They advocated rapid industrialisation of the country at a time when the offi-cial policy was to promote agrarian growth. The leading members of the left opposition were Trotsky, Evgeny Preobrazhensky (their most influ-ential economist), Zinoviev and Kamenev. They were defeated in 1927 by a Stalin-led coalition and their leading lights lost their Party and government posts. They all lost their lives during the show trials of the 1930s. Trotsky, in Mexico, was murdered by one of Stalin's agents in 1940.

Lenin's Testament

This refers to the notes that Lenin dictated on 24–25, 26 and 30 December 1922 and 4 January 1923 and was intended to be considered at the next Party Congress, the 12th. Seriously ill, after a stroke, partly paralysed and only able to speak with great effort, Lenin assessed the merits of his possible successors. Stalin had concentrated 'unlimited authority' in his hands and it was not certain that he was always 'capable of using that authority with sufficient caution'. Trotsky was distinguished by 'outstanding abilities' and, as a person, was probably the 'most able man on the Central Committee (CC) at present' but he had revealed 'excessive self-assurance and demonstrated excessive preoccupation with the purely administrative side of the work'. Lenin expected these two outstanding members of the CC to disagree to the point where they would cause a split in the CC. The two most outstanding younger members of the CC were Bukharin and Pyatakov. The former was not only the 'most valuable and most powerful theorist in the Party' but was also regarded 'rightly as the darling of the whole Party', but his theoretical views could only be qualified as Marxist with 'considerable reserve'. There was something scholastic about him and he had never studied and had 'never fully understood the dialectic'. Pyatakov was too attracted to administration to be relied upon in a 'serious political question'.

On 26 December Lenin recommended that the number of CC members be increased to 50 or 'even 100' in order to train more in CC work and avoid a split. On 30 December he was worried by reports of conflict between the Party and the Communist Party of Georgia, which had resulted in blows being struck. He described the typical Russian bureaucrat as a 'Great-Russian chauvinist and a rascal and a tyrant'. The small number of Soviet and sovietised workers would drown in that 'tide of chauvinistic Great-Russian riffraff like a fly in milk'. On 4 January Lenin concluded that Stalin was 'too rude' and this defect was 'intolerable in the post of General Secretary'. Lenin invited members to remove Stalin from that post and replace him with a comrade who was 'tolerant, more loyal, more polite and more considerate to his comrades, less capricious, etc.'. This was necessary to avoid a split in the CC. Lenin's Testament was not brought to the attention of the 12th Party Congress, mainly because of the tension in the country, which required the Party to display unity. However, Trotsky missed a great opportunity to downgrade Stalin. Nadezhda Krupskaya, Lenin's widow, presented it to the 13th Congress in 1924, and Stalin formally offered his resignation. It was rejected, with his supporters arguing that he had mended his ways. The leadership then placed the papers in the Party archives and so the comments remained unknown to the ordinary Party member until they were published in *Kommunist*, no. 9, 1956, after the 20th Party Congress.

Leninism

The expression, used in a pejorative sense, originated among Lenin's political foes inside the Party, who took umbrage at his dogmatism and intolerance in debates on organisation and tactical questions. The term becomes positive after 1917 and refers to the translation of Marxist ideas into political practice. Zinoviev referred to Leninism as the realisation that the Russian peasantry could become the tactical allies of the working class in the socialist revolution. Stalin in 1924 defined Leninism as the Marxism of the epoch of imperialism and the proletarian revolution. This concept raised Leninism to the level of theory which developed Marxism further. Gradually this view predominated and Moscow laid down that the Soviet model of revolution was applicable to the whole world and hence became obligatory. This led to the dropping of the term Leninism in Soviet usage and its replacement with Marxism–Leninism. Henceforth the two could not be separated. Another definition was that Leninism was the Marxism of the twentieth century. Leninism means the rule of the Party, a Party of a new type, which was strictly disciplined, was run along the lines of democratic centralism, mobilised the masses, and acted as the vanguard of the proletariat. It later became a party of the whole Soviet people. Leninism, as an ideology, evolves gradually and passes through two distinct phases.

Phase One

(i) Lenin regarded monopoly capitalism (banks and enterprises which enjoyed a monopoly and ran the state in their own interest) as a stepping stone to socialism. He wrote in 1916:

> the big banks are the state apparatus which we need to bring about socialism, and which we take ready made from capitalism. . . . A single State Bank, the biggest of the big, with branches in every rural district, in every factory, will constitute as much as nine tenths of the socialist apparatus. This will be country wide bookkeeping, country wide accounting of the production and distribution of goods, this will be. . . . the skeleton of socialist society. . . . We can lay hold of and set in motion this state apparatus . . . at one stroke, by a single decree, because the actual work of bookkeeping, control, registering, accounting and counting is

performed by employees, the majority of whom themselves lead a proletarian or semi-proletarian existence.

(ii) The state could not be reformed. Monopoly capitalism and the state were like Siamese twins and in order to smash monopoly capitalism the state had to be smashed as well. The model for Lenin was the Paris Commune of 1871. A commune state could come into being in Russia with the soviets running it. Unlike conventional states it did not need a bureaucracy or a standing army or the divisions of power between the legislature, the executive and the judiciary. Public business would be carried out by elected officials accountable to their constituents, liable to be recalled at any time and paid an average workman's wages. Police functions would be performed by a militia formed from a universally armed people. Socialism here meant democracy from below. This vision is expressed in the April Theses. One of the reasons for changing the name of the Party to Communist Party was Lenin's obsession with the Paris Commune, whose objective had been to dissolve the state into society. This simplistic view of the state – the bearer of everything that was evil and wrong in the world – was to have an immense influence on the future development of Russia. It put out of bounds any discussion about improving its institutions and procedures, making its officials accountable and subjecting its decisions to judicial review. Lenin regarded the state and politics as having no autonomy or permanence. Both would disappear as exploitation of man by man disappeared. Hence the goal of Lenin in power was economic rather than political – to eliminate exploitation and thereby eliminate classes. When this had been done there would be no need for the state or politics.

(iii) Economic goals would be decided by the Party leadership and not through debate or dispute. The available resources (capital and labour) would be allocated, in a planned and rational manner, in order to achieve an optimal outcome. The allocation of rewards within society would depend on the contribution of individuals and groups to the production achieved by society. Hence Lenin never suggested that economic priorities be debated by society but would be decided by the Party leadership in consultation with economists, engineers and other specialists. Lenin had nothing but contempt for politics.

Phase Two

(i) In 1920–21 Lenin (together with Trotsky and Bukharin) reformulated the Soviet view of the state. They agreed that socialism could no longer be identified with mass popular participation in the management of political, economic and social affairs. Proletarian power was to cease being identified with workers' control, factory committees, trade unions, soviets, people's militias and cooperatives. They agreed that the above was merely the first, destructive phase of the revolution because it had produced nothing positive – the country was on the verge of economic ruin. Lenin now concluded that socialism had no longer anything to do with altering the power relations between men but rather transforming their productive relations so that economic growth would eventually lead to abundance and hence social freedom. For the first time Bolshevik leaders made a distinction between socialism and communism – hitherto the terms had been used almost interchangeably. The desperate times led to new slogans: iron discipline, ruthless and firm leadership, one-man management and universal labour mobilisation.

(ii) The dictatorship of the proletariat was redefined. The dictatorship could not be exercised by the working class as a whole. The dream of a commune state with universal participatory democracy was no longer valid. Only the avant-garde of the class, endowed with special knowledge and wisdom, was capable of leading the proletariat and running the state. That avant-garde was to be found in the Party. Communists were a small minority in Russia and this led to the view that allowing competing political views or a free press would result in the Bolsheviks losing power. They had to be suppressed. As Lenin put it succinctly: 'We have no desire to commit suicide'. Lenin then defined what he meant by dictatorship: 'nothing more or less than authority untrammelled by any laws, absolutely unrestricted by any rules whatsoever, and based directly on force. The term dictatorship has no other meaning than this'. Anyone who opposed the Bolsheviks was classified as 'bourgeois' and hence could be legitimately destroyed. This included socialists, such as Mensheviks and SRs. Lenin (and Trotsky and Bukharin), in 1920, agreed that the Russian proletariat had become déclassé (declassed) and had ceased to exist as a proletariat. The result of this sad state of affairs was that the proletarian state would have to use coercion to re-educate the working class. The Kronstadt uprising was a graphic example of this policy in action. The Kronstadters wanted to revert to commune democracy but Lenin wanted his new dictatorship.

(iii) Insisting on a monopoly of power, given very limited public support, led to state terror and coercion. Lenin and Bukharin acknowledged that they were behaving in the manner of the imperialist state they wished to destroy throughout the world.

(iv) Socialism was redefined in 1920–21 not as mass participation in administering the state but as the most efficient means for allocating capital and labour to maximise output. Democracy was a luxury which could be dispensed with. Lenin was blunt: 'industry is indispensable, democracy is not'. As long as the conflict between capitalism and socialism lasted, Lenin and the Bolsheviks did not promise any 'freedom or any democracy'.

(v) The essential element of the consolidation of the workers as a class was their consolidation into a single political party. The Communist Party would instil a socialist consciousness and organise the workers nationally, without which they could not exist as a class. The Party would purge the workers of their illusions and educate them through propaganda.

(vi) As Russia developed economically politics would recede into the background. As Lenin put it: 'Henceforth less politics will be the best politics'.

(vii) As Lenin lost faith in the creative potential of the proletariat, his faith in science grew.

(viii) Lenin hated pluralism and always believed that there was one correct view, the working class had only one will to realise its role in history, there was only one path to paradise and only the Party, and the Party alone, knew the way and could guide the proletariat to cornucopia and freedom.

(ix) At the 2nd Congress of the Comintern, in July 1920, Lenin laid down, for the first time, the organisational structures of a Communist Party. The core of this organisation was democratic centralism. No individual or lower Party body was to dissent from or oppose instructions from a superior body. The penalty for this offence was expulsion. Lenin, at the 10th Party Congress in 1921, fumed: 'we want no more opposition . . . we are not a debating society'. A resolution was passed banning factionalism (opposition). The penalty again was expulsion from the Party.

Marxism–Leninism

The official ideology of the Soviet Union and the socialist states which acknowledged Moscow's leadership. Based on the teachings of Marx, Engels and Lenin on state and society, Stalin also made his contributions and it was known as Marxism–Leninism–Stalinism for a time. Other leaders of the CPSU, from Khrushchev to Gorbachev, developed the ideology but without adding their name to it. The concept of Marxism–Leninism was adopted in the mid-1920s and originally signified the development of Marxism by Lenin (Bolshevism) in a direction different from that of Russian and west European social democracy. There was Marxism and Leninism. In his desire to strengthen his credentials as the leading pupil of Lenin, Stalin, in 1924, defined Leninism as the Marxism of the epoch of imperialism and proletarian revolution. In the search for an expression which would underline the differences between the Soviet understanding of Marxism and that of non-Soviet Marxists and the need to demonstrate that Marxism and Leninism formed a unity, V. V. Adoratsky coined the expression Marxism–Leninism in an article in 1926. It was then taken over as the name of the official state ideology.

Marxism–Leninism claimed to be a universal doctrine which consisted of various laws determining the evolution of world society. Among these were the transition from capitalism to socialism during the proletarian revolution, the peaceful, competitive coexistence of states with differing social systems, the increasing role of the masses in history and the increasing exacerbation of the class conflict on a world scale. According to Marxism–Leninism these laws had become universal laws and therefore would apply to all societies throughout the world. Research concentrated on confirming these universal laws and the inevitable victory of socialism. All uprisings, conflicts, revolutions and other conflicts world-wide were analysed as rungs in the ladder of world revolution and confirmation that the laws of Marxism–Leninism were valid.

Marxism–Leninism was more than Marxism and Leninism and over time acquired various encrustations. As new problems arose, so the ideology was adapted. During the 1920s and 1930s Marxism–Leninism fitted rather loosely together, but in the 1940s and 1950s great efforts were undertaken to unify the ideology. In the 1960s the concept of scientific communism was adopted to embrace all the changes in communist construction and the expansion of Soviet influence into the Third World, as well as the puzzle of why capitalism was proving so resilient. Marxism–Leninism was then divided into three sections: the philosophy of dialectical and historical materialism; the political economy of capitalism and socialism; and scientific communism. Brezhnev introduced developed socialism and thereby revised the existing understanding of Marxism–Leninism. According to him Soviet society was not on the threshold of communism but was only beginning the completion of developed socialism. Gorbachev paid little attention to ideology but did replace developed socialism with developing socialism, thereby conceding that the Soviet economy was less well developed than hitherto had been claimed. The world-wide appeal of Marxism–Leninism was fatally damaged during the Soviet and Warsaw Pact invasion of Czechoslovakia in August 1968. The Czechoslovak socialism with a human face was more appealing than the Soviet version. After Khrushchev's attack on Stalin at the 20th Party

Congress in 1956, the Communist Party of China continued to use the term Marxism–Leninism–Stalinism, but this was dropped later.

Menshevik

Those social democrats in the minority when the RSDRP split at the 2nd Congress in London in 1903.

Ministries

Originally the Bolsheviks tried to avoid the creation of ministries and in October 1917 established a Council (Soviet) of People's Commissars (Sovnarkom), which was to function as a provisional workers' and peasants' government (until the Constituent Assembly was convened). Commissions were to be established to deal will all state affairs, guided by the people's commissariats, and in close contact with the mass organisations of the workers, soldiers and peasants. It was hoped that the resolutions of the 2nd Congress of People's Deputies would be implemented in this way. However, the commissions never came into being as the people's commissariats simply took over the functions of the previous ministries and their staffs. The RSFSR constitution of June 1918 listed 17 people's commissariats and corresponded closely to the same areas of competence as the old ministries. The establishment of the Soviet Union in 1922 saw some people's commissariats responsible for the whole of the country (foreign affairs, foreign trade, military and marine, posts and transport) and others had their counterparts in the other republics and regions (supply, labour, finance, etc.). The 1936 constitution accepted this division and distinguished between USSR people's commissariats, responsible for the whole of the country, and the Union republican people's commissariats with one at the centre to coordinate affairs and a separate commissariat in each republic. As the Soviet economy expanded so did the number of commissariats (in 1946 renamed ministries). In 1937 there were 18 and in 1947 there were 58. Khrushchev tried to cut back on this expansion of bureaucracy and in 1957 launched the sovnarkhoz reforms, which decentralised decision-making, so that in December 1963 there were only 11 ministries (three all-Union and eight Union republican), but alongside there were a plethora of state committees. After his removal in October 1964, the Soviet Union soon returned to the old system and in the 1970s there were over 70 ministries.

National communism

National communism was influential in the 1920s as the Soviet nationality policy sought to promote the flowering of the non-Russian nations.

Many of the national communist leaders were from parties which had been obliged to dissolve after 1921. They were enthusiastic about the prospects of building socialism in their own nations as a way of escaping Russian imperialism. There was never any all-Union movement, rather influential groups within their own nations. Their golden era was the 1920s but after 1929 Stalin concentrated more and more on centralisation and the bolshevisation of national elites. The determination to develop the USSR uniformly, according to a central plan, was the death knell for national communism. The leading figure was Sultan Galiev, a Tatar, and he became the first leading functionary to be expelled from the Communist Party for nationalism, in 1923, and was arrested. The national communists favoured a weak central authority and wide-ranging autonomy in political, economic, social and cultural affairs for each nation. They also wished to stop Russian immigration into their territories. Sultan Galiev was accused of pan-Turkism and pan-Islamism and of placing the interests of Muslims above those of the Party. National communists were most influential in Georgia, Ukraine and Tatarstan.

National self-determination

An important plank in the platform of the Bolshevik Party before 1917 as Lenin sought to win over the non-Russian nationalities in Imperial Russia and thereby promote revolution. The Bolsheviks promised all peoples the right of self-determination, which also included the right to secede from the state. Who was to decide? If there was no proletariat then the whole nation could vote. When there was a proletariat then it was the decision-maker. Of course, Lenin expected the proletariat to vote to stay within a future socialist state. The desire of many nations to leave Soviet Russia after 1917 was a shock to Lenin and Bolshevik policy changed. Whereas before the revolution secession was regarded as progressive, it now became counter-revolutionary. However, Poland left the Soviet Union and armed attempts by the proletariat to establish Soviet power in Finland, Estonia, Latvia and Lithuania failed and led to these states becoming independent. The 1936 Soviet constitution conferred on republics the right to secede, but this was only on paper. There developed a tension between the Soviet policy of supporting national self-determination in the Third World (developing world) and denying the same right to nations in the Soviet Union. National movements developed, from the 1960s onwards, in the Baltic republics, Armenia and Georgia. All deported peoples were permitted to return to their homelands except the Volga Germans and the Crimean Tatars. The latter began agitating for permission to return but only a small proportion had returned by the mid-1980s, mainly because their properties had been taken over by Russians and Ukrainians. Nationalism flowered after Gorbachev came to power and eventually led to the break-up of the Soviet Union as many nations sought to implement their right to self-determination. They could point to the 1977 Soviet constitution, which conferred this right on them.

Nomenklatura (also nomenclature)

The cadres policy which permitted the Party to secure all the leading positions in government, administration, economy and society. There were positions which could only be filled by the Party and others which could be filled in consultation with the Party. The same applied to the removal of persons from nomenklatura positions. Various Party bodies were responsible for these appointments and the seniority of the Party body was directly related to the seniority of the post. They were filled according to nomenklatura lists. The Politburo took the key decisions (appointment of Soviet ambassadors to Washington, for instance), besides those affecting the Party and government. Most decisions were taken by the Central Committee, which appointed secretaries at various levels, important posts in the government, the armed forces, the mass organisations, important enterprise directors and police chiefs. Party committees at krai and oblast level had their own lists to fill. Over time more and more positions were filled at the local level. The whole system was undermined at the 19th Party Conference, in June 1988, when Gorbachev removed the Party from the management of the state and economy.

October Revolution

The October Revolution of 25 October 1917 (renamed the Great October Socialist Revolution by Stalin in 1934) marked the transition from the parliamentary republic of the Provisional Government to the rule by soviets, understood by Lenin as the people taking over the state. It was mass, participatory democracy and saw the setting up of the Soviet or commune state. The Bolsheviks, supported by the left SRs, had a majority in the Petrograd soviet, founded the Military Revolutionary Committee (MRC), and planned the seizure of power using the latter as their instrument. For the Bolsheviks it was the end of the bourgeois revolution and the beginning of the transition to the socialist revolution. Lenin won a vote in the Bolshevik Central Committee for an armed uprising (Lenin did not call the events of October a revolution) on 10 October. The uprising was timed to coincide with the convening of the 2nd All-Russian Congress of Soviets on 25 October. The MRC, headed by Trotsky, seized the initiative and occupied key targets. The army and the Provisional Government, under Kerensky, were indecisive and weak, and this ensured the success of the takeover without much blood being shed. At

10 a.m. on 25 October Kerensky left the capital to summon military help and during the afternoon Lenin delivered his first speech welcoming the takeover. The cruiser *Aurora* fired a blank cartridge at 9.45 p.m., the signal for the attack on the Winter Palace, the seat of the government. It was taken without much effort. The 2nd Congress convened at 11 p.m., the moderate socialists walked out in protest against the violence, and the Congress was left to Lenin and the Bolsheviks, and their supporters. Most Petrograders woke up on the morning of 26 October unaware of the fact that a world-shattering event had taken place. All six dead were Bolsheviks. On 26 October the Congress passed the decrees on peace and land, and in the evening the first Bolshevik government, the Sovnarkom, was formed, headed by Lenin, with Trotsky as People's Commissar for Foreign Affairs. On 27 October Kerensky, heading the committee for the salvation of the fatherland and the revolution, composed mainly of moderate socialists with some right wingers and Cossacks, moved from Gatchina towards Petrograd but they were soon dealt with. In Moscow, the soviets of workers' deputies and the soviet of soldiers' deputies had not been fused, as in Petrograd, and the soldiers refused to follow the Bolsheviks. Fighting lasted until 3 November. Elsewhere there was little conflict. The Bolsheviks claimed the revolution cost them about 500 dead. The above analysis treats the revolution as having taken place on one day but it is also possible to regard the October Revolution as beginning in October 1917 and ending in 1932, at the end of the first FYP. This analysis is based on the completion of the economic and social revolution as well. By then, a new ruling class, the nomenklatura, had come into being.

Orgburo

The organisation bureau was set up in early 1919 to concentrate exclusively on problems of Party organisation: the selection and development of Party cadres, contact with local and regional Party bodies, collecting reports on Party activity and information. Hitherto this work had been in the Secretariat. The Politburo had taken the key decisions. The Orgburo was elected by the plenum of the Central Committee, consisted of five persons, and was to meet at least three times a week and once every two weeks report to a plenum of the Central Committee. In effect the Orgburo concentrated on basic Party organisation and cadres. The fact that Stalin was a member of the Orgburo, the Secretariat and the Politburo meant that he was the only top Bolshevik in all three leading bodies. He skilfully used his position and knowledge to build up his position in the Party apparatus by appointing cadres loyal to him. At the 19th Party Congress in 1952 the Orgburo was dissolved and its functions transferred to the Secretariat.

Parties

The October Revolution transferred power to the soviets, dominated by the Bolsheviks, and the latter regarded all other parties which opposed their seizure of power as petty-bourgeois, bent on returning Russia to semi-feudalism and capitalism. The 'bourgeois' press was a special target. The Kadets (Constitutional Democrats), the liberal party, were labelled the party of the enemies of the people. Their press was banned soon after the revolution and their leaders were arrested in December 1917. This policy met with considerable opposition within the Party Central Committee. These Bolsheviks opposed the banning of the press and favoured the formation of a coalition socialist government (with the SRs and Mensheviks) to replace the Bolshevik Sovnarkom. When Lenin refused to concede any ground, five CC members, including four people's commissars, resigned. In December 1917 some left SRs did join Sovnarkom and it thereby became a coalition government. It lasted until the signing of the Treaty of Brest-Litovsk, which was strongly opposed by the left SRs. They quit the government and the Bolsheviks again formed the government on their own. This situation remained until the end of the Soviet Union in 1991, although under Gorbachev non-Party members could become ministers. During the desperate days of the Civil War the SRs and Mensheviks were gradually eliminated from soviets and other representative institutions. The SRs staged a military revolt, shooting Lenin, during the summer of 1918, and they also entered into coalitions with bourgeois parties in the White-controlled areas during the Civil War (for example, the Ufa Directorate). The SRs and Mensheviks were separate entities and did not agree on core questions: the October Revolution, the possibility of working with the Bolsheviks, coalitions with non-socialist parties, etc. Victory in the Civil War confirmed the Bolsheviks as the party of power. The first great show trial took place in 1922 with the SRs as the accused. The Kadets, SRs and Mensheviks, in emigration, founded their own parties and they debated long on whether they should come to terms with Stalin's regime. The Menshevik journal, *Sotsialistichesky vestnik*, survived until the 1950s. Under Gorbachev, unofficial (unregistered) organisations and movements emerged and article 6 of the 1977 USSR constitution was amended, ending the monopoly of the Party. Opposition parties thereby became legal in 1990.

Partiinost (party-mindedness)

A basic element of Marxism–Leninism, requiring members always to act in the interests of proletarian class interest. Until the 1930s there was some plurality in Soviet literature, culture and science, but partiinost was also applied to these areas in the early 1930s. It required members to contribute more to the building of socialism and to portray this struggle in an inspiring manner in works of literature and art. Socialist realism was an aspect of it. Partiinost was not effectively applied to science until the 1950s, when it penetrated philosophy and the social sciences. Partiinost declined during the 1970s as conflict between writers and artists, and cultural bureaucrats intensified. The expression fell out of use during the Gorbachev era. Partiinost was based on the view that all forms of social consciousness were influenced by class interests and that a person's thinking and behaviour were conditioned by these interests. Lenin also maintained that capitalism had its own partiinost, which rejected the social laws of development and distorted social development. Only proletarian class-consciousness, which grasped the reality of social processes, could attain objective knowledge and truth.

Party Central Committee

This was elected at each Party Congress to 'direct the activity of the Party and its local organs', to select and appoint leading cadres (nomenklatura) and to guide the 'work of the central state organisations and the mass organisations of the workers through their Party groups'. The CC represented the Party in relations with other parties and was to meet at least once every six months in a CC plenum. It was to report to each Party Congress, which after 1971 took place every five years. The CC after its election at a Party Congress then elected the General Secretary, the Politburo (Presidium 1952–66), the Secretariat and the Party Control Commission. The 28th Party Congress, in July 1990, adopted a new Party statute which did not alter the above. The 4,683 delegates elected a 412-person CC, of whom only 15.3 per cent had been members of the CC in 1986 (when the CC consisted of 309 members). The CC existed before 1917 but only then began to meet on a regular basis. The 7th Congress in March 1918 elected 15 full and eight candidate members to the CC and the 8th Congress 19 full and eight candidate members. The CC was instructed to elect a Politburo, an Orgburo and a Secretariat. The CC was to meet at least twice a month and to discuss all political and organisational questions at these plenums, providing they did not require immediate solution. The Politburo, Orgburo and Secretariat were to report to the CC. All these arrangements were confirmed in the Party statute which was adopted in the same year. The Party statute, adopted in 1922, passed the responsibility of deciding the size of the CC to the Party Congress. In 1925 over 100 full and candidate members were elected, in 1930 over 140 and in 1952 over 230. It was a deliberate tactic of Stalin to increase the size of the CC since it made it more difficult to discuss matters in detail and it provided him with the opportunity of promoting his clients.

The larger the CC became, the less often it met. In the 1922 statutes, there were to be CC plenums at least every two months, in 1934 this was reduced to one every four months and in 1952 it was decided that two a year were sufficient. This rule was not observed even under Gorbachev. Power passed from the CC to the Politburo, Orgburo (abolished 1952) and Secretariat as the CC met less frequently. The Secretariat was divided into departments and headed by a secretary. Groups of departments were headed by a secretary who sometimes became a member of the Politburo. The General Secretary was, *ex officio*, head of the Secretariat but it was not usual for him to chair sessions of the Secretariat. This duty was performed by a 'second' secretary, the last of whom was Egor Ligachev.

Party Conference

The 1st Conference of the RSDRP took place in Tammerfors, Finland (then part of the Russian Empire), in December 1905. The distinction between a Conference and a Congress was that whereas the latter brought together all delegates who were entitled to attend, the former only brought together a proportion. This was often due to the need to meet at short notice, the long distances and difficulties of travel. A Conference could not elect members to the Central Committee. The 2nd Conference was also held at Tammerfors, in November 1906 (it was also referred to as the 1st All-Russian Conference). The 3rd Conference took place at Kotka, Finland, in July 1907 (the 2nd All-Russian Conference); the 4th Conference (3rd All-Russian) at Helsingfors (Helsinki), in November 1907; the 5th Conference in Paris, in December 1908; the 6th (Prague) Conference, in Prague, in January 1912; the 7th (April) All-Russian Conference, in Petrograd in April 1917; the 8th All-Russian Conference, in Moscow, in December 1919; the 9th All-Russian Conference, in Moscow, in September 1920; the 10th All-Russian Conference, in Moscow, in May 1921; the 11th All-Russian Conference, in Moscow, in December 1921; the 12th All-Russian Conference, in Moscow, in August 1922; the 13th Conference, in Moscow, in January 1924; the 14th Conference, in Moscow, in April 1925; the 15th Conference, in Moscow, in October–November 1926, the 16th Conference, in Moscow, in April 1929; the 17th Conference, in Moscow, in January–February 1932; the 18th Conference, in Moscow, in February 1941; and the 19th Conference, in Moscow, in June 1988. If one compares the dates of the conferences and congresses of the Party until 1941 a pattern emerges. Conferences were normally held between Congresses and can be regarded as mini-Congresses. Gorbachev chose to call a Conference in 1988 instead of a Congress in order to remove the Party from management of the economy, nomination of candidates for election to soviets and control over ministerial and other state appointments.

Party Congress

The supreme body of the Party which, according to the Party statutes, was to meet at least once every five years. The Congress laid down the Party line and state policy in domestic and foreign policy, passed the Party programme and statutes, considered the reports of the central Party bodies, the Central Committee and the Central Control Commission (CCC) and elected a new CC and CCC. At the final Congress, the 28th, in July 1990, 5,000 delegates represented about 16 million members. (At the 26th Congress in February–March 1986, the delegates had represented 18.4 million members.) The 1st Congress of the RSDRP took place in Minsk in 1898 and counted nine delegates. Three of these were elected to the newly formed Central Committee. At the 2nd Congress in Brussels and London in 1903 the Party split into Bolshevik and Menshevik factions but they held joint Congresses until 1907. At the 6th Conference in Prague in 1912 the factions decided to merge. However, when the 6th Congress met in Petrograd in July–August 1917 the two factions were far apart and coalesced into separate parties. At the 7th Congress, in March 1918, the name of the Party was changed from RSDRP to Russian Communist Party (Bolsheviks). A new Party programme and statutes were adopted at the 8th Congress, in March 1919, resolved to expand the central and regional Party organisations and to set up the Comintern. The 10th Congress was a watershed as it adopted the resolution on Party unity which banned factionalism in the Party. It also introduced NEP. The 11th and 12th Congresses continued NEP. The 13th, 14th, 15th and 16th Congresses, 1924–30, were the stage for the conflict between Stalin, the left opposition and the right opposition, and the implementation of socialism in one country. Rapid industrialisation and enforced collectivisation were decreed at the 15th and 16th Congresses.

The nature of Congresses changed dramatically over time. In the immediate post-revolutionary years they were forums for discussion and heated debate, but the 16th set a trend by becoming a stage for acclamation of the Party leadership's (Politburo and CC) decisions. They also became a forum for the vilification of Stalin's opponents and his personal glorification. Over time they grew in size. At the 8th Congress, in March 1918, there were 104 delegates, but at the 15th Congress, in December 1927, there 1,669 delegates. According to the Party statutes, adopted in 1919, Congresses were to take place annually but this rule went by the board in 1926 and was not included in the new Party statutes, adopted at the 17th Congress in 1934. It was then decided Congresses would meet every three years and the Party Conference, which traditionally met between Congresses, was abandoned. However, the next Congress, the 18th, was postponed until 1939. The 17th Congress was hailed as the Congress of Victors but was, in reality, the Congress of the

Condemned: 1,108 of the delegates were arrested afterwards and accused of being counter-revolutionaries and 98 of the 139 candidate and full members of the Central Committee did not survive 1937–38.

There were no Congresses between 1939 and 1952, when the 19th met. The latter resolved to convene once every four years. It also dissolved the Orgburo, created a Politburo out of the previous Presidium, and changed the name of the Party to Communist Party of the Soviet Union. In so doing it gave up its suffix, Bolsheviks. It also passed the FYP which launched vast projects and hydroelectric stations to boost energy output. The 20th Congress, in February–March 1956, was the occasion for Khrushchev's secret speech, which pilloried Stalin's record after 1934 and accused him of developing a cult of personality. The 21st Congress adopted the Seven Year Plan (1959–65) and the 22nd, in 1961, (referred to as an extraordinary Congress), adopted a new programme which looked forward to the foundations of communism being built by 1980. This would mean that per capita output would be higher than in the USA. The Palace of Congresses, in the Kremlin, was ready for the 22nd Congress and permitted 4,800 delegates to attend. It became virtually impossible to hold a debate given the huge number of those present. The 23rd Congress, in 1966, reversed many of Khrushchev's Party reforms (bifurcation of the Party, officials only permitted to stay in office for specific periods), much to the delight of middle-level Party functionaries. The Party Presidium reverted to its former name Politburo, and the head of the Party, First Secretary, was again called General Secretary (this title had been abandoned in 1934 and until his death, Stalin was referred to as merely Secretary). The 24th Congress decided to call Congresses once every five years, in order to adopt a new FYP, among other things. The 25th and 26th Congresses, 1976 and 1981, were very boring for onlookers and epitomised the stagnation of the late Brezhnev era. The 27th Congress, in 1986, was quite different and marked Gorbachev's new style and approach. The 28th Congress, in July 1990, was the last and was characterised by open dissent and confrontation between the various factions within the Party. The Congress demonstrated that the Party was no longer monolithic but was in reality a series of parties within a party. The leadership of the Party supported the attempted coup of August 1991 but afterwards Gorbachev held to the view that the Party could be reformed and become democratic.

Party Control Commission

Such was the level of dissent and dissatisfaction among members, the 9th Party Conference in September 1920 resolved to propose to the next Party Congress that a Party Control Commission (PCC) be elected and be made subordinate only to the Party Congress. The PCC was not to be subject to the Central Committee or its decrees and was to collect complaints from members. These were to be discussed with the Central Committee and at Congresses. Regional Party bodies also had their own PCCs. The reorganisation of the workers' and peasants' inspectorate (Rabkrin), discussed at the 12th Party Congress in April 1923, led to the merging of state and Party control to form the People's Commissariat of Workers' and Peasants' Inspectorate, with the PCC being responsible for Party members. The 17th Party Congress in January 1934 removed the PCC from the People's Commissariat and set up a commission for party control in the Party Central Committee. It was renamed the committee for party control of the Central Committee at the 19th Party Congress in 1952. In November 1962 it became the Party Commission of the Central Committee. In 1962 an attempt was made once again, this time by Khrushchev, to merge state and Party control in one organisation, the committee for Party and state control, subordinate to the Party Central Committee and the USSR Council of Ministers. In 1965 the new leadership split the committee and a separate committee for party control emerged.

Permanent revolution

A theory of revolution developed by Lev Trotsky in an article, 'Results and Perspectives', published in 1906. It takes as its starting point the revolutionary theory of Karl Marx, who posited that revolutions follow a pattern, from slave-owning to feudalism, to capitalism, to socialism and communism. Trotsky maintained that the bourgeois-capitalist phase of development, in an economically backward state such as Russia, could be circumvented or at least reduced in length, if the proletariat took power during the democratic revolution (when it took power). It was possible for the working class to establish hegemony over the weak bourgeoisie during this period, introduce the dictatorship of the proletariat and begin building a socialist society. The success of this revolution, indeed the final victory of socialism, is only possible if a permanent process of revolution takes place in all capitalist countries. This will lead to the formation of a powerful socialist economic union, without which the revolution in Russia cannot be completed. Hence the success of the revolution in Russia is inextricably linked to successful revolutions abroad. This flew in the face of all arguments in favour of socialism in one country, espoused by Stalin after 1924. However, it was not Stalin but Bukharin who first articulated the concept of socialism in one country. Trotsky, Zinoviev and their supporters pilloried Stalin for this concept but Stalin was astute enough to make a distinction between socialism in one country and the final victory of socialism in Russia. The latter, Stalin confirmed, would only take place after the world-wide socialist revolution. There are strands of socialism in one country in Lenin, who placed the interests of Soviet Russia ahead of everything else, including promoting revolution abroad.

Politburo

The Political Bureau (Politburo) was the key decision-making body of the Party and the state (known as the Presidium between 1952 and 1966). According to article 6 of the 1977 Soviet constitution, the Party enjoyed a monopoly of political power. Hence it took precedence over the government, the USSR Council of Ministers. In July 1987 there were 14 full and six candidate (they could participate, speak but not vote) members of the Politburo. It usually met weekly, being chaired by the General Secretary. It was elected anew at each Party Congress by the newly elected Central Committee. In October 1917 the top Bolsheviks formed themselves into a seven-man Political Bureau but it was only at the 8th Party Congress, in March 1919, that it was formally established. It was to deal with all questions which needed urgent attention. Those elected full members were: Kamenev, Krestinsky, Lenin, Stalin and Trotsky, and Bukharin, Zinoviev and Kalinin were made candidate members. It acquired greater significance in that Lenin, as head of Sovnarkom, permitted commissars to appeal to the Politburo. It was normal practice for commissars to send their deputies to Sovnarkom meetings to go themselves to Politburo meetings. All key political, economic, military and foreign affairs questions were debated and decided in the Politburo.

After Lenin's death Stalin, lacking a majority in the Politburo, preferred to debate economic questions in Sovnarkom. The deliberate expansion of the number of delegates attending Party Congresses (in 1925, already over 1,300) and the enlarged Central Committee (in 1925, over 100 members and candidates) meant that decision-making was concentrated in the Politburo and the Secretariat. It gradually became the practice for the Central Committee to discuss (guided, of course, by the Politburo) and the Congress to confirm. The battle over NEP led to the removal of the left and then of the right opposition by 1929–30. Their places were taken predominantly by Stalin's men and a few women. The emergence of Stalin as the vozhd (boss) by 1936 weakened the Politburo and it ceased to perform its previous role of collective discussion and decision-making. Stalin preferred to meet small groups to discuss issues. At the 19th Party Congress, the Politburo was dissolved (it had 11 full and one candidate members) and succeeded by a Presidium of 25 full and 11 candidate members. Some observers see this dramatic increase in the membership as a harbinger of another purge. Until 1957 the Politburo had a majority of members performing governmental and state functions. After the defeat of the Anti-Party Group, Khrushchev removed his opponents and replaced most of them with Party officials. Henceforth Party officials were in the majority in the Politburo. Some non-Party officials always belonged to the Politburo: the Prime Minister, the head of state and the head of the KGB. In 1973 the Minister of Foreign Affairs and the Minister of Defence joined. The First Party Secretary in Ukraine was always a member from Khrushchev onwards. A striking fact about the Politburo was that its members grew older and older under Brezhnev but also non-Russians gradually disappeared. The primacy of the Politburo as a decision-making body was undermined by Gorbachev when he introduced the USSR Congress of People's Deputies into Soviet life. His becoming executive President also weakened the Politburo. The 28th Party Congress, in July 1990, revamped the Politburo, removing all non-Party officials.

For instance, all republican Party leaders became members. Only Gorbachev and Ivashko, the Ukrainian leader, survived from the pre-Congress Politburo. Candidate membership was abolished. The attempted coup of August was the kiss of death for the Politburo as most members had supported the *putsch*.

Propaganda

In Lenin's eyes propaganda was an important aspect of the activities of the Party. In contrast with agitation, which was concerned with the practical aspects of motivating the population, propaganda was a constituent part of education and sought to impregnate people's minds with Marxism-Leninism. A target was to ensure that popular behaviour conformed to the goals set society and that everyone accepted the legitimacy of the Party and the Soviet state. Soviet propaganda was based on the tenets of Marx, Engels and Lenin, the decrees of the Party, the Party programmes and the main pronouncements of the world communist movement (before it splintered in the 1960s; thereafter the pro-Moscow parties). Propaganda attempted to link the Marxist–Leninist Weltanschuung to communist morality, the leading role of the working class and Party, and to motivate everyone to work harder and more effectively and to respect socialist property. It was always hostile towards western imperialist ideology and the policies of western governments. It was most effective in the early years of the revolution but was astutely but cynically used by Stalin to legitimise his policies. Its power to influence the population declined in the 1950s as the population became better educated and had access to foreign ideas. It fought a losing war against western jazz, pop music and western fashions. A counter-culture emerged in the 1970s which challenged accepted norms. Education led to greater individualism and access to foreign languages fuelled the desire to learn more of the outside world. The presentation of the outside world in stark black and white terms was unconvincing as more and more Soviet citizens experienced life outside the Soviet Union or through transistor radios. Traditional Russian values proved more resilient and propaganda faded into the background once glasnost was launched under Gorbachev.

Popular Front

A tactical alliance of communists and all anti-fascists which was adopted in 1935 because of the threat of fascism in Germany and elsewhere. There were Popular Front governments in France but it made little impact on international politics due to the legacy of the hostility of the communists to social democracy and other forces before 1935.

Rada

The word means council or soviet in Ukrainian and Belarusian. The Ukrainian Central Rada was set up on 17 March 1917 in Kiev as the centre of the revolution in Ukraine. A Ukrainian National Congress, which met on 19–21 April 1917, declared the Rada to be the supreme national institution. It represented the interests of the Ukrainian people and was to aim at achieving autonomy for the republic. Most influential in the Rada were the non-Bolshevik social democrats, the Ukrainian SRs and the Ukrainian Socialist Federalists. The Rada and its executive, the general secretariat, chaired by V. Vynnychenko, found little enthusiasm in Petrograd among members of the Provisional Government for its goal of autonomy. After the October Revolution the Rada proclaimed the Ukrainian People's Republic and it declared itself independent on 25 January 1918. It signed the Treaty of Brest-Litovsk in March 1918 with Germany and its allies. The latter's troops had occupied almost all of Ukraine by the beginning of May 1918 and protected the People's Republic from defeat by the Bolsheviks. The German authorities dissolved the Rada and its institutions on 28 April 1918 and replaced it by a regime headed by hetman P. Skoropadsky.

Right opposition

Known also as the right deviation, this was the name given by the Soviet authorities to those groups which opposed the rapid industrialisation and forced collectivisation of agriculture and preferred the continuation of NEP, the retention of the class alliance between workers and peasants (smychka) and industrial development through a 'dynamic equilibrium' of consumers' and investment interests. Opposition to the repressive policy towards the peasants, the constantly rising tempo of industrial expansion, the concentration on the development of heavy industry and the neglect of consumption was widespread and was articulated in the Politburo by Bukharin, A. I. Rykov and M. P. Tomsky. As head of the trade unions, Tomsky spoke for the material interests of workers, Bukharin defended the peasants and Rykov was chairman of Sovnarkom. They were all removed from the Politburo and their posts in 1929–30 and were executed during the purges.

Russian political parties after 1991

Over 100 political parties and movements had been established under communism, but parliamentary elections were not held in Russia until December 1993. President Yeltsin did not attempt to found a presidential party and no new constitution was forthcoming. A consequence of the above was the appearance of highly fragmented parties and movements with narrow support bases and fractious leaderships. This resulted in another phenomenon, the transitory nature of parties, coalitions and alliances. A prime example was the democratic Russia (DemRossiya) bloc. It was established in October 1990 by nine political parties, including the Social Democratic Party of Russia, the Republican Party of Russia, the Democratic Party of Russia, the Free Democratic Party, the Russian Christian Democratic Movement, and the Constitutional Democratic Party, and 18 social movements. The bloc fractured in November 1991 over whether it should support the break-up of the Soviet Union or not. DemRossiya proved incapable of developing into a national, democratic party. Disillusionment with economic reform by nationalists and communists led to the formation of the Civic Union in June 1992 and in October 1992 they established the National Salvation Front. Several parties were set up which have survived to the present. The Agrarian Party of Russia, the communists in the countryside, was set up in February 1992. The Communist Party of the Russian Federation (led by Gennady Zyuganov) was established in February 1992 but only registered in March 1993. The Liberal Democratic Party of Russia (headed by Vladimir Zhirinovsky) was established in 1989. The Duma elections of December 1993 brought many new parties and blocs into existence. Most significant was the Russia's Choice bloc, set up in October 1993 and led by Egor Gaidar. The Women of Russia bloc was registered in October 1993. The Yavlinsky–Boldyrev–Lukin bloc (Yabloko) appeared in October 1993. Discord among the democrats led to the formation of Our Home is Russia, headed by Viktor Chernomyrdin, to contest the second Duma elections in December 1995. Political parties have been slow to develop along western lines and this underlines the personal nature of Russian politics. It is personalities who count not parties.

Russian (RSFSR) Congresses of People's Deputies

I Congress (16 May–22 June 1990)

Some 94 per cent of the deputies had never been RSFSR-level deputies before, but over half had previous experience of local government. Of the 1,059 deputies elected from the 1,068 electoral districts by late April 1990, 78.3 per cent were Russian; 4.4 per cent Ukrainians, 6.2 per cent Tatar, 1.5 per cent Jews, 1 per cent Mordovian, etc.; 86.7 per cent of deputies were members of the CPSU. The scientific and creative intelligentsia, staff from universities, scientific institutes, technical colleges, schools and other educational establishments accounted for 19.5 per cent of deputies; officials from Party, soviet and social organisations made up 24.8 per cent; those from law enforcing agencies accounted for 5.6 per cent and the military 4.3 per cent of deputies; 5.6 per cent were workers and 6 per cent peasants. For the first time there were representatives from various faiths, five deputies in all. Women made up 5.3 per cent of deputies. Some 92.7 per cent of deputies had enjoyed higher education. There were three members of the USSR Academy of Sciences, 65 doctors of science (DSc) and 150 PhDs. Four-fifths of the deputies were between 36 and 55 years of age; only 16 deputies were over 60 years of age. Congress can be regarded as a super parliament and it elected a standing parliament, the Supreme Soviet. This was bicameral, consisting of the Council of the Republic and the Council of Nationalities. Each house had 126 members. Members of Congress and the Supreme Soviet were often called MPs. Deputies to the Council of the Republic were elected from territorial districts and those to the Council of Nationalities from national territorial districts. Some deputies to the Supreme Soviet were changed at each Congress. The aim was to rotate all MPs so that everyone eventually became a member of the Supreme Soviet. Over time radical deputies were gradually eased out and more conservative ones voted in. The Supreme Soviet had a Presidium and in April 1992 there were 32 members. The Presidium had one committee (on granting pardons) and one commission (on Soviet Germans). The Supreme Soviet, in July 1990, confirmed 18 committees and chairmen in office. A committee embraced both houses and each house had its own commissions. Over time deputies formed themselves into groups, factions and associations. In October 1991 there were 27 groups and factions and 14 of these, during the V Congress, formed themselves into political associations, such as the agrarian union, Democratic Russia (DemRossiya), communists for democracy, radical democrats, Russia and sovereignty and equality. Other associations were set up to promote professional and religious interests, such as group of the military, medical workers, union of Russian workers Chernobyl and Sever (north).

Democratic Russia (DemRossiya) seized the initiative and held two preparatory meetings to form a bloc in Congress; over 200 attended but up
to 350 deputies supported the DemRossiya position. The democrats won
a key vote in Congress when Boris Yeltsin was elected chairman of the
Supreme Soviet, making him chairman of the Presidium of the Supreme
Soviet. Yeltsin and the democrats seized the initiative and secured the
passage of the decree on power, which claimed sovereignty for Russia.
It was also claimed that Russian legislation took precedence over Soviet
legislation. This decree stopped short of claiming full sovereignty for
Russia or the independence of Russia, but it can be seen as dealing a
serious, if not fatal, blow to the continued existence of the USSR. One
estimate of the voting blocs in the I Congress states that there were two
equal blocs – the democrats, and the defenders of the old, communist
order – and about 20 per cent of deputies in the middle. Legislative success accrued to those who could win over the middle ground. In order
for legislation to be passed, a majority of elected members was necessary
(not a majority of those present and voting). Amendments to the constitution required a two-thirds vote of all elected deputies.

II Congress (27 November–15 December 1990)

By the time the II Congress convened in November 1990 the political
climate had changed. Gorbachev had abandoned radical economic transformation and had aligned himself with the hardliners who wished to
preserve the Union and make no concessions to republican sovereignty.
The Russian Congress coincided with the USSR Congress and Eduard
Shevardnadze resigned in December 1990 warning of a looming dictatorship. The conservatives were on the offensive and democrats were being
blamed for their inability to halt the continuing decline of the economy
at local and national levels. Democratic forces began to disintegrate and
form mutually critical factions. The conservatives attempted to remove
Yeltsin and demanded a third, extraordinary Congress, which was to
hear and vote on a report by Yeltsin.

III Congress (28 March–5 April 1991)

However, before Congress convened, a national referendum was held
(17 March 1991) which altered the balance of forces. Yeltsin used his
position as chairman of the Presidium of the Russian Supreme Soviet to
propose and have accepted an additional question: were Russian voters
in favour of a popularly elected President of Russia? In the event, about
three-quarters of all Union voters supported the continuation of the
USSR but 71 per cent of Russian voters favoured the introduction of a
popularly elected Russian presidency. Congress convened because of the

communist desire to oblige Yeltsin to report to Congress and thereby force a vote which they hoped would remove him as chairman. Gorbachev, acceding to the wishes of his advisers, who informed him that the pro-Yeltsin forces were planning a coup, ringed the Kremlin on 28 March with tanks and armoured vehicles, the opening day of Congress. This worked in Yeltsin's favour, who again stressed the sovereignty of Russia, and communists, including Aleksandr Rutskoi, supported him. Rutskoi formed the 'communists for democracy' faction. Yeltsin won key votes at Congress, most importantly the constitutional amendments needed to define the powers of the President. The result was a strong presidency and this can be regarded as a victory for the democratic forces and the conservatives who wished to enhance the sovereignty of Russia *vis-à-vis* the USSR.

IV Congress (21–25 May 1991)

Held after the Novo-Ogarevo agreement on a new union was initialled. It debated the office of presidency and the law on the presidential election. Yeltsin secured a crucial victory in that the presidential election was to be held in June rather than later which would have allowed opposition candidates more time to campaign. The campaign began when Congress ended.

V Congress (10–17 July, 28 October–4 November 1991)

Voting behaviour was different from that at the first four Congresses. The bipolar dimension eroded and both right and democrats splintered over the issue of a strong executive presidency. Yeltsin neglected to cultivate his constituency and even threatened, shortly after Congress ended, to disband Congress. He did not attempt to form a coalition to support the government and himself. During the first session of Congress, Yeltsin failed to win support for Ruslan Khasbulatov as speaker. He was opposed by the democrats, especially by those who worked with him as full-time members of parliamentary committees. Congress adjourned after a week and agreed to reconvene in the autumn. The attempted August 1991 coup intervened and fundamentally changed the political situation. In the aftermath of the failed coup Yeltsin's legitimacy and power increased while that of Gorbachev was fatally weakened. The power of the all-Union structures also suffered greatly. Yeltsin took more and more power from the Union, refused to finance the Union government and made any future Union agreement dependent on Russia's consent. Yeltsin's position in the legislature was weakened by the departure of his supporters to key positions on the presidential staff. One of these was Sergei Shakhrai, who was chairman of the committee on legislation. In all, over

100 deputies eventually left to accept positions in the executive. Those who held full-time positions in the Supreme Soviet had to resign from them to do so.

VI Congress (6–21 April 1992)

Liberalisation, spending cuts, tax increases and financial austerity provoked opposition and Khasbulatov sided with the critics, referring to the young economic ministers as 'boys' and 'worms'. Yeltsin claimed that Russia needed a presidential republic because a parliamentary republic would be tantamount to 'suicide'. Yeltsin reached a compromise with Sergei Filatov, Khasbulatov's deputy, according to which Congress was to agree a resolution permitting the government to continue with its economic reforms, but with modifications, and the government was to stay in office. For the first time it was clear that Yeltsin did not command a two-thirds majority in Congress to pass a resolution dissolving it and introducing a new constitution. From now on governmental legislation could be passed only if the President were willing to make concessions.

The balance of power in Congress had changed. Almost 200 deputies had moved from the democratic to the communist wing. Some democrats were pushed out as Khasbulatov consolidated his position. Other deputies were appointed the President's regional representatives or chiefs of administration (governors) or became members of the presidential staff.

VII Congress (1–14 December 1992)

Two phenomena were visible at the last three Congresses: increasing confrontation between the President and parliament, and the growth of the anti-Yeltsin bloc in Congress. Congress pressed for control over the executive and voted consistently against radical economic reform, including the private ownership of land. Support for Yeltsin almost exactly correlated with support for radical reform. Valery Zorkin, head of the Constitutional Court, promoted an agreement between Congress and the President which envisaged a popular referendum to decide the nature of a new constitution. Yeltsin conceded that he could not win approval for Gaidar as Prime Minister and surprised his supporters by accepting Viktor Chernomyrdin as Prime Minister. The latter was viewed as a representative of industrial interests. However, he promised to push on with reform and Yeltsin appointed several pro-reform economic ministers before the law requiring Supreme Soviet confirmation came into effect. Yeltsin got his way on a referendum in April 1993 but the Supreme Soviet was to approve the questions.

VIII Congress (10–13 March 1993)

Congress began with a strong attack on the President by Khasbulatov, who accused him of acting unconstitutionally. Congress voted to amend the constitution, strip Yeltsin of many of his powers and cancel the proposed April referendum. Yeltsin made some concessions. He signed a decree which conferred cabinet rank on Viktor Gerashchenko, head of the Russian Central Bank, and three other officials. This was in accordance with a decision of the Congress but these new ministers were to be subordinate to parliament, in the first instance. The President stalked out of Congress and determined to hold the referendum despite Congress objections. He then addressed the nation, stating that he was introducing a 'special regime'. He bitterly attacked parliament, accusing it of trying to restore the old communist order. Vice-President Aleksandr Rutskoi condemned the President's move and Valery Zorkin and the Constitutional Court declared that he was acting unconstitutionally. However, they had overlooked the fact that the statement only became law when published. It was published a few days later but the offending term was omitted.

IX Congress (26–29 March 1993)

Congress began with a virulent attack on the President by Khasbulatov. Yeltsin conceded that he had made mistakes and appealed for a compromise, but he was rejected contemptuously by Congress. The anti-Yeltsin lobby clearly believed that they had the necessary two-thirds majority to impeach the President. However, they fell 72 votes short of the 689 necessary. When it became known that Khasbulatov had cut a deal with the President abandoning the April referendum and the holding of simultaneous presidential and parliamentary elections in November 1993, it turned on him and one-third of the deputies voted for his removal. The referendum would go ahead, but Congress voted that in order to win, the President needed to obtain 50 per cent of the whole electorate, not 50 per cent of those who voted. The Constitutional Court supported Yeltsin and ruled that the President required only a simple majority on two issues: confidence in him, and economic and social policy; he would need the support of half the electorate in order to convene new presidential and parliamentary elections.

In order to outmanoeuvre parliament Yeltsin convened a constitutional assembly in June. After much hesitation, the constitutional committee of Congress decided to participate. Some 700 representatives adopted a draft constitution on 12 July that envisaged a bicameral legislature and the dissolution of Congress. The Supreme Soviet immediately rejected the draft and declared that Congress was the supreme law-making body and hence would decide on the new constitution.

The Supreme Soviet was very active in July, when the President was away on vacation, and passed many decrees that revised economic policy in order to 'end the division of society'. It also launched investigations into the activities of key presidential advisers, on suspicion of corruption. The President returned from vacation in August and declared that he would deploy all means, including circumventing the constitution, to achieve his aim of new parliamentary elections. The President launched his offensive on 1 September when he temporarily suspended General Aleksandr Rutskoi as Vice-President. Two weeks later he declared he would agree to early presidential elections if parliament agreed to early parliamentary elections. Parliament ignored him. Yeltsin then brought Egor Gaidar back into government as deputy Prime Minister and Minister for the Economy. Predictably the Supreme Soviet rejected this appointment. On 21 September the President dissolved Congress and the Supreme Soviet and set new elections to a bicameral legislature (Federal Assembly consisting of a lower house, Duma, and an upper house, Council of the Federation) on 11–12 December 1993. The Duma would have 450 deputies, half elected on the first-past-the-post principle and the other half on proportional representation. The Council of the Federation would contain representatives from each of Russia's 89 subjects.

The reaction of the Supreme Soviet was instantaneous. During an all-night session, chaired by Khasbulatov, it declared the presidential decree null and void. Rutskoi was sworn in as President. He dismissed Yeltsin and the 'power' ministers, Grachev (Defence), Golushko (Security) and Erin (Internal Affairs). Russia now had two Presidents, two Ministers of Defence, of Security and of Internal Affairs. This was dual power with a vengeance.

The political conflict developed into an armed conflict on 3 October after Moscow police failed to control a demonstration near the White House. Demonstrators then marched towards Ostankino, the TV centre. Rutskoi, Khasbulatov and others barricaded themselves in the White House. The army, after initially hesitating, began to shell the White House on 4 October. By the evening it was all over. The President moved quickly to consolidate his position. He banned many political parties and newspapers which had supported parliament, and the Constitutional Court was suspended, with Zorkin being forced to resign. A pro-Yeltsin lawyer was named Procurator General. A new draft constitution was to be put to a national referendum on 12 December.

The Congress period was characterised by a gradual confrontation between the legislature (Congress and Supreme Soviet) and the executive (government and President). A division of powers was gradually emerging. Parliament did not compromise in its aim of destroying the President and his concessions were conceived as signs of weakness. Eventually the confrontation between the legislature and the executive led to the demise of the legislature.

Secretariat of the Party Central Committee

The Secretariat was the brain of the Party and, according to article 38 of the Party statute, was responsible for the day-to-day work of the Party Central Committee. Its chief functions were the selection of cadres and ensuring the implementation of Party decrees and instructions. The Secretariat had around 20 departments (propaganda, agriculture, science, culture, economy, international relations, etc.), which paralleled the Soviet ministries which they supervised. The head of a department was the secretary and the head of all departments the General Secretary. It was normal for the more senior secretaries of the Central Committee (who supervised a number of departments) to be elected to the Party Politburo. In 1987 there were 11 secretaries, headed by Gorbachev. It was the practice for the 'second' (an unofficial title) secretary to chair meetings of the Secretariat, at that time Egor Ligachev. At the 19th Party Conference in June 1988 Gorbachev removed the Party from the management of the economy. This crucial decision weakened the Secretariat, which had now to concentrate on political matters. Also Gorbachev did not realise that the Party was the glue which kept the Soviet system together and thereby hastened not only the demise of the Party but also the Soviet state. The Secretariat was set up at the 8th Party Congress in 1919, along with the Orgburo and the Politburo. The head of the Secretariat was to be a member of the Central Committee and also a member of the Orgburo. He had five secretaries and many other Party functionaries to carry out the Secretariat's duties. Its first task was to set up departments and by December 1919 there were eight departments with about 80 staff, including agit-prop, personnel, organisational and finance departments. The Secretariat quickly established itself as superior to the Orgburo, which restricted itself to organisational questions. The Secretariat set out to establish contact with all regional Party committees but this was not achieved by the end of the Civil War. Things changed in April 1922 when Stalin was made head of the three-person Secretariat. He was also a member of the Orgburo and the Politburo. Stalin developed a card index system which permitted him to influence the selection of cadres and which gave Lenin pause for reflection in his Testament. Lenin died in 1924, before he could remove Stalin from the centre of the Party bureaucracy. Stalin skilfully used the Secretariat to build up a support base, which contributed to his success over his rivals for the leadership of the Soviet Union. The Secretariat was the instrument which permitted the transformation of the Party from a revolutionary one to a ruling one and eventually to a state Party. The Party nomenklatura was conceived and built up in the Secretariat, as was the state nomenklatura. The Party grew rapidly, exceeding one million members (full and candidate) in the 1920s and then over two million in the 1930s. The Secretariat masterminded this advance. Its role increased as the Party swelled and Central Committee plenums and Party Congresses became larger and larger. The 17th Party Congress decreed in the new statutes that Congresses were to convene every three years and Central Committee plenums every four months. In 1952 this was amended to every four years and six months. This underlined the importance of the Secretariat. Despite the increased workload the Secretariat remained small. In 1934 there were only three Secretaries, Stalin (who lost his title of General Secretary and was referred to as a Secretary), Zhdanov and Kirov. In March 1953 there were only five Secretaries. Khrushchev's victory over the Anti-Party Group in June 1957 contributed to the rapid expansion of the Secretariat and the number of departments grew from the eight, laid down in 1934, to over double this number. This underlined the fact that under Khrushchev the Party took precedence over the government and gradually became responsible for supervising the economy. This situation remained until 1988, when the Party was removed from operative control of the economy. The agenda of the Politburo was drafted in the Secretariat and it provided situation papers. It also carried out soundings so that a consensus could be reached before a policy was discussed in the Politburo. If no consensus could be attained, the matter did not go forward. The Secretariat quickly lost influence after 1988 and by 1991 it was a skeleton of its former self.

Socialism in one country

Lenin envisaged that the October Revolution would be the spark which ignited the world socialist revolution. He waited impatiently for the message that the German proletariat had taken over Berlin but this never happened. World capitalism was seen as a chain with Russia as its weakest link. However, Lenin opposed the left communists who wanted to come to the aid of foreign comrades in their pursuit of revolution. Instead he advocated a separate peace with Germany, irrespective of the price to be paid. He believed that securing Soviet power was the main prerogative and it must never be put at risk. Victory in the Civil War and the recovery of NEP nourished the belief that Soviet Russia could survive without a world-wide revolution. The concept of socialism in one country stems from Bukharin but it was Stalin who turned it into policy. In the mid-1920s he proclaimed the construction of socialism in one country, quoting Lenin and Bukharin. He was virulently opposed by Trotsky and the left opposition, who regarded the concept as nonsense. However, they were incapable of coming up with a viable alternative. The polemics over socialism in one country during the 1920s were, first and foremost, about the succession to Lenin. Stalin understood how to nourish the pride of Soviet workers by claiming that it was possible to build socialism at home. The claim could thus be made that Soviet Russia was the most advanced country socially in the world – an intoxicating thought. However, Stalin was careful enough not to claim that socialism could be secure in Soviet Russia. This would only occur when the final victory of socialism world-wide became reality. The concept of socialism in one country made it possible to reconsider Russian history and culture, to introduce Soviet patriotism and reach a reconciliation with the Russian Orthodox Church. However, it also led to some conclusions which exacted great sacrifices from the Soviet population – such as Stalin's law that claimed that as socialism strengthens so opposition to it intensifies. Forced collectivisation and the cultural revolution of the early 1930s could be justified by the above claim.

Socialist camp

The expression originated at the beginning of the Cold War and came to mean all the states and communist parties which were opposed to the USA and its 'imperialist camp'. Andrei Zhdanov, at the constituent congress of the Cominform in 1947, divided the world into two camps: the socialist, peace-loving camp, and the capitalist, aggressive camp. He placed some countries outside both camps, such as India and Indonesia, and they became part of the non-aligned movement. The speech was a reaction to the proclamation of the Truman Doctrine and the Marshall Plan. The conflict between socialism and capitalism had developed into a worldwide confrontation with Washington, the leader of the capitalist enemy. The task for the Soviet Union and the new 'democracies' (in eastern and south-eastern Europe) was to unite all anti-imperialist and peace-loving forces in the spirit of proletarian internationalism against US imperialism and its allies. Countries which made up the socialist camp were the Soviet Union, Poland, the GDR, Czechoslovakia, Romania, Bulgaria, Yugoslavia, Albania, China, the People's Democratic Republic of (North) Korea, North Vietnam, Mongolia and Cuba and all pro-Moscow communist parties. In the 1970s these were joined by the ex-Portuguese colonies in Africa, the People's Democratic Republic of (South) Yemen, Ethiopia, Congo (Brazzaville) and others. The expression communist Third World was coined to describe these. There was never any time when all communist states and parties belonged to one organisation or recognised one centre. The Comintern expelled Yugoslavia in 1948. Comecon (1949) and the Warsaw Pact (1955) were regional associations dominated by the

Soviet Union. The integration of the socialist camp always failed because of ideological, political and economic differences. The sovietisation of eastern and south-eastern Europe led to the conflict with Yugoslavia in 1948 and Moscow kept a tight rein on the region until 1953. Khrushchev adopted a different stance and attempted to achieve two goals: increase the autonomy of the people's democracies and thereby make them more loyal to Moscow and, in so doing, make the Soviet model more attractive to other states, especially in the Third World. He improved relations with China (1954) and Yugoslavia (1955–56), but his attack on Stalin at the 20th Party Congress in 1956 undermined the legitimacy of communist leaders in eastern and south-eastern Europe. An early warning was the uprising in the GDR on 17 June 1953, but the Hungarian uprising (now called revolution) in 1956 was much more serious. There were clearly limits to the autonomy these states could be afforded as they all wished to develop their own socialist systems. These tensions surfaced at the Moscow conference of 12 ruling communist parties in November 1957. The resolutions accepted that there could, within limits, be different roads to socialism but all parties were called upon to fight revisionism and dogmatism. The Soviet Union, at the instigation of the Chinese, was declared the leader of the socialist camp. However, Yugoslavia declined to sign this declaration and serious Sino-Soviet tensions surfaced in and after 1958. The socialist camp was fractured down the middle as China and the Soviet Union fought for world dominance. Armed conflict between China and the Soviet Union led to a break in relations in 1963–64. The Soviet-led invasion of Czechoslovakia in August 1968 proved a fatal blow to the solidarity of the socialist camp. It gave rise to the Brezhnev doctrine whereby the Soviet Union claimed the right to intervene in any socialist state in the Warsaw Pact in which it believed socialism to be under threat. At the Congress of Communist and Workers' Parties in 1969 it was no longer possible for Moscow to gain support from all participants for its policy towards China and Czechoslovakia. West European communist parties developed into Eurocommunist parties which rejected the Brezhnev doctrine and were critical of aspects of Soviet policy. Under Brezhnev the socialist camp disintegrated as Moscow dropped class interests as the basis of its foreign policy and espoused universal human values, interdependence of all states and the renunciation of force in international relations. In eastern and south-eastern Europe ruling parties were afforded autonomy and the Soviet army was not to intervene militarily in support of these parties. This undermined the legitimacy of these regimes and, coupled with the inability of the Soviet Union to fulfil its economic commitments, they collapsed one after the other. When Comecon and the Warsaw Pact were dissolved in mid-1991 the socialist camp passed into history. The Soviet Union and China achieved a rapprochement under Gorbachev by agreeing not to interfere in one another's domestic affairs. The ideological war between the Communist Party of China and the CPSU was over.

Soviet of Nationalities

One of the chambers of the USSR Supreme Soviet, established in 1936 (the other was the Soviet of the Union). The number of deputies in the Soviet of Nationalities was laid down by the 1936 constitution according to whether the territorial-administrative entity was a Union republic, autonomous republic, and so on. Those nationalities which had no territorial-administrative entity, such as the Germans, the Crimean Tatars or the Poles, were not represented. The Soviet of Nationalities appeared in the 1924 USSR constitution and emerged from the RSFSR People's Commissariat for Nationalities, which functioned from 1917 to 1923. From 1920 the People's Commissar convened this consultative body, consisting of representatives of non-Russian nationalities. In the 1924 constitution each Union republic sent five representatives, the Autonomous Republics of Ajaria and Abkhazia and the autonomous oblasts sent one each. A Presidium of the Soviet of Nationalities functioned between 1924 and 1936 as a constitutional organ, permanently in session, and made many attempts to articulate non-Russian interests. It disappeared in the 1936 constitution. In the 1936 constitution the Soviet of Nationalities was placed on an equal footing with the Soviet of the Union and its deputies directly elected. Between 1957 and 1966 an economic commission, permanently in session, of the Soviet of Nationalities existed to represent the interests of the Union republics and sometimes did just this. According to the 1977 Soviet constitution each Union republic was to send 32 deputies, the autonomous republics 11 each, autonomous oblasts five each and the autonomous okrugs one each to the Soviet of Nationalities. The Soviet of Nationalities was found wanting, after 1985, when confronted with finding a solution to the increasing number of ethnic conflicts in the Soviet Union.

Soviet of the Union

The formation of the Soviet Union in 1922 resulted in a new constitution (1924) which declared the USSR Congress and its USSR Central Executive Committee (TsIK) to be the supreme legislative body. The TsIK was bicameral, consisting of a Soviet of the Union and a Soviet of Nationalities. Conflict in the TsIK was to be resolved by an arbitration commission, a joint session of both houses or by the Congress of Soviets. The 371 members of the Soviet of the Union were to be elected by the Congress of Soviets from the representatives of the republics according to the size of the republic. The Soviet of the Union elected a seven-person presidium

and together with the Soviet of Nationalities elected a 21-person presidium of the TsIK (the members of the presidium of the Soviet of the
Union entered *ex officio* the presidium of the TsIK). The 1936 constitution retained the bicameral arrangement for the newly created USSR
Supreme Soviet; thus there was a Soviet of the Union and a Soviet of
Nationalities. Deputies to the Soviet of the Union were now to represent
constituencies, each consisting of 300,000 citizens. Both chambers enjoyed
equal rights. Each elected a chair and two deputies and in joint sessions
the chair rotated between the two houses. They elected a 41-person presidium of the USSR Supreme Soviet. Each chamber set up a mandate
commission (concerned with checking deputies' credentials) and as many
other commissions as was judged necessary. The 1977 constitution made
no changes to this legislative system but decided that the two houses
should have the same number of deputies. The rise in population had
led to the Soviet of the Union expanding while the Soviet of Nationalities had remained constant. By the 1980s there were about 750 deputies
in each chamber. These arrangements remained after the constitutional
changes of 1988 and 1990, which provided for the election of a USSR Congress of Deputies and it in turn elected a USSR Supreme Soviet consisting of two chambers, a Soviet of the Union and a Soviet of Nationalities.

Soviets

Literally council, they were the short form of the workers', soldiers' and
peasants' councils which sprang up in 1917. They first emerged spontaneously during the 1905–7 Revolution and thereafter all soviets based
themselves on this form. Soviets became influential, first and foremost,
in Petrograd among workers, and soldiers in the garrisons. Soviets were
also set up in middle-class areas of Petrograd and their representatives
were elected to the Petrograd soviet. The Petrograd soviet of workers'
deputies and the soviet of soldiers' deputies merged very soon, but in
other cities, such as Moscow, this did not happen until after the October
Revolution. The 1st Congress of Soviets convened in Petrograd in July
1917 and it elected an All-Russian Central Executive Committee (TsIK).
Lenin viewed the soviets, in the April Theses, as the core of a new proletarian, democratic state, one in which democracy from below would
take over and run things. When the Bolsheviks secured a majority in
the Petrograd and Moscow soviets in September 1917, the possibility of
an armed uprising became a reality. The Bolshevik seizure of power
was guided by the Military Revolutionary Committee of the Petrograd
soviet, chaired by Trotsky. The date chosen for the uprising (Lenin never
referred to it as a revolution) was 25 October, the day the 2nd Congress
of Soviets was to convene. When the Bolsheviks took power they handed
it to the Congress of Soviets and hence it became a Soviet takeover. The

other main socialist parties, the SRs and Mensheviks, had no desire to take power, the former because when the Constituent Assembly convened it would be the largest party since it represented the peasants, 80 per cent of the population. The Mensheviks regarded the taking of power by the workers in an underdeveloped industrial state such as Russia as nonsense. Lenin and Trotsky pre-empted the Constituent Assembly elections since they knew that the Bolsheviks would be a minority there. The October Revolution was made in the name of the soviets but power rested with the Bolsheviks. The Congress of Soviets also elected a government, Sovnarkom, and a Central Executive Committee (TsIK), which was to act in the name of the soviets between Congresses. There were three institutions which wielded power, the TsIK, Sovnarkom and the Communist Party.

The dream of a Soviet republic soon faded as soviets sought to gain control over their own territory and ignore Moscow. In the villages, the peasants kept to their traditional assembly, the skhod, and ignored the soviets. The first Soviet constitution of July 1918 declared that supreme state power rested with the soviets and failed to mention the Communist Party. Soviets were to be elected in villages and cities and these were the basic organisations of proletarian self-administration. Congresses were to be held in regions, guberniyas and oblasts and these elected their own executive committees. At the centre was an All-Russian Congress and its TsIK. Sovnarkom was subordinate to it. The division of responsibilities between soviets and the government was never clarified – neither was the competence of the Party.

The Civil War fundamentally altered the situation and the government began to concentrate power in its own hands and overrule local or regional agencies. Special commissions were set up to cope with new problems as they arose and they rode roughshod over local authorities. Since many soviets were dominated by SRs and Mensheviks, the Bolsheviks took them over by placing their own members in the executive committees. After the Civil War the soviets were recreated in many areas and it was the centre which organised them. The Congress of Soviets remained but gradually the TsIK took precedence and then the presidium of the TsIK. Constitutionally the government was subordinate to the TsIK but by 1921 the roles, in practice, had been reversed. The centre of decision-making passed to the Politburo of the Party. This situation prevailed until the 1936 constitution, which abolished elections to the Congress and replaced it with a bicameral USSR Supreme Soviet, consisting of the Soviet of the Union and the Soviet of Nationalities.

Khrushchev moved from the dictatorship of the proletariat to an all-people's state. This was toned down in the early Brezhnev years but found expression in article 2 of the 1977 constitution. This stated that all power rested with the people and they exercised this through the soviets of people's deputies, which formed the political base of the Soviet Union. At the 19th Party Conference, in June 1988, Gorbachev made clear that he envisaged a return to the original form of the Congress of Soviets. In March 1989 a 2,250-member USSR Congress of People's Deputies was elected and it, in turn, elected a bicameral USSR Supreme Soviet. In 1990 all republics elected their own Supreme Soviets, only the RSFSR electing a Congress and a Supreme Soviet. These institutions quickly became parliaments and proved much too radical for the Soviet leadership. Those in the Baltic republics voted for independence and the Russian parliament declared that its laws took precedence over Soviet laws. Hence soviets moved full circle in the Soviet Union, from democratic institutions in 1917, to emasculated bodies later, and finally to genuine parliaments under Gorbachev. The irony was that the last soviets helped to weaken central power and hastened the collapse of the Soviet Union. After 1991 in Russia soviets were renamed dumas, the pre-1917 term.

Sovnarkom

The Council of People's Commissars; the government of Soviet Russia and later of the USSR. It was appointed by the 2nd Congress of Soviets in October 1917 and was to be subordinate to it, but soon proved stronger. All the members of the first Sovnarkom were Bolsheviks and picked by Lenin himself. There was a brief coalition government between December 1917 and March 1918 when some SRs joined. After March 1918, only Bolsheviks were commissars or ministers (under Gorbachev there was one minister who was not a member of the Party). It was renamed the USSR Council of Ministers in April 1946. According to the 1936 and 1977 constitutions, the government was to resign at the end of each legislative period, but this was a mere formality. These constitutions also laid down that each republic and autonomous republic (ASSR) was to elect its own government or Council of Ministers to underline the federal nature of the Soviet state, but in reality the USSR Council of Ministers dominated. Sovnarkom was the dominant body in the state when Lenin was well, but it was superseded by the Politburo in 1922.

Stalinism

The term was coined in the Soviet Union in the 1930s at the height of the cult of the personality to place the political achievements of Stalin on a par with those of Lenin. It disappeared in the USSR after Khrushchev's attack on Stalin at the 20th Party Congress in 1956 but reappeared under Gorbachev in a purely negative sense. The term was used by western scholars from the 1940s onwards to describe the totalitarian aspirations of Stalin and is also quite negative. It embraces the theory and practice of a Marxist–Leninist regime which practised terror as well as analysing the form of that dictatorship. Fundamental aspects of Stalinism were the elevation of Leninism to a position where it presented the Marxism of the nineteenth century and, taking into consideration the developments of state monopoly capitalism and imperialism, developed it in the twentieth century to a new level, called Marxism–Leninism. A popular slogan was: Leninism is the Marxism of the twentieth century. Those who rejected this claim and instead based their arguments on Marxist texts were dismissed as dogmatists.

Whereas Marx claimed that his theory was universally relevant, Stalinism is associated with one country, the Soviet Union, and the development of socialism there. This is summed up in the concept of socialism in one country. This involved rapid industrialisation, forced collectivisation and the cultural revolution of the 1930s. Stalinism diverges from Marxism in its analysis of the state. Whereas Marx expected the state to decline gradually as socialism was built, Stalinism rejected this and claimed that the state had to become stronger as socialism was approached. This was because the Soviet Union was surrounded by hostile capitalist powers all eager to destroy it. Another trait of Stalinism was the claim that the struggle intensified as socialism was being constructed. It reached a crescendo when socialism had proved victorious in the Soviet Union. This legitimised the murderous purges and show trials of the 1930s. Stalinism signifies the use of force to implement polices and the use of mass terror to cow the population. Millions were sent to the gulag and over 50 nations were deported to the east. Stalin did not permit any challenge to his authority or his policies and to quote Stalin was to be guaranteed success.

From 1936 Stalin established a personal dictatorship and relegated the collective leadership of the Party to history. Central Committee plenums and Party Congresses did not take place according to Party statutes. Stalin was the first Party leader to use terror against the Party leadership. He underestimated the threat of German national socialism and his non-aggression pact with Hitler almost destroyed the Soviet Union. Stalin's expulsion of Tito and Yugoslavia from the Cominform in 1948 was the first split in the socialist camp and his lack of respect for Mao Zedong when he visited Moscow in 1950 stored up trouble for the future.

There have been many attempts to define Stalinism. Two examples are given below. This is by Roi Medvedev, a Russian who wrote much about the origins of Stalinism and was a dissident in the Soviet Union.

(i) Stalinism was the cult of the state and the worship of rank, the irresponsibility of those who held power and the population's lack of rights, the hierarchy of privileges and the canonisation of hypocrisy, the barrack (only orders) system of social and intellectual life, the suppression of the individual and the destruction of independent thought, the environment of suspicion and terror, the atomisation of people and notorious 'vigilance', the uncontrolled violence and the legalised cruelty.

From R. A. Medvedev, *On Socialist Democracy* (Basingstoke, Macmillan, 1975), p. 553. This definition is by Graeme Gill, an Australian political scientist:

  (i) A formally highly centralised, directive economic system characterised by mass mobilisation and an overriding priority on the development of heavy industry.
 (ii) A social system initially characterised by significant fluidity, most particularly in the form of high levels of social mobility which brings the former lower classes into positions of power and privilege; subsequent consolidation of the social structure results in the dominance of rank, status and hierarchy.
(iii) A cultural and intellectual sphere in which all elements are meant to serve the political aims laid down by the leadership and where all areas of culture and intellectual production are politically monitored.
 (iv) A personal dictatorship resting upon the use of terror as an instrument of rule and in which the political institutions are little more than the instrument of the dictator.
  (v) All spheres of life are politicised, hence, within the scope of state intervention.
 (vi) The centralisation of authority is paralleled by a significant measure of weakness of continuing central control, resulting in a system which, in practice, is in its daily operations loosely controlled and structured.
(vii) The initial revolutionary ethos is superseded by a profoundly conservative, status quo orientation.

From Graeme Gill, *Stalinism* (Basingstoke, Macmillan, 1975), pp. 57–8.

Trotskyism

A negative term in the Soviet Union to denigrate the views of Lev Trotsky and to demonstrate that his 'left' views were inimical to those of the Party. It arose during his conflict with Stalin over who should succeed Lenin as leader of the Party and Soviet Russia. Trotsky had views on the proletarian revolution, support for the international proletariat and the structure of the Party and the Soviet state which collided head on with those of Stalin and others. Stalin and his supporters coined expressions such as the Trotskyist opposition to vilify Trotsky and his views during the period 1924–27. Trotsky was expelled from the Party on 14 November 1927 on the grounds that he had revised Leninism, had denied the possibility of constructing socialism in one country (the Soviet Union), was undermining the alliance of the working class and the peasantry, and had been involved in factional activity within the Party. His views were labelled left deviation.

Trotsky's views found expression in the 4th (Trotskyist) International, which was founded in 1938 and was consistently attacked by the Soviet Party. The core of Trotskyism is the theory of permanent revolution, which maintains that in countries such as Russia where capitalism is under-developed, it is possible to cut short that phase and move to socialism after a successful workers' revolution. The building of socialism can begin after the imposition of the dictatorship of the proletariat and be completed after the final victory of socialism world-wide. Lenin adopted Trotsky's concept of permanent revolution in his April Theses (April 1917) when he claimed that the specific feature of the present situation in Russia was that it represented a 'transition from the first stage of the revolution' to the 'second stage, which must place power in the hands of the proletariat and poor strata of the peasantry'. This revised Trotsky's view that the peasantry was a reactionary class. When Stalin began to argue in 1924 that it was possible to construct socialism in one country, he clashed violently with Trotsky and his supporters. The latter maintained that socialism could only succeed in Russia after a victorious revolution in western Europe, because Russia needed aid from western industrial states to build up its own economy. Another important aspect of Trotskyism was its critique of the Soviet Party and state. In 1923 he began attacking the increasing alienation of Party officials from the rank and file members. This was the consequence of more and more decisions being taken at the centre with little consultation with the base. The growth of the Party and state bureaucracy was to him a deformation of the Soviet revolution. He demanded the return of intra-Party democracy and the replacment of state functionaries by workers.

After expulsion from the Soviet Union in 1929 (together with his archive) Trotsky had plenty of time to brood on the essence of Stalin-ism. He came to the conclusion that the revolution in Russia from cap-italism to socialism had come to a halt somewhere and was stuck there. The Party and state apparatuses were responsible for this catastrophic state of affairs. This was called the theory of transitional society. Soviet bureaucracy had become a ruling stratum by taking over the administrat-ive apparatus and nullifying workers' control and was using Soviet insti-tutions to carry out its interests. The only way to overcome this state of affairs was another political revolution which would cast the bureaucratic dictatorship aside and restore the socialist revolution. Trotsky expected that a German invasion of the Soviet Union would lead to the collapse of the Stalinist system but this did not come about. Trotsky did not live to see it, since one of Stalin's agents had put an ice pick into his skull in Mexico in 1940. The virulence of the Soviet attacks on Trotsky and Trotskyism hinted at a realisation that Soviet workers would find his views attractive. It is interesting that while many were rehabilitated by the Party under Gorbachev, it could never bring itself to rehabilitate Trotsky and Trotskyism.

Union of Sovereign States

A USSR Congress of People's Deputies was convened immediately after the failure of the August 1991 attempted coup and it resolved to speed up the transition of the Soviet Union to a Union of Sovereign States. The new Union was to be based on the principles of independence and territorial integrity, human and civil rights, social justice and democracy. The desire of the states to be recognised in international law and to join the UN was to be supported. The USSR State Council formally recognised the independence of Estonia, Latvia and Lithuania and supported their application to join the UN on 6 September 1991. Yeltsin and other republican leaders in the USSR State Council agreed that the new Union should be a confederation on 14 November. However, on 25 November Yeltsin and Shushkevich (Belarus) refused to initial the treaty on the confederation which had been negotiated, on 25 November. When Yeltsin, Shushkevich and Kravchuk (Ukraine) met in the Belovezh Forest, outside Minsk, on 7–8 December 1991 and agreed to leave the Soviet Union and establish the Commonwealth of Independent States, the Union treaty became a dead letter.

United Front

A tactical alliance between communists and social democrats brought about by the threat of fascism. The united front from above was with the social democratic leadership; the united front from below was with the social democrat rank and file, over the heads of their leaders. The policy had little impact.

USSR Congress of People's Deputies

In December 1988 both houses of the USSR Supreme Soviet passed an amendment to the 1977 Soviet constitution by which a USSR Congress of People's Deputies would become the supreme organ of Soviet power. It was to be elected for five years and to meet normally once a year. The republics of the Union altered their own constitutions accordingly. There were 2,250 deputies, one-third to be elected in territorial constituencies, one-third in national-territorial constituencies, and one-third of the seats were reserved for social organisations such as the CPSU (which had 100 seats), the trade unions, the Komsomol, etc. Hence two-thirds were elected directly and one-third indirectly. The Congress was to decide amendments to the constitution, could hold referenda, adopt perspective plans, take the main decisions in domestic and foreign policy, elect a bicameral USSR Supreme Soviet, with 271 deputies in each to serve as a standing parliament and elect a chair (or speaker) who would be the Soviet head of state. Elections were held in March 1989 and resulted in many leading communist candidates being defeated. At the first session on 25 May–9 June 1989, Gorbachev was elected chair. The debates, due to glasnost, were unlike anything since the 1920s and were carried live on TV. So popular were they that labour productivity dropped by about 20 per cent as workers turned up bleary-eyed for their shift thanks to the Russian habit of debating through the night. Factions were formed and these contributed to the ending of the power monopoly of the CPSU. Two factors undermined the authority of the Congress: the increasing power of the Soviet President Gorbachev (from 1990) and the centrifugal flow of power from the centre to the republics and regions as they claimed sovereignty. There was always tension between the Congress and the President and the latter was not able to impose an austerity programme to restore economic equilibrium against the wishes of the Congress, which became populist and passed many decrees increasing wages, pensions, etc. The election of Congresses of People's Deputies in the Union republics in 1990 led to a war of laws, with the republican Congresses ruling that their laws took precedence over USSR laws. The most dangerous competitor for the USSR Congress was the RSFSR Congress, which elected Boris Yeltsin its chair. The chair of the USSR Congress during the attempted coup of 18–21 August 1991 was Anatoly Lukyanov, one of the plotters. On 5 September 1991 the USSR Congress voted for an amendment to the USSR constitution, the law on the organs of state power and the government of the USSR during the transition period. This law did not envisage any role for the USSR Congress.

USSR Council of Ministers

The Soviet government was responsible for the administration of the country and hence performed executive functions. All key political, economic, social and security decisions were taken in the Party Politburo and the government was charged with implementing them (the chair of the USSR Council of Ministers or Prime Minister was always a full member of the Politburo). The government could promulgate its own decrees, instructions and regulations, sometimes in conjunction with the Party Central Committee. The USSR Council of Ministers was elected at a joint session of the two houses (Soviet of the Union and Soviet of Nationalities) of the USSR Supreme Soviet, immediately after the latter's election. When a legislative period ended (every five years), the government resigned and was reappointed by the new parliament. The USSR government consisted of the chair, first deputy chair, deputy chairs and ministers and chairs of USSR state committees. The full government normally had over 100 members. Each republic and autonomous republic had is own Council of Ministers. The USSR Council of Ministers began as the Council (Soviet) of People's Commissars (Sovnarkom), established in October 1917, as a provisional government. After the dissolution of the Constituent Assembly in January 1918 it dropped the appellation provisional. Sovnarkom was subordinate to the Congress of People's Deputies and its Central Executive Committee (TsIK). When the USSR was established in 1922 there was a USSR Sovnarkom and one in each republic and autonomous republic. In the 1936 constitution Sovnarkom was made subordinate to the USSR Supreme Soviet. The expansion of the number of commissariats led to the formation of an inner cabinet, and after 1949 a Presidium. The Presidium was first mentioned in the 1977 constitution and became the key economic decision-making body.

USSR Supreme Soviet

This was established by the 1936 constitution as the supreme organ of state power. It was elected by general, equal, direct and secret voting and replaced the USSR Congress of People's Deputies, which had been elected indirectly (by local and regional soviets and according to different weights – urban voters elected more deputies per head of population than rural – with certain social groups, such as priests, excluded from the franchise). The Central Executive Committee of the Soviet Union (TsIK) also disappeared. The USSR Supreme Soviet was to be elected for four years and to convene twice a year. It was bicameral, consisting of the Soviet of the Union and the Soviet of Nationalities. They elected, in joint session, the chair of the Presidium and he acted as head of state. It was responsible for everything not expressly the responsibility of Sovnarkom (in 1946 renamed the USSR Council of Ministers) and the various people's commissariats (in 1946 renamed ministries). The USSR Supreme Soviet drafted and promulgated legislation, it passed the FYPs and the budget, elected judges (for five years) to the USSR Supreme Court, the USSR Public Prosecutor (for seven years) and appointed the USSR government. In all Union republics and autonomous republics the Supreme Soviets replaced the Congress of People's Deputies and their Central Executive Committees. All these Supreme Soviets were unicameral. The USSR Supreme Soviet was in many ways similar to a western parliament but there were important differences: the leading role of the Communist Party was constitutionally laid down; the great importance of the Presidium of the Supreme Soviet; the lack of clarity about the laws it could pass; the short sessions of the Supreme Soviet, which excluded meaningful debate on the legislation under review. During the 1950s, 1960s and 1970s the USSR Supreme Soviet normally met for only a week a year. The turnover of deputies meant that there was little time to accumulate experience. About half the deputies were female. The 1st session in 1937 brought together 1,100 deputies and this rose to over 1,500 by the beginning of the 1980s. About three-quarters of deputies were members of the Party or communists and this proportion remained constant. The USSR Congress of People's Deputies, elected in March 1989, elected from its members a USSR Supreme Soviet, consisting of 542 deputies, half in the Soviet of the Union and half in the Soviet of Nationalities. This standing parliament was to be in session for three or four months a year.

Workers' and Peasants' Inspectorate (Rabkrin)

The name of a people's commissariat between 1920 and 1934. It was set up by the Soviet Central Executive Committee as part of the reorganisation of the People's Commissariat for State Control, which had been set up in December 1917. Rabkrin was charged with combating the increasing bureaucratisation and ensuring that state decrees were implemented. In 1923 Lenin severely criticised Rabkrin and merged it with the Central Control Commission of the Communist Party. Rabkrin was responsible for supervision of the Party and the state and economic apparatuses. However, during the inner Party debates in the 1920s and the purges of 1925, 1929–30 and 1933, the Central Control Commission played a more important role. Both were charged with supervising the implementation of the first Five Year Plan (1928–32). The 17th Party Congress in 1934 dissolved Rabkrin and the Central Control Commission, and replaced them with a commission for Party control of the Party CC and a commission for state control of Sovnarkom.

Law

Civil rights

Civil rights and guarantees were included in all Soviet constitutions (except the Union constitution of 1924). Rights included freedom of conscience, opinion, associations and coalitions. However, they were not perceived as universal human rights which could be upheld if the state encroached on them, but rather as ways of securing the loyalty of the citizen to the Soviet state. In the Soviet Russian constitution of 1918, civil rights were restricted to the workers and poor peasants. Hence rights were class-based. This disappeared in the 1936 constitution as it was claimed that socialism had been essentially achieved and there were no antagonistic classes any more. The franchise was extended to the whole population. The 1977 constitution expanded the rights of the Soviet citizen and whereas these came at the end of the 1936 constitution they were now in second place. Basic rights included equality of the sexes, nationalities, education, religion and so on. There were socio-economic rights (work, leisure, health, accommodation, culture, etc.), political rights (freedom of speech, press and association, including the right to demonstrate), the inviolability of the home, letter and telephone communication, and freedom of conscience. However, the goal of all these rights was the strengthening and development of the socialist order and these rights were linked with a list of social duties. By ratifying both UN conventions on human rights (1973) and signing the Helsinki Final Act (1975) the Soviet Union committed itself to a wider definition of human rights than hitherto and a consequence of this was that human and civil rights groups sprang up in the Soviet Union requesting that the USSR meet its international obligations.

Constitution (Soviet)

Lenin, in his April Theses (April 1917), envisaged that the Provisional Government would be replaced by a Soviet republic and hence proclaimed all power to the soviets. Power was handed to the 2nd Congress of Soviets in October 1917 and soviets were to be vehicle of the dictatorship of the proletariat and the poor strata of the peasantry. The soviets would be elected at all levels and at the centre would be a Congress of Soviets and its Central Executive Committee (TsIK). The government, Sovnarkom, was to be elected by the Congress of Soviets and to be subordinate to it. This amounted to a commune state or one which was administered by the population itself. Workers' control, cooperatives, soviets, factory committees, trade unions, revolutionary tribunals and other organisations would represent democracy from below. There would be no need for a state bureaucracy or a standing army. However, it quickly became evident that the Bolsheviks could not effect their policies through this commune state and they began to conceive of an economic mechanism – it became the Supreme Economic Council – which would manage industry from the centre through economic councils at all levels. This required the nationalisation of industry. When the Constituent Assembly convened in January 1918 the Bolsheviks demanded that it recognise the new soviet order, and when it refused to accept the Reds' declaration on the rights of the labouring and exploited people, Lenin's supporters left the Assembly. It was dispersed by force the following day. This indicated that the Bolsheviks would not accept a western parliamentary republic and a division of powers between the legislature, executive and judiciary.

In April 1918 the Bolsheviks began work on drafting a new constitution. The constitution of the RSFSR of July 1918 envisaged the main task as establishing the dictatorship of the proletariat and the poor strata of the peasantry, the suppression of the bourgeoisie and the elimination of the exploitation of man by man. When all this had been achieved, socialism, meaning the elimination of classes and state power, would begin. Power would rest with soviets at all levels. Village and city soviets would be directly elected. At the oblast, raion and guberniya level, congresses of soviets would convene and they would elect the relevant soviets. Supreme power rested with the Congress of Soviets. It elected a TsIK which acted in the name of the Congress between Congresses. The TsIK elected a government, Sovnarkom. Only those engaged in productive labour had the right to vote. The establishment of the USSR in 1922 necessitated a new constitution and it extended the RSFSR model to the whole of the USSR. The supreme organ was the USSR Congress of Soviets and its deputies were from the four Union republics (RSFSR, Ukrainian Socialist Soviet Republic, Belorussian Socialist Soviet Republic and the Transcaucasian Socialist Federal Soviet Republic). The new USSR Congress of Soviets was bicameral, consisting of the Soviet of the Union and the Soviet of Nationalities. The Soviet of the Union was elected by the USSR Congress of Soviets and the Soviet of Nationalities by the Congress of Soviets of the Union republics. The Soviet of the Union and the Soviet of Nationalities together elected the Presidium of the TsIK. Foreign policy, defence, foreign trade, transport, post and telegraph were the responsibility of the Union. Agriculture, justice, internal affairs, health and education fell within the competence of the Union republics. Supply, labour, finance, the economy and state control were under dual control, the Union and the republics. The constitution permitted each republic to secede from the Union. In 1935 the USSR Congress of Soviets set up a commission to draft a new constitution which would correspond to the socialist development of the state.

The new constitution of 1936, often called the Stalin constitution, was mainly drafted by Bukharin and was claimed to be the most democratic in the world. This was true, at least on paper. The constitution was based on the belief that socialism had in essence been achieved and that there were no more antagonistic classes in the USSR. It became possible to enfranchise all citizens and introduce the general, equal, direct and secret right to vote. The Congresses of Soviets were abolished and replaced by a directly elected Supreme Soviet in each republic and at Union level. The new constitution abandoned the concept of a Soviet or commune state. The practice of the constant election and recall of deputies to soviets was given up in the early 1920s as Lenin's new concept of the state took over. This reflected the lack of support for the Bolsheviks among the population. The commune state was to be replaced by one in which the Communist Party would dominate, but not the whole membership, only the avant-garde of the Party. It would instil, from without, socialist consciousness into the working class. To reflect this, the Party was mentioned in the constitution for the first time. However, its dominant role in the state and the economy was only obliquely referred to. There were now 11 Union republics and they, as before, had the right to secede from the Union.

In 1959 Khrushchev declared that a new constitution was needed to reflect changes since 1945 and to look ahead to communism. This was in contrast to Stalin's constitution, which reflected the situation in 1936. A 96-person constitutional commission began work drafting a new constitution in 1962. It was chaired by Khrushchev and after his removal in 1964 Brezhnev took over. It proved very difficult to agree as Khrushchev's concept of the all people's state was dropped but later accepted. The result was the 1977 Soviet constitution, which had been widely discussed in draft form, and some changes had been made in the light of citizens' comments. It proclaimed the all people's state. State power was exercised by the people through the soviets. The Party was moved up to article 6 and its true role was spelled out for the first time. It was acknowledged as the leading and guiding force of the country. As before, republics (now 15) had the right to secede. In December 1988 the USSR Supreme Soviet adopted an amendment to the constitution which brought into being the USSR Congress of People's Deputies and a new USSR Supreme

Soviet. In 1990 another constitutional amendment established an executive presidency in the Soviet Union.

Constitution (Russian)

The RSFSR constitution of 1978 served as the Russian constitution until
December 1993. It was amended in line with the 1977 USSR constitution, and included a Congress of People's Deputies and an executive
presidency. The constitution was amended over 300 times between 1991
and 1993 and reflected the conflict between the legislature (Congress)
and executive (President). The President unconstitutionally dissolved
the Congress and Supreme Soviet in September 1993 and proposed that
a draft constitution be put to a referendum on 12 December 1993. This
constitution had emerged from a Constitutional Conference during the
summer of 1993 and there were several drafts. The Congress proposed
a parliamentary republic and the President a presidential republic. The
Congress and Supreme Soviet were replaced by the federal Assembly,
consisting of a lower house, the State Duma, and an upper house, the
Council of the Federation. The federal structure of Russia was retained,
although all references to the sovereignty of the subjects of the federation disappeared.

Under the new constitution the President has enormous power; he
can issue decrees and regulations, providing they do not conflict with
the constitution or federal laws. If there is doubt, the matter is resolved
by the Constitutional Court. International treaties are solely the responsibility of the President. He now appoints the Prime Minister but the Duma
has to accept his nomination. If it rejects it three times, the President
shall appoint the Prime Minister, dissolve the Duma and call new elections. The Prime Minister proposes ministers to the President. The government has to present the budget to the Duma for approval and also
the President's nomination for chair of the Russian Central Bank. The
budget is sometimes not passed until the year in question has begun.
The refusal of the Duma to accept Tatyana Paramonova as chair of the
Central Bank in November 1995 resulted in the President dismissing her
and nominating Sergei Dubinin, who was duly confirmed by the Duma.
The first Duma twice passed votes of no confidence in the government
but shied away from confrontation with the President. Had three votes
of no confidence been passed the President would then have either dismissed the government or dissolved the Duma. It is now virtually impossible to impeach the President. A balance of power has not been achieved
in this constitution. Power rests with the President. However, the President has been careful to use his power sparingly. Over time the Duma has
established the practice of inviting government ministers to appear before

its committees to question them on policy. They are not constitutionally required to do so but it is rare now for a minister to refuse.

Death penalty

The death penalty was abolished immediately after the February Revolution but reintroduced in July 1917 in the army and navy in a vain attempt to impose greater discipline. On 26 November 1917 the 2nd Congress of Soviets annulled this regulation so that technically there was no death penalty for any crime. However, in the early period of the revolution this was a fiction as the bourgeoisie and others were killed during the struggle against counter-revolution and sabotage. The Cheka, formed in December 1917, freely used the death penalty, as did the revolutionary tribunals. The first criminal code of the RSFSR, passed in 1922, regarded the death penalty as temporary until it was abolished by the All-Russian Central Executive Committee (TsIK). The same formulation was retained in the second criminal code of the RSFSR in 1926. The death penalty applied to crimes against the state and its agencies and also economic crimes. During the 1930s the number of crimes for which the death penalty could apply increased. The USSR Supreme Soviet abolished the death penalty on 26 May 1947. The severest penalty now became incarceration in a corrective labour camp for 25 years. However, in January 1950 the death penalty was back for 'traitors, spies and saboteurs'. On 30 April 1954 a decree permitted execution in particularly gruesome murder trials. A new USSR criminal code was introduced under Khrushchev in 1958 and all Union republics followed suit. These codes permitted execution in exceptional cases such as treason, spying, terrorist acts and murder. In 1961–62 the number of crimes for which it could be applied was extended to the embezzlement of state and social property, bribery, hard currency smuggling, forgery of currency and attacks against militia personnel. This revealed that these phenomena had become sufficiently widespread to merit drastic measures against them. Corruption grew rapidly under Brezhnev and involved many in official positions. Under Gorbachev there were several high-profile corruption cases but when found guilty the accused was always sentenced to imprisonment.

Gulag

The main administration for corrective labour camps, Gulag is the name of the organisation in the 1930s under which all labour camps were subordinated. Until the late 1920s there were two types of camp: one for criminals, subordinate to the People's Commissariat of the Interior (NKVD), and the other for political prisoners, subordinate to the OGPU (secret police). The number of prisoners increased quickly at the end of the 1920s and the beginning of the 1930s as a result of collectivisation, and anyone sentenced to over three years was placed under the OGPU. A gulag was set up within the OGPU in 1930. In December 1930 the NKVD in the Union republics was dissolved and the task of supervising the NKVD camps passed to the Union republican People's Commissariats for Justice. In 1934 an all-Union NKVD was set up and the OGPU was made part of it and all labour camps became OGPU's responsibility. A vast network of camps evolved, which Alexander Solzhenitsyn described in his novel as the Gulag Archipelago. There were over 100 gulags with between 2 and 20 million prisoners, according to the western estimate chosen. The gulags played an important economic role in the timber, mining, zinc, phosphate and lead industries. The prisoners built roads and canals (the White Sea and Volga–Don Canals). Khrushchev abolished the gulags in 1956.

Industrial Party

As part of the process of intimidation of specialists, a trial took place in late October 1930, involving bourgeois economists and engineers, and the collective name the prosecution gave to them was the Industrial Party. The founders, according to *Pravda*, were the engineers Plachinsky, Fedorovich and Rabinovich, who had links to émigré capitalist circles in Paris and capitalists who had remained in the Soviet Union. They allegedly had penetrated to the top of Gosplan and the Supreme Economic Council (VSNKh). Their goal was to provoke bottlenecks in industry and transport, slow down the tempo of growth and sow discontent among workers. Their overall goal was to overturn the dictatorship of the proletariat and restore capitalism in the Soviet Union. Of the eight accused, five were sentenced to death and the others to long periods of imprisonment. The death sentences were commuted into long prison sentences. The whole trial was a fabrication.

Justice

A Bolshevik decree of 22 November 1917 abolished all courts and investigative judges and lawyers. New courts were to be set up and judges elected by the people, and every citizen could act as prosecutor or defence lawyer. Law was to be guided by revolutionary conscience and revolutionary legal consciousness. Revolutionary tribunals were set up and soon became the responsibility of the Cheka (secret police). During the Civil War the revolutionary tribunals dispensed rough justice, as did the Cheka as it applied the Red terror. Under NEP there was a dramatic change in thinking and the goal was to introduce order, socialist legality. Lawyers reappeared and the revolutionary tribunals disappeared. In the 1930s justice became an instrument of the class struggle and sought out saboteurs of socialist construction and this led to the show trials. Judges did not decide sentences in criminal cases; the secret police or even Stalin did. The de-Stalinisation campaign under Khrushchev radically altered the legal system and all Party and state organs were again instructed to observe socialist legality, meaning to observe the law. The special laws which the secret police had used were abolished. New court procedure, criminal and civil codes were issued between 1958 and 1964. The constitution of 1977 stressed that only courts could administer justice and that judges were independent (this was qualified by the fact that almost all judges were Party members and hence subject to Party discipline).

Katyn

The place near Smolensk, western Russia, where German troops discovered a mass grave with the bodies of over 4,000 Polish officers, in April 1943. They were men who had been taken prisoner by the Red Army after the invasion of east Poland on 17 September 1939. About 15,000 officers were placed in three camps and most of them were murdered in April–May 1940. German reports about Katyn led to the Polish government in exile in London calling for an international enquiry. The Soviet Union used this as a pretext to break off relations with the government on 25 April 1943. Moscow maintained that the Germans had committed the crime. Under glasnost a lively debate developed between Polish and Soviet historians about the question of guilt. Gorbachev acknowledged the Soviet Union's guilt, handing over documents in 1991 which confirmed Stalin's direct involvement. In November 1996 the Russian government announced that a memorial to the Polish victims of Katyn and Mednoe, Tver oblast, would be erected.

KGB   *see* Secret police

Militia

The civil police who were responsible for public order, the protection of socialist property and the rights and legal interests of citizens, enterprises and organisations. The People's Commissariat of the Interior, on 28 October 1917, instructed all soviets to set up workers' militias to act as a police force and to be subordinate to the workers' and soldiers' soviets. They were to replace the bourgeois police force which had formed after the February Revolution. They remained subordinate to local soviets until 1931 but were subordinate, in turn, to the People's Commissariat of Internal Affairs (NKVD), later Ministry of Internal Affairs (MVD). In order to overcome rising crime, Khrushchev established voluntary people's militias (druzhina) in the late 1950s, but they proved a mixed blessing as they began to take the law into their own hands.

Purges

In Russian the word chistka means purge and was originally used to describe the process of checking the membership of the Party in order to weed out careerists and other undesirables. A Party Control Commission was set up in 1920 to perform this task and it developed a network of local control agencies to help it. Article 51 of the Party statutes of 1919 permitted not only the expulsion of a comrade but if his offence was sufficiently grave he could be handed over to the legal authorities. The first general purge was carried out in 1921 and removed about a quarter of the Party membership, about 160,000, of whom only 10 per cent went voluntarily. Reasons for expulsion included misuse of office, blackmail, fraud, unparty behaviour such as acting as a careerist, indulging in bourgeois or dissolute styles of life or attending religious ceremonies, ignoring Party directives and being passive and not defending the interests of the Party. It became customary to carry out regular Party purges thereafter in various institutions, such as Soviet and higher educational Party groups in 1925 and village cells in 1926. A special target were members of the right and left opposition.

On the other hand, purges in western literature refer to the expulsion of most of the pre-1917 Bolsheviks from the Party and the great show trials of the 1930s. Many of these comrades lost their lives as well as their Party cards. The purges were sparked off by the murder of Sergei Kirov, the Leningrad Party leader, on 1 December 1934. Stalin skilfully used the event to take in all his political opponents. There were three great show trials (so called to underline the propagandistic effect of the trials, which were conducted with scant respect for legal norms and were based on confessions, often extorted under torture, from the accused): the first was in August 1936 and involved the Trotskyist–Zinovievist Terrorist Centre (or the trial of the 16); the second was in January 1937 against the Anti-Soviet Trotskyist Centre (also the trial of the 17); and the third was in March 1938 against the Anti-Soviet Bloc of the Right and Trotskyists (also the trial of the 21) in which Kamenev, Zinoviev, Pyatakov, Radek, Sokolnikov, Rykov and Bukharin were accused of the most outlandish crimes and found guilty. The purges also affected top-level politicians. Khrushchev stated at the 20th Party Congress in 1956 that of the 1,966 delegates to the 17th Party Congress in 1934, 1,108 had been arrested on counter-revolutionary charges and 70 per cent (98 out of 139) of Central Committee candidates and full members elected at the Congress had been executed in 1937–38. This bloodletting may have been linked to the vote at the Congress in which Kirov had come top in elections to the new Central Committee. Kirov had been approached to stand against Stalin as leader of the Party but declined and informed Stalin. As a result of these purges Party membership fell from 3.5 million in 1933 to

1.9 million in 1938. Another target for the purges were the armed forces and in 1937–38 three out of five marshals, all eight admirals, and all eleven deputy commissars for defence were purged, to name only a few examples. In all, about 35,000 or half the officer corps were either shot or arrested. The non-Russian nationalities also suffered in 1937–38. For example, in the Checheno-Ingush Autonomous Republic 14,000 were arrested, or practically the whole educated elite.

The term purge can also be used to describe the deportation of hundreds of thousands of successful farmers (kulaks) during collectivisation and the trials of the Shakhty engineers in 1928, the Industrial Party in 1930 and the Metro-Vickers engineers in 1933. The bloodiest purges of the period are linked to the name of Ezhov, head of the NKVD, in the late 1930s. The late 1940s also saw purges of thousands of officials, Jews, etc. Precise numbers of victims will probably never be known, but at least half a million were shot and several million ended up in the gulag during the 1930s and 1940s. It is worth remembering that the campaign against nationalists was not exclusively against non-Russians. Russian nationalists were among the first to be put in labour camps in the 1920s. Lenin, for one, feared they might undermine Soviet power as they rejected Marxism as a foreign import.

Secret police

The western designation for the Soviet term, organs of state security. Most popularly known as the Committee of State Security (KGB) from 1954 to 1991, the organisation's origins go back to the founding of the Cheka, the Russian Extraordinary Commission for the Struggle against Counter-Revolution and Sabotage, headed by Feliks Dzerzhinsky. It was ruthless during the Civil War and exercised the Red terror in response to White terror. It was dissolved after the Civil War and its functions assumed by the State Political Administration (GPU), part of the People's Commissariat of the Interior, in 1922 but this became the Unified State Political Administration (OGPU) during the winter of 1922–23, when it again became an independent institution. The secret police were used by Stalin to enforce collectivisation, stage manage the show trials and eliminate any opposition to his dictatorship. It became the most feared institution in the country. In 1934 the People's Commissariat of the Interior and the OGPU were fused but eventually the secret police dominated the whole police service. The NKVD carried out the purges after the murder of Sergei Kirov in December 1934. In 1936 Yagoda, the chief, fell from favour and was replaced by Ezhov, who became even more brutal. He, in turn, was replaced by Beria in 1938. Both Yagoda and Ezhov were executed. The secret police were also responsible for the forced labour camps, the gulag. After Stalin's death Beria was arrested and the political police brought under Party control by establishing the KGB. Each republic and autonomous republic had a KGB head. A high-profile chief of the KGB was Yury Andropov, who headed the organisation from 1967 to 1982. The last head of the KGB, Vladimir Kryuchkov, was a member of the extraordinary committee which organised the attempted coup of 18–21 August 1991 against Gorbachev.

Trotskyist–Zinovievist Terrorist Centre

A centre, invented by Stalin, to which Trotsky and his supporters belonged and whose goal was the violent overthrow of Soviet power. It supposedly came into existence after 1927 when Trotsky and others were expelled from the Party. Stalin grasped the opportunity, afforded him by the assassination of Sergei Kirov in December 1934, of disposing of the left opposition. A show trial in August 1936 linked Trotsky (in absentia), Zinoviev, Kamenev and 14 other supporters together in the centre. They were held accountable for the murder of Kirov and other terrorist acts (including an attempt on Stalin's life). Their goal was to seize power in the Soviet Union. All 16 of the accused present were sentenced to death and executed.

Universal human values

These were linked to perestroika and emphasised that the Soviet leadership no longer thought in terms of class or national interest. This was now replaced by universal human values whose tasks included preventing war and resolving the economic, social and political problems of the world. Elements of these common human values were freedom, social justice and solidarity, and respect for human and minority rights. Hence the Soviet Union began to adopt the concepts of the developed world. The Soviet constitution guaranteed many rights but they remained on paper until Gorbachev came to power. According to the constitution the state granted these rights to the citizen but they could be withdrawn. When the USSR ratified the UN agreement on human rights in 1973, and signed the Helsinki Final Act, Moscow accepted the western definition of human rights for the first time. In the Soviet Union, Helsinki Monitoring Committees were established during the 1970s, pressing for the implementation of the human rights agreed at Helsinki. The KGB moved against these groups and imprisoned many of their members. Academician Andrei Sakharov and his wife, Elena Bonner, became leading campaigners. This led to Sakharov being exiled to Gorky (Nizhny Novgorod), which was a closed city because of its defence industries, and only his wife was allowed to visit and contact him. Gorbachev released him and brought him back to Moscow.

SECTION THREE

Foreign affairs and security

Wars and uprisings

Armed forces

In the April Theses Lenin stated that the army was to be abolished. It was to be replaced by a territorial militia recruited from a universally armed population. This was the phase when Lenin expected the commune or Soviet state to form and the state to be dissolved in society. Democracy from below was the order of the day. A Sovnarkom decree of December 1917 abolished all military ranks, orders and medals. There were to be no more ranks and soldiers were to elect their commanders. The declaration of the rights of the labouring and exploited people of 3 January 1918 stated that a workers' and peasants' socialist Red Army would be formed. A Sovnarkom decree of 15 January 1918 made this a reality. The new army was to consist of volunteers from the most politically conscious and best organised strata of the workers and peasants, was to prepare the way for a national militia and to render aid to the ever-advancing socialist revolution in Europe. A socialist red workers' and peasants' navy was set up on 29 January 1918. Soldiers organised themselves along the lines of the workers' detachments and the factory red guards.

However, it soon became clear that this motley assortment of men was incapable of resisting the regular German army. This led the Soviet government in the spring of 1918 to abandon the idea of a national militia and to begin building up a traditional, regular army. Election of superiors by the men was abandoned and voluntary service replaced by obligatory national service (the bourgeoisie was excluded). Discipline became rigorous. This new army could not do without ex-Tsarist officers and recruited them as military specialists. Military commissars were to supervise the new officers closely and to ensure the implementation of Party decrees and orders. Revolutionary military councils (soviets) were set up at soviet level but independent of them and a Revolutionary Military Council of the Republic (Revvoensovet) had overall command. The People's Commissariats for the Army and the Navy were subordinate to the Revvoensovet and Trotsky chaired it until 1925. The Red Army grew from 200,000 men in April 1918 to over 5 million at the end of 1920.

After the Civil War the Bolsheviks did not revert to the concept of a militia but proceeded to build up a professional army. The military reforms of 1924–25 paved the way but territorial militias did come into being. They were to provide reserves and only required a short period of service. The main reason for this was the lack of resources available for defence. In 1934 the Revvoensovet was dissolved, and the People's Commissariats for the Army and the Navy were merged in a People's Commissariat for Defence and the Staff of the Red Army became the General Staff in 1935. In the same year military ranks were reintroduced. The 1936 constitution made all citizens responsible for the defence of the motherland. The new oath of 1939 deleted all references to the international revolution and obliged all men and women to carry out orders without demur. The military suffered during the purges, with Stalin apparently believing that officers might refuse to obey his orders. Military commissars were again introduced as a political check, but they were abolished in August 1940. After the German invasion of June 1941 they were again set up, revealing that Stalin was still unsure of the loyalty of the military. In late June 1941 a state committee for defence (GKO) was formed to fight the war and all resources were placed at its disposal. Stalin chaired it and also became People's Commissar for Defence. The link between the military and the Party was strengthened by easing the conditions for entry. Soldiers were recruited at the front and those who distinguished themselves were immediately invited to join. The number of military in the Party rose from 1.3 million in 1941 to 3.3 million in 1945. During the autumn of 1942 the military commissars were transformed into deputy commanders for political affairs. Many new orders and awards were created to mark the victorious advance of the Red Army. Guard regiments were introduced in 1942 and in 1943 the old Tsarist division of the military into soldiers, NCOs, officers and generals reappeared. In 1945 the Red Army and Navy became the Soviet armed forces.

Stalin was concerned to build his own atom and hydrogen bombs and thereby to end the American monopoly. Sputnik demonstrated that the Soviets were ahead in space rocketry. By the early 1960s Khrushchev was boasting of nuclear superiority and the Cuban Missile Crisis of October 1962 brought the world to the brink of nuclear war. The Americans conceded nuclear parity in 1972. The collapse of the Portuguese empire in Africa in 1975 led to a rash of new communist and pro-Moscow states in Africa. The Soviet intervention in Afghanistan in December 1979 added impetus to the new Cold War and the Soviet military gained unprecedented influence over security and foreign policy under the ailing Brezhnev. Economic growth rates in the Soviet Union declined during the 1970s and defence expenditure reached, possibly, 18 per cent of GDP by the early 1980s (the comparable US figure was 6 per cent with an economy 2.5 times that of the USSR). The superpowers began negotiations about arms limitations in the late 1960s and this led to the SALT I and SALT II agreements during the 1970s. Talks about mutually balanced force reductions (MBFR) began in Vienna in 1973 but did not result in agreement.

The arrival of Gorbachev in March 1985 transformed the situation as he had come to the conclusion that the arms burden was crippling the Soviet Union. International relations could not improve without agreement on nuclear arms. He proposed a 50 per cent cut in strategic missiles at Geneva during his first meeting with President Reagan in September 1985. In Reykjavik in October 1986 he stunned Reagan by his radical proposals, but agreement just eluded them. One of the reasons why the two leaders could not agree was the Soviet demand that the Americans drop the Strategic Defence Initiative (SDI). In December 1987 Reagan and Gorbachev signed the Intermediate Range Nuclear Force (INF) treaty, which was to reduce their numbers. Negotiations on the Conventional Forces in Europe (CFE) treaty were concluded in November 1990. The Soviet Union agreed to abandon its superiority in conventional arms but this was never implemented as the Soviet military moved its tanks east of the Urals and hence into Asia. There was tension between Gorbachev and the military but it remained loyal until the attempted coup of August 1991 when Marshal Yazov, Minister of Defence, was involved. The Soviet armed forces disintegrated in December 1991 with the dissolution of the Soviet Union and most passed into the Russian armed forces. In December 1991 there were four nuclear states, Russia, Belarus, Ukraine and Kazakhstan, but Belarus and Kazakhstan soon agreed to pass their weapons to Russia.

Civil War

The Civil War began in spring 1918 and lasted until late 1920. Whites and Reds fought one another to a standstill but the Whites were not organisationally united. There were also the blacks, the anarchists, strongest in Ukraine (Makhno movement, Antonov uprising). Many foreign states intervened (among them the USA, Great Britain, France, Japan, Germany). A volunteer White army formed during the winter of 1917–18 in the south (not controlled by the Bolsheviks) under generals Kornilov and Alekseev. They linked up with the Don Cossacks under their hetman Kaledin. General Denikin took over command after Kornilov was killed in 1918. The first phase of the Civil War began in May 1918 when the Bolsheviks failed to disarm the Czechoslovak legion and return them to their homeland. This encouraged Denikin to push eastwards. The Whites took Kazan and the gold reserves of the State Bank and moved down the Volga. The Reds hit back and they defended Tsaritsyn (later Stalingrad) successfully and drove Denikin back to the south. The second phase began in the spring and summer of 1919. Admiral Kolchak ruled Siberia and moved eastwards. The Allies recognised Kolchak in June 1919 and Denikin acknowledged him as leader. General Yudenich almost took Petrograd and in the summer of 1919 the Reds seemed defeated. In December 1919 the Czechoslovaks handed Kolchak over to the Reds and he was executed in February 1920. Denikin's forces in the south were exhausted from fighting the Reds and also Makhno, and in spring 1920 most of his men embarked for the Crimea. The third phase began in April 1920 with the Polish attack and conquest of Kiev, but the Reds counter-attacked and reached the outskirts of Warsaw. Here the 'miracle of the Vistula' occurred when the Poles defeated the Reds, who had expected the Polish workers to welcome them as liberators but who were instead regarded as Russian imperialists. Wrangel was defeated in the Crimea and the Reds, against all the odds, had won (see also Chronology pp. 9–11).

Chechnya

Dzhokhar Dudaev was elected President in October 1991 but the RSFSR Supreme Soviet declared the election invalid and in November 1991 a state of emergency was declared. Dudaev declared martial law and the Chechen national guard took over roads, communications and the airport. His goal was independence for Chechnya. After various failed attempts to remove Dudaev by force, Russia invaded on 11 December 1994 declaring Dudaev a bandit. The death of Dudaev, killed in a Russian air raid on 21 April 1996, opened up the possibility of a negotiated settlement. General Aleksandr Lebed and Aslan Maskhadov, Chechen Chief of Staff, negotiated a truce in the conflict in June 1996. All Russian troops were to leave Chechnya and they completed their withdrawal in January 1997. On 27 January 1997 Aslan Maskhadov was elected President of Chechnya. The conflict was a disastrous defeat for Russia and resulted in the deaths of over 50,000, many of them civilians. The Russians bombed Grozny to rubble and in so doing killed many ethnic Russian inhabitants. The three services that were in Chechnya, the military, Ministry of Internal troops and the security forces, failed to coordinate their efforts.

Czechoslovakia, August 1968

In January 1968 the Czechoslovak Communist Party sacked Antonin Novotny and elected Alexander Dubcek First Secretary. Moscow acknowledged the decision but it had underestimated the reform tendencies of the new leader. In March the Warsaw Pact states warned him against granting too many concessions to the reformers and he planned a conference for September 1968 to initiate major reforms. Various meetings with the Warsaw Pact members followed but Dubcek did not sense that the Pact would invade. On 21 August 1968 the Soviet Union, Poland, the GDR, Hungary and Bulgaria invaded. Romania refused to join them. The Prague Spring had become the Prague Winter. In April 1969 Dubcek was removed and replaced by Gustav Husak, who remained loyal to Moscow until the end of communism. The invasion underlined the limited sovereignty of communist states and the Brezhnev Doctrine emerged to legitimise Soviet intervention when Moscow perceived Soviet-style socialism was in danger. The invasion had a catastrophic effect on the standing of the CPSU world-wide.

Cold War

The expression which describes the world-wide confrontation between the Soviet Union and the USA, between communism and pluralist democracy, which dates from 1947 to the mid-Gorbachev era. Conflict arose over the post-war settlements between the two leading world powers mainly because the wartime conferences and the Potsdam conference failed to resolve many burning issues. The traditional western view was that it was all the fault of Stalin, who was bent on expansionism. A western revisionist view developed in the 1960s and blamed Washington for the Cold War because it was bent on extending American influence and capitalism into eastern Europe. A post-revisionist view regards the Cold War as almost inevitable given the conflicting world views of Moscow and Washington. In post-communist Russia many writers blame Stalin for the Cold War. An important role in forming America's view of the Soviet Union was played by George Kennan, who warned in 1946 about the expansionist ideology adhered to by Moscow. He declared that containment of communism was necessary. The Cold War can be seen as beginning with the Truman Doctrine in 1947 in which the US President declared that any nation under communist threat would be helped by America. The Marshall Plan divided east and west, and Comecon came into being in the east and NATO in the west. The Soviet Union established a cordon sanitaire of people's democracies in eastern and southeastern Europe and Europe was divided in two. The Berlin Blockade was one of the results of this tension but the 17 June 1953 uprising in East Berlin against communist rule resulted in no western aid being extended. It became accepted that the Soviet Union held sway in eastern Europe. The Hungarian Revolution of 1956 and the invasion of Czechoslovakia in August 1968 were also accepted by the west. However, the latter mortally weakened the appeal of Soviet communism and the pro-Moscow regimes collapsed in 1989. This was a direct result of Gorbachev's new political thinking, which involved no Soviet military aid for communist regimes. The Cold War was over. Some writers refer to the period 1979–85 as the new Cold War brought about by Soviet intervention in Afghanistan in December 1979 and the confrontation over the placing of SS20 missiles in the east and the desire of the west to counter by stationing Cruise and Pershing missiles in the west.

Great Patriotic War, 1941–45

On 21 June 1941 the Germans and their allies attacked the Soviet Union without warning and set in train the Soviet part of the Second World War. Stalin had failed to heed numerous warnings about an imminent German attack and was taken completely by surprise. Great Britain signed an assistance pact on 12 July 1941, as did the USA on 2 August 1941. The Soviet Union became a beneficiary of the Lend Lease Act on 7 November 1941. An Anglo–Soviet alliance was agreed on 26 May 1942 and an assistance and cooperation treaty was signed with the USA on 11 June 1942. Tension developed over the second front in Europe as the British and Americans chose North Africa as their route to Europe. A turning points was the battle of Moscow in December, which ended the German concept of a Blitzkrieg (a lightning war). German strategy had to be reoriented towards a longer conflict. Surrender at Stalingrad in February 1943 was the greatest land defeat ever suffered by German forces. In July 1943 the battle of the Kursk salient resulted in the defeat of German armour (the greatest tank battle in history up to that time). Afterwards it was only a matter of time before the Germans were expelled from the Soviet Union. There was some doubt in the west about the Red Army continuing to Berlin, but it took the German capital on 2 May 1945. The war ended with the German capitulation on 9 May (8 May in the west) 1945. The war may have resulted in the premature deaths of 28 million Soviet citizens or one in seven of the pre-war population (see also Chronology, pp. 21–7).

Hungarian Revolution

Demonstration on 23 October 1956 against Ernö Gerö, First Secretary of the Hungarian United Workers' Party, the communists, in favour of a return to power of Imre Nagy, the former Prime Minister, were countered by Gerö, who made an aggressive speech. Police fired into the crowd and the revolution was under way. The army joined the demonstrators and distributed arms. Outside Budapest councils sprang up and peasants reclaimed their collectivised land. Soviet troops withdrew from the country. Nagy was appointed Prime Minister and on 1 November declared that Hungary had withdrawn from the Warsaw Pact and requested the UN to recognise Hungary as a neutral state. However Nagy and János Kádár, the Party leader, did not satisfy the demands for reform. Concessions were made but Soviet troops began re-entering Hungary and on 3 November Kádár broke with Nagy and formed a pro-Moscow government. On 4 November the Soviet army entered Budapest. Nagy took refuge in the Yugoslav embassy and Cardinal Mindszenty, the Hungarian Primate, entered the US legation. By 11 November the Russians were in control and over 3,000 were dead and over 200,000 had fled to the west. Nagy was arrested and later executed. Moscow had been uncertain about how to react to the crisis. Khrushchev and the Soviet Presidium (Politburo) decided on 28 October, and again on 30 October, to seek a peaceful solution by withdrawing the Soviet army and begin negotiations about the Finlandisation (turning Hungary into a neutral country which did not join any western political, economic or military alliance) of the country.

All members of the Presidium voted for the peace option, even though Kliment Voroshilov and Vyacheslav Molotov privately favoured the military option. On 31 October the Presidium reversed its decision in favour of the peace option and decided on the military option. The reason for this change of course is uncertain. The east European leaders, especially Walter Ulbricht of East Germany, pressed for the military option. Between 24 and 31 October a Chinese delegation was in Mosow and underlined Mao Zedong's warning that the Chinese would protest officially in strong terms against a Soviet military intervention in Hungary. Mao seems to have changed his mind on 31 October after hearing reports from the Chinese ambassador in Hungary and western reports which indicated that Hungary could fall into the hands of the capitalists. Khrushchev met Marshal Tito of Yugoslavia secretly on the island of Brioni on 2–3 November and Tito, like other east European leaders, pressed for the military option. Another reason for Khrushchev's change of mind appears to have been his fear that if he abandoned Hungary (and also Nasser during the Suez conflict) that this would lead to a split in the Presidium. The west, engaged in the Suez conflict, could not intervene.

Kronstadt uprising
The first, serious conflict the Bolsheviks encountered with those who supported Soviet power. Most of the sailors on the island fortress in the bay of Petrograd were SR supporters and they were unhappy with the dictatorial policies of the Bolsheviks. On 28 February 1921 local sailors demonstrated and passed a resolution which was adopted on 1 March by a mass meeting of 15,000 sailors, soldiers and civilians. Mikhail Kalinin, sent by the Bolsheviks to plead with the crowd, was not permitted to speak. The Kronstadters demanded new elections to the soviets, freedom of speech and the press, left-wing parties, including the anarchists, to be permitted to reappear, and the Communist Party not to have a privileged position in the state. They had little interest in a Constituent Assembly as they supported the principles of a soviet republic of workers and peasants. On 2 March a five-member provisional revolutionary committee was elected and took power in Kronstadt. The Cheka centre was taken over and Communist Party members arrested. Lenin and Trotsky dismissed the events as a White Guardist, anti-soviet and counter-revolutionary mutiny. Martial law was declared there and on 5 March (later marshal) Tukhachevsky was ordered to suppress it. Only on 17–18 March did the Red Army succeed in taking the island. About 50,000 Red Army soldiers and some delegates to the 10th Party Congress charged over the ice to Kronstadt. This was the first time that the Bolsheviks had shed the blood of their own supporters and revealed how ruthless the Party had become. It would not tolerate any challenge to its monopoly on power.

Makhno movement

An anarchist uprising and revolutionary movement which emerged at the end of 1917 in small groups in Ekaterinoslav and then spread through the rural population of neighbouring areas between the rivers Don and Dniester, in Ukraine. Nestor I. Makhno bcame its leader in October 1918 and he was inspired by the anarchist writings of Mikhail Bakunin and Kropotkin. The Reds were the communists, the Whites were the anti-Reds and the Blacks were the anarchists. At its height the movement had about 20,000 fighters behind its black banners. They advocated the nationalisation of all land and its distribution among the peasantry and a federation of local communities (soviets), which would have far-reaching autonomy to regulate their own affairs. The anarchists were caught in a vice, they were vigorously opposed by the Whites and therefore entered into tactical alliances with the Reds. However, the Reds also wanted to destroy them and when the Whites had been beaten they turned on Makhno's men. They were finally defeated by the Reds in August 1923.

Military commissars (war commissars)

Representatives of the Communist Party and Soviet leadership in units of the Soviet armed forces. The Supreme Military Council, set up on 4 March 1918, served as a model as it had a military commander, a general, and two political commissars. The Red Army and all military institutions were reorganised according to this principle in April 1918. It was usual for a military specialist (usually a former Tsarist officer) to be paired with a military commissar. Since the Reds were often dependent on former Tsarist officers during the Civil War, the military commissars, dedicated communists, played a vital role in ensuring that military orders from above were implemented. Military commissars disappeared during the 1920s after single commanders became the norm. They reappeared in May 1937 at the height of the military purges as an instrument of control. This changed again in May 1940 when they were almost phased out and the armed services reverted to single commanders, but shortly after the German invasion of June 1941 they were reintroduced in divisions, regiments, general staffs and other military institutions. Together with the commander they were held responsible for the battle preparedness of the troops and to ensure that they did not retreat unless given orders to do so. In October 1942 military commissars were phased out for the last time and demoted to deputies of the commanders, responsible for political questions (politruks).

Partisans

They played an important role during the Great Patriotic War. Stalin, in his address to the nation on 3 July 1941, called for the unleashing of a partisan war everywhere in areas occupied by the enemy. On 18 July 1941 the Party Central Committee published a special decree on the 'organisation of the struggle behind German lines' which expanded on an earlier decree of 29 June. A Central Staff of the Partisan Movement was established on 30 May 1942 and it functioned until 1944 with the staffs of the partisan movement in the various regions and republics being subordinated to it. It was headed by P. K. Ponomarenko, with the rank of Lieutenant General. The Soviets were unprepared for a partisan war as they had expected to be fighting on enemy territory. There was general confusion and the initial defeats hindered the emergence of the movement, so that it took until the end of 1941 for it to take shape. There were an estimated 90,000 active partisans in early 1942 and by the autumn of 1942 this had grown to 150,000. As the Red Army advanced so the partisan movement expanded, and during the summer of 1944 it had about 280,000 members. The military significance of the partisans is a matter of debate. Soviet authors praised their role and especially their spectacular successes in preventing German reinforcements reaching the front, in 1943 for example. Western authors are more sceptical: while giving due credit for their sabotage in the German rear and tying down German troops, they point out that their successes were not commensurate with their size. Stalin's attitude was ambivalent, since there was a risk that partisans, having organised under German rule, would wish to play an important role after liberation, especially in areas which had been added to the Soviet Union between 1939 and 1940.

Politruk

This was an abbreviation for politichesky rukovoditel (political leader). They were persons who were responsible for the political education of the members of companies, batteries and other units in the Soviet armed forces. They were established by decree of the Revolutionary Military Council of Soviet Russia on 14 October 1919. The politruk was the personnel chief of his unit and was on a par with the military commander, and his function was similar to that of a military commissar in large units and institutions. His main function was to ensure the implementation of Party directives in the armed forces. In the mid-1920s, when the military also went over to one-man management (edinonachalie), the politruk lost prestige and became merely an auxiliary for political questions of the commander. The politruk regained his equal status with the military commander between 10 May 1937 and 12 August 1940, and again between 16 July 1941 and 9 October 1942. He was on a parallel with the military commissar but was subordinate to him. The politruk was replaced by the deputy commander for political affairs. There were junior and senior politruks as well.

Russian–Polish War (1919–20)

Initiated by the Polish army penetrating into territory which the Red Army was attempting to occupy. The Russian Civil War began in the summer of 1918 and the goal of the Bolsheviks was to win control of the territory of the former Russian Empire. The Poles moved towards Lithuania, Belorussia and Ukraine, where the Reds were trying to defeat nationalist forces and take over from the Germans (they, according to the Treaty of Brest-Litovsk, controlled the republic) who had abandoned the territory after the armistice of November 1918 in the west. The new Polish Republic, headed by J. Pilsudski, promoted the formation of a federation of states on its eastern borders, running from the Baltic to the Black Sea. In April 1919 the Poles attacked the Lithuanian–Belorussian Soviet Republic, which had just come into being, and took Vilna (Vilnius). They then moved eastwards. In June 1919 the Poles intervened in Ukraine at a time when the conflict between the Rada and Denikin, the Russian White commander, was at a critical stage. The Poles took East Galicia. The Supreme Allied Council decided that Poland's eastern frontier should be along the Curzon Line, on 8 December 1919. Although Polish troops were well east of this line, Soviet Russia offered, on 22 January 1920, to recognise the territorial status quo. While Pilsudski was negotiating with the Bolsheviks he was also in talks with the Ukrainian Directory, which was under great pressure from the Red Army. The result was the Polish–Ukrainian pact of 21 April 1920 and five days later Polish troops attacked and occupied Kiev on 7 May. However, Budenny's First Cavalry Army and a counter-offensive by Tukhachevsky (2 July) changed the situation. This opened up the prospect for Soviet Russia of carrying the revolution to central Europe and Germany, and on 28 July, in occupied Bailystok, a Polish Provisional Revolutionary Committee was established. Peace negotiations, proposed by the Poles, got under way, with the Curzon Line as the proposed frontier. However, the situation was transformed when Pilsudski counter-attacked on 16 August and forced Tukhachevsky to retreat (the miracle on the Vistula) and Soviet Russia to make territorial concessions. This defeat was partly due to the inability of Stalin to link up with Tukhachevsky's forces. A preliminary peace in Riga on 12 October 1920 moved the Polish frontier 150 km east of the Curzon Line into Belorussia and Ukraine. This was formally recognised in the Treaty of Riga on 18 March 1921. This frontier remained until September 1939, when the Red Army moved into Poland and the regions east of the Curzon Line were again added to Belorussia and Ukraine.

Sino–Soviet border conflicts, 1969–89

The Sino–Russian border, laid down in the sixteenth to the nineteenth centuries, always benefited Russia because of its military power. There was always tension between Mao Zedong and the Moscow communist leadership, with the Chinese leader believing that neither he nor China were treated with the respect they deserved. The Cultural Revolution in China, which got under way during the mid-1960s, escalated tension and

China began complaining that the Sino–Soviet border had been laid down under unequal treaties. It also rankled China that Soviet influence predominated in the People's Republic of Mongolia (the second communist state set up, in 1924, and pro-Moscow). The main sources of conflict were the rivers Ussuri and Amur with the border changing several times. This was partly due to the fact that the the river beds marking the border kept changing. Fighting broke out on Damansky Island on the Ussuri in March 1969 when the Chinese opened fire on Russian border guards. Moscow weighed up the nuclear option and enquired how Washington would react if it did attack. Another source of Sino–Soviet tension was the belief by the Chinese that Moscow had promised it an atomic bomb, something which Khrushchev denied. Relations improved in the 1970s but in 1979 tension increased again on the Ussuri, China invaded North Vietnam and talks on the border dispute were broken off in 1980. Under Gorbachev, the talks began again in February 1987 and a settlement was reached in November 1988. Two of China's preconditions, the withdrawal of Soviet troops from Mongolia and a reduction in Soviet forces along the Sino–Soviet border, were met by Gorbachev. The border conflict was a by-product of the growing estrangement between the CPSU and the Communist Party of China after 1960. This conflict paralleled a bitter ideological dispute between the two communist parties.

Soviet–Finnish War
This comprises the Winter War of 1939–40 and the continuation war of 1941–44. The secret protocol of the Nazi–Soviet Pact of August 1939 provided the Soviet Union with future control of eastern Poland, the Baltic States, Bessarabia and northern Bukovina, thus meeting its security needs. The only outstanding problem was Finland as the Finnish border was very close to Leningrad. The Soviet Union, in October 1939, proposed that Finland should cede a considerable piece of territory to it and that the two countries should sign treaties on the stationing of troops and mutual aid. Finland prevaricated and only offered limited territorial concessions. In November 1939 the Soviets arranged a border incident and attacked on 30 November 1939 in Karelia, and on 1 December a Finnish people's government, headed by Otto Kuusinen, was proclaimed in occupied Finnish territory. The intention was that this government could take over the whole of Finland if and when that possibility presented itself. The Finns, however, held up the advance of the Red Army along the Mannerheim Line and encircled other advancing Soviet units. The League of Nations expelled the USSR on 14 December 1939 because of its aggression and Great Britain and France approved a plan to send an expeditionary force to Scandinavia, ostensibly to help Finland but in reality to seize Swedish iron ore mines (ore being exported to Germany) and open a second front against Germany in Scandinavia.

To do this they required a request for military assistance from Finland. The Finns considered the Anglo–French offer and deemed it insufficient. Sweden refused to help. The Finns flew to Moscow and, on 12 March 1940, a peace treaty was signed in which Finland conceded most of the strategic and territorial demands made by Moscow in late 1939. The Soviets had lost over 200,000 dead and the Finns 25,000. Had they continued the war they could have achieved total victory but decided to end hostilities, possibly because of nervousness about Anglo–French intentions. Stalin continued to apply pressure on Finland but the latter put out feelers to Germany in response. German troops landed in Finland and the latter received military and civil aid. On 25 June 1941, three days after Germany attacked the Soviet Union, Finland continued the Winter War against the USSR. Initial successes led in late 1941 to the reconquest of all territory lost in 1940 and a line of defence was established in east Karelia which resisted all Soviet attacks. After Stalingrad the Finns realised that the Germans could not win and began peace feelers, but the Soviets broke off talks in February 1944. In June 1944 a massive Soviet offensive drove Mannerheim back and emergency aid had to be purchased from Germany by promising not to make a separate peace with Moscow. The front was stabilised in August, roughly on the line of the 1940 frontier. Finland reneged on its promise to Germany and an armistice was signed on 19 September 1944. This restored the 1940 treaty, substituted Porkkala for Hanko, and the remaining German troops were to be disarmed and evacuated. Heavy reparations were imposed and the special relations between the Soviet Union and Finland, which lasted until 1991, came into being. Finland, alone among Germany's allies during the war, escaped Soviet occupation and the imposition of a people's government. Under Gorbachev, it was freely admitted that the USSR would have been much better off had the Finnish model been imposed in eastern and south-eastern Europe.

Warsaw Pact
The name used in the west to describe the Soviet-led counter to NATO. It was set up by the treaty on friendship, cooperation and mutual assistance, signed in Warsaw on 14 May 1955. It followed the admission of West Germany to NATO on 23 October 1954, which thereby fully integrated the Federal Republic into the western alliance system. The Soviets argued that the pact was necessary since the west had declined to reach an understanding with them on the future of Germany and Europe. However, if a system of collective security in Europe was achieved, the Pact would dissolve. The original signatories were the Soviet Union, Poland, Czechoslovakia, the GDR, Romania, Bulgaria and Albania (it left in 1968). These states recognised the principle of equal sovereignty and were obliged to consult one another when international crises arose.

They had to come to the aid of a member state when necessary, were not permitted to interfere in the domestic affairs of member states and were not permitted to join other alliance systems. A united supreme command and a political consultative committee were to be established. The treaty was for 20 years and if not annulled to be extended for another 10 years. For the Soviet Union, the Pact performed functions which the Cominform and Comecon did not. However, Moscow revealed little interest in developing the consultative political committee into a body which could contribute to the further integration of the east and south-east European communist states. It met at infrequent intervals. The supreme command was a different matter. It was always in Moscow and the Commander-in-Chief of the Pact was always a Soviet Marshal and, *ex officio*, a deputy USSR Minister of Defence. Military cooperation between the Soviet Union and its allies had been laid down in the bilateral treaties signed between 1944 and 1947 and renewed in the 1960s. The Pact required agreements on the stationing of Soviet troops and these were concluded in 1956–57. The agreement with the GDR permitted Soviet troops to enter and leave the country without reference to the GDR authorities. There were no Soviet troops stationed in Czechoslovakia. There were Soviet troops stationed in Poland, Hungary and Romania but the Romanians managed to convince them to leave. The Warsaw Pact intervention in Czechoslovakia in August 1968 was based on the perception that socialism was in danger and thus required the help. This became known as the Brezhnev doctrine and limited the sovereignty of member states. Gorbachev abandoned the Brezhnev doctrine and refused to permit the use of Soviet forces to shore up national communist parties. This ensured that the revolutions in eastern and south-eastern Europe in 1989 were bloodless. The GDR left the pact when Germany reunited in October 1990 and other post-communist regimes were also concerned to leave. The Pact was dissolved on 1 July 1991.

Whites
The main opponents of the Reds or communists during the Russian Civil War (1981–20). See entry on Civil War for details.

Conferences and summits

Bandung Conference, 18–24 April 1955

This was the first international meeting of developing states and provided a forum for anti-colonialism and non-alignment. It laid the foundations for the Third World movement. It took place in the former Dutch colony of Indonesia and was attended by 29 Afro-Asian states. Nehru, India's leader, played a major role at the conference and the meeting adopted his five principles of cooperation. Western states were sharply criticised. This paved the way for Khrushchev's and Bulganin's tour of Afghanistan, Burma and India in November 1955. They discovered that courting the Third World could pay dividends and thus began a policy which was abandoned only by Gorbachev.

Beijing Summit, 15–18 May 1989

Relations between the Soviet Union and China had deteriorated after 1959, when Kosygin had met Mao Zedong. The Chinese listed three conditions for the improvement of Sino–Soviet relations: a Soviet withdrawal from Afghanistan, the end of Vietnamese dominance over Kampuchea (Cambodia) and a reduction in Soviet forces along the Sino–Soviet border. Gorbachev addressed all these after 1985. His main objective in meeting Deng Xiaoping was to normalise relations with China and establish personal contact. Gorbachev confirmed Soviet force reductions along the frontier. The visit deeply embarrassed the Chinese leaders as Gorbachev was mobbed as a hero of democracy. This forced changes in the itinerary. The student demonstrations had begun on 18 April, three days after the death of Hu Yaobang, the General Secretary of the Communist Party of China. The Party leadership was deeply split over its reaction to the demonstrations and Gorbachev's presence exacerbated the situation. Shortly after Gorbachev's departure martial law was proclaimed and on 3–4 June 1989 the students, demonstrating for democracy, were mown down.

Camp David Summit, 26–27 September 1959

This was the first Soviet–American summit without any other great powers being present. In August 1959, in the wake of tension over Berlin, President Eisenhower suddenly invited Nikita Khrushchev, the Soviet leader, to America. Eisenhower hoped that Khrushchev would moderate his hostility to all things American if he were exposed to a dose of the American way of life. The trip was the first by a Soviet leader to America and impressed Khrushchev greatly. He picked up some useful tips on growing maize and was so taken by overnight sleeper trains that they were introduced widely afterwards in the Soviet Union. The two leaders met at Camp David after a previous meeting in Washington and agreed that a great power summit should take place in 1960. Khrushchev backed away from his ultimatum on Berlin and it was agreed that problems should be solved by peaceful means. There was no agreement, however, on Germany or disarmament.

Geneva Conference, 26 April–21 July 1954

The death of Stalin breathed new life into east–west relations as the new Soviet leaders competed with one another for supremacy. One of the by-products of this was a search for a less confrontational foreign policy and this was the first meeting of Soviet and Allied foreign ministers since 1949. The main goal was a peace treaty with Germany but the window of opportunity did not open and no agreement was reached. Had Beria won the power struggle in 1953 he might have moved towards a unified, neutral Germany, but Khrushchev revealed little appetite for this approach. The Soviets wished to preserve East Germany in a united Germany, thereby hoping to expand communist influence and exert Soviet pressure on the evolution of the new German state. This was as vain a hope in 1954 as it proved in 1990. The summit also discussed the draft Austrian peace treaty, Korea and Indo-China. It was agreed to meet in April 1954 to discuss the last two issues.

Geneva Summit, 18–23 July 1955

Khrushchev's first meeting with President Eisenhower and his first summit in the west. It was the first meeting of the victorious allies since the Potsdam conference in July–August 1945. It was attended by Khrushchev and Bulganin (Khrushchev was still sharing power at this time), Eisenhower, Anthony Eden (later Lord Avon) and Edgar Faure (France), as well as their foreign ministers. In his memoirs, Khrushchev relates that the Soviet delegation felt a bit inferior on arrival. The leaders got on well and the spirit of Geneva was born. An Austrian peace treaty, providing for Austrian neutrality, had been signed in May 1955 and Moscow would have liked a similar agreement on Germany. The major Russian fear was that a united Germany would fall into the western camp and become a threat to the Soviet Union. The west, especially German Chancellor Konrad Adenauer, were concerned lest a neutral Germany break away from its pro-western moorings with Germany playing off the east against the west. The Soviets did not alter their views on how a united Germany should come about: East and West Germany agreeing and then elections.

The west wanted elections and then an all-German government. Moscow proposed that NATO and the Warsaw Pact be abolished and replaced by a collective security system. This found no favour with the west. On disarmament Eisenhower proposed an open skies policy of allowing the USA and USSR to collect aerial photographs of the other's territory to verify any arms deal. Moscow shied away from this.

Geneva Summit, 19–20 November 1985

The first summit for six years and the first between President Ronald Reagan and Mikhail Gorbachev. The main goal of the meeting was to establish personal contact and improve the dismal state of Soviet–American relations. They hit it off after they retired to have a fireside chat and agreed to meet again. Various agreements were signed on the landing rights of civilian aircraft, cultural exchanges and the opening of new consulates.

Glassboro', New Jersey, Mini-Summit, 23–25 June 1967

This was the only top-level meeting between the Soviets and the Americans between 1961 and 1972. Prime Minister Aleksei Kosygin, in the USA for a meeting of the UN on the Arab–Israeli war just ended, met President Lyndon Johnson on 23 and 25 June. They discussed the Middle East and Vietnam but there was no meeting of minds. At this time Kosygin spoke for the Soviet Union on foreign affairs but was pushed aside after the Warsaw Pact invasion of Czechoslovakia in August 1968 by Brezhnev.

Helsinki Summit, 9 September 1990

The third Gorbachev–Bush summit took place as a result of Saddam Hussein's invasion of Kuwait. It was referred to as the first post-Cold War summit. The two presidents demanded that Saddam withdraw from Kuwait and agreed that economic sanctions should be applied to Iraq. Gorbachev was keen to prevent a military confrontation with a former ally of the Soviet Union and wanted more time for talks. The USA proposed military action. Gorbachev was concerned about Soviet military advisers in Iraq and whether the USA would withdraw militarily from Saudi Arabia when the crisis was over.

Malta Summit, 2–3 December 1989

Gorbachev was concerned about the long delay in arranging a summit with the new US President George Bush. The President needed time to reassess American foreign policy but US public opinion was becoming restive as the Soviet leader enjoyed wide popularity among ordinary Americans. The summit took place after the opening of the Berlin Wall and the collapse of communism in eastern and south-eastern Europe. The weather was dreadful and this epitomised Gorbachev's prospects in the Soviet Union. No agreements were signed and no communiqué was issued, but the two leaders got on well. Both declared the Cold War was over.

Moscow Summit, 22–26 May 1972
The first summit between Leonid Brezhnev and President Richard Nixon, which was marked by the signing of the strategic arms limitation treaty (SALT I). Besides SALT, agreements were signed on health, a joint space adventure (the 1975 Apollo–Soyuz mission), an agreement on avoiding accidents at sea and the setting up of a commercial commission. The two sides also agreed on certain basic principles regulating their relations, including restraint during times of crisis and the avoidance of confrontation. This marked the high point of Soviet power and the Soviets viewed it as America conceding nuclear parity with them.

Moscow Summit, 27 June–3 July 1974
Watergate overshadowed the third and final Brezhnev–Nixon summit. They reached agreement on one nuclear arms question: both sides were to restrict themselves to one anti-ballistic missile field instead of the two agreed in the 1972 ABM treaty. There was also an agreement on energy research, a ban on small nuclear tests and discussion of the START II treaty.

Moscow Summit, 29 May–2 June 1988
This was the last of the Gorbachev–Reagan summits and was marked by the exchange, on 1 June, of the instruments of ratification which implemented the INF treaty. The two superpowers agreed to apprise one another of nuclear missile launches. They began to lay the ground for a reduction in strategic nuclear arms.

Moscow Summit, 30 July–1 August 1991
The centrepiece of the fourth and last Gorbachev–Bush summit was the signing of the START II treaty. Gorbachev had returned empty-handed from the G7 meeting in London earlier in July, having failed to obtain any firm promises of credits from the west, and was under great pressure at home. Bush pressed for a more liberal policy towards the Baltic republics and advised that the Soviet economy should move more rapidly towards the market. There was a tentative agreement on a Middle East peace conference. The summit was a great success personally for the two leaders and developed further the cooperation between the superpowers. President and Mrs Bush were made aware of the demands of President Yeltsin of Russia when he ignored protocol at an official dinner. Yeltsin made it clear he objected to not being seated at the top table.

New York Summit, December 1988
On 7 December Gorbachev, at the UN, announced that the Soviet Union would reduce its armed forces by 500,000 within two years without requiring reciprocal moves by the USA or its allies. He also stressed that the common interests of mankind and freedom of choice are universal human principles. Later he met President Reagan and President-elect Bush on Governors Island. He had to cut his visit short after receiving news of an earthquake in Armenia.

Paris Summit, May 1960
The summit was proposed at the Camp David meeting of the US and Soviet leaders in September 1959. However, Chancellor Adenauer and French President de Gaulle had doubts about the advisability of such a meeting, presumably fearing that America might make concessions to Khrushchev on Germany and other matters. On 1 May 1960 a US U2 spy plane was shot down over Sverdlovsk and the pilot, Gary Powers, captured alive. Khrushchev used the incident to demand an apology from Eisenhower, who had initially denied the existence of such an aircraft over the Soviet Union. The British Prime Minister, Harold Macmillan, pointed out to Khrushchev that the President of the United States could not make such an apology. Khrushchev used the incident to scupper the summit. The leaders arrived in Paris on 11 May but the meeting was cancelled within 48 hours.

Potsdam Conference, 17 July–2 August 1945
The last meeting of the Big Three (USSR, USA and Britain) between 17 July and 2 August 1945 outside Berlin, at which decisions on the military and political goals of the anti-Hitler coalition were taken. Tension had been building up before the end of hostilities. The US objective was to get Stalin to agree to Soviet intervention in the war against Japan and to join a world body, the UN. The Soviet aspiration of acquiring east and south-east Europe as a cordon sanitaire for military security clashed with the American and British view that there should be no closed zones of influence. Moscow moved quickly in the occupied territories to install pro-communist regimes and Washington and London began to practice containment – blocking the expansion of the Soviet Union outside its existing zones of influence. The ending of Lend Lease on 11 May 1945 can be seen as the first step in this policy. Some agreements were reached however: the west recognised Poland's takeover of the territories east of the rivers Oder and Neisse and the expulsion of the German population from Czechoslovakia, Poland and Hungary. The frontier between Germany and Poland was to be agreed at a separate peace conference. The Yalta agreement that although Germany was to be divided into occupation zones, it was to be treated as an economic entity was reconfirmed.

The Allies were not able to agree on reparations. The disagreements between the USSR and the USA which surfaced at Potsdam were continued at the London Conference of foreign ministers and proved to be incapable of resolution. The final protocol – always referred to as the Potsdam treaty by Moscow – papered over some of the cracks but was an unsatisfactory document which gave rise to conflict during the Cold War. Stalin dominated proceedings as Churchill had given way to Clement Attlee as British Prime Minister and President Truman had taken over from Franklin D. Roosevelt, who had died on 12 April 1945.

Reykjavik Summit, 11–12 October 1986

Gorbachev proposed the summit in September and since neither leader was willing to go to the other's capital, Reykjavik, the Icelandic capital, seemed an ideal half-way house. The summit was preceded by Soviet–American tension, which began with the arrest of a Soviet intelligence officer, with the Soviets responding by arresting Nicholas Daniloff , a US journalist. Various US and Soviet personnel were then expelled from the respective countries. The two men were exchanged on 29 September. Gorbachev made dramatic proposals for nuclear weapons reductions but agreement eluded them as the USA would not give up its Strategic Defence Initiative (SDI). The USA regarded the summit as a failure until Gorbachev, at a press briefing afterwards, portrayed it as quite a success. The Americans then concurred.

Tehran Conference, 28 November–1 December 1943

The first meeting of the Big Three (Stalin, Churchill and Roosevelt) took place at Tehran from 28 November to 1 December 1943 and began a process of consultation between the Allied leaders which lasted to Potsdam in June 1945. By Tehran it was clear that Germany was going to be defeated and hence the conference was about the spoils of the post-war era. There had been sharp disagreements between the partners about war aims in the past but the successes of the Red Army in July 1943 strengthened Stalin's hand. At the Moscow conference of foreign ministers on 19–30 November 1943 the USA and Britain had prepared the way for concessions to Moscow. At Tehran the USA and Britain finally committed themselves to the second front in Europe in 1944 and the recognition of the Curzon Line (with northern East Prussia to be added) as the frontier between Poland and the Soviet Union. The Americans wanted in return a Soviet commitment to enter the war against Japan after the defeat of Germany. No agreement was reached on the Soviet desire for a zone of influence in eastern Europe and the occupation of Germany. The western Allies were concerned to avoid conflict with Stalin lest the Red Army, for example, stop at the frontiers of the Soviet Union and leave the Allies to fight the rest of the war in Europe. The shape of post-war Europe was agreed, in principle, at the conference of Yalta.

Vienna Summit, 3–4 June 1961

The only meeting between President Kennedy and Khrushchev was marked by the Soviet leader's heavy-handed treatment of the US President. Khrushchev thought that Kennedy's youth and lack of political experience would permit him to gain the upper hand. Kennedy was on the defensive after the Bay of Pigs fiasco, when Cuban exiles had invaded and been trounced by Castro's Cuban forces. They could not agree over Khrushchev's demand that the USA recognise East Germany but they did agree that there should be a neutral and independent Laos. Kennedy kept his head. Khrushchev misjudged Kennedy and this was revealed during the Cuban Missile Crisis.

Vienna Summit, 15–18 June 1979

The only summit between President Jimmy Carter and Leonid Brezhnev was marked by the signature of the START II treaty. There was considerable opposition in the USA to the treaty, with some commentators seeing détente as a one-way street – all the benefits to the USSR and none to the USA – and the Soviets were nervous about Sino–American collaboration. By this time Brezhnev's physical faculties were failing him and he was not capable of establishing a rapport with the American President. The Soviet invasion of Afghanistan in December 1979 killed détente and a new Cold War descended on Soviet–Americans relations.

Vladivostok Summit, 23–24 November 1974

This was the only summit between President Gerald Ford and Leonid Brezhnev and followed a tour by President Ford of East Asia. The meeting had been arranged by Henry Kissinger to provide the two leaders with an opportunity to become acquainted. The meeting produced a 'base agreement' on the SALT II treaty, with both sides accepting a limit of 2,400 strategic missiles and bombers, of which 1,320 could have multiple warheads. The Chinese took umbrage at the summit and slowed the Sino–American rapprochement. The expected visit to America by Brezhnev in 1975 did not materialise.

Washington Summit, 16–24 June 1973

This was the second Brezhnev–Nixon summit and the Soviet leader's first trip to America. It took place during the Watergate hearings, which were suspended for the summit. The first meeting was in Washington, the next in Camp David, and the two leaders also met in San Clemente, California. There were agreements on agriculture, transport and cultural exchanges, and the framework for START II talks and a treaty, and both countries promised to consult one another if nuclear war ever threatened to involve one or both of them. It could not match the first Moscow summit for drama but it helped to establish the fact that superpower summits were becoming normal.

Washington Summit, 7–10 December 1987
Talks on reducing intermediate-range nuclear forces (INF) in Europe between George Shultz, the US Secretary of State, and Edvard Shevardnadze, the Soviet Foreign Minister, on 15–18 September 1987, progressed well and produced a framework for an INF treaty. The treaty was signed at the summit, the first signed by the US and Soviet leaders on arms since 1979. It was a highly successful summit with Americans taking to Gorbachev; indeed one can say that Gorbymania was born there. Gorbachev had been warned, in a KGB briefing, that Americans were reserved towards him and the Soviet Union. He grasped the opportunity to stop his car, get out and meet and talk to ordinary Americans. This experience had quite an impact on him.

Washington Summit, 30 May–4 June 1990
The second Bush–Gorbachev summit was conducted in a friendly atmosphere, symbolising that the two superpowers were now partners and not adversaries, and major strategic arms reductions were agreed in principle. There were also discussions about conventional arms cuts in Europe and the control of chemical weapons. Gorbachev held to the Soviet view that the reunification of Germany was premature, and if it did occur the new Germany should not be in NATO. He was irritated by US criticism of Soviet policy in the Baltic republics (there were diasporas in the USA). The Soviet leader continued his efforts to secure US loans to bail out the Soviet economy.

Yalta Conference, 4–11 February 1945
This took place on 4–11 February 1945 in the Crimea and was the second and last meeting of Stalin, Roosevelt and Churchill, as Roosevelt died on 12 April 1945 (the first conference had been at Tehran). The topics discussed were the concluding phases of the Second World War and the post-war settlement. Stalin was in a stronger position than at Tehran due to the rapid progress of the Red Army and its penetration of eastern Europe. The USA was keen to involve the Soviet Union in the war against Japan and to win its cooperation in the UN. The Big Three agreed that the Curzon Line should be Poland's eastern frontier and that the Soviet-backed Polish provisional government would be recognised when a few members of the exiled Polish government in London were added. The agreement on German occupation zones of 14 November 1944 was confirmed (now including France). Decisions on breaking

Germany up, the eastern border with Poland and reparations were left for future resolution. A declaration on liberated Europe was issued which guaranteed all nations democracy and self-determination. This had little impact as the occupying power determined the form of government which would take power.

Treaties and agreements

ABM Treaty, 1972

The American–Soviet summit in Moscow in May 1972 completed the drafting and the signature of two treaties. Firstly, an Anti-Ballistic Missile Treaty which restricted both sides to building two ABM fields, of a hundred missiles each, one around their capital cities and one to protect their intercontinental ballistic missile (ICBM) sites. The ABM treaty was ratified by the US Senate on 3 August 1972. Secondly, there was an interim agreement on offensive missiles, with a freeze on existing numbers of strategic (long-range or intercontinental) weapons as follows: 1,054 ICBMs for the USA and 1,618 for the Soviet Union; 656 submarine launched ballistic missiles (SLBMs) for the USA and 740 for the Soviet Union; 455 strategic (capable of reaching the Soviet Union) bombers for the USA and 140 for the Soviet Union. The treaty was to cover five years. These two treaties form the Strategic Arms Limitation Treaty (SALT I). They were important advances in nuclear arms control but attracted criticism from several quarters. They did not involve new strategic systems, such as the multiple independently targetable re-entry vehicles (MIRVs). The USA had a sizeable lead in the number of nuclear warheads. The Soviet Union, on the other hand, had more ICBMs and SLBMs. The treaty did not cover the Soviet deployment of new heavy missiles, such as the SS19. In 1973 the Soviet Union tested its own MIRV, something that surprised the Americans.

Anglo–Soviet Alliance, 1942

The treaty was signed by British Foreign Secretary, Anthony Eden (later Lord Avon), and his Soviet counterpart, Vyacheslav Molotov, in London on 26 May 1942. It was preceded by tough negotiations during which Britain refused to recognise the USSR frontiers at the start of the war with Germany in June 1941 (Britain had agreed with the US view that such questions should be resolved after the war). The two parties agreed that no armistice or peace with Germany or its Axis allies would be negotiated or concluded by one party without the consent of the other. Other clauses stated that the parties were bound by the two principles of not seeking territorial aggrandisement for themselves and of non-interference in the internal affairs of other states. There were also clauses about joint action after the war. The treaty followed the Anglo–Soviet agreement of 12 July

1941, when the two parties agreed not to conclude an armistice except by mutual consent and a commitment by Britain to help the USSR with material support.

Austrian Peace Treaty, May 1955

The Anschluss (union of Austria and Germany in 1938) was declared null and void by the Allies in 1943. The same arrangement as for Germany was agreed: that is, four occupation zones (USA, USSR, Britain and France), and the division of the capital, Vienna, into four sectors. Vienna, just like Berlin, was inside the Soviet zone. The Soviets set up a provisional government, under the social democrat Karl Renner, in April 1945 and the Allies recognised this government in October. A similar government for Germany could not be agreed. Under Stalin Soviet policy on Germany and Austria was similar: it wanted them neutral and united with communists maintaining influence. Khrushchev gauged that Moscow had much to gain from a united Austria in the western camp. NATO's lines of communications between West Germany and Italy ran through Austria and Austrian neutrality would cut this link. A peace treaty was signed and this provided for the withdrawal of all foreign troops. This was the first occasion after 1945 that Soviet troops had left any part of Europe willingly.

Berlin Treaty, 24 April 1926

The treaty, signed by the Soviet Union and Germany on 24 April 1926, confirmed the provisions of the treaty of Rapallo and both parties committed themselves to neutrality, renouncing aggression and not becoming involved in any boycott measures. The initiative for the treaty was Soviet and was an attempt by Moscow to ensure that the capitalist world did not unite against it. Germany supported the Soviet Union in the League of Nations and extended large credits to Moscow. However, Germany began to reorient its foreign policy in Europe and this led the Soviet Union to seek a policy of peaceful coexistence with Europe and to sign non-aggression pacts wherever possible.

Brest-Litovsk Treaty, 3 March 1918

The signing of the treaty on 3 March 1918 with Germany, Austria-Hungary, Bulgaria and Turkey ended Soviet Russia's involvement in the First World War. Attempts to end the war had begun immediately after the Soviet seizure of power with the decree on peace, passed by the 2nd Congress of Soviets on 26 October 1917. Trotsky offered the Central Powers a cease-fire on 13 November 1917 and appealed to the Allies to do the same. They refused and Soviet Russia had to go it alone. A cease-fire of 2 December 1917 prepared the way for talks and these began on 9 December in Brest-Litovsk. The Soviet side hoped to avoid losing territory but the Central Powers demanded Ukraine, Poland and west Latvia.

There was considerable conflict within the Bolshevik Party over negotiating with the capitalist powers. Bukharin advocated revolutionary war
(peace at no price), Lenin peace at any price and Trotsky neither peace
nor war. Lenin had his way and after additional German demands the
treaty was accepted. Soviet Russia gave up Poland, Estonia, Latvia, Lithuania, Finland and Ukraine and the regions in the Caucasus demanded
by Turkey. Russia lost about 30 per cent of the population of the Russian
Empire and most of its raw materials, industry and railways. Lenin justified the sacrifices by claiming they were interim losses since after the
victory of the proletariat in Berlin they would all return. The Treaty of
Brest-Litovsk was annulled by the Bolsheviks after Germany's defeat in
the west on 11 November 1918.

Briand–Kellogg Pact, 27 August 1928
An international agreement signed on 27 August 1928 outlawing war as
a means of pursuing political goals which the Soviet Union joined shortly
afterwards. It was named after the French Foreign Minister and the US
Secretary of State. Germany proposed that the Soviet Union be invited to
join but France and Great Britain strongly opposed this. Moscow joined
and thereby overcome its isolation, which had been compounded by the
activities of the Comintern. The pact was a departure for the Soviet Union
in its policy of peace and collective security, enunciated by Stalin at the
15th Party Congress in December 1927.

Comecon (or CMEA)
The Council for Mutual Economic Assistance was set up on 25 January
1949 and the founding members were the Soviet Union, Bulgaria, Hun-
gary, Poland, Romania and Czechoslovakia. Albania joined on 23 Feb-
ruary 1949 (left 1962) and the GDR on 29 September 1950. Vietnam,
China (until 1966), North Korea and Cuba acquired observer status.
Mongolia became a member on 6–7 July 1962 and thus was the first non-
European state to join. Cuba joined in July 1972 and Vietnam in June
1978. On 17 September 1964 Yugoslavia became an associate member. In
East Berlin in October 1983 Afghanistan, Angola, Ethiopia, South Yemen,
Laos, Mozambique and Nicaragua attended as observers. Comecon grew
out of the Soviet desire to wean east European states away from economic relations with the west and to offer a substitute for the Marshall
Plan. Comecon languished until 1959, when goals and principles were laid
down. Comecon was to serve socialist economic integration and became
an economic organisation to enable governments to coordinate their
economic plans with other governments. The Soviet Union dominated,
producing about two-thirds of the social product, but in terms of per
capita social product the GDR was at the top, with Mongolia, Vietnam
and Cuba at the bottom. The secretariat was in Moscow and besides the

meetings, there was an executive committee, four special committees and 21 permanent commissions on various sectors of the economy. In the 1980s about 60 per cent of trade turnover of member states was through Comecon. The highest proportion was 96 per cent of trade turnover by Mongolia in 1984 and the lowest was 46.6 per cent in 1984 by Romania. As member states rejected communism and moved to the market economy, Comecon became less and less relevant. It dissolved itself at its 46th council meeting on 28 June 1991.

Cominform

The Communist Information Bureau was established in September 1947 at a conference of nine communist parties (the CPSU, the Polish, Czechoslovak, Hungarian, Bulgarian, Romanian, Yugoslav French, and Italian parties) in Szklarska Poreba, Poland. The tasks of the Cominform were more limited than those of the Comintern and it was restricted to Europe and formally only facilitated the transfer of information and coordinated the activities of its member parties. Its headquarters were in Belgrade, and then in Bucharest after the expulsion of Yugoslavia in June 1948. It had its own newspaper, *For a Lasting Peace, for People's Democracy*. The Cominform was to promote the integration of the people's democracies in the interests of the Soviet Union and oppose the Marshall Plan. The conflict between Stalin and Tito in 1948 seriously undermined the viability of the organisation and it declined in prestige from 1949 onwards. Tito informed Khrushchev that the dissolution of the Cominform was a necessary part of the normalisation of relations between the two countries. On 17 April 1957 the Cominform was officially dissolved.

Comintern

The Communist International was founded in March 1919 in Moscow as a successor to the 2nd Socialist International. When Lenin and his supporters failed to take it over, Lenin decided a new, more revolutionary international was necessary. Hence the Comintern was also called the 3rd International. The language of the Comintern until the early 1920s was German as it was assumed that the socialist revolution would soon be victorious in Berlin and the organisation would transfer there. Lenin always delivered his speeches to the Comintern in German, with Karl Radek helping him when he could not find the right German word. The 2nd Congress of the Comintern met in July–August 1920 and passed the 21 conditions necessary to qualify for membership. They represent the Bolshevisation of the international communist movement: every party was obliged to support first and foremost Soviet power. All were subordinate to the executive committee in Moscow. The principle of democratic centralism was to apply. The Comintern was useful to Moscow as it could claim that it did not control the organisation when foreign states complained about its activities. During the 1920s and 1930s the Comintern was brought into line with the goals of Soviet foreign policy. Under NEP the policy of limited coexistence with the capitalist world meant that the Comintern had to abjure radicalism. In 1928 communist parties were to target social democrats as their main enemy and social democracy was called social fascism. In 1935 the Comintern adopted the popular front policy of attempting to unite all forces against the rising tide of fascism. The Comintern became a hindrance to Stalin after the German attack of June 1941 as he wished to established working relations with capitalist states against Germany. It was dissolved on 15 May 1943 and most of its functions passed to what became the international department of the Party CC.

Commonwealth of Independent States (CIS)

The leaders of Russia, Ukraine and Belarus met in Belovezh forest near Minsk, Belarus, on 7–8 December 1991 and decided to dissolve the Soviet Union and replace it with the CIS. They claimed they were entitled to take this action as they were founder members of the USSR in 1922. On 12 December the Central Asian leaders, meeting in Ash-khabad (Ashghabat), Turkmenistan, requested membership of the CIS as founding members. On 21–22 December 1991 in Almaty these three were joined by another eight former Soviet republics and the CIS was expanded (Estonia, Latvia, Lithuania and Georgia did not attend). Gorbachev resigned as USSR President on 25 December and the Soviet Union ceased to exist on 31 December 1991. The Soviet Union could not cope with its ethnic problems and the elections of 1990 produced parliaments in the Baltic republics and elsewhere which were legitimate and could speak for the population. Republics and regions claimed sovereignty, but it was the declaration of sovereignty by Russia in June 1990 which was the decisive moment. Gorbachev attempted to broker a new Union of Sovereign States at Novo-Ogarevo, his dacha outside Moscow, but in vain. A Union of Sovereign States, a confederation, was negotiated in the USSR State Council but Yeltsin and Shushkevich (Belarus) refused to initial it on 25 November and this indicated that they had decided to break up the Soviet Union. Minsk was declared the capital of the CIS and its secretariat was also to be there. Meetings of members would take place in the various capitals, in rotation. The attempted coup of August 1991 accelerated the break-up of the Soviet Union as republics sought to leave before another possible coup succeeded.

Conventional Forces in Europe (CFE) Treaty, 1990

In January 1989 a Conference on Security and Cooperation In Europe meeting in Vienna agreed to reconvene conventional (non-nuclear) stability talks. These became the Conventional Forces in Europe (CFE) talks when they opened in March 1989 in Vienna between NATO and the Warsaw Pact. Simultaneously all CSCE members convened in a Conference on Disarmament in Europe to discuss confidence and security-building in Europe. While these were under way the Berlin Wall was breached and communist regimes in eastern and south-eastern Europe collapsed. This increased the significance of NATO to the west in a rapidly changing security environment. Gorbachev, on the other hand, mindful of the declining power of the Soviet Union, the disintegration of the Warsaw Pact, then withdrawal of Soviet forces from eastern and south-eastern Europe and the reunification of Germany, wanted the CSCE to assume greater responsibility for the security of Europe. This meant the downgrading of NATO. In Paris, in November 1990, two major agreements were signed:

(i)   The CFE treaty between NATO and the Warsaw Pact, signed on 19 November, was tilted in favour of NATO and promised to end the Soviet superiority in Europe in conventional weapons. Numbers of soldiers were not negotiated but there were limits on the amount of armament to be held by signatory states. For example, each alliance could have 20,000 tanks with no single state having more than 13,300. The Soviet military evaded their strict limits by transferring tanks and other equipment east of the Urals, and hence to Asia. Also some tanks were transferred to the navy.

(ii) CSCE states signed a declaration on individual rights and guaranteed democratic freedoms, including private property. A CSCE secretariat was established and a Conflict Prevention Centre was established in Vienna.

Cuban Missile Crisis

A confrontation between the Soviet Union and the United States which brought the world to the brink of nuclear war in October 1962. Khrushchev judged John F. Kennedy to be a young, cautious President after their meeting in Vienna in June 1961. There was, however, the danger that the Americans might permit the Cuban exiles to try again after the fiasco of April 1961 at the Bay of Pigs. In order to prevent this and also to overcome the lack of Soviet intercontinental nuclear missiles, Khrushchev began placing intermediate-range nuclear missiles on Cuba. At the 22nd Party Congress in October 1961 Marshal Malinovsky claimed military superiority for the USSR, but it was not true that the Soviets had more missiles than the Americans. The USA discovered the Cuban missiles on 18 October 1962 and on 22 October President Kennedy warned Khrushchev that any attack from Cuba would be treated in the same way as an attack from the Soviet Union. He then imposed a naval blockade to prevent any more missiles being delivered to Cuba. In reality all the missiles were already in place. Between 23 and 28 October Khrushchev and Kennedy exchanged letters. With the situation very tense Khrushchev, without consulting Castro, accepted the solution proposed by President Kennedy. Soviet missiles would be removed from Cuba in return for a promise by the USA and its allies that they would not invade Cuba. The USA would withdraw its Jupiter missiles from Turkey.

Curzon Line

The demarcation line which the Supreme Allied Council proposed to Russia, Poland and other warring states on 8 December 1919 as a provisional frontier. The British Foreign Secretary, Lord Curzon (1859–1925), presented the proposal again on 11 July 1920 as an ultimatum to the warring parties. However, the Treaty of Riga between Poland and Soviet Russia placed the eastern frontier of Poland much further to the east than the Curzon Line. The line again became a live issue at the Tehran conference when Stalin achieved recognition from the Allies for the Curzon Line to be the western boundary of the Soviet Union. It was confirmed as such, with a few minor changes, at the Potsdam conference.

Decree on land

The first decree of Soviet power, which was passed during the night of 26–27 October 1917 by the 2nd Congress of Soviets. It was based on the model of the 1st Russian Congress of Peasants' Deputies in 1917, with the addition of 242 amendments (mandates) by regional delegates. Although passed by a Bolshevik-dominated Congress, it was the programme of the Socialist Revolutionaries. The decree abolished the private ownership of land and confiscated the landed estates, all crown, church and monastery lands, together with their livestock and implements. All land was placed at the disposal of the land committees and soviets of peasants' deputies until the Constituent Assembly met. In reality much of the landlord estates had already been distributed among the peasants and this remained so until the advent of collectivisation, when it was the peasants who lost their land.

Decree on peace

The first decree by Soviet power on foreign policy and the second decree passed by the 2nd Congress of Soviets, on 26 October 1917. The Bolsheviks had campaigned before October under the slogans peace and land, and thereby promised to end the war. Lenin discovered that it takes two to make peace and the Treaty of Brest-Litovsk was not signed until March 1918.

Helsinki Final Act

NATO and the western Allies always treated Soviet proposals for a European security conference – the first proposal was made in 1954 – with suspicion. It was perceived as a tactic to separate the USA from western Europe and undermine NATO. On the other hand, Moscow never made up its mind whether it would be better off with the USA out of Europe or with the USA in Europe as a brake on German policy. In December 1971 the Atlantic Council accepted a proposal by the Warsaw Pact for a security conference on Europe. Preparatory talks got under way in November 1972 and in July 1973 a conference convened in Helsinki which was attended by 33 states, including NATO, the Warsaw Pact, non-aligned and neutral states. The only European state of any significance which boycotted the proceedings was Albania. NATO participation led to the USA and Canada also being present. On 30 July–1 August 1975 the Helsinki Final Act was discussed and signed by President Gerald Ford, Leonid Brezhnev (as General Secretary of the CPSU he was technically not a head of state or Prime Minister; in 1977 he assumed the role of Soviet head of state) and other leaders. There were three baskets:

   (i) On security issues, principles such as sovereignty and non-interference in the domestic affairs of states were underlined and European borders were referred to as inviolable. They could be changed, but only through negotiations. This was one of the goals of the Soviet Union, which wished to have the post-1945 frontiers, including the division of Germany, confirmed.

   (ii) Cooperation was to develop in trade, technology and cultural exchanges.

   (iii) The Soviet Union accepted for the first time that human rights were of a universal character and that there was to be a free exchange of ideas and people across Europe. Moscow made this concession in order to get the rest to accept basket one and the inviolability of post-war frontiers. Brezhnev lived to regret this concession as it opened the door to Helsinki monitoring groups in the Soviet Union and the flowering of human rights groups. Moscow had accepted that human rights in the Soviet Union were the legitimate concern of other states. This was then used by the west to criticise the Soviet record on human rights and to request improvements. A Conference on Security and Cooperation in Europe was to convene in follow-up meetings to monitor progress and promote further developments. The next meeting in Belgrade, in 1978, took place at a time of increasing east–west tension and there was no meeting of minds on human rights. The CSCE process was revived under Gorbachev and after the collapse of the Soviet Union the

CSCE became the Organisation for Security and Cooperation in Europe (OSCE).

Hitler–Stalin (Nazi–Soviet) Pact

The Nazi–Soviet Non-Aggression Pact was signed on 23 August 1939 and divided Europe into spheres of interest. Its origins go back to 1936 but it became a real possibility from April 1939 onwards. Stalin weighed up this option after the policy of collective security failed to guarantee the Soviet Union safety as war threatened. Britain guaranteed Poland's security on 31 March 1939 and began to seek a military alliance with the Soviet Union. Stalin was wary as he feared that he could be drawn into a war with Germany with Britain and also France standing on the sidelines. The Hitler–Stalin Pact included the clauses of the Berlin Treaty of 1926, which committed both parties to desist from aggression and observe neutrality in conflicts involving third parties. A secret protocol defined future spheres of influence with Estonia, Latvia and Bessarabia passing to the USSR as well as a part of east Poland. Lithuania was added later. On 17 September 1939 the Red Army moved into east Poland and a German–Soviet friendship and frontier treaty of 28 September 1939 laid down the new Polish border in the east. The Soviet Union forced the Baltic states (28 September, 5 and 10 October 1939) to sign treaties which permitted the stationing of Soviet troops on their territories, and Romania in June 1940 conceded Bessarabia and north Bukovina to the Soviet Union. Tension surfaced at the end of 1940 as Stalin's demands for an expansion of his sphere of influence into Scandinavia and south-east Europe collided with Germany's desire to expand there. A Soviet–German economic agreement was signed on 11 January 1941. Despite receiving numerous warnings from his own and foreign intelligence sources that a German attack on the Soviet Union was being planned, Stalin refused to believe that Hitler would attack the Soviet Union and open a new front before defeating Great Britain. The German attack of 22 June 1941 revealed this to be false. During perestroika in the Baltic republics the Pact again became a live issue. Estonia, Latvia and Lithuania based their declarations of independence in 1990 on the fact that their incorporation into the Soviet Union had not been voluntary and was in accord with the Pact.

INF Treaty, 1987

The intermediate-range nuclear forces treaty was signed in Moscow between the Soviet Union and the USA on 8 December 1987. It provided for the destruction of about 2,600 missiles stationed in Europe with a range of between 500 and 5,500 km, within 36 months. The treaty was the first major disarmament treaty between the superpowers since 1945; the ABM treaty of 1972 and the SALT I treaty of 1973 had merely set ceilings for further arms production. A 1974 treaty covered the conditional ending of atomic tests and SALT II was signed in 1979, but these two treaties were not ratified by the US Senate because of the stationing of new Soviet middle-range missiles (SS20s) and the Soviet invasion of Afghanistan. The USA pursued a double-track policy: offering the USSR talks with NATO about removing the SS20s but, if this failed, placing Cruise and Pershing missiles in western Europe. No progress was made until the advent of Gorbachev, who was willing to make concessions on the vexed problem of verification. The INF treaty resulted from the new START talks and was the first tangible fruit of the new political thinking.

Lend Lease Act

The act was passed by the US Congress on 11 March 1941 to permit President Roosevelt to provide war material to other countries involved in the Second World War, if the security of the USA required this. The Soviet request for help under this act on 30 June 1941 was met at first with strong resistance in Washington. However, President Roosevelt won over the opposition by demonstrating the decisive contribution the USSR could make to the war against Hitler. US deliveries began after the signing of the Moscow protocol of 1 October 1941 and a formal treaty was signed on 11 June 1942. Deliveries ended on 20 September 1945 and totalled about US$26 billion. The money was extended on credit but no counter political concessions were ever requested of Stalin. Tension arose during the Cold War but it was not until 18 October 1972 that a treaty was signed providing for partial compensation for the goods which remained in the Soviet Union in 1945.

Litvinov Protocol

An agreement signed in Moscow on 9 February 1929 by the Soviet Union, Poland, Romania, Estonia and Latvia (and later by Lithuania, Persia and Turkey) implementing the Briand–Kellogg Pact of August eliminating war as an instrument of national policy before it was ratified by the signatory powers. It was named after Maksim Litvinov, the USSR People's Commissar for Foreign Affairs. The protocol lost its significance in August 1929 when the Briand–Kellogg Pact was ratified. However, it was a significant move by the Soviet Union as it demonstrated its concern for non-aggression and collective security. It led to various non-aggression pacts being signed and entry into the League of Nations.

Moscow Treaty, 12 August 1970

The usual name of the Soviet–West German treaty of 12 August 1970 which laid the foundation for the political normalisation of relations between the Warsaw Pact and the Federal Republic of Germany, and prepared the way for the Polish–West German and GDR–West German treaties. It also produced the Four Power Agreement on Berlin. After the Cuban Missile Crisis, the Soviet-led intervention in Czechoslovakia and the Sino–American rapprochement, beginning in 1969, the Soviet Union was interested in a relaxation of tension in the German question. Bonn was prepared to normalise relations with the GDR and recognise the status quo in eastern Europe. The treaty acknowledged the existing states and the inviolability of all European frontiers, including the Oder–Neisse Line (the eastern border between the GDR and Poland) and the inner-German border (between East and West Germany). It did not, however, recognise the GDR in international law but it did confirm the existence of two German states. Bonn never recognised the GDR as a foreign state. The Moscow treaty was overtaken by the 2 (East and West Germany) + 4 (the USSR, USA, France and Great Britain) agreement of 1990, which permitted the unification of Germany on 3 October 1990 within the terms of the Federal constitution.

Non-aggression pacts

Beginning in 1927 the chief aim of Soviet foreign policy was to sign non-aggression pacts with as many states as possible. This underlined the Soviet state's peaceful intentions and also prevented capitalist states from uniting against and attacking the USSR. The onset of rapid industrialisation and collectivisation in 1929 required stability in foreign relations. Stalin thereby accepted that peaceful coexistence was possible between states with differing social systems (socialist and capitalist). The first fruits of this policy was the Litvinov Protocol in 1929, and the expansion of Japan in the Far East in 1931–32 added urgency. Between January and March 1932, pacts were signed with Finland, Latvia and Estonia and then with Poland on 25 July 1932, with France on 29 November 1932 and with Italy on 2 September 1933. The goal of these pacts was to secure agreements on the non-use of force, the refusal to participate in economic boycotts or to permit hostile propaganda, and to observe neutrality in conflicts involving third parties. Only the pacts with Finland and Estonia confirmed existing frontiers. These pacts prepared the way for the admission of the Soviet Union to the League of Nations and the policy of collective security of the mid-1930s.

Nuclear Non-Proliferation Treaty, 1 July 1968

The major nuclear powers had an interest in preventing the spread of nuclear weapons and this treaty was signed in Geneva by many countries. Nuclear powers were bound not to help any other state to acquire nuclear devices. Moscow thereby ensured that the USA would not provide West Germany with nuclear weapons. However, the impact of the treaty was limited by the fact that many states refused to sign it, including Israel, India, Pakistan, South Africa, Brazil and Argentina, all capable of developing their own nuclear weapons. At the signing ceremony, the USA and USSR announced that they were to begin strategic arms limitation talks (SALT).

Rapallo Treaty, 16 April 1922

The treaty, signed on 16 April 1922, brought together the two great out-casts of the post-war world, Germany and Soviet Russia. The latter was extremely keen to overcome its economic and political isolation by the rest of Europe and the world after the adoption of the New Economic Policy (NEP). Soviet Russia wished to attract foreign investment and know-how from the capitalist states and also to achieve peaceful coexist-ence with them. The trade treaty with Great Britain, signed on 16 March 1921, failed to achieve a breakthrough for Moscow. The western powers insisted that the normalisation of relations with the RSFSR was only pos-sible after Soviet Russia had recognised the foreign debts run up by its predecessor and was willing to pay compensation for property which had been nationalised. Despite compromises by the Soviet side at the Genoa conference, agreement could not be reached. German Foreign Minister Walter Rathenau and Georgy Chicherin, People's Commissar for For-eign Affairs, then moved to Rapallo and signed a treaty which had been negotiated in large part beforehand. Both sides agreed not to make any financial demands of the other, to establish political relations and to afford one another most favoured nation status in foreign trade. The economic impact of the agreement was not very great as Germany was short of capital, but the political consequences were of great significance. It provided both players with room for manoeuvre *vis-à-vis* the western powers, permitted a common policy towards Poland and strengthened the links between the Reichswehr and the Red Army. This special German–Russian relationship survived the intervention of the Comintern in German affairs in 1923 and was developed in the Berlin Treaty of 1924. It ended with the coming to power of Hitler in 1933.

Sino–Soviet Treaty, February 1950

Stalin would have preferred the communist victory in China to have been postponed until he was in a position to exercise major influence over the Communist Party of China. Mao Zedong went for power against the advice of Stalin. Mao came to Moscow in December 1949, two months after the proclamation of the People's Republic of China. As such he acknowledged the leading role of the Soviet Union but wanted aid from Moscow to develop China rapidly. Stalin attempted to demonstrate to Mao that he was master and the negotiations were long and arduous. It was much easier to agree on foreign policy than on economic policy. China and the Soviet Union agreed to assist one another if Japan, or countries allied to it, began acting aggressively. Mao wanted to end the

Soviet Union's right to control Port Arthur, Dairen and the railways in Manchuria, and Stalin had to concede this in principle. Mao wanted generous economic aid but Stalin did not want China to become a competitor and only agreed to a small loan. He even insisted the Chinese paid interest on it. Stalin forced Mao to agree to Soviet participation in Chinese companies (as in eastern and south-eastern Europe) as a way of monitoring and benefiting from Chinese industrial expansion. The treaty was to last 30 years. Hence Sino–Soviet tension existed from the very inception of the People's Republic of China. The Soviet Union and its east European allies unilaterally withdrew their specialists from China in 1959 and this, to all intents and purposes, ended this treaty.

Strategic Arms Limitation Treaty (SALT I), 1972
Strategic arms limitation talks, first proposed by President Lyndon B. Johnson in 1967, were accepted by the Soviet Union in the summer of 1968. Full-scale negotiations began in November 1969. The SALT I agreements were signed by President Richard Nixon and Leonid Brezhnev in Moscow on 26 May 1972. SALT I consisted of various agreements, the most important of which were the Anti-Ballistic Missile (ABM) Treaty and the Interim Agreement and Protocol on the Limitation of Strategic Offensive Weapons.

Strategic Arms Limitation Treaty (SALT II), 1979
Negotiations began in late 1972 and lasted seven years. A major problem for the negotiators was the asymmetry between the strategic forces of the two superpowers. The Soviet Union concentrated on missiles with large warheads while the USA had developed smaller missiles of greater accuracy. Technological advance was another problem, as was the thorny question of verification, including on-site verification. A draft SALT II agreement was floated at the Vladivostok summit between President Ford and Leonid Brezhnev in November 1974: there should be equal ceilings of 2,400 long-range weapons (missile launchers and bombers) for the Soviet Union and the USA, of which 1,320 could have a MIRV (multiple independently targetable re-entry vehicle) capability. Détente came under attack in the USA for allegedly conceding too much to the Soviet Union and this slowed progress on SALT II. Superpower relations were subject to some tension as the United States normalised its relations with China in December 1978. SALT II was signed in Vienna by President Jimmy Carter and Leonid Brezhnev on 18 June 1979. The Soviet invasion of Afghanistan in December 1979 led to President Carter withdrawing the treaty for ratification in the Senate in January 1980. However, both signatories pledged themselves to observe the treaty limits voluntarily. The next stage in disarmament talks, which opened in Geneva in June 1982, assumed the name of strategic arms reduction talks, or START.

Strategic Arms Reduction Treaty (START), 1991

Relations between the superpowers deteriorated after the Soviet invasion of Afghanistan in December 1979 and when President Reagan took over in 1981 he renamed the strategic nuclear weapons talks START, emphasising that they were about reducing the nuclear arsenals not merely limiting them. When talks began in June 1982 in Geneva, estimates of the strategic arsenals were as follows:

(i) The USA had 1,052 intercontinental, land-based missiles; 576 submarine-launched missiles; and 316 long-range bombers (with multiple warheads, about 9,000 warheads in all).

(ii) The Soviet Union had 1,398 intercontinental, land-based missiles; 989 submarine-launched missiles; and 150 long-range bombers (about 8,400 warheads in all).

A major stumbling block to START was the Strategic Defence Initiative (SDI or Star Wars), announced by President Reagan in March 1983. The talks were broken off in December 1983 after NATO's deployment of Cruise and Pershing missiles and only got under way again after Mikhail Gorbachev became Soviet leader. However, American interest was then focused on an Intermediate Nuclear Forces Treaty and it was signed in 1987. Star Wars was a constant theme during the talks and also at the Bush–Gorbachev summits. In 1989–90 attention tended to be concentrated on the Conventional Forces in Europe (CFE) Treaty. START problems were finally ironed out and Presidents Bush and Gorbachev met in Moscow on 31 July 1991 to sign the agreement. The main features of the treaty were:

(i) Ceilings were placed on launchers (ICBMs, SLBMs and bombers) at 1,600 each, and warheads, at 6,000 each. Of these 6,000 warheads, 4,900 were to be on ballistic systems, 1,540 on heavy missiles and 1,100 on mobile, land-based weapons.

(ii) Overall strategic arsenals were to be reduced by about 30 per cent. The total US missile and bomb arsenal was to be cut from 12,000 to about 9,000, that of the Soviet Union from 11,000 to about 7,000.

(iii) Submarine-launched Cruise missiles were limited to 880 each under a separate agreement.

(iv) The Soviet Union agreed to reduce warheads on heavy SS18s by 50 per cent.

(v) Limits were to be implemented over eight years, accompanied by verification, including on-site verification.

(vi) Nuclear technology should not be passed to third parties (except for US sales of Trident missiles to Britain).

The collapse of the Soviet Union on 31 December 1991 resulted in four successor states becoming nuclear powers, Russia, Belarus, Ukraine and Kazakhstan. Negotiations of these states with the United States resulted in a supplementary agreement, signed on 23 May 1992, by which the parties agreed to adhere to the 1991 treaty. In addition, Belarus, Ukraine and Kazakhstan agreed either to destroy their nuclear warheads or transfer them to Russia.

Test Ban Treaty, August 1963
Public concern about the negative effects of nuclear tests surfaced in 1954 after a Japanese fishing boat suffered radiation from a US test. The Campaign for Nuclear Disarmament in Britain became influential and in March 1958 the Soviet Union announced a moratorium on tests. In July 1958 the Soviet Union, the USA and Britain began discussing controls on nuclear tests in Geneva. In October, Washington and Moscow announced they would observe a voluntary moratorium. A sticking point was the refusal of the Soviets to permit on-site inspection of underground nuclear tests. In August 1961 Moscow began a series of tests in the atmosphere again. President Kennedy followed suit but also engaged in underground tests. The Cuban Missile Crisis was a sobering experience for all sides and a treaty was negotiated between the Soviet Union, the USA and Britain which banned them from nuclear tests in the atmosphere, underwater and in space.

SECTION FOUR

Main office holders

Major office holders

Imperial Russia, 1914–17

Government ministers 1914–17 (all dates are Old Style)

Chairman of the Council of Ministers (Prime Minister)
V. N. Kokovtsov	11 September 1911–30 January 1914
I. L. Goremykin	30 January 1914–20 January 1916
B. V. Sturmer	20 January 1916–10 November 1916
A. F. Trepov	19 November 1916–27 December 1916
N. D. Golytsin	27 December 1916–27 February 1917

Minister of the Interior
N. A. Maklakov	26 December 1912–5 July 1915
N. B. Shcherbakov	5 July 1915–26 September 1915
A. N. Khvostov	27 September 1915–3 March 1916
B. V. Sturmer	3 March 1916–7 July 1916
A. N. Khvostov	7 July 1916–16 September 1916
A. D. Protopopov	18 September 1916–27 February 1917

Minister of Finance
V. N. Kokovtsov	26 April 1906–30 January 1914
P. L. Bark	30 January 1914–27 February 1917

Minister of Foreign Affairs
S. D. Sazonov	14 September 1910–7 July 1916
B. V. Sturmer	7 July 1916–10 November 1916
N. N. Pokrovsky	30 November 1916–27 February 1917

Minister of War
V. A. Sukhomlinov	11 March 1909–13 June 1916
A. A. Polivanov	13 June 1915–15 March 1916
D. S. Shuvaev	15 March 1916–3 January 1917
M. A. Belyaev	31 January 1917–27 February 1917

Minister of Trade and Industry
S. I. Timashev	5 November 1909–18 February 1915
V. N. Shakhovsky	18 February 1915–27 February 1917

The Provisional Government, February–October 1917 (all dates are Old Style)

The First Provisional Government of 2 March 1917

Prince G. E. Lvov (Non-Party)	Minister-President and Minister of the Interior
P. N. Milyukov (Kadet)	Minister of Foreign Affairs
A. I. Guchkov (Octobrist)	Minister of the War and Navy
M. V. Nekrasov (Kadet)	Minister of Transport
A. I. Konovalov (Kadet)	Minister of Trade and Industry
M. I. Tereshchenko (Non-Party)	Minister of Finance
A. A. Manuilov (Kadet)	Minister of Education
V. N. Lvov (Centrist)	Ober-Procurator of the Holy Synod
A. I. Shingarev (Kadet)	Minister of Agriculture
A. F. Kerensky (SR)	Minister of Justice

The First Coalition Government of 5 May 1917

Prince G. V. Lvov (Non-Party)	Minister-President and Minister of the Interior
A. F. Kerensky (SR)	Minister of the War and Navy
P. N. Pereverzev (SR)	Minister of Justice
M. I. Tereshchenko (Non-Party)	Minister of Foreign Affairs
N. V. Nekrasov (Kadet)	Minister of Transport
A. I. Konovalov (Kadet)	Minister of Trade and Industry
A. A. Manuilov (Kadet)	Minister of Education
A. I. Shingarev (Kadet)	Minister of Finance
V. M. Chernov (SR)	Minister of Agriculture
M. I. Skobelev (Menshevik)	Minister of Labour
I. G. Tsereteli (Menshevik)	Minister of Posts and Telegraph
A. V. Peshekhonov (Popular Socialist)	Minister of Food
Prince D. I. Shakhovskoi (Kadet)	Minister of Welfare
V. N. Lvov (Centrist)	Ober-Procurator of the Holy Synod
I. V. Godnev (Octobrist)	State Controller

The Second Coalition Government of 24 July 1917

A. F. Kerensky (SR)	Minister-President and Minister of the War and Navy
N. V. Nekrasov (Kadet)	Deputy Minister-President and Minister of Finance
M. I. Tereshchenko (Non-Party)	Minister of Foreign Affairs
M. I. Skobelev (Menshevik)	Minister of Labour

A. V. Peshekhonov (Popular Socialist)	Minister of Food
V. M. Chernov (SR)	Minister of Agriculture
S. F. Oldenburg (Non-Party)	Minister of Education
A. S. Zarudny (Popular Socialist)	Minister of Justice
I. N. Efremov (Progressive)	Minister of Welfare
P. P. Yurenev (Kadet)	Minister of Transport
S. N. Protopovich (Menshevik)	Minister of Trade and Industry
A. M. Nikitin (Menshevik)	Minister of Posts and Telegraph
F. F. Kokoshin (Kadet)	State Controller
A. V. Karteshev (Kadet)	Ober-Procurator of the Holy Synod
N. D. Avksentev (SR)	Minister of the Interior

The Third Coalition Government of 25 September 1917

A. F. Kerensky (SR)	Minister-President
A. I. Verkhovsky (Non-Party)	Minister of War
D. V. Verderevsky (Non-Party)	Minister of the Navy
A. M. Nikitin (Menshevik)	Minister of the Interior, and Posts and Telegraph
M. I. Tereshchenko (Non-Party)	Minister of Foreign Affairs
S. N. Prokopovich (Menshevik)	Minister of Food
M. V. Bernatsky (Non-Party)	Minister of Finance
S. S. Salazkin (Non-Party)	Minister of Education
A. V. Liverovsky (Non-Party)	Minister of Transport
A. I. Konovalov (Kadet)	Minister of Trade and Industry
N. M. Kishkin (Kadet)	Minister of Welfare
P. N. Malyantovich (Menshevik)	Minister of Justice
K. A. Gvozdev (Menshevik)	Minister of Labour
S. L. Maslov (SR)	Minister of Agriculture
A. V. Kartashev (Kadet)	Minister of Confessions
S. A. Smirnov (Kadet)	State Controller
S. N. Tretyakov (Non-Party)	Chairman of the Economic Council

The Soviet government, November 1917–1991 (all dates are New Style)

Heads of state

Chair, Russian Central Executive Committee (November 1917–1922)

L. B. Kamenev	9 November 1917–21 November 1917
Ya. A. Sverdlov	21 November 1917–16 March 1919
M. F. Vladimirsky (acting)	16 March 1919–30 March 1919

Chair, USSR Central Executive Committee (1922–38) and from 1938 Chair, Presidium of the USSR Supreme Soviet (1938–89)

M. I. Kalinin	30 March 1919–15 March 1946
N. M. Skvernik	15 March 1946–15 March 1953
K. E. Voroshilov	15 March 1953–7 May 1960
L. I. Brezhnev	7 May 1960–15 July 1964
A. I. Mikoyan	15 July 1964–9 December 1965
N. V. Podgorny	9 December 1965–16 June 1977
L. I. Brezhnev	16 June 1977–10 November 1982
Yu. V. Andropov	16 June 1983–9 February 1984
K. U. Chernenko	14 April 1984–10 March 1985
A. A. Gromyko	2 July 1985–1 October 1988
M. S. Gorbachev	1 October 1988–25 May 1989

Chair, USSR Supreme Soviet (1989–91)

M. S. Gorbachev	25 May 1989–15 March 1990
A. I. Lukyanov	15 March 1990–22 August 1991

President of the USSR (1990–91)

M. S. Gorbachev	15 March 1990–25 December 1991

The government (RSFSR Sovnarkom, 8 November 1917–6 July 1923)

Chair (Prime Minister)

V. I. Lenin	8 November 1917–6 July 1923

Chair, USSR Sovnarkom (6 July 1923–15 March 1946)

V. I. Lenin	6 July 1923–21 January 1924
A. I. Rykov	2 February 1924–19 December 1930
V. M. Molotov	19 December 1930–6 May 1941
I. V. Stalin	6 May 1941–15 March 1946

Chair, USSR Council of Ministers (15 March 1946–26 December 1990)

I. V. Stalin	15 March 1946–5 March 1953
G. M. Malenkov	6 March 1953–8 February 1955
N. A. Bulganin	8 February 1955–27 March 1958
N. S. Khrushchev	27 March 1958–15 October 1964
A. N. Kosygin	15 October 1964–23 October 1980
N. A. Tikhonov	23 October 1980–27 September 1985
N. I. Ryzhkov	27 September 1985–26 December 1990

Prime Minister, USSR Cabinet of Ministers (27 December 1990–6 September 1991)

V. S. Pavlov	14 January 1991–22 August 1991

RSFSR People's Commissar of Foreign Affairs (8 November 1917–6 July 1923)

L. D. Trotsky	8 November 1917–8 April 1918
G. V. Chicherin	13 March 1918 appointed deputy People's Commissar
G. V. Chicherin	9 April 1918 acting People's Commissar
G. V. Chicherin	30 May 1918–6 July 1923

USSR People's Commissar for Foreign Affairs (6 July 1923–15 March 1946)

G. V. Chicherin	6 July 1923–25 July 1930
M. M. Litvinov	25 July 1930–4 May 1939
V. M. Molotov	4 May 1939–15 March 1946

USSR Minister of Foreign Affairs (15 March 1946–5 November 1991)

V. M. Molotov	15 March 1946–4 March 1949
V. Ya. Vyshinsky	4 March 1949–7 March 1953
V. M. Molotov	7 March 1953–24 December 1956
D. T. Shepilov	24 December 1956–14 February 1957
A. A. Gromyko	15 February 1957–16 July 1985
E. A. Shevardnadze	16 July 1985–20 December 1990
No Foreign Minister	21 December 1990–14 January 1991
A. A. Bessmertnykh	15 January 1991–23 August 1991
No Foreign Minister	24 August 1991–27 August 1991
B. D. Pankin	28 August 1991

The USSR Ministry of Foreign Affairs decided to dissolve on 9 September 1991 'to permit B. D. Pankin, the new Minister of Foreign Affairs, to form a new collective'. New collective formed on 14 September 1991.

USSR Minister of External Affairs (5 November–8 December 1991)

B. D. Pankin	5 November 1991–19 November 1991
E. A. Shevardnadze	19 November 1991–8 December 1991

RSFSR People's Commissar for Internal Affairs (NKVD) (8 November 1917–6 February 1922)

A. I. Rykov	8 November 1917–17 November 1917
G. I. Petrovsky	30 November 1917–30 March 1919
F. E. Dzerzhinsky	30 March 1919–6 February 1922

USSR People's Commissar for Internal Affairs (NKVD) (10 July 1934–15 March 1946)

G. G. Yagoda	10 July 1934–September 1936
N. I. Ezhov	September 1936–December 1938

L. P. Beria   December 1938–14 January 1946
M. N. Kruglov   14 January 1946–15 March 1946

USSR Minister of Internal Affairs (MVD) (15 March 1946–13 January 1960; 26 July 1966–22 August 1991)

S. N. Kruglov   15 March 1946–5 March 1953
L. P. Beria   6 March 1953–10 July 1953
S. N. Kruglov   8 August 1953–31 January 1956
N. P. Dudorov   31 January 1956–13 January 1960
N. A. Shchelokov   26 July 1966–17 December 1982
V. V. Fedorchuk   17 December 1982–January 1986
A. V. Vlasov   January 1986–3 October 1988
V. V. Bakatin   3 October 1988–2 December 1990
B. K. Pugo   2 December 1990–22 August 1991

Chair of Cheka (20 December 1917–6 February 1922)

F. E. Dzerzhinsky   20 December 1917–6 February 1922

Chair of GPU (Main Political Administration; absorbed into the RSFSR NKVD) (6 February 1922–15 November 1923)

F. E. Dzerzhinsky   6 February 1922–15 November 1923

Chair of OGPU (Unified State Political Administration) (15 November 1923–10 July 1934)

F. E. Dzerzhinsky   15 November 1923–20 July 1926
V. R. Menzhinsky   30 July 1926–10 July 1934

USSR People's Commissar for Internal Affairs (NKVD; OGPU absorbed into NKVD) (10 July 1934–3 February 1941)

G. G. Yagoda   10 July 1934–26 September 1936
N. I. Ezhov   26 September 1936–31 May 1939
L. P. Beria   8 December 1938–3 February 1941

USSR People's Commissar for State Security (NKVD was split into NKVD and People's Commissariat for State Security, NKGB, on 3 February 1941–20 July 1941)

N. Merkulov   3 February 1941–20 July 1941

USSR People's Commissar for State Security (GUGB) (within NKVD) (20 July 1941–14 April 1943)

V. N. Merkulov   20 July 1941–14 April 1943

USSR People's Commissar for State Security (14 April 1943–15 March 1946)

V. N. Merkulov   14 April 1943–15 March 1946

USSR Minister of State Security (MGB) (15 March 1946–7 March 1953)
V. S. Abakumov   15 March 1946–late 1951
S. G. Ignatev   late 1951–7 March 1953

Chair of GUGB (within USSR Ministry of Internal Affairs, MVD) (7 March 1953–13 March 1954)
S. G. Ignatev   7 March 1953–13 March 1953

Chair of Committee of State Security (KGB) (attached to the USSR Council of Ministers) (13 March 1954–5 July 1978)
I. A. Serov   13 March 1954–8 December 1958
A. S. Shelepin   25 December 1958–13 November 1961
V. E. Semichastny   13 November 1961–18 May 1967
Yu. V. Andropov   18 May 1967–5 July 1978

Chair of the KGB of the USSR (5 July 1978–11 October 1991)
Yu. V. Andropov   5 July 1978–24 May 1982
V. V. Fedorchuk   24 May 1982–December 1982
V. M. Chebrikov   December 1982–30 September 1988
V. A. Kryuchkov   30 September 1988–22 August 1991
V. V. Bakatin   23 August 1991–late October 1991

RSFSR People's Commissar of Nationalities (8 November 1917–7 July 1923)
I. V. Stalin   8 November 1917–7 July 1923

Chair of the Supreme Council of the National Economy (VSNKh) (25 December 1917–5 January 1932)
N. Osinsky   25 December 1917–28 March 1918
A. I. Rykov   28 March 1918–28 May 1921
P. A. Bogdanov   28 May 1921–6 July 1923
A. I. Rykov   6 July 1923–2 February 1924
F. E. Dzerzhinsky   2 February 1924–20 July 1926
V. V. Kuibyshev   5 August 1926–10 November 1930
G. K. Ordzhonikidze 10 November 1930–5 January 1932

RSFSR Committee on Military and Naval Affairs (November 1917)
V. A. Antonov-Ovseenko⎫
N. V. Krylenko   ⎬ 8 November 1917–November 1917
P. E, Dybenko   ⎭
N. I. Podvoisky   9 November 1917–November 1917

RSFSR People's Commissar of the Army (November–28 March 1918)
N. I. Podvoisky   November 1917–28 March 1918

RSFSR People's Commissar of the Navy
P. E. Dybenko   November 1917–28 March 1918

RSFSR War Commissar (Military Commissar of Army and Naval Affairs)
L. D. Trotsky   28 March 1918–6 July 1923
(also Chair, Military Revolutionary Council of the Republic)

USSR People's Commissar of the Army and Navy (6 July 1923–20 June 1934)
L. D. Trotsky   6 July 1923–26 January 1925
M. V. Frunze   26 January 1925–6 November 1925
K. E. Voroshilov   6 November 1925–20 June 1934

USSR People's Commissar of Defence (20 June 1934–25 February 1946)
K. E. Voroshilov   20 June 1934–7 May 1940
S. K. Timoshenko   7 May 1940–19 July 1941
I. V. Stalin   19 July 1941–25 February 1946

USSR People's Commissar of the Armed Forces(25 February 1946–15 March 1946)
I. V. Stalin   25 February 1946–15 March 1946

USSR Minister of the Armed Forces (15 March 1946–25 February 1950)
I. V. Stalin   15 March 1946–3 March 1947
N. A. Bulganin   3 March 1947–24 March 1949
A. M. Vasilevsky   24 March 1949–25 February 1950

USSR Minister of War (25 February 1950–15 March 1953)
A. M. Vasilevsky   25 February 1950–15 March 1953

USSR Minister of Defence (15 March 1953–22 August 1991)
N. A. Bulganin   15 March 1953–8 February 1955
G. K. Zhukov   9 February 1955–26 October 1957
R. Ya. Malinovsky   26 October 1957–31 March 1967
A. A. Grechko   13 April 1967–26 April 1976
D. F. Ustinov   26 April 1976–20 December 1984
S. L. Sokolov   20 December 1984–30 May 1987
D. T. Yazov   30 May 1987–22 August 1991

USSR People's Commissar of the Navy (30 December 1937–15 March 1946)
P. A. Smirnov   30 December 1937–28 April 1939
N. G. Kuznetsov   28 April 1939–25 February 1946

USSR Minister of the Navy (25 February 1950–15 March 1953)
I. S. Yumashev   25 February 1950–July 1951
N. G. Kuznetsov   July 1951–15 March 1953

The Communist Party of the Soviet Union

Members and candidate members of the Politburo (Presidium, 1952–66), 1917–91

Bureau for the Political Guidance of the Insurrection (Revolution); elected at the Central Committee (CC) Meeting on 10 (23) October 1917
V. I. Lenin; A. S. Bubnov; G. E. Zinoviev; L. B. Kamenev; G. Ya. Sokolnikov; I. V. Stalin; L. D. Trotsky

Elected by the 8th Congress, 25 March 1919
Members: L. B. Kamenev; N. N. Krestinsky; V. I. Lenin; I. V. Stalin; L. D. Trotsky
Candidate Members: N. I. Bukharin; G. E. Zinoviev; M. I. Kalinin
(E. D. Stasova, at the invitation of the Politburo and the Orgburo, was a temporary member of the Politburo between July and September 1919.)

Elected by the 9th Congress, 5 April 1920
Members: L. B. Kamenev; N. N. Krestinsky; V. I. Lenin; I. V. Stalin; L. D. Trotsky
Candidate Members: N. I. Bukharin; G. E. Zinoviev; M. I. Kalinin

Elected by the 10th Congress, 16 March 1921
Members: G. E. Zinoviev; L. B. Kamenev; V. I. Lenin; I. V. Stalin; L. D. Trotsky
Candidate Members: N. I. Bukharin; M. I. Kalinin; V. M. Molotov

Elected by the 11th Congress, 3 April 1922
Members: G. E. Zinoviev; L. B. Kamenev; V. I. Lenin; A. I. Rykov; I. V. Stalin; M. M. Tomsky; L. D. Trotsky
Candidate Members: N. I. Bukharin; M. I. Kalinin; V. M. Molotov

Elected by the 12th Congress, 26 April 1923
Members: G. E. Zinoviev; L. B. Kamenev; V. I. Lenin; A. I. Rykov; I. V. Stalin; M. M. Tomsky; L. D. Trotsky
Candidate Members: N. I. Bukharin; M. I. Kalinin; V. M. Molotov; Ya. E. Rudzutak
(V. I. Lenin died on 21 January 1924.)

Elected by the 13th Congress, 2 June 1924

Members: N. I. Bukharin; G. E. Zinoviev; L. B. Kamenev; A. I. Rykov; I.
V. Stalin; M. M. Tomsky; L. D. Trotsky

Candidate Members: F. E. Dzerzhinsky; M. I. Kalinin; V. M. Molotov; Ya.
E. Rudzutak; G. Ya. Sokolnikov; M. V. Frunze

(M. V. Frunze died on 31 October 1925.)

Elected by the 14th Congress, 1 January 1926

Members: N. I. Bukharin; K. E. Voroshilov; G. E. Zinoviev; M. I. Kalinin;
V. M. Molotov; A. I. Rykov; I. V. Stalin; M. M. Tomsky; L. D. Trotsky

Candidate Members: F. E. Dzerzhinsky; L. B. Kamenev; G. I. Petrovsky;
Ya. E. Rudzutak; N. A. Uglanov

(F. E. Dzerzhinsky died on 20 July 1926.)

Central Committee (CC) Plenum, 23 July 1926

G. E. Zinoviev expelled and replaced by Ya. E. Rudzutak.

Candidate Members: A. A. Andreev; L. M. Kaganovich; L. B. Kamenev;
S. M. Kirov; A. I. Mikoyan; G. K. Ordzhonikidze; G. I. Petrovsky; N. A.
Uglanov elected

**CC and Central Control Commission (CCC) Plenum, 23 October
1926**

L. D. Trotsky expelled as member and L. B. Kamenev expelled as candidate member.

CC and CCC Plenum, 3 November 1926

G. K. Ordzhonikidze demoted to chair the Central Control Commission;
replaced by V. Ya. Chubar as candidate member.

Elected by the 15th Congress, 19 December 1927

Members: N. I. Bukharin; K. E. Voroshilov; M. I. Kalinin; V. V. Kuibyshev;
V. M. Molotov; A. I. Rykov; Ya. E. Rudzutak; I. V. Stalin; M. M. Tomsky

Candidate Members: A. A. Andreev; L. M. Kaganovich; S. M. Kirov; S. V.
Kosior; A. I. Mikoyan; G. I. Petrovsky; N. A. Uglanov; V. Ya. Chubar

CC Plenum, 29 April 1929

N. A. Uglanov dropped and replaced by K. Ya. Bauman as candidate.

CC Plenum, 21 June 1929

S. I. Syrtsov expelled as candidate member.

CC Plenum, 17 November 1929

N. I. Bukharin expelled as member.

Elected by the 16th Congress, 13 July 1930
Members: K. E. Voroshilov; K. M. Kaganovich; M. I. Kalinin; S. M. Kirov;
S. V. Kosior; V. V. Kuibyshev; V. M. Molotov; Ya. E. Rudzutak; A. I.
Rykov; I. V. Stalin
Candidate Members: A. A. Andreev; A. I. Mikoyan; G. I. Petrovsky; S. I.
Syrtsov; V. Ya. Chubar

CC and CCC Plenum, 21 December 1930
A. I. Rykov expelled; A. A. Andreev demoted and elected chair of the
CCC; G. K. Ordzhonikidze elected to the Politburo.

CC Plenum, February 1932
Ya. E. Rudzutak demoted and elected chair of CCC; A. A. Andreev
elected member of Politburo.

Elected at 17th Congress, 10 February 1934
Members: A. A. Andreev; K. E. Voroshilov; L. M. Kaganovich; M. I.
Kalinin; S. M. Kirov; S. V. Kosior; V. V. Kuibyshev; V. M. Molotov; G.
K. Ordzhonikidze; I. V. Stalin
Candidate Members: A. I. Mikoyan; G. I. Petrovsky; P. P. Postychev; Ya.
E. Rudzutak; V. Ya. Chubar
(S. M. Kirov murdered on 1 December 1934. V. V. Kuibyshev died on 25
January 1935.)

CC Plenum, 1 February 1935
Members: A. I. Mikoyan; V. Ya. Chubar elected
Candidate Members: A. A. Zhdanov; R. I. Eikhe elected
(G. K. Ordzhonikidze died on 18 February 1937.)
Ya. E. Rudzutak expelled as member of the CC, 26 May 1937 (hence
cannot be a candidate member of the Politburo.)

CC Plenum, 12 October 1937
N. I. Ezhov elected as candidate member.

CC Plenum, 14 January 1938
P. P. Postychev expelled and N. S. Khrushchev elected as candidate
member.

Politburo decision, 16 June 1938
V. Ya. Chubar expelled.
S. V. Kosior executed on 26 February 1939.

Elected by the 18th Congress, 22 March 1939
Members: A. A. Andreev; V. E. Voroshilov; A. A. Zhdanov; L. M.
Kaganovich; M. I. Kalinin; A. I. Mikoyan; V. M. Molotov; I. V. Stalin;
N. S. Khrushchev
Candidate Members: L. P. Beria; N. M. Shvernik

CC Plenum, 21 February 1941
Candidate Members: N. A. Voznesensky; G. M. Malenkov; A. S. Shcherbakov
(A. S. Shcherbakov died on 10 May 1945.)

CC Plenum, 18 March 1946
Members: L. P. Beria; G. M. Malenkov
Candidate Members: N. A. Bulganin; A. N. Kosygin
(M. I. Kalinin died on 3 June 1946.)

CC Plenum, 26 February 1947
Member: N. A. Voznesensky

CC Plenum, 18 February 1948
Member: N. A. Bulganin

CC Plenum, 4 September 1948
Member: A. N. Kosygin
(A. A. Zhdanov died on 31 August 1948.)

CC Plenum, 7 March 1949
N. A. Voznesensky expelled as member.

Presidium elected by the 19th Congress, 16 October 1952
Members: V. M. Andrianov; A. B. Aristov; L. P. Beria; N. A. Bulganin; K. E. Voroshilov; S. D. Ignatev; L. M. Kaganovich; D. S. Korotchenko; V. V. Kuznetsov; O. V. Kuuisen; G. M. Malenkov; V. A. Malyshev; L. G. Melnikov; A. I. Mikoyan; N. A. Mikhailov; V. M. Molotov; M. G. Pervukhin; P. K. Ponomarenko; M. Z. Saburov; I. V. Stalin; M. A. Suslov; N. S. Khrushchev; D. I. Chesnokov; N. M. Shvernik; M. F. Shkiryatov
Candidate Members: L. I. Brezhnev; A. Ya. Vyshinsky; A. G. Zverev; N. G. Ignatov; I. G. Kabanov; A. N. Kosygin; N. S. Patolichev; N. M. Pegov; A. M. Puzanov; I. F. Tevosyan; P. F. Yudin
(I. V. Stalin died on 5 March 1953.)

CC Plenum, USSR Council of Ministers and Presidium of the USSR Supreme Soviet and confirmed by a CC Plenum, on 6 March 1953
Members: L. P. Beria; N. A. Bulganin; K. E. Voroshilov; L. M. Kaganovich; G. M. Malenkov; A. I. Mikoyan; V. M. Molotov; M. G. Pervukhin; M. Z. Saburov; N. S. Khrushchev
Candidate Members: M. D. Bagirov; L. G. Melnikov; P. K. Ponomarenko; N. M. Shvernik

CC Plenum, 6 June 1953
L. G. Melnikov dropped.

CC Plenum, 7 July 1953
L. P. Beria expelled from Presidium and candidate member M. D. Bagirov.
Candidate Member: A. I. Kirichenko elected.

CC Plenum, 12 July 1955
Members: A. I. Kirichenko; M. A. Suslov

Elected by the 20th Congress, 27 February 1956
Members: N. A. Bulganin; K. E. Voroshilov; L. M. Kaganovich; A. I.
   Kirichenko; G. M. Malenkov; A. I. Mikoyan; V. M. Molotov; M. G.
   Pervukhin; M. Z. Saburov; M. A. Suslov; N. S. Khrushchev
Candidate Members: L. I. Brezhnev; G. K. Zhukov; N. A. Mukhitdinov;
   E. A. Furtseva; N. M. Shvernik; D. T. Shepilov

CC Plenum, 14 February 1957
Candidate Member: F. R. Kozlov

CC Plenum, 29 June 1957
M. Malenkov; L. M. Kaganovich; V. M. Molotov; D. T. Shepilov expelled
   from the Presidium
Members: A. B. Aristov; N. I. Belyaev; L. I. Brezhnev; N. A. Bulganin; K.
   E. Voroshilov; G. K. Zhukov; N. G. Ignatov; A. I. Kirichenko; F. R.
   Kozlov; O. V. Kuusinen; A. I. Mikoyan; M. A. Suslov; E. A. Furtseva;
   N. S. Khrushchev; N. M. Shvernik
Candidate Members: Ya. E. Kalnberzin; A. P. Kirilenko; D. S. Korotchenko;
   N. Kosygin; K. T. Mazurov; V. P. Mzhavanadze; N. A. Mukhitdinov; M.
   G. Pervukhin; P. N. Pospelov;
N. S. Khrushchev elected First Secretary of CC, 7 September 1953.

CC Plenum, 29 October 1957
E. Zhukov expelled from the CC.

CC Plenum, 17 December 1957
Member: M. V. Mukhitdinov

CC Plenum, 18 June 1958
Candidate Members: N. V. Podgorny; D. S. Polyansky

CC Plenum, 5 September 1958
N. A. Bulganin expelled from the Presidium.

CC Plenum, 4 May 1960
N. I. Belyaev and A. I. Kirichenko expelled ås members.
Members: A. N. Kosygin, N. V. Podgorny; D. S. Polyansky

CC Plenum, 16 July 1960
K. E. Voroshilov expelled as member.

CC Plenum, 18 January 1961
Candidate Members: G. I. Voronov; V. V. Grishin
There were no elections at the 21st Extraordinary Congress, 27 January–
5 February 1959.

Elected by the 22nd Congress, 31 October 1961
Members: L. I. Brezhnev; G. I. Voronov; F. R. Kozlov; A. N. Kosygin; O.
   V. Kuusinen; A. I. Mikoyan; N. V. Podgorny; D. S. Polyansky; M. A.
   Suslov; N. S. Khrushchev; N. M. Shvernik
Candidate Members: V. V. Grishin; K. T. Mazurv; V. P. Mzhavanadze; Sh.
   R. Rashidov; V. V. Shcherbitsky

CC Plenum, 23 April 1962
Member: A. P. Kirilenko

CC Plenum, 23 November 1962
Candidate Member: L. N. Efremov

CC Plenum, 13 December 1963
V. V. Shcherbitsky dropped as candidate member.
Candidate Member: P. E. Shelest
(O. V. Kuusinen died on 17 May 1964.)

CC Plenum, 14 October 1964
N. S. Khrushchev dismissed as CC First Secretary; L. I. Brezhnev elected
   CC First Secretary.

CC Plenum, 16 November 1964
F. R. Kozlov dropped as candidate member.
Members: A. N. Shelepin; P. E. Shelest
Candidate Member: P. N. Demichev

CC Plenum, 26 March 1965
Member: K. T. Mazurov
Candidate Member: D. F. Ustinov

CC Plenum, 6 December 1965
Candidate Member: V. V. Shcherbitsky

Elected by the 23rd Congress, 8 April 1966
Members: L. I. Brezhnev; G. I. Voronov; A. P. Kirilenko; A. N. Kosygin; K. T. Mazurov; A Ya. Pelshe; N. V. Podgorny; D. S. Polyansky; M. A. Suslov; A. N. Shelepin; P. E. Shelest
Candidate Members: V. V. Grishin; P. N. Demichev; D. A. Kunaev; P. M. Masherov; V. P. Mzhavanadze; Sh. R. Rashidov; D. F. Ustinov; V. V. Shcherbitsky

CC Plenum, 21 June 1967
Candidate Member: Yu. V. Andropov

Elected by the 24th Congress, 9 April 1971
Members: L. I. Brezhnev; G. I. Voronov; V. V. Grishin; A. P. Kirilenko; A. N. Kosygin; F. D. Kulakov; D. A. Kunaev; K. T. Mazurov; A. Ya. Pelshe; N. V. Podgorny; D. S. Polyansky; M. A. Suslov; A. N. Shelepin; P. E. Shelest; V. V. Shcherbitsky
Candidate Members: Yu. V. Andropov; P. N. Demichev; P. M. Masherov; V. P. Mzhavanadze; Sh. R. Rashidov; D. F. Ustinov

CC Plenum, 23 November 1971
Candidate Member: M. S. Solomentsev

CC Plenum, 19 May 1972
Candidate Member: B. N. Ponomarev

CC Plenum, 18 December 1972
V. P. Mzhavanadze dropped as candidate member.

CC Plenum, 27 April 1973
V. I. Voronov; P. E. Shelest dropped as members.
Members: Yu. V. Andropov; A. A. Grechko; A. A. Gromyko
Candidate Member: G. V. Romanov

CC Plenum, 16 April 1975
A. N. Shelepin dropped as member.

Elected by the 25th Congress, 5 March 1976
Members: Yu. V. Andropov; L. I. Brezhnev; A. A. Grechko; V. V. Grishin; A. A. Gromyko; A. P. Kirilenko; A. N. Kosygin; F. D. Kulakov; D. A. Kunaev; K. T. Mazurov; A. Ya. Pelshe; N. V. Podgorny; G. V. Romanov; M. A. Suslov; D. F. Ustinov; V. V. Shcherbitsky
Candidate Members: G. A. Aliev; P. N. Demichev; P. M. Masherov; B. N. Ponomarev; Sh. R. Rashidov; M. S. Solomentsev
(A. A. Grechko died on 26 April 1976.)

CC Plenum, 24 May 1977
N. V. Podgorny dropped as member.

CC Plenum, 3 October 1977
Candidate Members: V. V. Kuznetsov; K. U. Chernenko
F. D. Kulakov died on 17 June 1978.

CC Plenum, 27 November 1978
K. T. Mazurov dropped as member.
Member: K. U. Chernenko
Candidate Members: N. A. Tikhonov; E. A. Sheveradnadze

CC Plenum, 27 November 1979
Member: N. A. Tikhonov
Candidate Member: M. S. Gorbachev
(P. N. Masherov fatally injured in a car crash on 4 October 1980.)

CC Plenum, 21 October 1980
A. N. Kosygin retired as member.
Member: M. S. Gorbachev
Candidate Member: T. Ya. Kiselev

CC Plenum, 24 May 1982
Candidate Member: V. I. Dolgikh
Yu. V. Andropov elected a secretary of the CC.
(L. I. Brezhnev died on 10 November 1982.)

Elected by the 26th Congress, 3 March 1981
Members: Yu. V. Andropov; L. I. Brezhnev; M. S. Gorbachev; V. V. Grishin;
A. A. Gromyko; A. P. Kirilenko; D. A. Kunaev; K. T. Mazurov; A. Ya.
Pelshe; G. V. Romanov; M. A. Suslov; N. A. Tikhonov; D. F. Ustinov;
K. U. Chernenko; V. V. Shcherbitsky
Candidate Members: G. A. Aliev; P. N. Demichev; T. Ya. Kiselev; V. V.
Kuznetsov; B. N. Ponomarev; Sh. R. Rashidov; M. S. Solomentsev; E.
A. Sheveradnadze
(M. A. Suslov died on 25 January 1982.)

Extraordinary CC Plenum, 12 November 1982
Yu. V. Andropov elected General Secretary of the CC.

CC Plenum, 22 November 1982
A. I. Kirilenko dropped as member.
Member: G. A. Aliev
(T. Ya. Kiselev died on 11 January 1983.)
(A. Ya. Pelshe died on 29 May 1983.)

CC Plenum, 15 June 1983
Candidate Member: V. I. Vorotnikov
(Sh. R. Rashidov died on 31 October 1983.)

CC Plenum, 26 December 1983
Members: V. I. Vorotnikov; S. M. Solomentsev
Candidate Member: V. M. Chebrikov
(Yu. V. Andropov died on 9 February 1984.)

Extraordinary CC Plenum, 13 February 1984
K. U. Chernenko elected General Secretary of the CC.
(D. F. Ustinov died on 20 December 1984.)
(K. U. Chernenko died on 10 March 1985.)

Extraordinary CC Plenum, 11 March 1985
M. S. Gorbachev elected General Secretary of the CC.

CC Plenum, 23 April 1985
Members: E. K. Ligachev; N. I. Ryzhkov; V. M. Chebrikov
Candidate Member: S. M. Sokolov

CC Plenum, 1 July 1985
G. V. Romanov dropped as member.
Member: E. A. Shevardnadze

CC Plenum, 15 October 1985
N. A. Tikhonov dropped as member.
Candidate Member: N. V. Talyzin

CC Plenum, 18 February 1986
V. V. Grishin dropped as member.
Candidate Member: B. N. Yeltsin

Elected by the 27th Congress, 6 March 1986
Members: G. A. Aliev; V. I. Vorotnikov; M. S. Gorbachev; A. A. Gromyko;
   L. N. Zaikov; D. A. Kunaev; E. K. Ligachev; N. I. Ryzhkov; M. S.
   Solomentsev; V. M. Chebrikov; E. A. Shevardnadze; V. V. Shcherbitsky
Candidate Members: P. N. Demichev; V. I. Dolgikh; B. N. Yeltsin; N. N.
   Slyunkov; S. L. Sokolov; Yu. F. Solovev; N. V. Talyzin

CC Plenum, 28 January 1987
D. A. Kunaev dropped as member.
Candidate Member: A. N. Yakovlev

CC Plenum, 26 June 1987
S. L. Sokolov dropped as candidate member.
Members: N. N. Slyunkov; A. N. Yakovlev; V. P. Nikonov
Candidate Member: D. T. Yazov

CC Plenum, 21 Octtober 1987
G. A. Aliev dropped as member.

CC Plenum, 18 February 1988
B. N. Yeltsin dropped as candidate member.
Candidate Members: Yu. D. Maslyukov; G. P. Razumovsky

CC Plenum, 30 September 1988
A. A. Gromyko, M. S. Solomentsev dropped as members; P. N. Demichev,
   V. I. Dolgikh dropped as candidate members.
Member: V. A. Medvedev
Candidate Members: A. P. Biryukova; A. V. Vlasov; A. I. Lukyanov

CC Plenum, 20 September 1989
V. P. Nikonov, V. M. Chebrikov, V. V. Shcherbitsky dropped as mem-
   bers; Yu. F. Solovev, N. V. Talyzin dropped as candidate members.
Member: V. A. Kryuchkov; Yu. D. Maslyukov promoted from candidate
   to member.
Candidate Members; E. M. Primakov; B. P. Pugo

CC Plenum, 9 December 1989
Member: V. A. Ivashko

Elected by the 28th Congress, 13–14 July 1990
M. S. Gorbachev; M. M. Burokevicius; G. G. Gumbaridze; S. I. Gurenko;
   A. S. Dzasokhov; V. A. Ivashko; I. A. Karimov; P. K. Luchinsky; A. M.
   Masaliev; K. Makhkamov; V. M. Movsiyan; A. N. Mutalibov; N. A.
   Nazarbaev; S. A. Niyazov; I. K. Polozkov; Yu. A. Prokofev; A. P. Rubiks;
   G. V. Semenova; E.-A. A. Sillari; E. E. Sokolov; E. S. Stroev; I. T.
   Frolov; O. S. Shenin; G. I. Yanaev
Candidate membership is abolished.

CC Plenum, 10–11 December 1990
E. E. Sokolov dropped as member of Politburo after ceasing to be first
   secretary, Communist Party of Belorussia
V. M. Movsisyan dropped as member of Politburo after ceasing to be
   first secretary, Communist Party of Armenia
A. A. Malofeev, first secretary, Communist Party of Belorussia, elected
   member of Politburo

S. K. Pogosyan, first secretary, Communist Party of Armenia, elected member of Politburo

CC Plenum, 31 January 1991

G. I. Yanaev leaves the Politburo after his election as Vice-President of the USSR

G. G. Gumbaridze dropped from Politburo after ceasing to be first secretary, Communist Party of Georgia

L. E. Annus, first secretary, Communist Party of Estonia (CPSU), elected a member of the Politburo

Politburo

M. S. Gorbachev   General Secretary
V. A. Ivashko   Deputy General Secretary
L. E. Annus; M. M. Burokevicius; S. I. Gurenko; A. S. Dzasokhov; I. A. Karimov; P. K. Luuchinsky; A. A. Malofeev; A. M. Masaliev; K. Makhkamov; A. N. Mutalibov; N. A. Nazarbaev; S. A. Niyazov; S. K. Pogosyan; I. K. Polozkov; Yu. A. Prokofev; A. P. Rubiks; G. V. Semenova; E.-A. A. Sillari; E. S. Stroev; I. T. Frolov; O. S. Shenin

CC and CCC Plenum, 24–25 April 1991

D. B. Amanbaev, first secretary, Communist Party of Kyrgyzstan, elected member of Politburo

G. I. Eremei, first secretary, Communist Party of Moldova, elected member of Politburo

M. S. Surkov, secretary of the All-Armenian Party committee, elected member of Politburo

A. M. Masaliev dropped from Politburo after ceasing to be first secretary, Communist Party of Kyrgyzstan

Politburo

M. S. Gorbachev   General Secretary
V. A. Ivashko   Deputy General Secretary
D. B. Amanbaev; L. E. Annus; M. M. Burokevicius; S. I. Gurenko; A. S. Dzasokhov; G. I. Eremei; I. A. Karimov; P. K. Luuchinsky; A. A. Malofeev; K. Makhkamov; A. N. Mutalibov; N. A. Nazarbaev; S. A. Niyazov; S. K. Pogosyan; I. K. Polozkov; Yu. A. Prokofev; A. P. Rubiks; G. V. Semenova; E.-A. A. Sillari; E. S. Stroev; M. S. Surkov; I. T. Frolov; O. S. Shenin

Post-communist Russia

President

B. N. Yeltsin   12 June 1991–12 June 1996
B. N. Yeltsin   12 June 1996–3 July 1996 (acting)
B. N. Yeltsin   3 July 1996–

Prime Minister (Chair of Government)

B. N. Yeltsin	November 1991–16 June 1992
E. T. Gaidar	16 June 1992–14 December 1992 (acting)
V. S. Chernomyrdin	14 December 1992–

First Deputy Prime Minister (First Deputy Chair of Government)

G. E. Burbulis	December 1991–April 1992
V. F. Shumeiko	June 1992–22 December 1993
O. N. Soskovets	28 April 1993–20 June 1996
O. I. Lobov	15 April 1993–16 September 1993
E. T. Gaidar	16 June 1993–16 January 1994
A. B. Chubais	16 November 1994–16 January 1996
A. B. Chubais	11 March 1997– (acting Prime Minister when Chernomyrdin is away)
V. V. Kadannikov	25 January 1996–15 August 1996
O. I. Lobov	20 June 1996–15 August 1996
V. Potanin	15 August 1996–17 March 1997
A. Bolshakov	15 August 1996–17 March 1997
A. Livshits	15 August 1996–17 March 1997
V. Ilyushin	15 August 1996–17 March 1997
B. E. Nemtsov	17 March 1997–

Minister of Economics

A. A. Nechaev	February 1992–26 March 1993
A. Shapovalyants	26 March 1993–10 January 1994
A. N. Shokhin	10 January 1994–4 November 1994
E. G. Yasin	8 November 1994–17 March 1997
Y. Urison	17 March 1997–

Minister of Finance

E. T. Gaidar	February 1992–24 April 1992
V. V. Barchuk	24 April 1992–26 March 1993
B. G. Fedorov	26 March 1993–26 January 1994
S. Dubinin	26 January 1994–4 November 1994
V. Panskov	4 November 1994–14 August 1996
A. Livshits	15 August 1996–11 March 1997
A. B. Chubais	11 March 1997–

Chair of the Russian Central Bank

V. V. Gerashchenko	August 1992–14 October 1994
T. Paramanova	18 October 1994–8 November 1995 (acting)
S. Dubinin	14 November 1995–

Ministry of Security and Internal Affairs (December 1991–10 January 1992)
V. Barannikov   December 1991–10 January 1992

Minister of the Interior
V. F. Erin   10 January 1992–29 June 1995
A. Kulikov   5 July 1995–   (also deputy Prime Minister)

Minister of Defence
P. S. Grachev   18 May 1992–1 June 1996
M. P. Kolesnikov   1 June 1996–17 July 1996 (acting)
I. N. Rodionov   17 July 1996–
I. Sergeev   22 May 1997–23 May 1997 (acting)
I. Sergeev   23 May 1997–

Minister of Foreign Affairs
A. V. Kozyrev   November 1991–5 January 1996
E. M. Primakov   9 January 1996–

Minister without Portfolio, Responsible for Long-Term Strategic Planning
E. Yasin   17 March 1997–

SECTION FIVE

Biographies

Biographies

Adzhubei, Aleksei Ivanovich (1924–): 'You can't go wrong if you marry the boss's daughter' – Adzhubei put this old adage to the test and it led to a glittering career as a journalist while Khrushchev was in power. He became known as the king of the Soviet press and became editor-in-chief of *Komsomoloskaya Pravda* and *Izvestiya*. He accompanied his father-in-law on many of his western jaunts, including the hugely successful visit to the United States in 1959. One of the accusations levelled against Khrushchev in October 1964 was that he had turned Adzhubei into a shadow foreign minister, who had attempted to meddle in diplomatic matters at the highest level, confusing the Soviet ambassadors. Adzhubei fell like a stone with Khrushchev in October 1964 and his official career was over.

Afanasev, Yury Nikolaevich (1934–): One of the most prominent reformers during the Gorbachev era, who eventually became frustrated with the Soviet leader's lack of consistency. He went into politics in March 1989, when he was elected to the USSR Congress of People's Deputies. As a radical communist, Afanasev became one of the leaders of the Inter-Regional Group in the parliament. As an effective and energetic speaker, he addressed many demonstrations and gained respect and support from a wide spectrum of opinion. Afanasev resigned from the Communist Party in April 1990, the first prominent person to do so. He was active in the Memorial Society, whose main task was to make known the repression of the Stalin era and to erect a memorial to its victims.

Aganbegyan, Abel Gazevich (1932–): One of the key Soviet economists during the early phase of Gorbachev's perestroika. An Armenian, he was born in Tbilisi, Georgia. Gorbachev had been introduced to some radical-thinking specialists, including Tatyana Zaslavskaya, in the early 1980s, and Aganbegyan in due course attended Gorbachev's discussion group. Aganbegyan was not as radical (pro-market) a reformer as others, and his star, which had been brightest in the early years of perestroika, waned and he was overtaken by Yavlinsky, Shatalin and others.

Akhromeev, Marshal Sergei Fedorovich (1923–91): He ended his brilliant military career by hanging himself in his Kremlin office after the failed coup against Gorbachev in August 1991. He accompanied Gorbachev to various summits but was regarded as more conservative than the Soviet leader. His view of the USA remained adversarial and when Gorbachev announced unilateral defence cuts at the United Nations in December 1988, Akhromeev resigned as Chief of the General Staff. However, he remained an adviser to Gorbachev and addressed the US Congress in July 1989. Held in high regard by western specialists, Akhromeev, however, could not move with the political times. He became one of the ringleaders of the attempted August coup against Gorbachev and became one of the few top conspirators to commit suicide.

Alliluyeva, Svetlana Iosefovna (also Stalina) (1926–): The daughter of Stalin and his second wife, Nadezhda Sergeevna Alliluyeva, Svetlana has led a peripatetic existence since her defection to the west in March 1967. She had a privileged upbringing in Moscow but she lost her mother to suicide in 1932. She was her father's favourite but she found it difficult to come to terms with the world she inhabited. Her second husband, Bradegh Singh, was an Indian communist and, surprisingly, the authorities permitted her to accompany his ashes back to his native India. Her defection caused a sensation inside and outside the Soviet Union and she vented her ire on the Soviet Union and its establishment in many television and newspapers interviews. In 1970 she married William Peters, an American architect (died 1991). Their daughter, Olga, was born in 1971. She lived in England from time to time and struck up a warm friendship with Malcolm Muggeridge, the English journalist. This led to some memorable interviews. She declined to see academics, whom she regarded as being only interested in her father, not in her.

Arbatov, Georgy Arkadevich (1923–): One of the most influential academics and journalists in the Soviet Union, and the leading specialist on the USA, especially in the Gorbachev era. He became an academician of the USSR Academy of Sciences. His institute blossomed under Gorbachev and was a major centre of the New Political Thinking, but it gradually lost its commanding position on policy towards the USA. Gorbachev's gifts in foreign policy presentation lessened his reliance on any one adviser and Arbatov's glory days were almost over. He continued to advise President Yeltsin after 1991.

Bagramyan, Marshal Ivan Khristoforovich (1897–1982): One of the successful Soviet commanders during the Great Fatherland War (1941–45). He was Chief of Staff to Timoshenko but was given command of an army in July 1942. He fought on the western front and at Kursk, in July 1943. In November 1943 he was made General and became commander of the First Baltic front. During the Belorussian campaign his armies killed

20,000 Germans and captured 10,000. His armies then moved into Latvia and in January 1945 he was ordered to take Königsberg. Stubborn German resistance held up the Red Army until April 1945 and the blame for the delay was placed on Bagramyan. After the war he became commander of the Baltic military district. He was appointed deputy Minister of Defence in 1954, later chief inspector of the Ministry of Defence and commander of the Rear Army.

Bakatin, Vadim Viktorovich (1937–): After the attempted coup of August 1991, he was appointed head of the USSR KGB with a brief to break it up. In 1988 Gorbachev brought him to Moscow as USSR Minister of Internal Affairs, a very sensitive post at a time of rising ethnic tension. In March 1990, at the 3rd USSR Congress of People's Deputies, he was nominated for the post of USSR President by the Soyuz group of parliamentary deputies, but withdrew and left the field to Mikhail Gorbachev. In December 1990 he was dismissed as USSR Minister of Internal Affairs in line with the swing to the right by President Gorbachev. He was not regarded by conservatives as willing to use sufficient force to maintain the continued dominance of the Communist Party. He was succeeded by General Boris Pugo, one of the leaders of the attempted coup of August 1991. He stood against Boris Yeltsin in the RSFSR presidential election in June 1991 and suffered the humiliation of coming bottom of the poll of six members, with 3.4 per cent of the votes. On 23 August 1991 he was made chair of the USSR KGB, renamed the Inter-republican Security Service, following the arrest of the KGB chief, Vladimir Kryuchkov, and the suicide of Boris Pugo. Bakatin's task was to liquidate the KGB and divide it up into three independent branches: law and order, intelligence, and counter-intelligence. Bakatin stated that he was not in favour of granting public access to KGB files but that the greater part of them should be transferred to national archives, something which has yet to happen.

Beria, Lavrenty Pavlovich (1899–1953): A gangster in politics, Beria served Stalin well but lost out in the succession struggle. Like Molotov he wore a pince-nez. He was born near Sukhumi, Georgia, into a Mingrelian family. He replaced Ezhov in 1938 as People's Commissar for Internal Affairs and replaced Ezhov as candidate member of the Politburo in 1939. When war broke out Beria became a member of the State Committee for Defence (GKO) and in 1944 he became its deputy chair. He was promoted to Marshal of the Soviet Union in July 1945, the highest rank below that of generalissimo, which Stalin had claimed for himself. There was no love lost between Beria and the military, and one of his main targets was Zhukov. At the end of Stalin's life his position was under threat and he was pleased when Stalin died in March 1953, earning the undying hatred of Stalin's daughter, Svetlana. Beria played a key role in developing the gulag (forced labour camps) system and the Sovietisation of eastern Europe after 1945. He was universally feared but was always obsequious to Stalin in company. He was highly intelligent, a master of intrigue and as deadly as a viper. He had a huge sexual appetite, having his agents pick girls off the streets if he fancied them. After Stalin's death, he fatally underestimated Khrushchev's abilities, writing him off as a moon-faced idiot. Khrushchev conspired with Malenkov against him and had him arrested (by Zhukov and other officers: this was sweet revenge for Zhukov), accusing him of attempting a coup (quite untrue) and smuggling him out of the Kremlin without his guards realising it. At his trial he was accused of, among other things, being a British agent and conspiring to undermine nationality relations in the Soviet Union. He was a coward at his trial and begged on his knees for his life to be spared but provided Khrushchev with much ammunition to use against his political opponents later. He was one of the monsters around Stalin and history will judge him harshly.

Boldin, Valery Ivanovich (1935–): One of the plotters during the attempted coup against Gorbachev in August 1991. Boldin was a personal assistant of Gorbachev in 1985–87, then became head of the general department of the Central Committee, a key appointment which involves close liaison with the General Secretary, including drafting the agenda for Politburo meetings and supplying the necessary background papers. In March 1990 Boldin was appointed one of the members of Gorbachev's Presidential Council, and was the President's Chief of Staff. He was a leading member of the Emergency Committee during the abortive coup of August 1991. Boldin was arrested after the coup collapsed but was released from prison in December 1991, for health reasons. His memoirs are very entertaining, but inaccurate, as he casts a caustic eye over the Gorbachev era. Gorbachev totally misjudged him and this proved fatal.

Brezhnev, Leonid Ilich (1906–82): Vain, an excellent mimic, Brezhnev was leader of the Soviet Union at the apogee of its powers and influence but presided over its precipitate decline. In October 1964 Brezhnev became First Secretary (renamed General Secretary in 1966) of the Party and by 1969 he was top dog. Soviet intervention in Czechoslovakia gave rise to the Brezhnev doctrine: the right of Moscow to intervene in any socialist country where it perceived communist power to be under threat. In the early 1970s Brezhnev took the lead in articulating Soviet foreign policy and made many visits abroad, including going to Washington in June 1973 and receiving two US Presidents, Nixon and Ford, in Moscow and Vladivostok. Various agreements were reached and the Americans accepted, for the first time, the concept of nuclear parity between the two superpowers. In Europe, Brezhnev searched for increased security and signed the Helsinki Final Act of 1975, which accepted that the post-1945 frontiers could only be changed by negotiation. Brezhnev once remarked that his strength was in cadres policy: finding the right men and a few women for important posts. He was not a man of bold initiatives and innovative thinking – one of the reasons why his comrades had chosen him to follow the quixotic Khrushchev. He appears to have become dependent on drugs in the mid-1970s, once remarking that the more he took the better he slept. The Soviet Union also went into physical decline. The tragedy for the Soviet Union was that at a crucial point in its decline, it was being run by a man who could only function part of the time from the late 1970s. Brezhnev became the butt for many cruel jokes. He comes into his Kremlin office one day and his embarrassed secretary says: 'Leonid Ilich, one of your shoes is blue and the other red'. Brezhnev beams: 'And I have another pair just like these at home!' Brezhnev instructs a clever assistant to write him a ten-minute speech. The next day Brezhnev is livid and abuses the unfortunate scribe. 'I told you to prepare me a ten-minute speech and it took me twenty minutes to read it. You idiot!' The assistant, in an embarrassed tone, rejoins: 'But comrade Brezhnev, I gave you two copies!'

Bukharin, Nikolai Ivanovich (1888–1938): In Lenin's phrase, the 'darling of the Party', Bukharin was a sophisticated, urban intellectual who became a leading economic theorist but proved no match for Stalin. After the October Revolution he became a prominent left communist, opposing a peace treaty with Imperial Germany and instead advocating revolutionary war. Bukharin came round to Lenin's views by the end of 1918 and he was as ruthless as he in persecuting perceived opponents of the regime. After Lenin's death in 1924, the strongest apparent contender for the succession was Trotsky. Bukharin entered into a tactical alliance with Stalin to vitiate the brilliant, far left firebrand. Bukharin was one of the first, if not the first, to use the expression 'socialism in one country'. This implied putting the interests of Soviet Russia ahead of world revolution. Bukharin was appalled by the prospect of forced industrialisation and the concomitant authoritarian state which would automatically emerge. The nightmare of forced collectivisation was something he did not envisage. In the Gorbachev era there was considerable interest in Bukharin's views and the possibility that they represented an alternative course to Stalin's policies. Many believe that he penned the 1936 Soviet constitution (the most democratic in the world, in Stalin's words, and it was – at least on paper). He was the principal target of the last great show trial in March 1938. After being promised that his and his young wife's lives would be spared by Stalin and Voroshilov, Bukharin confessed to the most extraordinary and ludicrous (when one reads them today) crimes. His widow described him as a 'sensitive, emotional man', in *Ogonek*, in late 1987. His farewell letter, addressed to a Future Generation of Soviet Leaders, was published in *Moskovskie Novosti* (Moscow News) on 3 December 1987 and described his 'helplessness in the face of a murderous machine seeking his physical destruction'. He was rehabilitated by the USSR Supreme Soviet, together with nine others, on 4 February 1988.

Chernenko, Konstantin Ustinovich (1911–85): He contradicted the rule that losers never made a political comeback in the Soviet Union. He failed in his attempt to acquire the top prize after Brezhnev's death, being edged out by Andropov, but managed to push Gorbachev aside in 1984, when Andropov favoured Gorbachev as his successor. If the American political dream was to move from log cabin to the White House, Chernenko actually did move from an izba (cottage) to the Kremlin. Some have unkindly said that the reason why he did get to the top was because he carried Brezhnev's briefcase, in other words, his patron made him. Despite Andropov favouring Gorbachev, Chernenko got the nod from the ageing Politburo, mindful of the fact that the 'young' man Gorbachev might sweep them all away. At the burial of Andropov, Chernenko cut a poor figure. He attempted to salute the dead leader and failed to get his arm above his shoulder. When it came to his oration, he could hardly get the words out, he was clearly suffering from emphysema. When he died, after 13 months in office, the baton then passed to Mikhail Gorbachev but by then the race was already lost.

Chernomyrdin, Viktor Stepanovich (1938–): An industrialist who became a successful Prime Minister of Russia after the collapse of the Soviet Union. Chernomyrdin was USSR Minister of the Gas Industry in 1985–89. In 1989 the ministry became the State Gas Concern (Gazprom), with Chernomyrdin as chair of the board. It had a monopoly on gas production and sales and provided about one-third of the Soviet Union's hard currency export earnings. Chernomyrdin was opposed to the break-up of the gas monopoly, by privatisation or other means. Chernomyrdin became deputy Russian Prime Minister, responsible for fuel and energy, in June 1992. He was appointed Russian Prime Minister in December 1992, replacing the acting Prime Minister, Egor Gaidar.

Chicherin, Georgy Vasilevich (1872–1936): The diplomat who afforded the Bolsheviks some respectability, Chicherin was of noble birth, well educated, spoke all the main European languages except English, and was a wizard at presenting the communist case. With him in full flow, who could believe that the Soviets were the major threat to world civilisation?

He was a natural in a dinner jacket, unlike most Bolsheviks. Chicherin articulated the view that diplomacy represented state interests, the Comintern represented international communist interests, and the Red Army represented the security of the state. These three entities acted independently of one another. Chicherin was signalling the end of Soviet Russia as a revolutionary state. Its diplomacy had become traditional and Soviet Russia was a normal state. Chicherin's star began to wane after the Treaty of Locarno (1925), which saw a German–French rapprochement. The rising star was Maxim Litvinov, who effectively took over in 1928. In retirement Chicherin devoted himself to writing a book on Mozart and playing his piano music. The book was published in Moscow in 1973. (Chicherin belonged to an era when there was more culture in the Commissariat of Foreign Affairs. It requires quite a feat of imagination to see either Molotov or Gromyko playing a Mozart étude almost as well as Schnabel.)

Chubais, Anatoly Borisovich (1955–): The father of Russian privatisation, Chubais was one of the leaders of the democratic movement in Leningrad in 1985, and he was one of the organisers of the Leningrad Perestroika Club in 1987. His elder brother, Igor, was a leading light of the Moscow Perestroika Club and more radical than Anatoly. As a member of the CPSU, Anatoly was regarded as too loyal to Mikhail Gorbachev. In 1991 he became the senior economic adviser to Anatoly Sobchak, the mayor of Leningrad (St Petersburg). In November 1991 Gaidar appointed Chubais head of the state committee for the administration of the state property of the Russian Federation (Goskomimushchestvo), which was to develop a programme for the privatisation of state property. For his pains, Chubais became a hated man, blamed by many Russians who regarded privatisation as organised theft. He was dismissed by Yeltsin in January 1996 but came back to head brilliantly Yeltsin's campaign team for re-election. As a reward he was made the President's Chief of Staff and became one of the most influential politicians in Russia.

Chuikov, Marshal Vasily Ivanovich (1900–82): He became famous at the battle of Stalingrad and afterwards occupied many high posts. He was appointed commander of the 62nd army at Stalingrad. His army was the mainstay of the defence of the city. It was honoured by being renamed the 8th Guards Army and he remained its commander until the end of the war, taking part in the battle for Berlin. He was deputy commander, then in 1949 commander of the Soviet occupation forces in (East) Germany. As such he played a role in suppressing the Berlin uprising of June 1953. His memoirs of the battle for Stalingrad, *The Beginning of the Road*, are a graphic and incisive account of that epic battle, one of the turning points of the Second World War.

Dzerzhinsky, Feliks Edmundovich (1877–1926): Many sobriquets were applied to Dzerzhinsky by the Bolsheviks: Iron Feliks, the Shield of the Revolution and so on. They illustrate his steel-like qualities, his single-minded dedication, his ruthlessness in protecting the revolution against its enemies. He was the first head of the political police, first called the Cheka, then OGPU and eventually the KGB. Dzerzhinsky came from a Polish landed family and like many Bolsheviks of 'bourgeois' origin, made up for it by zealously destroying the bourgeoisie and intelligentsia after October 1917. Lenin trusted him explicitly so he was given *carte blanche* to make Russia safe for Bolsheviks. Dzerzhinsky's Great Russian chauvinism surfaced to Lenin's dismay during the 1922–23 Georgian affair. The conflict was over whether Tbilisi would be directly subordinate to Moscow, as an autonomous republic of the RSFSR, or indirectly, as a sovereign Soviet republic. Had Lenin lived he would have sided with the Georgians against Dzerzhinsky and Stalin – the arch centralisers. When once made aware by an aide that everyone feared him, he appeared surprised and rejoined that no one who was not guilty need fear him. He was never Stalin's man and when he died suddenly of a heat attack in July 1926 the way was open for Stalin to attempt to take control of OGPU.

Ezhov, Nikolai Ivanovich (1895–1939): The 'bloody dwarf' and 'iron people's commissar', Ezhov gave his name to the bloodiest period of the purges, the Ezhovshchina. He succeeded Yagoda as People's Commissar for Internal Affairs in September 1936, after the latter's fall from grace. Stalin believed that the NKVD was 'four years behind' in applying mass repression and consequently there was a need to 'catch up'. Ezhov is reported to have spent his first six months in office liquidating about 3,000 of Yagoda's men. He was dismissed as People's Commissar in December 1938, being replaced by Beria. Ezhov was then appointed People's Commissar for Water Transport. The previously powerful head of the police attended meetings of his new commissariat but never said anything. He spent the time making paper airplanes and birds, tossing them into the air and then crawling under the table to retrieve them. The security police finally arrived for him, in the middle of a commissariat meeting, in March 1939. He is reported to have stood up, threw his gun on to the table and stated: 'I have been waiting for this for a long time'. He was taken away and never seen again. Stalin had decided he needed a scapegoat for the excesses of the purges, which were coming to an end in 1939. Ezhov was addicted to drugs and was rumoured to have shot Yagoda personally.

Frunze, Mikhail Vasilevich (1885–1925): A leading Red commander during the Civil War, Frunze was born in Pishpek, now known as Bishkek, in Kyrgyzstan. Pishpek was renamed Frunze in 1926. In October 1917

Frunze led workers and soldiers in the struggle for Moscow. He was then dispatched to the Urals, where he led the southern group of the Red Army in 1919. His troops inflicted a severe defeat on Admiral Kolchak's White forces and Frunze took over command of the eastern front. He then turned his attention to Turkestan (Central Asia) and disposed of the local Muslim leaders, including the emir of Bukhara. He led the Reds who routed General Wrangel in the Crimea in November 1920. He became People's Commissar for War in January 1925 when Trotsky resigned. He sided with Stalin against Trotsky on military affairs. Frunze was the author of the 'unitary military doctrine', which envisaged that the military should be trained for offensive action and dedicated to carrying out the goals of the Communist Party, world revolution. This meant disposing of the ex-Tsarist officers whom Trotsky, out of necessity, had recruited during the Civil War. Frunze helped lay the foundations of the efficient Soviet military machine by introducing conscription and standardising military formations and uniforms.

Furtseva, Ekaterina Alekseevna (1910–74): Under Khrushchev, she became the first woman to be elected to the Politburo and thus was the exception to the rule that only males could make it to the top. She was a special favourite of Nikita Sergeevich and he made her First Secretary of Moscow city Party organisation in 1954 (until 1957). This was a formidable position for a woman to occupy. In 1956 she was elected a secretary of the Central Committee and a candidate member of the Presidium (Politburo), attaining full membership of the highest Party organ the following year. Her career nose-dived in 1960 when she lost her secretaryship of the Central Committee and was made USSR Minister of Culture. In 1961 she also lost her Presidium membership. She was reported to have attempted suicide but was found in time. She stayed under Brezhnev and died in office in November 1974. This testifies to her conservative, conformist views on culture and indicates that her main function was to keep the cultural intelligentsia in line. Artists and intellectuals used to complain that the Soviet Union had a minister of culture who had no culture. This was unfair, she did like the circus.

Gaidar, Egor Timurovich (1956–): A leading Russian economist who rose to prominence under Yeltsin and became known as the father of shock therapy – moving quickly from a planned to a market economy. It produced little for the average Russian so it was dubbed all shock and no therapy. Gaidar was a member of Shatalin's team who helped draft the 500-day programme for Gorbachev, but the latter found it too radical to implement. Gaidar then established contact with Yeltsin and after the abortive coup of August 1991 vied with Yavlinsky to fashion a new market-oriented Russian economy. Gaidar won and became deputy Prime

Minister of the Russian Federation in November 1991, launching his shock therapy in January 1992. Gaidar had to retreat from government in December 1992, giving way to Viktor Chernomyrdin as Prime Minister.

Gerasimov, Gennady Ivanovich (1930–): One of the most colourful representatives of glasnost under Gorbachev as head of the press department of the USSR Ministry of Foreign Affairs. Very tall for a Russian, Gerasimov, a professional journalist, was always looking for the quotable phrase. He turned Frank Sinatra to good use by saying the Soviet Union was doing things its way. Once, when he fell off the podium, he scrambled back and quipped: 'now for my next trick'! In 1986 Gerasimov moved to the Foreign Ministry and remained as principal press spokesman until 1990. His removal was an indication that more conservative forces were becoming influential in Moscow. He went off to Lisbon as Soviet ambassador to Portugal and in 1992 became Russian ambassador there. In Lisbon he felt isolated and missed the contact with the world's press. An American organisation once named him communicator of the year, something which gratified him deeply.

Gorbachev, Mikhail Sergeevich (1931–): If Lenin was the father of the Soviet Union, Gorbachev was its grave-digger. A remarkable man for the Party to produce and then elect leader, he perceived that Stalinist socialism was doomed and set about democratising the system, including ending the Party's monopoly on power. He remains convinced that had it not been for the attempted coup in August 1991 he could have fashioned a Union of Sovereign States out of the moribund Soviet Union. The key to the Soviet Union's fate after August 1991 rested not with Gorbachev but with Boris Yeltsin of Russia and Leonid Kravchuk of Ukraine. Yeltsin's desire to be the boss in the Kremlin doomed Gorbachev to political oblivion. The Gorbachev era can be divided into three periods. The first period was 1985–88, when he believed that the planned economy and Communist Party could be reformed from within. Reform from above, perestroika, was then accompanied by reform from below, glasnost. In 1988, at the 19th Conference, the Party lost its key role as manager of the economy. The second period, 1988–90, saw rapid institutional change as Gorbachev sought to revitalise the soviets. The election of the USSR Congress of People's Deputies and its inner core, the USSR Supreme Soviet, in 1989, brought into being a functioning parliament. Economic reform began to lay the foundations of a market economy. These reforms shattered elite consensus about reform and led to fierce inter-elite conflict, which culminated in the attempted coup of August 1991. Gorbachev made himself executive President in 1990 in an effort to overcome conservative opposition to reform. Even more contentiously, the Party lost its monopoly on political power, enshrined in article 6 of the constitution.

Gorbachev needed an institution to manage the economy and implement top decisions, but never found one. Glasnost fuelled rising nationalism, and republican elections in 1990, especially in the Baltic states, produced parliaments dominated by national fronts whose objective became independence. The draft agreement on a Union of Sovereign States was ready for signing when the coup plotters struck. He stood for Russian President in June 1996 but received only 0.5 per cent of the votes. Abroad he continued to weave his magic and his *Memoirs*, published in English in 1996, served as a focus for an international tour which was hugely successful. A prophet abroad but not in his own country, this is now his fate.

Gorbacheva, Raisa Maksimovna (née Titorenko) (1932–): A highly intelligent, strong-willed woman who carved out for herself a political role in a male-dominated political system, she aroused jealousy inside the Soviet Union. On the one hand, male communists took umbrage at her influence over Mikhail Gorbachev, and on the other hand, many Soviet women bridled at her access to expensive western clothes and cosmetics. She was closely involved in a foundation for the preservation of Russian culture, headed by Academician Dmitry Likhachev. She found house arrest at Foros during the attempted coup very stressful and suffered a mild stroke, taking about two years to recover fully.

Gordievsky, Oleg Antonovich (1939–): He was probably the most successful double agent ever recruited by British Intelligence until his cover was blown by a CIA agent in 1985. As a KGB officer he was responsible for Great Britain and Scandinavia, specialising in 'illegals', KGB agents infiltrated in foreign countries to operate under cover. He was posted to Copenhagen in 1966 as a press attaché at the Soviet Embassy and it was probably during his time there that he was recruited. In June 1982 he moved to the Soviet embassy in London and in 1984 became *Rezident*, or head of the KGB there. When his cover was blown by a CIA agent he was recalled to Moscow but managed to escape back to Britain. He provided much information on Soviet agents but more importantly on how the KGB operated. After the collapse of the Soviet Union he abandoned his habit of appearing on TV in disguise and made a good living commenting on spying and crime.

Gorky, Maksim (1868–1936): Regarded by many as the father of Soviet literature, Gorky was born into a Russian family in Nizhny Novgorod (renamed Gorky 1932–90) and spent his time as a wanderer, turning his hand to many trades. These experiences provided him with valuable material for his novels and plays as he knew Russian life from the bottom up. He left for a lecture tour of the United States in 1906 and caused a scandal by cohabiting with the actress Mariya Andreeva, not at that time his wife. He lived on Capri from 1906, put up the money for a Bolshevik

Party school, and remained on close terms with Lenin. Gorky returned to Russia in 1913 and opposed violent revolution in 1917. Zinoviev and Kamenev published their reservations about an armed seizure of power in October in his newspaper, *Novaya Zhizn*. After the revolution he was critical of Bolshevik excesses but kept many members of the intelligentsia alive by providing them with translation work. He fell out with Zinoviev, the Party boss of Petrograd, and left Soviet Russia in 1921, living in Sorrento in 1924–31. He became the most famous communist writer in the world while, ironically, living in Mussolini's fascist Italy. He returned to the Soviet Union in 1931 and was proclaimed as the father of socialist realism. Unlike his criticisms of Lenin's Russia, he was quiet about Stalin's excesses, especially forced collectivisation. His death may have been due to the consequences of shooting himself through the lung in a suicide attempt during his youth. On the other hand, Stalin may have been involved as Gorky may have been on the point of changing his mind about the type of state that Stalin was fashioning.

Gromyko, Andrei Andreevich (1909–89): Known as Grim Grom (he always looked as if he had toothache) and Mr Nyet (he was wont to say no), Gromyko personified Soviet foreign policy for almost three decades. When Mikhail Gorbachev became Party leader in 1985 he wanted to implement his new political thinking and Gromyko became the unacceptable face of Soviet foreign policy. He was replaced in July 1985 by the Georgian, Eduard Shevardnadze, a more compliant, flexible official. Gromyko succeeded Molotov in 1957 when the latter (a leading member of the Anti-Party Group) took on Khrushchev but lost. Khrushchev treated Gromyko with scant respect and once told de Gaulle, in Gromyko's presence, that if he asked Andrei Andreevich to take off his trousers and sit on a block of ice he would obey. Would de Gaulle's Foreign Minister, Couve de Murville, do the same? Gromyko became a member of the Politburo in 1973 and gradually dominated decision-making in foreign policy. He cannot be classified as a successful Foreign Minister because tension increased between the superpowers and the arms race accelerated. He was much taken by Gorbachev and enthusiastically proposed him for the Party leadership in March 1985. He stated that Gorbachev had a nice smile but teeth of steel. Gromyko overlooked that he might be bitten and he was moved upstairs in July 1985 to become Soviet President. In 1988 Gorbachev decided to become President himself. So Gromyko had to go. Gromyko spoke beautiful Russian and enjoyed a wide culture, being especially well read in English literature. A British ambassador on one occasion was taken aback, after delivering a protest note from the British government, to hear Gromyko's response – he recited a Kipling poem flawlessly. Gromyko also had a sense of humour but he never practised this gift in public.

Kaganovich, Lazar Moiseevich (1893–1991): One of the hard men around Stalin, Kaganovich was ruthless with his subordinates. The only Jew to remain a member of Stalin's inner group until the end, Kaganovich was too conservative for Khrushchev, who had previously worked closely with him, and his career ended with the defeat of the Anti-Party Group in 1957. During collectivisation he acted as a fireman and stamped out opposition on various missions, revealing gross brutality. He did not speak up for his brother, Mikhail, USSR Minister of the Aviation Industry, who committed suicide on hearing that Beria intended to arrest him and have him shot. Jews complained of Kaganovich's anti-Semitism. He headed several ministries after 1935 and the reason for his appointment was always the same: the industry had become a bottleneck. Kaganovich broke the bottleneck. After Stalin's death Kaganovich was one of the Party elite but misjudged Khrushchev. He was packed off to manage a cement factory in the Urals in 1957 and after Khrushchev's removal he reapplied for Party membership but was turned down. He retired to Moscow where during the Gorbachev era he could be seen sitting on park benches. When asked about his past, he denied that he was a Jew and stoutly defended Stalin.

Kamenev, Lev Borisovich (1883–1936): The eternal moderate of the Bolshevik Party, Kamenev was born into a Moscow Jewish family. After the February Revolution Kamenev situated himself on the moderate wing of the Bolshevik Party and conflict with Lenin was inevitable when the Bolshevik leader managed to get back to Petrograd. Kamenev advocated caution in the run up to the October Revolution and went so far as to publish an article in Gorky's newspaper, *Novaya Zhizn*, warning against revolutionary adventurism. He became chair of the Moscow soviet after the revolution and remained there until ousted by Stalin. He was a leading light in the Politburo and often chaired meetings when Lenin was too ill to attend. As a moderate, he was always opposed to Trotsky's radicalism and he joined Stalin and Zinoviev to form the triumvirate whose aim was to prevent Trotsky succeeding Lenin, even though this was Lenin's wish. Later Kamenev sided with Trotsky against Stalin and also Zinoviev in his opposition to Stalin. He lost his place on the Politburo in 1925 and was dispatched to Rome as Soviet ambassador to Italy (1926–27). He suffered the same fate as Zinoviev in being expelled several times from the Party, being readmitted when he had made the ritual obeisance to Stalin. Kamenev and Zinoviev, and a supporting cast of minor officials, had the dubious honour of starring in the first great show trial in Moscow in August 1936. Kamenev confessed to having been behind the murder of Sergei Kirov in 1934 and given the opportunity would have topped Stalin as well. All this was nonsense but Kamenev had understood that confessions would spare his own and his family's lives. They did not and the whole Kamenev household perished. Kamenev was rehabilitated under Gorbachev on 13 June 1988.

Kerensky, Aleksandr Fedorovich (1881–1970): The great loser in twentieth-century Russian politics, Kerensky was blamed by an army of critics for the seizure of power by the Bolsheviks in October 1917. This weighed heavily on him and until his dying day it was impossible to carry on an objective conversation about the events of 1917 with him. He was liable to fly into a rage if his role was brought into question. His father was head-master of the school in Simbirsk (Ulyanovsk) where Lenin and his elder brother Aleksandr (executed for attempted regicide in 1887) studied. He studied history and law at St Petersburg University and in 1905 joined the Socialist Revolutionary Party (several of his wife's relatives were in the Party). He was elected to the Duma in 1912 as a Trudovik. Like many other top politicians, he became a freemason. The February Revolution afforded him central stage and he became the most important non-Bolshevik politician in 1917. In the first Provisional Government Kerensky was Minister of Justice and when Guchkov resigned as Minister of War and the Navy, Kerensky succeeded him. This afforded him a stage for his rhetoric and he toured the fronts attempting to enthuse the troops to victory. The bungled agreement with Kornilov was the kiss of death for Kerensky. He escaped arrest in the Winter Palace on 25 October 1917 by dressing up as a female nurse and attempted to rally loyal troops. He spent many years of his exile in Paris and, after 1940, in the United States.

Khrushchev, Nikita Sergeevich (1894–1971): An intelligent, cunning, rum-bustious Soviet leader who broke the Stalinist mould but was eventually removed by the nomenklatura. Khrushchev became the first Soviet leader to visit the United States and to promise that communism was round the corner in his homeland. Khrushchev was a political officer during the war and in 1944 was appointed Prime Minister and First Party Secretary of Ukraine with the task of rebuilding the shattered republic. In 1946 Khrushchev was replaced by Kaganovich as First Secretary but in 1948 he was back again as Party leader. Stalin brought him back to Moscow in 1949 to head the Moscow Party organisation and he also became a secretary of the Central Committee. This made him a key player after Stalin's death in March 1953 and by June 1957 he had outmanoeuvred Beria, Malenkov and Molotov to become a dominant, national leader. The defeat of the Anti-Party Group in June 1957 allowed Khrushchev to stack the Politburo with his appointees and marked the dominance of the Party apparatus over the government. In 1961 Khrushchev launched a new Party programme and expected the foothills of communism (to each according to need) to be reached by 1980. He was later to be the butt of much ridicule for this utopian prediction. In many ways his reforms presaged those of Gorbachev. Like the future Soviet leader he came to the conclusion that the Party apparatus was a brake on the economy and split it in 1962 into industrial and agricultural wings. Both wanted to afford industrial managers more latitude. There were considerable differences however. Khrushchev never questioned the leading role of the Party and would not contemplate any market-oriented reforms. Arguably in doing so, he doomed himself to failure. In foreign policy Khrushchev was very innovative but a high risk-taker. The 20th Party Congress demolition of Stalin infuriated Mao Zedong, who felt he should have been consulted beforehand. This contributed to the Hungarian Revolution of 1956 and weakened the communist edifice worldwide. The greatest crisis occurred in October 1962 when the superpowers almost began a nuclear war. In agriculture he launched the virgin lands programme, a vast expansion of the cultivated area, which increased output but at great expense. By 1963 he was importing grain from the United States. He was removed by the nomenklatura, whom he had almost totally alienated by October 1964.

Kollontai, Aleksandra Mikhailovna (née Domontovich) (1872–1952): The 'femme fatale' of the Russian Revolution, she scored many firsts in Europe: the first woman to join a government and the first woman ambassador. She will probably be remembered more for her role as a pioneer feminist and advocate of free love than for her revolutionary record. In 1914 she was in Berlin and later joined the left around Lenin, writing tirelessly against the war. She spent the war in Scandinavia and the USA but always maintained close contact with Lenin. In July 1917 she was elected to the Central Committee of the RSDRP. She supported the left communists around Bukharin, who opposed the Treaty of Brest-Litovsk as treason and a betrayal of internationalism. This cost her position on the Central Committee. She supported the workers' opposition. She belonged to the first Sovnarkom for a short time but as head of the women's section of the Central Committee from 1920 she exercised influence over policy towards women, families and health. She was elected deputy head of the international women's commissariat of the Communist International (Comintern). Many of her progressive innovations were put into reverse by Stalin. In 1923 Kollontai was sent to Oslo as Soviet representative, then to Mexico in 1926, and to Norway in 1927. She was well suited to this type of activity as she was an excellent linguist. In 1930 she was posted to Stockholm and in 1943–45 she was ambassador to Sweden. Kollontai had to accept that Stalin's Russia was male chauvinist and that the position of women declined over time.

Kosygin, Aleksei Nikolaevich (1904–80): The technically most competent Prime Minister the Soviet Union ever had, from 1964 to 1980, but as he lacked the guts for a political fight he was not very effective. In 1965 he launched reforms geared to increasing the decision-making role of enterprises. These reforms petered out after the Soviet-led invasion of Czechoslovakia in August 1968 led to a recentralisation of decision-making. Until 1968 Kosygin took the lead in representing the Soviet Union abroad but afterwards he conceded primacy to Brezhnev. Gorbachev found him cool, if not cold. This may be due to the fact that as a survivor of the purges of the 1930s and 1948 he avoided factional politics like the plague. When informed of the coup against Khrushchev his first question was about the position of the KGB. When told it was for, he said he was also for the coup.

Krupskaya, Nadezhda Konstantinovna (1869–1939): Lenin's wife but not his love (that was Inessa Armand). Krupskaya first encountered Lenin in St Petersburg social democratic circles in 1894. They were both arrested in 1895–96, and in Siberian exile Lenin proposed that she join him, informing the police that she was his fiancée. The police agreed, providing they marry immediately she arrived. They had to go through an Orthodox church ceremony in July 1898, much to Lenin's embarrassment, but it was a small price to pay for a companion and help-mate. There is no passion in his letters to her. Krupskaya faithfully followed Lenin into exile and around Europe (1901–16). She returned with Lenin to Petrograd in April 1917 but she evinced little enthusiasm for early insurrection. She did not accompany Lenin when he escaped to Finland after the July Days but did visit him twice in Helsinki. She was not an important emissary for Lenin – Stalin was already playing that role. They were reunited after the October Revolution but there was really no political role for her to play. She became deputy People's Commissar for Enlightenment under Lunacharsky. She was devoted to Lenin but lacked the resolve or the cunning to deal with Stalin, who treated her badly. After Lenin's death Stalin warned her that the Party was quite capable of designating someone else as Lenin's widow. An illness left her with protruding eyes. Her reminiscences of Lenin are remarkable for their lack of political insight and acumen.

Kozyrev, Andrei Vladimirovich (1951–): The Russian Foreign Minister before and after the collapse of communism in 1991, he came to personify the pro-western school of thought among Russian policy-makers. In October 1990 Ivan Silaev, RSFSR Prime Minister, invited him to leave the USSR Ministry of Foreign Affairs and become Russian Minister of Foreign Affairs. Previously this would have meant a demotion but in 1990 Russia was a rising power. He quickly established himself as a supporter of Russian sovereignty and during the autumn of 1991 he helped to draft the agreement which eventually set up the Commonwealth of

Independent States. He was a member of the Communist Party until 1991. As Russian Foreign Minister he was savagely attacked in the RSFSR Congress of People's Deputies for not defending Russians in the ex-Soviet republics (called the near abroad) and being too pro-western. This was known as the Atlanticist view as opposed to the Eurasian view of the Russian nationalists. Eventually Yeltsin had to dismiss him and he was succeeded by Evgeny Primakov in January 1996.

Kryuchkov, Vladimir Aleksandrovich (1924–): One of the many misjudgements by Gorbachev, who appointed him chair of the KGB in 1988. Kryuchkov became the leader of the attempted coup of August 1991. When Gorbachev was able to remove Chebrikov as KGB chief in 1988, he chose Kryuchkov to succeed him. This may have been due to the fact that Kryuchkov had been close to Andropov. Kryuchkov consistently misinformed Gorbachev about domestic and foreign policy. Gorbachev was later shocked to find that Kryuchkov had bugged his office. Gorbachev remains very bitter about being betrayed by Kryuchkov.

Lenin, Vladimir Ilich (1870–1924): One of the key political actors of the twentieth century, Lenin has left an indelible mark on Russian, European and world politics. A utopian Marxist socialist, he came to believe that will could triumph over everything else. A brilliant polemicist and tactician, Lenin had an unrivalled ability to analyse a political situation and evolve tactics to promote his Party's ends. He was deadly in dissecting and exploiting the weaknesses of his political opponents but he failed singularly to grasp the essence of Stalin or Trotsky. He lost his hair early and this contributed to his sobriquet as the 'old man' because of his seriousness and single-minded devotion to revolution. A member of the service nobility and a graduate in law at St Petersburg University, he nevertheless hated the intelligentsia – they were to him the chattering classes who never moved from word to deed. Another hatred was religion – he had been religious as a teenager. In private life he could be charming among his supporters but he could be as deadly as a viper towards his enemies. He was as bloodthirsty as a vampire during the early years of the revolution but mellowed in 1921. His declining years, partly the after effects of a failed assassination attempt in August 1918 and advancing arteriosclerosis, were painful and deeply frustrating. He died a saddened and worried man. Gorky once remarked that for humankind as a whole, Lenin had nothing but scorn. He treated the working class as a miner treats iron ore. Molotov, the only communist official to serve Lenin and Stalin throughout their time in power, when asked to compare the two, remarked that Lenin had been more severe. Lenin was an extraordinary mixture of incisive intelligence, erudition, messianic fervour, the morals of a Ghengis Khan, incredible misjudgements and utopian mania. In short, a visionary who refused to take men and women as he found them – he wanted to transform them in his image.

Ligachev, Egor Kuzmich (1920–): Ligachev and Gorbachev were moderate reformers in 1985–88, but then they parted company when Gorbachev became a radical reformer. Whereas until 1988 reform had been to improve the system, it then began to unravel the existing system. Ligachev found all this very disturbing, insisting on the leading role of the Party, the collective ownership of land and the dominance of the state in the economy. To his credit, Ligachev did not join the coup plotters in August 1991, even though he judged Gorbachev's policies to be disastrous to the socialist system. Andropov brought him to Moscow and in 1983 he became a secretary of the Central Committee. He was number two to Gorbachev after March 1985, chairing meetings of the secretariat. He was widely believed to be behind Nina Andreeva's letter to *Sovetskaya Rossiya* in March 1988, which Yakovlev called an anti-perestroika manifesto, but Gorbachev accepted that this was not true. Ligachev's attempt to become Gorbachev's deputy at the 28th Party Congress in July 1990 was stymied by the General Secretary himself. He was then not elected to the new-look Politburo, which contained only Party functionaries. Had Ligachev been more ruthless and ambitious he might have become an extremely dangerous opponent for Gorbachev.

Lysenko, Trofim Denisovich (1898–1976): The greatest charlatan of the Stalin and Khrushchev eras, Lysenko held back the development of Soviet agriculture. He founded agrobiology, a pseudo-science, in the 1920s, and promised to raise yields rapidly and cheaply. A passionate patriot, Lysenko's tragedy was that he lacked a rigorous scientific training and he fell victim to his ambition to make the Soviet Union bloom and himself the leading scientist. He reached his apogee in 1948 when genetics was banned, with Stalin playing close attention to the arguments used. Khrushchev was as blind as Stalin and would not listen to criticism of Lysenko. His nefarious influence extended to China, where Mao, in 1958, was much taken by his ideas such as planting deeply and densely on less land, grafting vegetables with fruit and the killing of all insect-eating birds. These ideas contributed to the Great Chinese Famine of 1959–61, when between 30 million and 60 million peasants died. It was only in 1965 that Lysenko was dethroned and genetics rehabilitated. Soviet scientists were later able to demonstrate that he had falsified his results.

Malenkov, Georgy Maksimilianovich (1902–88): The Gorbachev of his era, he promoted new political thinking at home and abroad as Prime Minister in 1953–55. He was a member of the group around Stalin who displayed great tactical skill but after Stalin's death was rather easily outmanoeuvred by Khrushchev. He became a Party official in the 1920s and was a protégé of Kaganovich during the 1930s. He was responsible for Party cadres and as such was deeply involved in the purges. He was a member of the Central Committee of the Communist Party from 1941. When war broke out he became a member of the State Defence Committee (GKO), responsible for technical supplies to the army and air force. In 1946 he was elected a secretary of the Central Committee and deputy Prime Minister. This underlined his considerable administrative talents and his political skill. He was a member of the Politburo in 1946–57. In the cut and thrust of the late Stalin era Malenkov proved ruthless in defending his own position and this earned the undying hatred of Khrushchev. On Stalin's death in March 1953, Malenkov became head of the Party and Prime Minister but was soon forced to give up one of these posts. He chose to remain Prime Minister and thus opened up the way for Khrushchev to challenge him for supremacy, using the Party as his base. Malenkov ushered in a period of détente at home and abroad, promoting a more consumerist approach to economic growth. At first, Beria and he worked closely together, but Khrushchev managed to attract Malenkov away from Beria. After Beria's arrest in June 1953 the contest between Malenkov and Khrushchev got under way in earnest. He sided with the Anti-Party Group (so called because they opposed the Party having a major say in running the economy) in July 1957 and their defeat meant the end of his active political career. He was dispatched to Ust Kamenogorsk, Kazakhstan, to manage the hydroelectric plant there. Malenkov soon returned to Moscow and he lived privately. There were reports that he attended Orthodox services. News of his death took some time to emerge as relatives had asked for the information to be withheld.

Mikoyan, Anastas Ivanovich (1895–1978): A master politician who exhibited great tactical skill and managed always to stay at the top, be it under Stalin, Khrushchev or Brezhnev. An Armenian, he formed a close alliance with Stalin early on and later played a key role in developing trade. There were many stories of his astuteness as Comrade Commerce. He is negotiating with Henry Ford and he is offered one of the new Ford models. He enquires about the price and is told it is 50 cents. He takes one but Ford apologises for not having 50 cents change. Mikoyan, quick as a flash, replies: 'That's alright, I'll take two!'. During the war he was chair of the committee of supply for the Red Army. He chose wisely in allying himself with Khrushchev after Stalin's death and Khrushchev sent him to Cuba, where he fell in love with Castro's revolution, saying that it reminded him of his youth. In October 1964 he rang Khrushchev in Pitsunda, north Caucasus, summoning him to a Politburo meeting to be dismissed. He had changed sides but he remained a friend. Mikoyan proposed that Khrushchev be given an honorific Party title, which Brezhnev rudely turned down. After defeat, Mikoyan kissed Khrushchev goodbye and they never met again. His son, Sergo, kept the information about Khrushchev's death from him, but he read about it in *Pravda*. He managed to send a wreath to the funeral. In 1988 Sergo Mikoyan became the first of the children of the old elite to acknowledge openly the responsibility of their parents for the terrible past.

Molotov, Vyacheslav Mikhailovich (né Scriabin) (1890–1986): Like many other true red Bolsheviks, he came from a middle class family and was related to the composer. He joined the Bolsheviks soon after the 1905 revolution and quickly identified with Lenin and later Stalin. Only in the Anti-Party Group against Khrushchev in 1957 did he emerge as a leader in his own right. Until then he had been the eternal bridesmaid and never the bride. He was an incongruous figure: a Bolshevik in a pince-nez. Obdurate, humourless (at least in public), he personified the unattractive side of Soviet foreign policy, especially in the immediate post-war years. His pseudonym, Molotov, means a hammer and this was apt. He displayed great political skill in his relations with Stalin and always kept his head. In retirement at Peredelkino, just outside Moscow, he was recognised while shopping by a woman who screamed at him: 'Why is this Stalinist criminal still at liberty?' Molotov did not utter a word but slowly turned and left the shop and Peredelkino for ever. Conversations with him were published in the 1980s but are disappointing. He never wavered in his conviction that everything Stalin had done was correct. When he was readmitted to the Party in July 1984, the in-joke was that Chernenko was smoothing the path for his successor! He became a member of the Politburo in 1925. Stalin chose him as chair of Sovnarkom in 1930 and he replaced Litvinov as Commissar for Foreign Affairs in 1939. Stalin became Prime Minister himself in 1941. The Soviet–German Non-Aggression Treaty of August 1939 is often referred to as the Molotov–Ribbentrop Pact. He was at Stalin's side during all the wartime conferences and at Potsdam. He was replaced in 1949 as Minister of Foreign Affairs by Andrei Vyshinsky but on Stalin's death in March 1953 he returned to the foreign ministry. Khrushchev used him to out-manoeuvre Beria, but Molotov was too conservative for the innovative Khrushchev. In 1957 Andrei Gromyko took over the foreign ministry. Molotov led the Anti-Party Group (so called because they resisted the Party assuming primacy in the state) in July 1957 and had the guts, in defeat, to refuse to acknowledge that he had been wrong. He was packed off to Ulan Bator as Soviet ambassador to Mongolia and later to Vienna as Soviet representative to the Atomic Energy Agency. He was vilified during the de-Stalinisation period and was expelled from the Party in 1964.

Ordzhonikidze, Grigory Konstantinovich (Sergo) (1886–1937): A prominent Georgian revolutionary who was influential in industrialising the Soviet Union. He supported Stalin and in 1926 moved to Moscow to become chair of the Central Control Commission and Rabkrin (responsible for discipline among Party and state officials) and in 1930 became chair of the Supreme Council of the National Economy (VSNKh). In January 1932 he became Commissar for Heavy Industry, the core of industrialisation. In 1926 he was elected a candidate member of the Politburo and in 1930 a full member, revealing that he was a member of Stalin's inner group. He fell out with Stalin over the purges, his brother was tortured and shot, and all around him were being arrested. He died suddenly, officially of a heart attack, but it is widely believed that he committed suicide.

Pasternak, Boris Leonidovich (1890–1960): World famous for his novel *Dr Zhivago*, which was turned into a successful film in the west. Pasternak was born in Moscow into a Jewish family which was very artistic, his father being a painter. He published his first poems in 1913 and proved a fine lyric poet. He wrote prose also but gradually found Stalin's Russia more and more uncongenial. Pasternak turned to translation, including Goethe and Shakespeare. His *Dr Zhivago* (in the Old Church Slavonic orthography, it would be *Dr Zhivogo* in modern Russian) hinted at spiritual values and the search for freedom. It was published in Italy in 1957. Pasternak was awarded the Nobel Prize in 1958. He was treated as a traitor by the Soviet establishment and had to decline the Nobel Prize. One doctor stated that the book was an insult to the medical profession, without having read it. The scandal shortened his life and Khrushchev, in his memoirs, regretted not having read the work himself at the time. *Dr Zhivago* was published in the Soviet Union in 1988, thus completing his rehabilitation as one of the great Russian poets and writers of the twentieth century.

Podgorny, Nikolai Viktorovich (1903–83): A member of the triumvirate which took over from Khrushchev in 1964 (the others were Brezhnev and Kosygin), Podgorny was an influential figure until 1977, when he fell out with Brezhnev. He sided with Brezhnev in 1964 and in 1965 was made chair of the Presidium of the USSR Supreme Soviet, or head of state. He exercised more influence as head of state than most former incumbents but it was not a real power base. When Brezhnev wanted to become head of state himself in 1977, he offered Podgorny the deputy's job, which the latter turned down flat. Podgorny was dismissed and also removed from the Politburo without a word of thanks for his long service. No pretense was made about his having resigned for reasons of health.

Polozkov, Ivan Kuzmich (1935–): Against Gorbachev's wishes he was elected the First Secretary of the Russian Communist Party at its founding congress in June 1990. He moved into Party work in 1962 and was elected to the USSR Congress of People's Deputies in 1989, and the RSFSR Congress of People's Deputies. In July 1990 he was elected to the CPSU Politburo. Polozkov was a great disappointment as he proved a colourless conservative apparatchik, close to the line pursued by Ligachev. His Party was banned by President Yeltsin in November 1991.

Popov, Gavriil Kharitonovich (1936–): A leading economist and politician of the Gorbachev era, he was born in Moscow into a family of Greek origin, graduated in economics from Moscow State University in 1959, and taught in the university in 1963–88, becoming dean of faculty in 1977. He campaigned for the introduction of business studies and was eventually successful. He was elected to the USSR Congress of People's Deputies in 1989, and became a leader of the Inter-Regional Group, a reform-minded group within the CPSU. In April 1990 he was elected chair of Moscow city council (Mossovet) and he left the Communist Party in July 1990. He was elected mayor of Moscow in June 1991 (with Yury Luzhkov as his deputy) and thereby became a prominent figure. He was a leading member of the Democratic Russia (DemRossiya) movement and was also chair of the All-Union Society of Soviet Greeks and the president of the USSR baseball and softball federation. He resigned as mayor of Moscow in June 1992.

Preobrazhensky, Evgeny Aleksandrovich (1886–1937): One of the leading Soviet economists until the late 1920s, when Stalin's rise meant his fall. He and Bukharin wrote the *ABC of Communism* and he was firmly on the left of the Party, siding with Trotsky against Stalin. He developed the concept of the primitive accumulation of capital, to be provided by the peasants. As such he was out of temper with NEP and favoured the introduction of a socialist economy. These ideas were not acceptable to Stalin and the right before 1927 but Trotsky's defeat meant that Stalin could move to the left and steal Preobrazhensky's ideas. He was expelled from the Party in 1927 and lost all his other positions as well. He recanted and was readmitted to the Party. He was a witness for the prosecution against Zinoviev in 1936 but was arrested in 1937, tried and executed.

Primakov, Evgeny Maksimovich (1929–): An astute politician who rose to prominence under Gorbachev and then played an even more important role in Yeltsin's Russia. In 1986 he was elected a candidate member of the Party Central Committee, in April 1989 a full member of the Central Committee, and in September 1989 a candidate member of the Politburo. In 1989 he was elected to the USSR Congress of People's

Deputies (nominated by the Communist Party) and the USSR Supreme Soviet, and from June 1989 to March 1990 he was chair (speaker) of the Soviet of the Union, one of the two houses of the USSR Supreme Soviet (and Gorbachev's nominee for the post). In March 1990 he was made a member of Gorbachev's Presidential Council. He was a frequent visitor to Iraq and some observers believe he had foreknowledge of Iraq's plan to invade Kuwait. From December 1990 to January 1991 he travelled to Baghdad and negotiated with Saddam Hussein in an effort to stave off the Gulf War. He also travelled to Baghdad during the war in an attempt to broker a settlement. In January 1992 President Yeltsin appointed him head of the Main Intelligence Administration (GRU) and in January 1996 he became Russian Foreign Minister, succeeding Andrei Kozyrev.

Pugo, Boris Karlovich (1937–91): One of the many Latvians to attain high political office in the Soviet Union. He was First Secretary of Riga Party city committee, 1975–76, and then became first deputy chair of the Latvian KGB in 1977–80, and chair in 1980–84. Yury Andropov had chosen him for these posts. Then in 1984–88 he was First Secretary of the Communist Party of Latvia, and became chair of the All-Union Committee of Party Control. In December 1990 he replaced Vadim Bakatin as USSR Minister of Internal Affairs. His appointment was regarded by liberals at the time as a bad omen and this turned out to be true as Pugo was one of the plotters in August 1991. Immediately after its failure he committed suicide by shooting himself. Pugo was one of the many appointments by Gorbachev which proved ill judged and the main reason appears to be that Gorbachev relied on personnel promoted by his patron Andropov.

Radek, Karl Berngardovich (1885–1939): A Polish Jew from Austrian Galicia, he was active in Polish and German social democracy before 1914. He became an adherent of Trotsky's theory of permanent revolution. He was elected to the Central Committee of the Communist Party in March 1919 but he never came to terms with developments within the Party and Russia. He sided with the left communists in their demands for instant socialism in the economy and opposed the Brest-Litovsk Treaty, favouring international revolution. His area of interest was observing international developments which could lead to socialist revolution. As secretary, from 1920, of the Communist International (Comintern), he was well informed and devoted great attention to the German left. The language of the Comintern under Lenin was German and when Lenin was lost for a German word, Radek, who was crouched under the podium, would come up with the relevant term. Radek supported Trotsky against Stalin. He was expelled from the Party in 1927 but was readmitted in 1929 after he had repented of his mistakes. He then became a passionate promoter of Stalin. He was again expelled from the Party in 1936 and arrested. In 1937 he was sentenced to 10 years imprisonment during the show trial against the Anti-Soviet Trotskyite Centre. He gave evidence against some of the other accused and this saved him from the executioner's bullet. He died in a labour camp and was rehabilitated in 1988.

Rasputin, Father Grigory Efimovich (1872–1916): The most infamous Orthodox priest of his generation, he established contact with the Romanov family in 1905. The Tsarevich Aleksei suffered from haemophilia, which he had inherited from his mother, who in turn had acquired it as a relative of Queen Victoria. Rasputin used hypnosis to staunch the internal bleeding, which caused excruciating pain. This led to the Tsarina regarding him as having been sent from God. Had he remained a healer, there would have been no scandal. However, he was a libertine (Rasputin is derived from this word) and he advocated sinning in order to experience repentance. His powerful presence made him very attractive to the noble women of the court and he engaged in sexual relations with many of them. (There is no conclusive evidence that he and the Tsarina were ever lovers.) His privileged position at court offered chances for financial and political gain and Rasputin was identified as early as 1912 as a baleful influence on the monarchy. When Tsar Nicholas II moved to Mogilev to assume command of the Russian armies in 1915 he left the Tsarina in Petrograd to cope with ministers. The Tsarina placed great faith in her 'friend's' counsel and this led to ministers and their deputies being sacked and replaced at whirlwind speed. Russian military defeats led to rumours that there was a German faction at court, headed by the Tsarina. This was nonsense but it was believed and damaged the royal family. Eventually, in December 1916, a relative of the Tsar conspired with others to poison – so much poison was administered that it worked as an antidote – then shoot Rasputin and drop him through a hole into the frozen River Neva. Rasputin lives on in many western films.

Reilly, Sidney (1874–1925): One of the most famous spies of the early revolutionary period, he was an agent for Britain and other countries and found the conspiratorial life irresistible. Born in Russia, he married an Irish widow in London in 1898 and changed his name to Reilly, thereby acquiring a British passport. He was a British intelligence officer in several countries and represented a German armaments company in St Petersburg until 1914. He was a British–Japanese double agent in the Far East. He was quite a society figure in St Petersburg and provided the Okhrana (Russian secret police) with information about revolutionaries, including, possibly, Stalin. He entered Russia in April 1918 on a Soviet passport given to him in London by Litvinov and, aided by

Bruce Lockhart, another British intelligence officer acting as a diplomat, established contact with the Cheka head of the Kremlin guard. The latter, under Chekist orders, pretended the Latvian troops guarding the Bolsheviks were disillusioned. Reilly fed him funds to promote an anti-Bolshevik coup. He acquired a Chekist passport and attempted to arrest Lenin and Dzerzhinsky. He crossed the Finnish–Soviet border in September 1925 and was immediately arrested by the Soviets. In 1966 a Soviet weekly stated that he had been executed in November 1925 in Moscow. Sam Neill played him in a British TV series.

Romanov, Grigory Vasilevich (1923–): A contender for the post of General Secretary in March 1985, his defeat by Gorbachev ended his political career. He moved into the Leningrad Party apparatus in 1955 and rose to be first secretary, Leningrad oblast committee, 1970–83. He had the reputation of being a tough administrator and gaining much defence investment for Leningrad. In 1973 he was elected a candidate member of the Politburo and in 1976 a full member. Andropov called him to Moscow in 1983 and made him a secretary of the Central Committee, where he was responsible for the armed forces and defence industry. Romanov supported Chernenko against Gorbachev in 1984. He was sacked in July 1985. It was put about that he had been involved in corruption, drunken bacchanalias and orgies, a familiar tale related after a political leader has fallen.

Romanov, Nikolai Aleksandrovich (Nicholas II, Tsar of all Russia) (1868–1918): A mild-mannered, self-effacing, politically unimaginative, family-loving man, completely out of his depth as Tsar, especially at such a critical juncture in his nation's history. He was forced into concessions during the 1905 Revolution and he always resented Witte's role in this, even though his autocratic powers were confirmed in the Fundamental Laws in April 1906. After the tercentenary celebrations of the Romanov dynasty in 1913, he even considered dissolving the Duma, even though it enjoyed only weak legislative powers. After the initial defeats of the Russian army, he determined in August 1915 to move to Mogilev, the headquarters of the General Staff, to become Commander-in-Chief. He was deaf to all pleas for a government of national confidence and it was only when he was abdicating in March 1917 that he conceded on this issue. When he abdicated he noted in his diary that he read Caesar's Gallic Wars (the Russian word Tsar is derived from Caesar). After the February Revolution, the royal family were kept at Tsarskoe Selo for five months, with Kerensky enquiring if they had collaborated with the Germans. In August 1917 they were moved to Tobolsk and in April 1918 they were taken to Ekaterinburg. Lenin gave the go ahead to murder them to the Ekaterinburg Bolsheviks and on 17 July 1918 all were butchered in a cellar and their bodies thrown down a disused mine shaft. The remains of the Tsar and his family were retrieved under Gorbachev and scientists confirmed that they were authentic in 1993. The Tsar was considered for canonisation by the Russian Orthodox Church.

Rutskoi, Aleksandr Vladimirovich (1947–): He became nationally prominent politically in 1989, advocating the military virtues of discipline, and was chosen by Boris Yeltsin as his Vice-President for the Russian presidential elections of June 1991. He was a hero during the attempted coup of August 1991 and was with Yeltsin in the White House. From 1985 to 1986 he was commander of an air force regiment in Afghanistan, and in 1988 he was commander of the air force of the 40th army in Afghanistan. He flew over 400 combat missions, was shot down twice, severely wounded, and was a prisoner of war of the mujahidin for six weeks in Pakistan. He returned to the Soviet Union a war hero and a Hero of the Soviet Union. He was elected to the RSFSR Congress of People's Deputies in March 1990, and the RSFSR Supreme Soviet. Rutskoi linked up with Yeltsin at the 3rd RSFSR Congress of People's Deputies in March 1991, and saved Yeltsin from defeat at the hands of the communists, who were trying to remove him as speaker. Rutskoi was chosen as Vice-President in the June 1991 presidential elections. During the attempted coup he appealed to all 'officers, soldiers and sailors' not to act against the people and not to 'support the conspirators'. He flew to Foros to 'liberate' Gorbachev and the Soviet President promoted him to Major-General. Gradually relations between Yeltsin and Rutskoi cooled and the latter felt slighted that Yeltsin did not offer him a prestigious post. Gradually a gulf opened and it culminated in October 1993 with Rutskoi being sworn in as President by the Congress of People's Deputies. Rutskoi was among those arrested after the storming of the White House but was amnestied later by the Duma.

Rykov, Aleksei Ivanovich (1881–1938): Stalin's ally in his struggle with Trotsky after Lenin's death, Rykov reaped the whirlwind later. Despite the fact that he advocated moderation, he was elected in September 1917 to the Bolshevik Central Committee and the Petrograd soviet. His skill as an administrator overcame Lenin's lack of faith in him and he was People's Commissar of the Interior in 1917–18, and then Chair of the Supreme Council of the National Economy (VSNKh) in 1918–20 and 1923–24. He was also Lenin's deputy on Sovnarkom, chairing meetings of the government when Lenin was too ill to attend. On Lenin's death, he was the obvious candidate to succeed him and remained as head of government until he fell foul of Stalin in 1930. Throughout the early Soviet period, Rykov maintained an independent, critical stance. As a moderate, it was not surprising that Rykov sided with Bukharin,

Tomsky and Stalin against Trotsky and Zinoviev after Lenin's death. He became a leading member of the right opposition, with Bukharin, against Stalin's policies, especially forced collectivisation. After the defeat of the right opposition, Rykov became for a time People's Commissar for Posts and Telegraph. In 1930 he was removed from all his posts and expelled from the Politburo in December 1930. He was arrested in 1937 and later tried for treason in the third great show trial, in 1938. He was found guilty of having formed a terrorist group in 1934, which had targeted Stalin, Molotov, Kaganovich and Voroshilov. He was sentenced to death and executed on 15 March 1938.

Ryzhkov, Nikolai Ivanovich (1929–): An industrial manager, Ryzhkov was Gorbachev's Prime Minister and supported perestroika until it became economically too radical for him. In September 1985 Gorbachev chose him as chair of the USSR Council of Ministers, where he remained until a heart attack forced him to retire in January 1991. He was elected to the USSR Congress of People's Deputies in 1989 as a nominee of the CPSU. In June 1991 he stood against Yeltsin in the Russian presidential elections and polled 16.9 per cent and came second. Ryzhkov was a moderate reformer whose industrial and planning experience gave him insights into the difficulties of moving to a market economy. He was never in favour of moving rapidly and opposed the Shatalin–Yavlinsky 500-day programme, proposing a more moderate variant called the regulated market approach. He did not support the private ownership of land and Russia accepting western credits as this would lead to the west enslaving Russia.

Sakharov, Andrei Dmitrievich (1921–89): The father of the Soviet hydrogen bomb, he became the most famous dissident in the Soviet Union until recalled by Gorbachev to Moscow, where he devoted his last years to active support of democracy. In the 1960s he became involved in the dissident movement through his second wife, Elena Bonner. He published an article in 1968 in the west advocating close Soviet–American cooperation and a convergence of the two social systems. This resulted in his removal from secret work but he carried on research at the Lebedev Institute on other matters. He actively supported human rights in the 1970s and was awarded the Nobel Peace Prize in 1975. He was a thorn in the flesh of Yury Andropov but he could not jail him as American scientists warned that such action would lead to a curtailment of scientific contacts between the two countries. Andropov came up with the astute solution of exiling Sakharov to Gorky (now Nizhny Novgorod) in January 1980, which, as a closed city, could not be visited by the western media. His wife acted as his conduit with the outside world. Gorbachev needed the intelligentsia on his side against the bureaucrats during glasnost and invited Sakharov back to Moscow in December 1986. Sakharov gave qualified support but wanted more radical reforms. He was elected to the USSR Congress of People's Deputies and became a leading democrat, condemning, for instance, the war in Afghanistan. He enjoyed immense moral authority. His fellow scientists regarded him as often politically naïve.

Shelepin, Aleksandr Nikolaevich (1918–94): Shelepin was a ruthlessly ambitious politician, schooled under Stalin, who never hid his talents under a bushel. He became the archetypal Soviet politician, heavy-handed, domineering and capable of arousing awe and revulsion in his subordinates and ideological foes. Khrushchev used him to bring the KGB under political control but he became one of the organisers of the coup which removed him in October 1964. Rumours circulated that Shelepin had been promised the post of First Secretary but this was eventually filled by Leonid Brezhnev. If this is so he was double-crossed by Brezhnev and the other conspirators on the grounds that he was potentially too dangerous to exclude from the plot. The Politburo was aware that Shelepin's reputation in the western world was not unlike that of Ghengis Khan and Himmler. As head of the Soviet trade unions he attended a get together in Geneva in 1975 and Len Murray, TUC General Secretary, invited him to Britain. Shelepin was pinned in Transport House by demonstrators, with the embarrassed Len Murray failing to raise the siege. When he returned to Moscow he was dismissed from the Politburo and disappeared into political oblivion. Given the opportunity to give his side of the story in and after 1991 he chose to remain silent. A broken man he had no fight or ambition left in him.

Shelest, Petr Efimovich (1908–): A close ally of Khrushchev, Shelest had to cope with the increasing resentment of the Ukrainian intelligentsia at what it regarded as Russification. Under Khrushchev this was not a problem but it became one under Brezhnev, who regarded Shelest as too lax in combating nationalism. Khrushchev chose him as First Secretary, Communist Party of Ukraine, in 1963, and in December 1963 he was elected candidate member of the Presidium (Politburo), becoming a full member in November 1964. In the wake of the suppression of the 'Prague Spring' in August 1968, Shelest came down hard on any manifestation of political dissent or democratic thinking but tried to compensate by being more accommodating in cultural affairs. This did not please Brezhnev and he replaced Shelest with Shcherbitsky in May 1972.

Shevardnadze, Eduard Amvrosievich (1928–): Gorbachev's Foreign Minister who was responsible for implementing the new political thinking abroad until he resigned in December 1990 warning about the possibility of a right-wing coup. He was born into a Georgian family in Mamati,

Georgia. As a Party secretary he collected information on the criminal activities of the Georgian Party leader, M. P. Mzhavanadze, showed it to Brezhnev and was rewarded by being given Mzhavanadze's post in 1972. In March 1985 Shevardnadze was a staunch supporter of Gorbachev and soon became a full member of the Politburo. Gorbachev astonished the world in July 1985 when Shevardnadze replaced Andrei Gromyko as Soviet Foreign Minister. After all Shevardnadze knew no foreign languages other than Russian and had no diplomatic experience. However, he soon proved an excellent advocate for the new political thinking. He was a welcome change from Grim Grom Gromyko and added a dash of flair to diplomacy. He became a member of the Presidential Council in March 1990, but left the Politburo in July 1990, when it was reorganised to include only Party officials. He resigned from the Communist Party in June 1991. He remained loyal to President Gorbachev after the failed August 1991 coup and was reapppointed Soviet Foreign Minister in November 1991, but was overtaken by the dissolution of the Soviet Union the following month. He then returned to Georgia where he later became head of state.

Shostakovich, Dmitry Dmitrievich (1906–75): A great Russian composer, with an international reputation, who managed to continue composing Russian music while appearing loyal to the Stalinist regime. He was involved in many conflicts with the official cultural norms of the regime but managed to retain his creative talents undimmed. The Party expected great things from him and the glorification of the achievements of the Five Year Plans. He composed his first opera, *The Nose* (based on Gogol's story), in 1928. His *Lady Macbeth of Mtsensk* (reworked as Ekaterina Izmailova) was attacked as a 'mess instead of music', probably the result of Stalin's anger on hearing the work. He was saved from imprisonment in 1937 by the arrest of his investigator. Shostakovich composed his great 7th symphony (the Leningrad symphony) to commemorate the resilience of the city under German siege. 'My symphony is about the Leningrad Stalin destroyed and Hitler almost finished off', he confessed in private. However, this was nothing compared to his travails after the Party decree on music in 1948, which condemned him, Khachaturyan and Prokofiev for anti-popular formalism. Shostakovich's music was proscribed. Only in 1958 were the accusations against Shostakovich withdrawn. Many were disappointed when he signed a letter against Academician Andrei Sakharov in 1973. He received an honorary doctorate from the University of Oxford. He was a sensitive, emotional man who was nevertheless a master of manoeuvre.

Sobchak, Anatoly Aleksandrovich (1937–): He shot to prominence after being elected to the USSR Congress of People's Deputies and the USSR

Supreme Soviet, for Leningrad, in 1989, and established himself as an accomplished parliamentarian. He took advantage of the fact that the country was falling apart to challenge the establishment (for instance, Nikolai Ryzhkov, the Prime Minister), and his legal skills were put to forensic use. In 1989, after election to the new Soviet parliament, he joined the Inter-Regional Group of Deputies, among whose other members was Boris Yeltsin. In May 1990 he was chair of the Leningrad city soviet. In June 1991 he was elected mayor of Leningrad and during the summer of 1991 he was one of the founders of the movement for democratic reforms. During the attempted coup of August 1991 he appealed to all not to implement the decisions of the Emergency Committee and arranged with the military commander for forces to leave the city. He then declared there was no state of emergency in the city. In August 1991 he was made a member of Gorbachev's Presidential Council and headed USSR delegations to Estonia and Ukraine. In September 1991 he was appointed head of administration (governor) of St Petersburg by President Yeltsin. He was elected mayor of St Petersburg but was voted out of office in mid-1996.

Solzhenitsyn, Aleksandr Isaevich (1918–): The leading Russian writer of his generation. In 1948, in Moscow, he was employed in the acoustics laboratory of the top secret scientific research institute and this provided the material for his novel, *The First Circle*. Then, in 1950, he was exiled to Kazakhstan. In 1955, while still in Kazakhstan, he began work on *The First Circle*. In exile, he contracted cancer but, remarkably, aided by sheer will power, he was completely cured. The experience is related in *The Cancer Ward*. His experiences in Kazakhstan also provided some background for *One Day in the Life of Ivan Denisovich*. Solzhenitsyn became famous in 1962 when *One Day in the Life of Ivan Denisovich* was published in the prestigious literary journal, *Novy Mir*. No less a person than Nikita Khrushchev had given his approval to publication as he believed that it would harm Stalin and benefit himself. The novel was an overnight sensation and broke the taboo of not describing the reality of the gulag. The KGB and the official literary establishment regarded Solzhenitsyn as a subversive and after Khrushchev was removed in 1964 persecution was stepped up. In 1970 he was awarded the Nobel Prize for Literature but decided not to accept it in person, fearing that he would not be permitted to re-enter the Soviet Union. The Soviet authorities decided against imprisoning him because of the international furore it would have caused, and instead stripped him of his citizenship in February 1974 and put him, in handcuffs, on a special plane to Frankfurt am Main. His wife and four children followed about six weeks later and his archive also went west. He became the spokesperson for anti-communism and Russian nationalism in the west. In 1976 he moved to the USA. A strict Orthodox

Christian, he and his family went to church every Sunday. He became a sharp critic of American democratic values. Glasnost changed the country's attitude to him and his writings were published in the USSR in the late 1980s and early 1990s. He was, at last, recognised as the greatest living Russian writer. He returned to Russia from exile but soon became a prophet whom Russians ignored.

Stalin, Iosif Vissarionovich (1879–1953): One of the dominant political actors of the twentieth century who has left an indelible mark on Russia and the world. The system he spawned, Stalinism, lived after him. Short of stature, with a pock-marked face, Stalin did not speak Russian until the age of eleven. A Georgian by birth, he came to dominate Soviet Russia in a manner that no communist leader had done before or after him. The Stalin cult presented Stalin as a god. He was very well read, possessed of an elephantine memory and never forgot a slight. He was highly intelligent and had a great facility to grasp an argument, draft memoranda and penetrate to the core of any matter. His Russian prose is clear and fluent. He was a master of intrigue and a shrewd tactician. He was a Hercules Poirot when it came to detecting the human weaknesses of an opponent. Stalin then ruthlessly and mercilessly exploited his advantage. Trotsky, intellectually more gifted, was nevertheless like a rabbit being mesmerised by Stalin the stoat. He immediately returned to Petrograd from exile after the February Revolution, and after Lenin's return in April, adopted his position and became one of his closest collaborators. At Lenin's funeral he delivered a quasi-religious eulogy to the dead leader and thereafter claimed to be Lenin's chief pupil. His skill at coalition politics produced victories over the left-leaning Trotsky, Kamenev, Zinoviev and finally the right-leaning Bukharin. This made Stalin the main political actor but Stalinism did not really take root until 1936.

The German invasion of June 1941 stunned him and Molotov made the announcement of the attack to the Soviet people. The wartime conferences with the Allies made him very popular in the West (he was known as Uncle Joe and it had to be explained to him that this was an affectionate sobriquet). The Russians acquired another empire after 1945, in eastern and south-eastern Europe, and the rule was that the Party set up shop after the Red Army had finished its work. Stalin did not want Mao Zedong and the communists to take power in China until he had established some type of control over them. Stalin failed to develop good relations with the west after 1945 and the Cold War took hold in 1947. This began an arms race which eventually proved a great economic liability for Moscow. Stalin's declining years saw him withdraw from the public gaze and become erratic and indeed paranoid. His death was slow and painful. It was his custom to lock himself in his quarters for the night. He suffered a stroke during the night and was only found in the morning. There was still a record on the gramophone. Stalin had spent his last hours listening to Chopin, played by a Russian pianist.

Suslov, Mikhail Andreevich (1902–82): A desiccated ideological calculating machine, the *éminence grise* of Soviet ideology, the sea green incorruptible of the Soviet establishment – all these fit the formidable guardian of Soviet political and moral orthodoxy. He was temperamentally unsuited to coexist with Khrushchev but managed it and was much more at home with Brezhnev's more orthodox, conservative style. He did not seek the company of westerners and once at a Kremlin reception placed tables between himself and foreign diplomats. He and Andropov were competitors and Suslov's death permitted Andropov to come back into the Central Committee secretariat and challenge for leadership of the Party. He gave the Czechoslovak communists a dressing down after the August 1968 Warsaw Pact invasion of their country. He protested against the increasing corruption among the Soviet nomenklatura but could do little other than berate the perpetrators.

Sverdlov, Yakov Mikhailovich (1885–1919): A brilliant Bolshevik administrator who carried most of the information about Party members in his head, his early death allowed Stalin to take over as chief of the Party apparatus. He was one of the few Old Bolsheviks (Party members before 1917) and Jews whose reputation remained untarnished during the treacherous 1930s. After the February Revolution Lenin instructed him to build up the Party Secretariat. He was more a practical administrator than a theoretician and built up a network of Party officials around the country. Sverdlov, a Jew, opposed Trotsky becoming Commissar for Internal Affairs because as a Jew he would have fuelled anti-Semitism in Russia. He also did not favour Trotsky becoming head of the Party press and instead proposed him as Commissar for Foreign Affairs, the post he occupied in the first Sovnarkom. Lenin was unhappy with the lenient line adopted by Kamenev as chair of the Central Executive Committee (TsIK) of the soviets and chose Sverdlov as his hard man. The latter then brought the TsIK into line and, among other things, gave the Secretariat precedence. This inevitably weakened the TsIK and the decline of the soviets was under way. Sverdlov then set about the task of establishing secretariats in local Party committees, all reporting to Moscow. Lenin and he became fast friends and their organisational views were remarkably similar. So good was Sverdlov at anticipating what Lenin wanted that on occasions he replied: 'Already done, already done', when the Bolshevik leader instructed him to do something. He contracted Spanish flu and died in March 1919. Had he lived he would have been the natural candidate for the post of General Secretary of the Party in 1922, pushing Stalin aside.

Tereshkova, Valentina Vladimirovna (1937–): The first woman in space when she made her one and only space flight in *Vostok 6* in June 1963. As a cosmonaut she was a military officer and continued her education, graduating from the Zhukovsky Aviation Academy in 1969. In 1992 she was appointed chair of the Presidium of the Russian Association for International Cooperation. She was elected to the USSR Congress of People's Deputies in 1989. In 1963 she married fellow cosmonaut Adrian Nikolaev and she took the name Nikolaeva-Tereshkova. When their daughter was born in 1964 she became the first child in the world whose parents were both cosmonauts. Tereshkova later divorced her husband, citing drunkenness. She represented the Soviet Union abroad at many conferences and was known as a formidable, business-like woman. A crater on the reverse side of the moon is named after her.

Tikhonov, Nikolai Aleksandrovich (1905–97): When Gorbachev became Soviet leader in 1985, the Prime Minister was 80 years old, older than the Soviet Union itself. Tikhonov was a classic example of the rule of the gerontocrats, having succeeded Kosygin in 1980. In 1965 he was one of the deputy chairs of the USSR Council of Ministers, under Kosygin, and in 1976 he progressed to become first deputy chair. When Kosygin retired he took over. In 1978 he was made a candidate member of the Politburo and then a full member a year later. He did his utmost to prevent Gorbachev becoming General Secretary. The latter pushed him aside in September 1985 to make way for Nikolai Ryzhkov.

Tomsky, Mikhail Pavlovich (1880–1936): The only fully-fledged worker among the top Bolsheviks after Lenin's death, Tomsky was a moderate who was drawn to Bukharin and perished with him. He was a leading trade unionist and resisted the notion that the unions should be mere transmission belts for conveying the Party's instructions to the working class. The number of strikes during the Civil War had convinced Tomsky that less pressure not more should be applied to workers. In 1920 Tomsky became chair of the All-Russian Central Council of the Trade Unions. Tomsky followed Lenin's line on the trade unions but in 1921 Lenin fell out with him on the role of unions under the New Economic Policy. Lenin even demanded the exclusion of Tomsky from the Central Committee and even the Party itself, in line with the resolution on Party unity passed at the 10th Congress. However the matter was allowed to fade into the background. He was soon rehabilitated as Lenin no longer feared the trade unions could undermine NEP and Tomsky was elected to the Politburo at the 11th Party Congress, 1922. He was one of the coffin bearers at Lenin's funeral. As a supporter of Bukharin, Tomsky lost his Politburo place at the 16th Party Congress, 1930. Along with Bukharin and Rykov, he should have played a starring role in the second great show trial but no longer able to bear his changed circumstances he shot himself in August 1936.

Trotsky, Lev Davidovich (né Bronstein) (1879–1940): The most gifted orator and writer among the Bolsheviks, he was second only to Lenin in October 1917 and afterwards, but the leader's illness from 1922 onwards also marked Trotsky's political demise. He was a great bridesmaid but was quite incapable politically of ever becoming the bride. He is the classic case of the intellectual in politics who is easily outmanoeuvred by the more mundane, party machine man. A talented organiser, he threw himself with immense energy into tasks which interested him, but these were followed by periods of lassitude. Stalin hated and feared him and relentlessly attempted to denigrate him in the eyes of Lenin. Trotsky was in New York when the February Revolution broke out and got back to Petrograd in May 1917. He merged his own group, Mezhraionka, with the Bolshevik Party and set sail under Bolshevik colours. One reason why he was reconciled with Lenin was that the latter had adopted Trotsky's theory of permanent revolution. As head of the Military Revolutionary Committee, the General Staff of the revolution, in Petrograd, Trotsky played a vital role in the Bolshevik success. He was Commissar for Foreign Affairs in the first Sovnarkom and in March 1918 was appointed Commissar for War and president of the Supreme War Council. He organised the Red Army from scratch and played the key role in ensuring that the Bolshevik regime survived. During the Civil War he clashed repeatedly with Stalin. Trotsky sided with the left in economics and advocated aid to revolutionary movements outside Russia. Stalin supported socialism in one country, which Trotsky ridiculed. He was exiled in 1928 and eventually went abroad, eventually finding refuge in Mexico in 1937, until Stalin's agent put an ice pick through his head in August 1940.

Tukhachevsky, Marshal Mikhail Nikolaevich (1893–1937): One of the architects of the Red Army, Tukhachevsky's brilliant career was cut short by suspicions about his loyalty to the Soviet Union. He had a brilliant Civil War and led the Red Army invasion of Poland, where he crossed swords for the first time with Stalin. There were serious differences of opinion and Stalin was partly blamed for the Soviet defeat on the Vistula. He headed the troops who crushed the Kronstadt revolt and the peasant uprising in Tambov guberniya. He was made head of the military academy in 1921 and this permitted him to begin the comprehensive retraining of the Red Army. He recognised early the significance of tanks and armoured vehicles. He was Chief of the General Staff in 1925–28, and from 1936 first deputy Commissar for Defence. He was very popular in the military and became a Marshal of the Soviet Union in 1935. Stalin never trusted the top military and in June 1937 Tukhachevsky was arrested and executed for high treason and conspiring with the military leaders of foreign powers. Tukhachevsky's execution led to the mass slaughter of the top ranks of the Soviet military. He was rehabilitated under Gorbachev.

Ustinov, Marshal Dmitry Fedorovich (1908–84): A very influential administrator of the Soviet defence sector, winning for it during the Brezhnev years an unprecedented proportion of the Soviet state budget. When Marshal Grechko died in 1976 Ustinov was chosen to succeed him as USSR Minister of Defence. Ustinov, a civilian, broke the tradition that a military man should be Defence Minister. He was promoted Marshal a few months afterwards because, according to some sources, the top military would not talk to a mere non-professional military general. Ustinov remained in office until he died. In his memoirs, Gorbachev relates that discussion of the military budget and burden to the country was taboo at Politburo meetings.

Voroshilov, Marshal Kliment Efremovich (1881–1969): Close to Stalin from the Civil War, he proved a great survivor until Khrushchev decided he no longer had any need of him. Voroshilov succeeded Frunze as People's Commissar for War and Navy in 1925. He was People's Commissar for Defence in 1934–40, and a close ally of Stalin during the latter's purging of the armed forces. Voroshilov became responsible for the mechanisation of the Red Army. He gave way to the more able Timoshenko in May 1940 as part of the reorganisation of the Red Army. When Stalin set up the State Defence Committee (GKO) in July 1941, its members were Stalin, Voroshilov, Molotov and Beria. GKO was responsible for the overall running of the war and the mobilisation of domestic Soviet resources. As a member of Stavka he was involved in talks with the Allies on the possibility of an Allied air force in Transcaucasia in August 1942. He attended the Tehran Conference in November 1943. He signed the armistice with Hungary for the Allies and later headed the Allied (Soviet) Control Commission in Hungary in 1946–47. He was chair of the presidium of the USSR Supreme Soviet (which made him head of state) in 1953–60. He was a member of the Anti-Party Group against Khrushchev in July 1957, but because of his willingness to engage in self-criticism and his long-term association with Khrushchev, he kept his position. He was a member of the Central Committee of the Communist Party in 1921–61, and a member of the Politburo in 1926–60.

Voznesensky, Andrei Andreevich (1933–): An immensely popular poet in the early 1960s, when he could fill stadia to hear him declaim his verse. He was born into a Russian family in Moscow and graduated from the Moscow Architectural Institute in 1957. He began publishing in the late 1950s and was a member of a group of promising young poets which also included Evgeny Evtushenko and Bella Akhmadulina. After the appearance of *Parabola* in 1960, he was criticised for formalism but it did not harm his career. Other works, such as *The Three Cornered Pear*, 1962, contributed to his reputation. He adapted one of his poems into a rock musical and it was successful in the Soviet Union and the United States. After 1985 he was recognised in the Soviet Union as one of the leading poets of his generation.

Vyshinsky, Andrei Yanuarevich (1883–1954): A merciless, venomous state prosecutor who gained world-wide notoriety for his courtroom behaviour during the great purge trials in the 1930s during which he humiliated some former communist leaders. While teaching at Moscow State University he honed his skills as a prosecutor in trials of alleged saboteurs and counter-revolutionaries. He became well known abroad during the Metro-Vickers trial in 1933, when several British engineers were accused of attempting to wreck the construction of Soviet hydroelectric stations. He starred during the three great show trials (1936–38), featuring, among many others, Zinoviev, Kamenev, Bukharin and Rykov. He exhibited great skill in keeping his head at a time when many of his high-profile contemporaries were losing theirs. In 1940, as deputy Commissar for Foreign Affairs, he supervised the incorporation of Latvia into the USSR and supervised the advent to power of the communists in Romania in 1945. Vyshinsky was Soviet representative on the Allied Mediterranean Commission and attended the Yalta Conference in 1945. In 1949 he became USSR Minister of Foreign Affairs and the permanent Soviet representative at the United Nations, where he turned his venom on the United States, especially during the Korean War of 1950–53. After Stalin's death, Molotov took over again as Foreign Minister and Vyshinsky dropped to being his first deputy. However, he remained at the United Nations and he died of a heart attack in New York. He died unloved in the west and Leonard Schapiro once described him, memorably, as the nearest thing to a human rat he had ever seen!

Yagoda, Genrikh Grigorevich (né Yehuda, Heinrich) (1891–1938): One of Stalin's bloodiest police chiefs who himself fell victim to the executioner's bullet. He joined the Cheka in 1920 and advanced to deputy head of the GPU (KGB) in 1924. He was referred to by some as Mephistopheles from the (Jewish) Pale. Stalin made him head of the NKVD (KGB) from 1934 to July 1936 and he was the implementer of the early purges, until he was dismissed and replaced by Ezhov. Stalin, just to keep him dangling before he decided to strike, made him People's Commissar for Posts and Telegraph in 1936–37, but then had him arrested. (He treated Ezhov in the same way later.) Yagoda was one of the main defendants at the trial of the Anti-Soviet Bloc of Rightists and Trotskyites. He was shot in the Lubyanka. When the defendants were rehabilitated by a Party commission in 1988, Yagoda's name was missing.

Yakovlev, Aleksandr Nikolaevich (1923–): The father of glasnost, he was a committed reformer who eventually came to realise that Marxism–Leninism was a brake on Soviet society and the country should move forward to social democracy. Yakovlev was Soviet ambassador to Canada in 1973–83. He accompanied Mikhail Gorbachev on an agricultural tour of Canada and made quite an impression on the future Soviet leader. Andropov brought Yakovlev back from exile and made him director of the Institute of World Economy and International Relations. In July 1985 Gorbachev made him head of the Central Committee propaganda department, a key centre from which to promote perestroika. In July 1988 Yakovlev took over as supervisor of the USSR's international policy in the Central Committee apparatus, as chair of the commission on international policy He stepped down from the Central Committee at the 28th Party Congress in July 1990, and thus forfeited his seat on the Politburo and his secretaryship of the Central Committee. By 1991 he was Gorbachev's senior adviser. Yakovlev was pushed aside in the last days of the Soviet Union but after the failed coup of August 1991 he remained loyal to Gorbachev. In 1992 he became Vice-President of the Gorbachev Foundation but later moved over to the Yeltsin camp

Yanaev, Gennady Ivanovich (1937–): He became notorious when he took over from Mikhail Gorbachev during the August 1991 attempted coup but was found wanting. His nervousness at the first press conference, announcing Gorbachev's retirement for 'health reasons', was evident when the drumming of his fingers on the table attracted attention. In December 1990 Gorbachev took the fateful step of choosing him as his Vice-President but he was not accepted during the first round of voting. Yanaev was a member of the USSR Security Council from March to August 1991. He was declared President by the Emergency Committee on 19 August but only lasted until 21 August, when the attempted coup failed. He was arrested but later amnestied by the Russian Duma.

Yavlinsky, Grigory Alekseevich (1952–): One of the leading radical economists who rose to prominence under Gorbachev but proved too radical for the Soviet leader. In 1987 he took part in drafting the USSR law on state enterprises but his draft was rejected by the commission, headed by Gaidar Aliev. In early 1990 he and other radical economists began drafting a programme for the stabilisation and reform of the Soviet economy, and when Boris Yeltsin heard of this Yavlinsky was made deputy chair of the Russian Federation government in July 1990. Academician Shatalin and Yavlinsky headed the team which drafted what became known as the 500-day programme for the Soviet economy, envisaging the transition to a market economy in 500 days, something which was highly improbable. In 1991 he became chair of the Council of the Centre for Economic and Political Research (Epitsentr). In late August 1991 he was appointed by President Mikhail Gorbachev as head of the committee on the operational management of the Soviet economy and in September 1991 he drafted a treaty on the economic union of the Soviet republics, but Yavlinsky's programme, based on the retention of a single Soviet economic space, became inoperative after the collapse of the USSR. Yavlinsky became active politically in post-communist Russia and in the December 1993 elections to the lower house, the Duma, his party Yabloko did reasonably well, regarding as its constituency the rising middle-class professionals.

Yazov, Marshal Dmitry Timofeevich (1923–): One of the ringleaders of the attempted coup in August 1991, something which he came to regret bitterly. He was born into a Russian family in Omsk oblast and joined the Red Army in 1941, graduated from the Frunze Military Academy in 1956 and the Academy of the General Staff in 1967. He was engaged in the personnel department, USSR Ministry of Defence, in 1974–76, after which he became first deputy commander, Far East military district. In 1979 he was appointed commander of the Central Group of Armies in Czechoslovakia and in 1980 he became commander of the Central Asian military district. In 1981 he was elected a candidate member of the Central Committee. In 1984 he returned to the Soviet Far East military district as commander. He impressed Gorbachev and the Soviet President made him USSR Minister of Defence in 1987. His promotion was swift as he was viewed as an officer of a new type committed to perestroika in the armed forces. He was elected a full member of the Central Committee in June 1987, a candidate member of the Politburo in September 1989–July 1990, a member of the Presidential Council in March 1990, and a Marshal of the Soviet Union in April 1990. His illustrious career came to an ignominious end in August 1991 when he was a member of the Emergency Committee. He was arrested, charged with treason, but was amnestied by the State Duma later.

Yeltsin, Boris Nikolaevich (1931–): The first democratically elected President of Russia, leader of the opposition to the attempted coup against President Mikhail Gorbachev in August 1991, his star began to wane in the mid-1990s when he was dubbed Tsar Boris, adrift in his Kremlin court. Yeltsin, a Russian, was born near Sverdlovsk (Ekaterinburg) and had an unprivileged childhood, growing up in workers' huts on construction sites. As the first secretary of Sverdlovsk obkom he knew Gorbachev, and when the latter became General Secretary of the Party in March 1985

Yeltsin was one of the first to be summoned to Moscow. Yeltsin became head of the construction department of the Central Committee secretariat in June 1985, and when Gorbachev wanted his own man to take over the Moscow Party apparatus (gorkom) he chose Yeltsin. During the summer of 1987 Yeltsin sent Gorbachev a letter intimating that he wished to resign but this did not please the General Secretary. Gorbachev asked Yeltsin to curb his tongue and bide his time but this was beyond the emotional Yeltsin. In October 1987 Gorbachev threw him to the wolves. Yeltsin suffered a heart attack on 9 November 1987. Still ill, he was called to account by the Moscow gorkom and given another dressing down. In February 1988, at Gorbachev's suggestion, he lost his seat as a candidate member of the Politburo. This episode led to an unbridgeable gap between Gorbachev and Yeltsin and henceforth the country was too small for both of them, one of them had to destroy the other. Yeltsin was elected a delegate, from Karelia, to the 19th Party Conference in June 1988, despite attempts by the leadership to prevent it. The 19th Party Conference was carried live on TV and, on the last day, Yeltsin asked for the floor and delivered a detailed apologia of his position, requesting that the Party rehabilitate him now, not posthumously. This was a fine piece of cheek by Yeltsin and made him the most popular politician in the country. Yeltsin won a stunning victory, 89.6 per cent of the vote, in his Moscow constituency, in elections to the USSR Congress of People's Deputies. Yeltsin became active in the Party's democratic platform, an opposition group within the parliament. In March 1990 Yeltsin was elected to the RSFSR Congress of People's Deputies, and chair or speaker of the RSFSR Supreme Soviet in May 1989. President Gorbachev held a referendum on 17 March 1991, seeking support for a new Union of Sovereign States. Republics added their own questions and Yeltsin asked Russian voters if they were in favour of a directly elected Russian President, which they were. Yeltsin became President of Russia in June 1991. His hour of glory came in August 1991 when he became the people's champion by leading the opposition to victory over the Emergency Committee. Skilfully he had demanded that President Gorbachev be restored to power, but when he did return to Moscow Yeltsin was the victor. He banned the activities of the Communist Party, with Gorbachev protesting in vain, and the Party itself in November 1991. When Gorbachev stepped down in December 1991, Yeltsin and Russia were there to take over from him and the Soviet Union. His popularity fell among Russian voters after mid-1993 as pain mounted without any gain. A brilliantly orchestrated re-election campaign by Anatoly Chubais saw him re-elected President in July 1996.

Zhdanov, Andrei Aleksandrovich (1896–48): The guardian of Stalinist cultural orthodoxy, from socialist realism to the xenophobia of the late

1940s, known as the Zhdanovshchina. When Sergei Kirov was murdered in December 1934, Stalin chose Zhdanov to succeed him as Party leader in Leningrad. At the 1st Congress of the USSR Union of Writers in 1934, Zhdanov, speaking for Stalin, laid down the new cultural rules, known as socialist realism. Culture was to be a weapon in the struggle for socialism and was to be didactic and optimistic. He led the defence of Leningrad during the siege in 1941–44. He had formidable political enemies in Malenkov and Beria. Stalin played one off against the other. The period from 1946 to August 1948, when Zhdanov expired, is known as the Zhdanovshchina. It is a period of gross cultural intolerance and anti-Semitism. Zhdanov's brief extended to the world communist movement and he presided at the founding congress of the Communist Information Bureau (Cominform), in Poland, in 1947. His death was sudden and caught everyone by surprise.

Zhirinovsky, Vladimir Volfovich (1946–): Known as Mad Vlad, the Russian Hitler, and some other unflattering sobriquets, he has made a dazzling career as an extreme Russian nationalist, appearing at times to be anti-Semitic, xenophobic and imperialist. He quips that his father was a lawyer but his mother was Russian. Many observers accept that he is part-Jewish but he denies this. He has been politically active since 1967 but never joined the Communist Party. His political career took off in 1988 when he was one of the founders of the Liberal Democratic Party of the USSR. The party nominated him for President of the RSFSR in June 1991. He polled 6.2 million votes and came third to Boris Yeltsin and Nikolai Ryzhkov. His party, now the Liberal Democratic Party of Russia (the usual comment was that it was neither liberal nor democratic), came second in the December 1993 elections to the State Duma, the lower house, causing consternation among President Yeltsin's supporters and foreign observers. Long feared as a threat to the security of the post-Soviet states and indeed the world at large (he once referred to Russian soldiers bathing their feet in the Indian Ocean) but he was, in reality, the Russian voice of protest at the pain, suffering and disorientation of the late Gorbachev and the early Yeltsin eras. He was one of the also-rans in the presidential elections of June 1996.

Zhukov, Marshal Georgy Konstantinovich (1896–1974): The most prominent and successful Red Army commander during the Great Fatherland War. He came to international notice as commander of Red Army forces at Khalkin Gol, Mongolia, in 1939, against the Japanese. This was one of the two decisive battles which led to the Japanese deciding not to press on with their attack into the Soviet Union. Zhukov was made Chief of the General Staff and deputy Commissar for Defence, January–July 1941. In October 1941 he replaced Voroshilov as commander of the northern sector, and was personally responsible for the defence of Leningrad. He was then moved to Moscow and made Commander-in-Chief of the entire western front, where he successfully repelled two German offensives against the capital. He counter-attacked in December 1941, drove the Wehrmacht back, and reached a standstill by February 1942. He was responsible for the defence of Stalingrad and took part in the planning of the offensive in November 1942 which broke through the German lines and eventually encircled Paulus's 6th army. He participated in the battle of Kursk in July 1943, the greatest tank battle the world until then had witnessed. He was in overall command in Ukraine and by April 1945 his troops had crossed the river Oder and launched the final assault on Berlin. He was the Soviet representative at the signing of the surrender of the German armed forces. He then became the first commander of the Soviet occupation forces in Germany. Zhukov emerged as a brilliant and decisive commander, very cautious in the beginning but very daring at the end of the war. He was enormously popular with his troops and struck up a close relationship with General Eisenhower, the US Commander-in-Chief. He could be rude, abrasive and ruthless. Stalin demoted him to commander of the Odessa military district after the war. After Stalin's death he was part of the conspiracy against Beria and was involved in his arrest. Zhukov was most valuable to Khrushchev during the struggle for power in June–July 1957. He ensured that Khrushchev's supporters in the Central Committee got to town to take part in the crucial Central Committee meeting which saved Khrushchev. Khrushchev rewarded Zhukov by making him USSR Minister of Defence, but dismissed him in October 1957. Zhukov's memoirs, published in 1974, disappointed many.

Zinoviev, Grigory Evseevich (né Radomyslsky) (1883–1936): In Trotsky's memorable phrase, Zinoviev was either in seventh heaven or in the depths of despair. A volatile politician, a passionate orator, he proved no match for the master game player, Stalin. He went into hiding with Lenin in Finland after the July Days but, together with Kamenev, he opposed the Bolshevik armed uprising in October. After the October Revolution Zinoviev favoured the formation of a broad socialist coalition government and opposed Lenin's insistence on a Bolshevik government. He was elected chair of the executive committee of the Communist International (Comintern) at its first congress in 1919. During the Kronstadt uprising Trotsky found him in a panic and he was saved by Trotsky and Tukhachevsky. Stalin drew him and Kamenev into a tactical alliance against Trotsky after Lenin's death, but after Trotsky's defeat Stalin turned on his erstwhile allies. In 1926 Zinoviev lost his place on the Politburo and his Comintern post and was expelled from the Party in November 1927. He was readmitted to the Party in 1928 after recanting his views and praising Stalin to the skies. He was expelled again in 1932. He (and

Kamenev) were tried in secret in January 1935 and he was sentenced to 10 years imprisonment. In April 1936 he was the main accused in the first show trial. He cut a pathetic figure but abject submission did not save him from the executioner's bullet. He was rehabilitated under Gorbachev.

Zyuganov, Gennady Andreevich (1944–): One of the leaders of the Russian Communist Party under Gorbachev who emerged as its leader under Yeltsin. He was born into a Russian family in Orlov oblast and graduated from the Orlov State Pedagogical Institute and the Academy of Social Sciences of the Party Central Committee. In 1967 he moved into trade union, Komsomol and Party work. In 1982 he moved into the department of propaganda, Central Committee Secretariat in Moscow, until 1989. Then he was deputy head of the ideology department, Central Committee, 1989–90. When the Communist Party of the Russian Federation was established in July 1990 he was elected a secretary of its Central Committee and its Politburo. Gorbachev was very disappointed with the leadership of the Russian Communist Party, seeing them as the enemies of perestroika. He became a Russian nationalist after 1991 and he was elected chair of the coordinating council of the national patriotic forces of Russia in 1992, and also co-speaker of the Duma of the Russian National Assembly, as well as co-chair of the political council of the front of National Salvation of Russia. Later he emerged as the leader of the Russian Communist Party and stood for President in June 1996, coming second to Yeltsin in the second round, on 3 July 1996.

SECTION SIX

Statistics

Statistics

Table 1. Population of the Soviet Union

	Total population (millions)	Urban (%)
1913 (Empire)	166.0	18.0
1913 (post-1945 frontiers)	159.0	18.0
1920 (inter-war frontiers)	137.0	15.0
1926	148.5	18.0
1937	162.7	32.0
1939	167.3	32.0
1940	194.1	33.0
1950	178.5	39.0
1959	208.8	47.8
1970	241.7	56.4
1979	262.4	62.7
1989	286.7	65.8
1991	290.0	65.9

Sources: Vestnik Statistiki, no. 7, 1990, p. 37; *Sotsialisticheskie issledovaniya,* no. 8. 1990, p. 51

Table 2. Russian and Soviet gross national product (GNP), 1913–40

	GNP, billion rubles at 1937 factor cost	Population mid-year, millions	GNP per head, rubles
(A) Pre-1918 frontiers			
1913	134.1	166.0	810
(B) Pre-1939 frontiers			
1913	113.0	139.9	810
1928	123.7	153.2	810
1929	127.0	156.1	810
1930	134.5	158.6	850
1931	137.2	160.8	850
1932	135.7	162.4	840
1933	141.3	159.8	880
1934	155.2	157.5	990
1935	178.6	159.2	1120
1936	192.8	161.3	1200
1937	212.3	164.0	1290
1938	216.3	167.0	1300
1940	223.6	173.1	1290
(C) 1940 frontiers			
1940	250.5	194.0	1290

Source: R. W. Davies, M. Harrison and S. G. Wheatcroft, eds, *The Economic Transformation of the Soviet Union 1913–1945,* Cambridge University Press, Cambridge, 1994, p. 269

The GNP is a western estimate and the GNP per head is arrived at by dividing the GNP by the population. The population figures are official Soviet data.

Table 3(a) Gross domestic product (GDP) per head of the USSR in international comparison, 1913–40 ($ and 1980 prices)

	1913	1928	1932	1937	1940
Japan	800	1,150	1,130	1,330	1,660
Russia (USSR)	900	900	930	1,440	1,440
Italy	1,550	1,780	1,740	1,960	2,070
Germany	1,960	2,280	1,880	2,740	3,190
France	2,000	2,550	2,280	2,590	2,330
UK	2,970	3,110	2,990	3,610	3,980
USA	3,790	4,690	3,450	4,570	4,970

Source: Davies *et al.*, *Economic Transformation of the Soviet Union*, p. 270

The Soviet Union was above Japan in GDP per head in 1913 but behind in 1940. Apart from Japan, however, the Soviet Union was growing faster than the other countries. This was partly due to the fact that mature economies grow more slowly than those which begin from a small base. Real GDP by sector of origin reveals that industry by 1944 contributed almost as much as in 1937 – a remarkable achievement given the war and dislocation.

Table 3(b) Real GDP by sector of origin, 1937–44 (billion rubles and 1937 factor cost)

	1937	1940	1941	1942	1943	1944
Agriculture	63.0	69.9	42.3	25.3	30.4	45.0
Industry:	65.4	73.8	70.3	51.1	59.2	66.5
defence industry	3.4	8.3	14.2	28.1	35.0	38.7
civilian industry	62.0	65.5	56.2	22.9	24.2	27.8
Construction	10.5	10.6	6.9	3.2	3.4	4.4
Transport, communications	16.8	19.3	17.8	10.2	11.8	13.7
Trade, catering	10.4	11.1	9.3	3.8	3.5	4.1
Civilian services	33.1	42.0	35.3	22.1	23.4	28.8
Military services:	3.7	7.3	10.4	16.6	17.3	17.9
army, navy	3.4	6.8	9.8	15.8	16.6	17.2
NKVD	0.3	0.5	0.6	0.8	0.7	0.7
NDP	202.9	234.0	192.3	132.4	149.1	180.5
Depreciation	9.4	13.6	14.0	11.7	11.8	11.7
GDP	212.3	247.6	206.3	144.1	160.9	192.2

Source: M. Harrison, *Soviet Planning in Peace and War, 1938–1945*, Cambridge University Press, Cambridge, 1985, Table 1

Table 4. Real burden of defence outlays, 1940–44 (billion rubles at 1937 factor cost)

	1940	1941	1942	1943	1944
GDP	247.6	206.3	144.1	160.9	192.2
Net imports	0.0	0.0	9.0	30.9	35.6
Defence outlays:	45.3	66.9	110.1	133.8	145.3
Munitions	16.6	28.3	61.6	82.3	90.2
Pay	6.8	9.8	15.8	16.6	17.2
Food	9.9	14.1	16.1	19.0	19.1
Clothing, etc.	4.4	5.1	6.4	5.3	6.3
Fuel	1.5	2.1	2.4	2.7	3.1
Transport	0.9	1.1	1.4	2.6	3.0
Construction	2.4	2.6	2.0	1.1	1.5
Other, including repairs	2.7	3.8	4.5	4.2	4.8
Defence outlays, less net imports	45.3	66.9	101.1	102.9	109.7
Defence outlays, % of GDP:					
Domestic supply	18	32	70	64	57
Foreign supply	0	0	6	19	19

Source: Harrison, *Soviet Planning in Peace and War*, Table 4 and D-1

The Soviet Union paid a heavier price in human and material resources during the war than any other belligerent country.

Table 5. Labour productivity in large-scale industry, 1913–21

	Production (million rubles 1913 prices)	Employment (millions)	Labour input (adjusted for hours worked)	Output/ labour (rubles)[b]	Per cent of 1913[b]
1913	6,391	2.44	2.44	2,619	100
1914	6,429	2.48	2.40	2,679	102
1915	7,056	2.58	2.50	2,822	108
1916	7,420	2.87	2.84	2,613	100
1917	4,780	2.89	2.57	1,860	71
1918	2,160	2.25	1.91	1,131	43
1919	955	1.54	1.28	746	28
1920	818	1.54	1.32	620	24
1921	1,080	1.30	1.10	982	37

Notes:
[a] Figures relate to USSR pre-1939 territory.
[b] Colum 1 divided by column 3.
Source: Davies et al., Economic Transformation of the Soviet Union, p. 319

This table reveals that 1920 was the worst year followed by some recovery in 1921, mainly due to NEP. In production terms, 1920 was easily the worst, only recording just under 13 per cent of the 1913 output.

Table 6. Fulfilment of the principal goals of the Stalinist Five Year Plans 1928–50 (%)

	First Five Year Plan (1928–1932)	Second Five Year Plan (1933–1937)	Fourth Five Year Plan (1946–1950)
National income			
Official Soviet estimate (1926/27 prices)	91.5	96.1	118.9
Jasny estimate (1926/27 'real' prices)	70.2	66.5	
Bergson estimate			89.9
Nutter estimate			84.1
Industrial production			
Official Soviet estimate (1926/27 prices)	100.7	103.0	116.9
Jasny estimate	69.9	81.2	
Nutter estimate	59.7	93.1	83.8
Kaplan and Moorsteen estimate	65.3	75.7	94.9
Official Soviet estimate, producer goods (1926/27 prices)	127.6	121.3	127.5
Official Soviet estimate, consumer goods (1926/27 prices)	80.5	85.4	95.7
Agricultural production			
Official Soviet estimates (1926/27 prices)	57.8	62.6–76.9	89.9
Jasny estimate	49.6	76.7	
Nutter estimate	50.7	69.0	76.4
Johnson and Kahan estimates	52.4	66.1–69.0	79.4
Transport			
Railway freight traffic (tonne/km)	104.0		113.2
Employment			
National economy, workers and employees	144.9	93.4	116.1
Industry, workers and employees	173.9		118.9

Table 6. (cont'd)

	First Five Year Plan (1928–1932)	Second Five Year Plan (1933–1937)	Fourth Five Year Plan (1946–1950)
Wages (workers and employees, nat. economy)			
Average money wage	143.9	173.6	127.8
Average real wage, official Soviet estimate	31.9	102.6	89.1
Average real wage, Zaleski estimate	26.0	65.8	
Labour productivity, industry			
Official Soviet estimate	65.1		100.7
Jasny estimate	41.8		
Nutter estimate	36.3		
Kaplan and Moorsteen estimate			80.0
Cost of production			
Industry (current prices)	146.1	121.1	134.2
Investment			
In constant prices	54.0		122

Source: E. Zaleski, *Stalinist Planning for Economic Growth 1933–1952*, Macmillan, Basingstoke, 1980, p. 503

Soviet economic growth is a contentious issue and various estimates are provided over the years above. The official Soviet figures were inflated so as to boost morale and also to demonstrate to the outside world that the Soviet Union was becoming a strong economy. One can argue that the major goal of the plans was to enhance the security of the USSR and frighten away potential enemies. This is an explanation for the emphasis placed on heavy industry and the neglect of light and consumer goods industry. Jasny, Bergson, Nutter, Kaplan, Moorsteen, Johnson and Kahan are western economists. Figures are given in percentages.

Various estimates are now given of economic growth.

Table 7. The main economic indicators

(a) Russian and Soviet GNP per head 1885–1985 (%)

Trend growth, 1885–1913, per year	1.7
Drop in level, 1914	−26.9
Trend growth, 1928–40, per year	3.6
Drop in level, 1941	−10.7
Trend growth, 1950–74, per year	3.6
Trend growth, 1974–85, per year	0.5

Source: M. Harrison, *Accounting for War: Soviet Production, Employment, and the Defence Burden, 1940–1945*, Cambridge University Press, Cambridge, 1996

(b) Performance 1955–87

	Average annual growth (%)					
	1955–65	1966–70	1971–75	1976–80	1981–83	1984–87
Population growth	1.6	0.9	0.9	0.8	0.9	0.9
Gross NP	5.4	5.2(5.0)	3.7(3.1)	2.7(2.2)	2.3	1.6
Industry	7.5	6.3	5.9(5.4)	3.4(2.6)	1.5	2.1
Agriculture	3.5	3.5(3.7)	−2.3(−0.6)	0.3(0.8)	4.2	0.8
Services	4.0	4.2	3.4	2.8	2.1	–
Consumption	4.7	5.3	3.6	2.6	1.7	2.4
Investment	9.1	6.0	5.4	4.3	4.2	3.0

Sources: 1955–80: US Congress, Joint Economic Committee *USSR: Measures of Economic Growth and Development, 1950–80*, Washington DC, 1982; 1981–87: *Handbook of Economic Statistics*, Washington DC, 1983 and 1988; figures in brackets: recalculations from 1988 publication; Population: *Narodnoe Khozyaistvo SSR*, various years

(c) Performance 1928–90 according to G. I. Khanin

(i) Soviet national income growth 1928–87: alternative
estimates (change over period, % per year)

	TsSU	CIA, Moorsteen & Powell	Khanin
1928–40	13.9	6.1	3.2[a]
1940–50	4.8	2.0	1.6[b]
1928–50	10.1	4.2	2.5
1950–60	10.2	5.2	7.2
1960–65	6.5	4.8	4.4
1965–70	7.7	4.9	4.1
1970–75	5.7	3.0	3.2
1975–80	4.2	1.9	1.0
1980–85	3.5	1.8	0.6
1985–87	3.0	2.7	2.0
1950–87	6.6	3.8	3.8
1928–87	7.9	3.9	3.3

Notes:
[a] 1928–41.
[b] 1941–50.
Source: M. Harrison, 'Soviet Economic Growth Since 1928: The
Alternative Statistics of G I Khanin', *Europe-Asia Studies*, vol. 45, no. 1,
1993, p. 146. TsSU is the offical Soviet statistical administration

G. I. Khanin, a Soviet economist, created a sensation when he published
some estimates in the Soviet Union in 1987, claiming, *inter alia*, that
Soviet national income had not multiplied 84.4 times the level of 1928,
as the official statistics claimed, but only 6.6 times.

(ii) Soviet inputs and productivity, 1928–90 (change over period, % per year)

	Stock of fixed assets	Capital productivity	Output per worker	Materials intensity
(A) TsSU				
1928–40	8.7	4.8	11.9	−0.3
1940–50	1.0	3.1	4.1	−0.2
1950–60	9.4	0.8	8.0	−0.5
1960–65	9.7	−3.0	6.0	−0.2
1965–70	8.2	−0.4	6.8	−0.4
1970–75	8.7	−2.7	4.6	0.6
1975–80	7.4	−2.7	3.4	0.0
1980–85	6.5	−3.0	3.0	0.0
1985–87	4.9	−2.0	3.0	0.4
1928–87	7.2	0.5	6.7	−0.2
(B) Khanin				
1928–41	5.3	−2.0	1.3	1.7[a]
1941–50	2.4	−0.8	1.3	1.1
1950–60	5.4	1.6	5.0	−0.5
1960–65	5.9	−1.4	4.1	0.4
1965–70	5.1	−1.0	3.0	0.4
1970–75	3.9	−0.6	1.9	1.0
1975–80	1.9	−1.0	0.2	1.0
1980–85	0.6	0.0	0.0	1.0
1985–87	0.0	2.0	2.0	−0.5
1928–87	3.9	−0.6	2.2	0.8
1980–82	1.5	−3.6	-2.5	2.5
1982–88	1.9	−0.2	1.4	0.7
1988–90[b]	−0.5	−4.1	−4.1	3.4

Notes:
[a] 1.7–2%
[b] Preliminary.
Source: Harrison, 'Soviet Economic Growth', p. 151

Table 8. National composition of the population
(thousands)

| | 1970 | 1979 | 1989 | Percentage increase or decrease | |
				1970–79	1979–89
Total USSR population	241,720	262,085	286,731	8.4	9.4
Russians	129,015	137,397	145,155	6.5	5.6
Ukrainians	40,753	42,347	44,186	3.9	4.3
Uzbeks	9,195	12,456	16,698	35.5	34.1
Belorussians	9,052	9,463	10,036	4.5	6.1
Kazakhs	5,299	6,556	8,136	23.7	24.1
Tatars	5,931	6,317	6,649	6.5	5.3
Azerbaidzhanis	4,380	5,477	6,770	25.0	23.6
Armenians	3,559	4,151	4,623	16.6	11.4
Georgians	3,245	3,571	3,981	10.0	11.5
Moldavians	2,698	2,968	3,352	10.0	12.9
Tadzhiks	2,136	2,898	4,215	35.7	45.4
Lithuainans	2,665	2,851	3,067	7.0	7.6
Turkmenis	1,525	2,028	2,729	33.0	34.6
Germans	1,846	1,936	2,039	4.9	5.3
Kirgiz	1,452	1,906	2,529	31.3	32.7
Jews	2,151	1,811	1,449	−15.8	−20.0
Chuvash	1,694	1,751	1,842	3.4	5.2
Latvians	1,430	1,439	1,459	0.6	1.4
Bashkirs	1,240	1,371	1,449	10.6	5.7
Mordovians	1,263	1,192	1,154	−5.6	−3.2
Poles	1,167	1,151	1,126	−1.4	−2.2
Estonians	1,007	1,020	1,027	1.3	0.7

Sources: 1970–79: based on Ann Sheehy, Radio Liberty Research no. 123/80 and calculated; 1989: *Naselenie SSSR po Dannym Vsesoyuznoi Perepisi Naseleniya 1989* g., Moscow, 1990, pp. 37–40 and calculated. There are about 80 other smaller nationalities.

Note that the most rapid increase in population was recorded by Muslims, followed by the Armenians. These growth rates far outstripped that of the Russians, who only made up just over 50 per cent of the Soviet population in 1989. Had the Soviet Union survived, Muslims would eventually have formed over half the Soviet population, an alarming state of affairs for Russians.

SECTION SEVEN

Bibliography

Bibliography

General surveys

Most surveys of twentieth-century Russia begin in 1917 with a backward glance at the First World War. E. Acton, *Russia: The Tsarist and Soviet Legacy*, 2nd edn (London, Longman, 1995) is stimulating; H. Carrère d'Encausse, *A History of the Soviet Union, 1917–53*, 2 vols (London, Longman, 1981) is particularly good on nationality affairs; Geoffrey Hosking, *A History of the Soviet Union*, rev. edn (London, Fontana Press/Collins, 1990) concentrates on domestic affairs and omits foreign and security policy; M. McCauley, *The Soviet Union 1917–1991*, 2nd edn (London, Longman, 1993) is wide-ranging; see also his *Who's Who in Russia since 1900* (London, Routledge, 1997); the standard work on economic history is A. Nove, *An Economic History of the USSR*, rev. edn (Harmondsworth, Penguin, 1992).

The decline of Tsarist Russia to 1917

The best book on the origins of the First World War and Russia is D. C. B. Lieven, *Russia and the Origins of the First World War* (London, Macmillan, 1983); N. Stone, *The Eastern Front* (London, Hodder and Stoughton, 1975) is excellent on Russia's performance in the war; A. de Jonge, *Life and Times of Grigorii Rasputin* (London, Collins, 1982) is a colourful account of the most influential cleric of the time; L. H. Siegelbaum, *The Politics of Industrial Mobilization in Russia 1914–17* (London, Macmillan, 1983) and K. Neilson, *Strategy and Supply: The Anglo-Russian Alliance 1914–17* (London, Allen & Unwin, 1984) study key aspects of the war effort; F. A. Golder, ed., *Documents of Russian History 1914–1917* (Gloucester, MA, P. Smith, 1969) provides many insights; M. McCauley, ed., *Octobrists to Bolsheviks 1905–1917* (London, Edward Arnold, 1984) is wide-ranging; O. Figes, *A People's Tragedy: The Russian Revolution 1891–1924* (London, Jonathan Cape, 1996) is excellent.

The Russian Revolution 1917–24

The most useful reference source for the Russian Revolution is H. Shukman, ed., *The Blackwell Encyclopedia of the Russian Revolution*, rev. edn

(Oxford, Blackwell, 1990); M. McCauley, ed., *The Russian Revolution and the Soviet State 1917–1921: Documents*, rev. edn (London, Macmillan, 1995) provides the main documents. On the February Revolution T. Hasegawa, *The February Revolution: Petrograd 1917* (Seattle, University of Washington Press, 1981) is detailed and suggests that the soviets were not as powerful as presented in many accounts; M. Ferro, *The Russian Revolution of February 1917* (London, Routledge and Kegan Paul, 1972) and *October 1917: A Social History of the Russian Revolution* (London, Routledge and Kegan Paul, 1980) were highly original when published and are still worth studying; S. Fitzpatrick, *The Russian Revolution* (Oxford, Oxford University Press, 1982) surveys the period 1917–32 as the span of the revolution; L. Schapiro, *1917: The Russian Revolutions* (London, Temple Smith, 1984) concentrates on power, its acquisition and retention; R. Service, *The Russian Revolution 1900–1927* (London, Macmillan, 1986) is an excellent survey; J. D. White, *The Russian Revolution 1917–1921* (London, Edward Arnold, 1994) is useful; J. Keep, *The Russian Revolution: A Study in Mass Mobilization* (London, Weidenfeld & Nicolson, 1976) is scholarly but needs to be read in conjunction with later studies which concentrate on a specific area or group such as R. Suny, *The Baku Commune 1917–1918* (Princeton, NJ, Princeton University Press, 1972), O. Figes, *Peasant Russia, Civil War: The Volga Countryside in Revolution 1917–1921* (Oxford, Oxford University Press, 1989) and R. Snow, *Bolsheviks in Siberia 1917–1918* (Rutherford, NJ, Fairleigh Dickinson University Press, 1977). E. Acton, *Rethinking the Russian Revolution* (London, Edward Arnold, 1990) is a useful commentary on recent scholarship on the Russian Revolution.

R. Abraham, *Alexander Kerensky* (New York, Columbia University Press, 1987) is a good biography of the great loser in 1917; W. Rosenberg, *Liberals in the Russian Revolution* (Princeton NJ, Princeton University Press, 1974) studies the Kadets in the period 1917–21; the SRs are covered by O. H. Radkey, *The Agrarian Foes of Bolshevism* (New York, Columbia University Press, 1958); and the anarchists are examined by P. Avrich, *The Russian Anarchists* (Princeton, NJ, Princeton University Press, 1967). The soviets are researched by O. Anweiler in *The Soviets* (New York, Pantheon Books, 1974); D. Koenker, *Moscow Workers and the 1917 Revolution* (Princeton, NJ, Princeton University Press, 1969) is very informative; D. Mandel has devoted much effort to studying workers in Petrograd: *The Petrograd Workers and the Fall of the Old Regime* (London, Macmillan, 1983) and *The Petrograd Workers and the Soviet Seizure of Power* (London, Macmillan, 1984); an edited collection is D. Kaiser, *The Workers' Revolution in Russia 1917: The View from Below* (Cambridge, Cambridge University Press, 1987); S. A. Smith, *Red Petrograd: Revolution in the Factories 1917–1918* (Cambridge, Cambridge University Press, 1983) concludes that workers took over the factories to protect their jobs but did not know what to do after this. W. Lincoln, *Red Victory* (New York, 1989) and E. Mawdsley, *The Russian Civil War* (Cambridge, Cambridge University Press, 1987) are good on this topic; M. Malet, *Nestor Makhno in the Russian Civil War* (London, Macmillan, 1986) examines a major cavalry figure.

Lenin

The most scholarly work on Lenin is R. Service, *Lenin: A Political Life*, 3 vols (London, Macmillan 1991–95); but needs to be supplemented by R. Pipes, ed., *The Unknown Lenin From the Secret Archive* (New Haven, CT, Yale University Press, 1996) which reveals how violent Lenin really was and that Stalin merely continued his work; D. Volkogonov, *Lenin: A New Biography* (New York, The Free Press, 1994) is very critical; N. Harding, *Leninism* (London, Macmillan, 1996) is excellent; the best study of the Cheka is G. Leggett, *The Cheka: Lenin's Political Police* (Oxford, Oxford University Press, 1981); T. H. Rigby, *Lenin's Government: Sovnarkom 1917–1922* (Cambridge, Cambridge University Press, 1979) is penetrating.

Stalin and Stalinism

R. McNeal, *Stalin: Man and Ruler* (London, Macmillan, 1988) is very good; R. Conquest, *Stalin: The Breaker of Nations* (Weidenfeld & Nicolson, London, 1991) is stimulating; A. Bullock, *Hitler and Stalin: Parallel Lives* (London, HarperCollins, 1991) is long and intriguing; D. Volkogonov, *Stalin: Triumph and Tragedy* (London, Weidenfeld & Nicolson, 1991) puts the case for the prosecution; I. Deutscher, *Stalin: A Political Biography*, 2nd edn (Oxford, Oxford University Press, 1972) is still worth perusing; R. Tucker, *Stalin as Revolutionary 1879–1929* (Cambridge, Cambridge University Press, 1973) and *Stalin in Power* (New York, W. W. Norton, 1990) attempt to penetrate Stalin's psyche and suggest Stalin modelled himself on Peter the Great and Ivan the Terrible; E. Radzinsky, *Stalin* (London, Hodder & Stoughton, 1996) uses new recently available sources. On Trotsky see I. Deutscher's three-volume work: including *The Prophet Armed 1921–1929* (Oxford, Oxford University Press, 1959); also B. Knei-Paz, *The Social and Political Thought of Leon Trotsky* (Oxford, Oxford University Press, 1978) is revealing; on Bukharin, see the sympathetic biography by S. F. Cohen, *Bukharin and the Bolshevik Revolution: A Political Biography 1888–1938* (Oxford, Oxford University Press, 1973) but it ignores the brutal side of Bukharin; M. Lewin's *Lenin's Last Struggle* (London, Faber & Faber, 1969) is excellent on Lenin and Stalin; N. Tumarkin, *Lenin Lives!* (Cambridge, MA, Harvard University Press, 1983) analyses the Lenin cult in fascinating detail. E. H. Carr, *The Russian Revolution from Lenin to Stalin* (London, Macmillan, 1979) is a useful summary; G. Gill, *Stalinism* (London, Macmillan, 1990) is a succinct summary; his *The*

Origins of the Stalinist Political System (Cambridge, Cambridge University Press, 1990) is more detailed; N. Lampert, *Stalinism: Its Nature and Aftermath* (London, Macmillan, 1991) is excellent and thought-provoking; M. McCauley, *Stalin and Stalinism*, 2nd edn (London, Longman, 1995) is a brief overview.

Industrialisation and collectivisation

E. H. Carr and R. W. Davies, *Foundations of a Planned Economy 1926–1929*, 2 vols (London, Macmillan, 1969); R. W. Davies, M. Harrison and S. G. Wheatcroft, eds, *The Economic Transformation of the Soviet Union 1913–1945* (Cambridge, Cambridge University Press, 1994) is a valuable statistical source; R. W. Davies, *The Industrialisation of Soviet Russia*, vol. 1: *The Socialist Offensive: The Collectivisation of Soviet Agriculture 1929–30* (London, Macmillan, 1980), vol. 2: *The Soviet Collective Farm* (London, Macmillan, 1980) and vol. 3: *The Soviet Economy in Turmoil 1929–30* (London, Macmillan, 1989) are detailed studies of the momentous decision to engage in forced collectivisation, a decision from which Soviet farming never recovered; compare M. Lewin, *Russian Peasants and Soviet Power* (New York, W. W. Norton, 1975), which is sympathetic to the peasants; S. Fitzpatrick, *Stalin's Peasants' Resistance and Survival in the Russian Village after Collectivisation* (New York, Oxford University Press, 1994) is essential reading; J. Hughes, *Stalin, Siberia and the Crisis of the New Economic Policy* (Cambridge, Cambridge University Press, 1991) considers a key area.

Nationalities, science and technology

R. E. Pipes, *The Formation of the Soviet Union*, 2nd edn (Cambridge, MA, Harvard University Press, 1954) analyses the important nationalities topic, a problem which was never solved; see also d'Encausse above; on the new technical elite see K. E. Bailes, *Technology and Society under Lenin and Stalin* (Princeton, NJ, Princeton University Press, 1978); on the important subject of science see his *Science in Russian Culture* (Bloomington, IN, Indiana University Press, 1990); N. Lampert, *The Technical Intelligentsia and the Soviet State* (London, Macmillan, 1979) examines managers and technicians; on the nefarious scientific and political influence of Lysenko see D. Joravsky, *The Lysenko Affair* (Cambridge, MA, Harvard University Press, 1970); Z. A. Medvedev, *The Rise and Fall of T. D. Lysenko* (New York, Columbia University Press, 1969) follows the career of Russia's greatest charlatan; R. Lewis, *Science and Industrialisation in the USSR* (London, Macmillan, 1979) considers scientific research 1917–40; for railway buffs J. N. Westwood, *Soviet Locomotive Technology during Industrialisation in the USSR* (London, Macmillan, 1982) is required reading.

Labour

D. Filtzer, *Soviet Workers and Stalinist Industrialization* (London, Pluto Press, 1986) is sympathetic to workers and sober reading for believers in Stalin's revolution; L. Siegelbaum, *Stakhanovism and the Politics of Productivity in the USSR* (Cambridge, Cambridge University Press, 1988) is a revealing study which underlines the fact that Stalin treated labour as a cheap resource; H. Kuromiya, *Stalin's Industrial Revolution: Politics and Workers* (Cambridge, Cambridge University Press, 1988) is good on the labour problems of the regime in the first Five Year Plan.

The Party and the purges

C. Merridale, *Moscow Politics and the Rise of Stalin* (London, Macmillan, 1990) examines the formative period of 1925–32; D. Thorniley, *The Rise and Fall of the Soviet Rural Communist Party 1927–1939* (London, Macmillan, 1988) demonstrates the growing urban attempt to control the countryside; on the history of the Communist Party, the most authoritative source is L. Schapiro, *The Communist Party of the Soviet Union*, 2nd edn (London, Eyre & Spottiswoode, 1970); see also G. Gill, *The Collapse of the Single-Party System* (Cambridge, Cambridge University Press, 1994); on the purges, R. Conquest, *The Great Terror* (London, Hutchinson, 1990) is the leader among those who believe that it was orchestrated from above; J. Arch Getty, *Origins of the Great Purges* (Cambridge, Cambridge University Press, 1985) is a leader among those who perceive the purges to be mainly from below, to replace conservative elites by more radical cadres; N. Mandelshtam, *Hope Against Hope* (Harmondsworth, Penguin, 1975) and *Hope Abandoned* (Harmondsworth, Penguin, 1976) are by someone who suffered the purges at first hand; E. S. Ginzburg, *Into the Whirlwind* (London, Collins, 1967) is a personal memoir of suffering; A. Solzhenitsyn, *The Gulag Archipelago 1918–1956* (London, Collins, 1974–78) is a multi-volume oeuvre by a leading Russian novelist.

Religion and law

W. Kolarz, *Religion in the Soviet Union* (London, Macmillan, 1961) is good on the sects; W. C. Fletcher, *The Russian Orthodox Church Underground 1917–1970* (Oxford, Oxford University Press, 1990) is a record of the illegal church; on the legal system 1917–39 see E. Huskey, *Russian Lawyers and the Soviet State* (Princeton, NJ, Princeton University Press, 1986).

Second World War 1941–45

Albert Axell, *Stalin's War Through the Eyes of His Commanders* (London, Arms and Aronour, 1997) includes personal interviews with top generals;

J. Erickson, *The Road to Stalingrad* (London, Weidenfeld & Nicolson, 1976) and *The Road to Berlin* (London, Weidenfeld & Nicolson, 1983) are detailed and authoritative; a good general account by an eyewitness is A. Werth, *Russia at War* (New York, Carroll and Graf, 1964); L. Goure, *The Siege of Leningrad* (Stanford, CA, Stanford University Press, 1962) relates a painful episode; H. Salisbury, *Leningrad* (London, Secker & Warburg, 1969) is immensely long; J. A. Armstrong, *Soviet Partisans in World War II* (Madison, WI, University of Wisconsin Press, 1964) examines an interesting topic; W. Strik-Strikfeld, *Against Stalin and Hitler* (London, Macmillan, 1970) presents the dilemma which faced many; C. Andreyev, *Vlasov and the Russian Liberation Movement* (Cambridge, Cambridge University Press, 1987) is good on the highest ranking turncoat in the Red Army; S. Newland, *Cossacks in the German Army 1941–1945* (London, Frank Cass, 1991) follows the fate of Russians who were never trusted by the Germans; M. Harrison, *Accounting for War: Soviet Production, Employment and the Defence Burden 1940–1945* (Cambridge, Cambridge University Press, 1996) is the definitive source; J. Barber and M. Harrison, *The Soviet Home Front 1941–1945* (London, Longman, 1992) is revealing on the effect of the war on ordinary people; W. Moskoff, *The Bread of Affliction* (Cambridge, Cambridge University Press, 1990) looks at rationing during the war; war memoirs are collected in S. Bialer, *Stalin and His Generals* (London, Souvenir, 1970).

High Stalinism 1945–53

T. Dunmore, *Soviet Politics 1945–1953* (London, Macmillan, 1984); his *The Stalinist Control Economy* (London, Macmillan, 1980) argues that the ministries had become stronger and Stalin could not command as before; W. G. Hahn, *Post-War Soviet Politics: The Fall of Zhdanov and the Defeat of Moderation 1946–53* (Ithaca, NY, Cornell University Press, 1982) sees Zhdanov as a moderate rejected by Stalin, prompted by Malenkov; W. O. McCagg, Jr., *Stalin Embattled 1943–1948* (Detroit, Wayne University Press, 1978) follows the above in suggesting Stalin did not command but concentrated on balancing interest groups; G. D. Ra'anan, *International Policy Formation in the USSR* (Hamden, CT, Archon Books, 1983) sees two competing foreign policies during these years; D. Marples, *Stalinism in Ukraine in the 1940s* (New York, St Martin's Press, 1991) examines collectivisation in western Ukraine; C. Kaplan, *The Party and Agricultural Crisis Management in the USSR* (Ithaca, NY, Cornell University Press, 1978) is revealing on the role of local Party secretaries in the late Stalin era; R. A. Medvedev, *Let History Judge* (London, Macmillan, 1972) and his *On Stalin and Stalinism* (New York, Columbia University Press, 1983) attack Stalin from a Leninist perspective; on nuclear power, D. Holloway, *Stalin and the Bomb* (New Haven, CT, Yale University Press, 1994) is the classic account; on the Jews, B. Pinkus, *The Soviet Government and the Jews, 1948–1967* (Cambridge, Cambridge University Press, 1967) and his *The Jews of the Soviet Union* (Cambridge, Cambridge University Press, 1988) are authoritative; Ia. Rapoport, *The Doctors' Plot* (London, Fourth Estate, 1991) is by one of the Jewish doctors involved; on literature, E. J. Brown, *Russian Literature since the Revolution* (Cambridge, MA, Harvard University Press, 1982) is useful; A. Kemp-Welch, *Stalin and the Literary Intelligentsia 1928–1939* (London, Macmillan, 1991) is good.

The Khrushchev era, 1953–64

The most up-to-date biography of Khrushchev is W. J. Tompson, *Khrushchev: A Political Life* (London, Macmillan, 1995); R. A. Medvedev, *Khrushchev* (Blackwell, Oxford, 1984) is by an insider; see also M. McCauley, ed., *Khrushchev and Khrushchevism* (London, Macmillan, 1987) and his *The Khrushchev Era 1953–1964* (London, Longman, 1995); J. G. Richter, *Khrushchev's Double Bind* (Baltimore, MD, Johns Hopkins University Press, 1994) is good on the interplay of domestic and foreign policy; R. Kolkowicz, *The Soviet Military and the Communist Party* (Princeton, NJ, Princeton University Press, 1967) reveals the tension between Khrushchev and the generals; John C. Ausland, *Kennedy, Khrushchev, and the Berlin-Cuba Crisis 1961–1964* (Scandinavian University Press, Oslo, 1996) examines the event which brought the world to the brink of a nuclear catastrophe; agriculture is covered by M. McCauley, *Khrushchev and the Virgin Lands Programme 1953–1964* (London, Macmillan, 1976); on housing see G. Andrusz, *Housing and Urban Development in the USSR* (London, Macmillan, 1984); on labour D. Filtzer, *The Khrushchev Era: De-Stalinization and the Limits of Reform in the USSR, 1953–1964* (London, Macmillan, 1993) is very good; on science see G. Fortescue, *The Communist Party and Soviet Science* (London, Macmillan, 1986) and P. Kneen, *Soviet Scientists and the State* (London, Macmillan, 1984); on literature M. Hayward and E. L. Crowley, eds, *Soviet Literature in the Sixties* (London, Methuin, 1965) is enjoyable; Khrushchev produced several entertaining volumes of memoirs; *Khrushchev Remembers*, 3 vols (Boston, MA, Little, Brown, 1970, 1974 and 1990); his son Sergei produced fascinating memoirs, *Khrushchev on Khrushchev: An Inside Account of the Man and his Era, by his Son* (Boston, MA, Little, Brown, 1992).

The Brezhnev era, 1964–85

There is no up-to-date biography of Brezhnev, a neat commentary on the man. G. W. Breslauer, *Khrushchev and Brezhnev as Leaders* (London, Macmillan, 1982) concentrates on authority building; D. Doder, *Shadows and Whispers* (London, Harrup, 1986) is good on the atmospherics of the twilight period of the early 1980s; on Andropov J. Steele and E. Abraham, *Andropov in Power* (Oxford, Robertson, 1983) and Z. Medvedev, *Andropov* (Oxford, Blackwell, 1983) are interesting; R. F. Byrnes, ed., *After Brezhnev: Sources of Soviet Conduct in the 1980s* (London, Pinter, 1983) is excellent; M. Matthews, *Class and Society in Soviet Russia* (London, Allen Lane, 1972) and his *Privilege in the Soviet Union: A Study of Elite Life-Styles under Communism* (London, Allen & Unwin, 1978) tackle important topics; A. McAuley, *Women's Work and Wages in the Soviet Union* (London, Allen & Unwin, 1981) is revealing on a neglected topic, and his *Economic Welfare in the Soviet Union: Poverty, Living Standards and Inequality* (London, Allen & Unwin, 1979) rewards study; A. W. Knight, *The KGB* (Boston, MA, Unwin Hyman, 1988) is excellent; J. Dunlop, *The Faces of Contemporary Russian Nationalism* (Stanford, CA, Stanford University Press, 1983) is first-class on an important topic; on dissent see P. Reddaway, *Uncensored Russia: The Human Rights Movement in the Soviet Union* (London, Cape, 1972), S. Bloch and P. Reddaway, *Russia's Political Hospitals* (New York, Basic Books, 1977) and M. S. Shatz, *Soviet Dissent in Historical Perspective* (Cambridge, Cambridge University Press, 1980).

The Gorbachev era, 1985–91

Mikhail Gorbachev, *Perestroika: New Thinking for Our Country and the World* (London, Collins, 1987) was immensely successful; his *Memoirs* (Doubleday, London, 1996) reveal the confusion of the last years of the Soviet Union; A. Brown, *The Gorbachev Factor* (Oxford, Oxford University Press, 1996) is an immensely scholarly case for the defence; V. Boldin, *Ten Years That Shook the World* (New York, Basic Books, 1995), by Gorbachev's Chief of Staff, puts the case for the prosecution; Y. Ligachev, *Inside Gorbachev's Kremlin* (Boulder, CO, Westview Press, 1996) is the case for conservative communism; A. S. Grachev, *Final Days: The Inside Story of the Collapse of the Soviet Union* (Boulder, CO, Westview Press, 1996), by Gorbachev's press secretary, is interesting and revealing; E. Shevardnadze, *The Future Belongs to Freedom* (London, Sinclair-Stevenson, 1991) was written hastily but is of some value; R. Gorbachev, *I Hope* (London, HarperCollins, 1991) is interesting; Jack F. Matlock, Jr., *Autopsy on an Empire* (New York, Random House, 1995), by the last US ambassador, is shrewd and very enjoyable; G. Ruge, *Gorbachev* (London, Chatto & Windus, 1991) is well informed; A. Sobchak, *For a New Russia* (London, HarperCollins, 1991) is by one of the stars of the democratic firmament who fell to earth in 1996; on history R. W. Davies, *Soviet History in the Gorbachev Revolution* (London, Macmillan, 1989) is rewarding; A. Nove, *Glasnost in Action* (Boston, MA, Unwin Hyman, 1989) is excellent; Geoffrey Hosking, *The Awakening of the Soviet Union* (London, Heineman, 1990) is good on social factors; V. Shlapentokh, *Public and Private Life of the Soviet*

People: Changing Values in Post-Stalin Russia (New York, Oxford University Press, 1989) is stimulating; on the travails of the economy, A. Åslund, *Gorbachev's Struggle for Economic Reform*, 2nd edn (London, Pinter, 1991) is by a leading pro-market western economist and, needless to say, finds Gorbachev sadly wanting; A. Aganbegyan, *The Challenge of Perestroika* (London, Hutchinson, 1988) is by the most influential economist in the early Gorbachev era; D. Filtzer, *Soviet Workers and the Collapse of Perestroika* (Cambridge, Cambridge University Press, 1994) reveals the problem facing Gorbachev; V. Tolz, *The USSR's Emerging Multiparty System* (New York, Praeger, 1991) is good on a complex subject; R. Sakwa, *Gorbachev and His Reforms 1985–1990* (London, Philip Allan, 1990); is a valuable source; S. White, *Gorbachev and After*, 3rd edn (Cambridge, Cambridge University Press, 1992) is comprehensive; J. Miller, *Mikhail Gorbachev and the End of Soviet Power* (London, Macmillan, 1993) is interesting but concentrates on political events; D. Remnick, *Lenin's Tomb: The Last Days of the Soviet Empire* (New York, Random House, 1993) is interesting; T. Zaslavskaya, *The Second Socialist Revolution: An Alternative Strategy* (London, I. B. Tauris, 1990) is revealing about the problems Gorbachev had to face; on the nationality question see A. J. Motyl, *Sovietology, Rationality, Nationality: Coming to Grips with Nationalism in the USSR* (New York, Columbia University Press, 1990) and his edited collection, *Thinking Theoretically about Soviet Nationalities* (New York, Columbia University Press, 1992); B. Nahaylo and Victor Swoboda, *Soviet Disunion: A History of the Nationalities Problem in the USSR* (London, Hamish Hamilton, 1990); G. Smith, ed., *The Nationalities Question in the Soviet Union* (London, Longman, 1990); G. W. Lapidus and V. Zaslavsky, eds, *From Union to Commonwealth: Nationalism and Separatism in the Soviet Republics* (Cambridge, Cambridge University Press, 1992); G. Suny, *The Revenge of the Past: Nationalism, Revolution and the Collapse of the Soviet Union* (Stanford, CA, Stanford University Press, 1993); Michael Urban, *The Rebirth of Politics in Russia* (Cambridge, Cambridge University Press, 1997) is very informative; see also G. Hosking, J. Aves and P. J. S. Duncan, eds, *The Road to Post-Communism: Independent Political Movements in the Soviet Union 1985–1991* (London, Pinter, 1992); on religion the leading study is M. Bourdeaux, *Gorbachev, Glasnost and the Gospel* (London, Hodder & Stoughton, 1990); on crime see A. Vaksberg, *The Soviet Mafia* (London, Weidenfeld & Nicolson, 1991) which provides many insights; on Gorbachev's summits with Reagan and Bush, R. L. Garthoff, *The Great Transition: American-Soviet Relations and the End of the Cold War* (Washington, DC, Brookings Institution Press, 1994) is valuable; C. D. Blacker, *Hostage to Revolution: Gorbachev and Soviet Security Policy, 1985–1991* (New York, Council on Foreign Relations, 1993) is excellent; S. Talbott, *At the Highest Levels: The Inside Story of the End of the Cold War* (London, Little, Brown, 1993) is revealing and valuable; M. McGwire, *Perestroika and Soviet National*

Security (Washington, DC, Brookings Institution Press, 1991) is well informed; C. Andrew and O. Gordievsky, *KGB: The Inside Story of its Foreign Operations from Lenin to Gorbachev* (London, Hodder & Stoughton, 1990) is as good as any spy thriller; M. Galeotti, *The Age of Anxiety: Security and Politics in Soviet and Post-Soviet Russia* (London, Longman, 1993) is a critical review; M. McCauley, *Gorbachev* (London, Longman, 1998) reassesses his record; Caroline McGiffert Ekedahl and Melvin A. Goodman, *The Wars of Eduard Shevardnadze* (London, Hurst, 1997) reveals how complex Gorbachev's foreign minister is.

Foreign policy, 1917–91

On foreign policy before 1945 the best overall survey is A. B. Ulam, *Expansion and Coexistence: Soviet Foreign Policy, 1917–73* (New York, Praeger, 1974); see also R. C. Raack, *Stalin's Drive to the West, 1938–1945* (Cambridge, Cambridge University Press, 1996), which argues that Stalin expected a general European war and that Hitler's war would lead to the internal collapse of the warring nations, clearing the way for soviet revolutions; on the period after 1945 the leader is J. L. Nogee and R. H. Donaldson, *Soviet Foreign Policy since World War II*, 4th edn (New York, Pergamon, 1992); S. Bailer, *The Soviet Paradox: External Expansion, Internal Decline* (London, I. B. Tauris, 1985) is good; S. R. Ashton, *The Politics of East–West Relations since 1945* (London, Macmillan 1989) is an excellent survey; any book by J. L. Gaddis is worth reading, especially *Russia, the Soviet Union and the United States*, 2nd edn (New York, McGraw-Hill, 1990) and *The Long Peace: Inquiries into the History of the Cold War* (Oxford, Oxford University Press, 1987); J. W. Young, *Cold War Europe 1945–89: A Political History* (London, Edward Arnold, 1991) is interesting; a briefer survey is M. McCauley, *The Origins of the Cold War 1941–1949*, 2nd edn (London, Longman, 1995); for a more detailed bibliography see J. W. Young, *The Longman Companion to Cold War and Détente* (London, Longman 1993). Ben Fowkes, *The Rise and Fall of Communism in Eastern Europe*, 2nd edn (London, Macmillan, 1995) is good.

The Yeltsin era, 1992–

On the Yeltsin era see B. Yeltsin, *Against the Grain: An Autobiography* (London, Jonathan Cape, 1990) and his *View from the Kremlin* (London, HarperCollins, 1994); J. Morrison, *Boris Yeltsin* (London, Penguin, 1991) is good; J. Steele, *Eternal Russia: Yeltsin, Gorbachev and the Mirage of Democracy* (London, Faber & Faber, 1994) is sceptical; A. Saikal and W. Maley, eds, *Russia in Search of its Future* (Cambridge, Cambridge University Press, 1995) is very good; on post-communist Russia there are several reference books: B. Szajkowski, ed., *Political Parties in Eastern Europe, Russia and the*

Successor States (London, Longman, 1994) provides detailed information on political parties in early 1994; M. McCauley, ed., *Directory of Russian MPs* (London, Longman, 1992) provides information on deputies in the Russian Supreme Soviet in April 1992; M. McCauley, ed., *Longman Biographical Directory of Decision Makers in Russia and the Successor States* (London, Longman, 1993) includes biographies of over 700 leading personalities; R. Sakwa, *Russian Politics and Society*, 2nd edn (London, Routledge, 1996) is the best textbook; A. Saikal and W. Maley, eds, *Russia in Search of its Future* (Cambridge, Cambridge University Press, 1995) is good; J. Dunlop, *The Rise of Russia and the Fall of the Soviet Empire* (Princeton, NJ, Princeton University Press, 1993) is stimulating; S. White, *After Gorbachev*, 4th edn (Cambridge, Cambridge University Press, 1994) is comprehensive; S. White, A. Pravda and Z. Gitelman, eds, *Developments in Soviet and Post-Soviet Politics* (London, Macmillan, 1994) includes interesting material; T. Remington, ed., *Parliaments in Transition* (Boulder, CO, Westview Press, 1994) has excellent material on Russia; J. Hough *et al.*, *The 1996 Russian Presidential Election* (Washington, DC, Brookings Institution Press, 1996) is succinct and informative; A. Åslund, *How Russia Became a Market Economy* (Washington, DC, Brookings Institution Press, 1995) is a positive evaluation of events; L. D. Nelson and I. Y. Kuzes, *Property to the People: The Struggle for Radical Economic Reform in Russia* (Armonk, New York, M. E. Sharpe, 1994) is an eye-opener; G. Fiorentini and S. Peltzman, eds, *The Economics of Organised Crime* (Cambridge, Cambridge University Press, 1996) includes a revealing chapter on Russia; N. Malcolm, A. Pravda, R. Allison and M. Light, *Internal Factors in Russian Foreign Policy* (Oxford, Oxford University Press, 1997) is illuminating.

The Commonwealth of Independent States (CIS)

K. Dawisha and B. Parrot, *Russia and the New States of Eurasia* (Cambridge, Cambridge University Press, 1994) is very informative; I. Bremner and R. Taras, eds, *New Nations New Politics* (Cambridge, Cambridge University Press, 1997) is the leader in the field.

SECTION EIGHT

Maps

Map 1 Political–administrative map of the USSR until 1991
Source: M. McCauley, *The Soviet Union 1917–1991* (London, Longman, 1993)

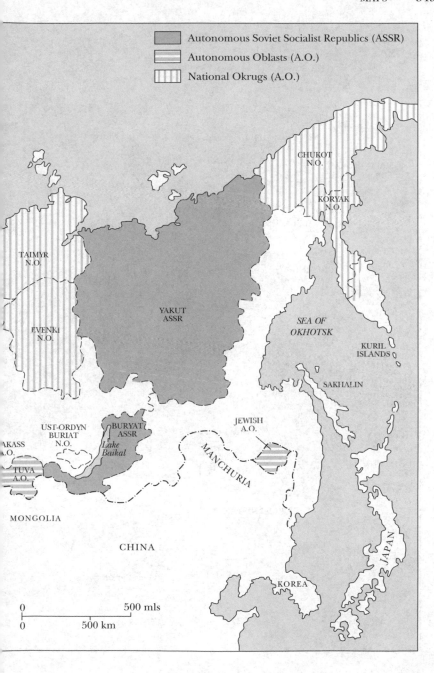

Map 2 The Commonwealth of Independent States
Source: Russia and the Successor States Briefing Service.

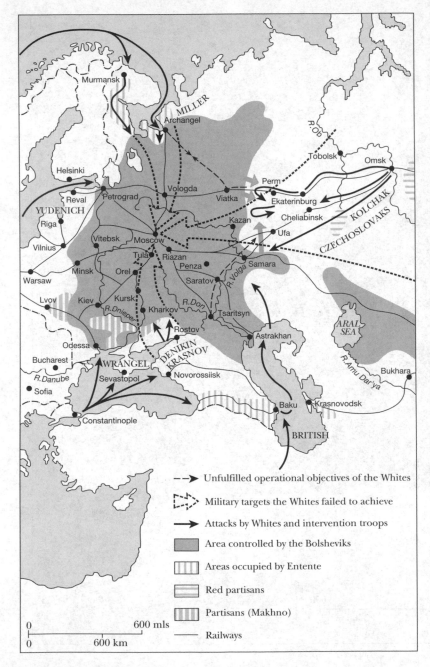

Map 3 The Civil War
Source: M. McCauley, *The Soviet Union 1917–1991* (London, Longman, 1993)

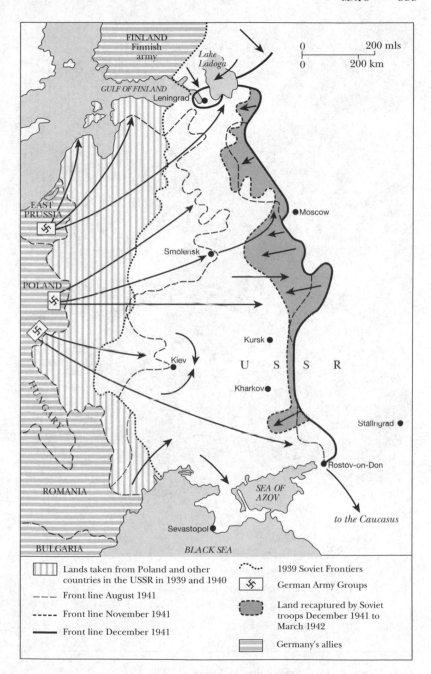

Map 4 The German invasion of the USSR, 1941–42
Source: M. McCauley, *The Soviet Union 1917–1991* (London, Longman, 1993)

Map 5 Soviet territorial gains in Europe 1939–1949
Source: M. McCauley, *The Soviet Union 1917–1991* (London, Longman, 1993)

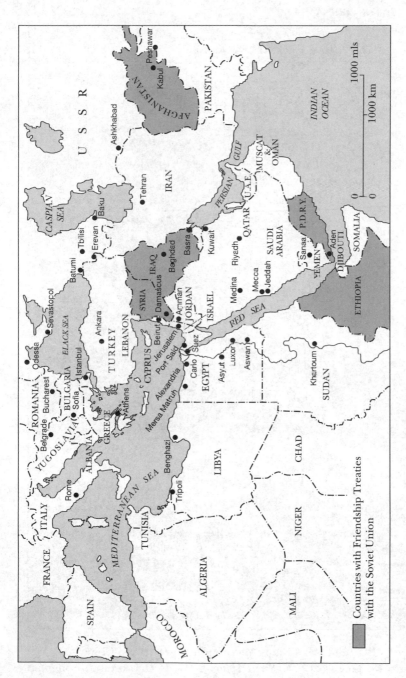

Map 6 The Soviet Union and the Middle East
Source: M. McCauley, *The Soviet Union 1917–1991* (London. Longman, 1993)

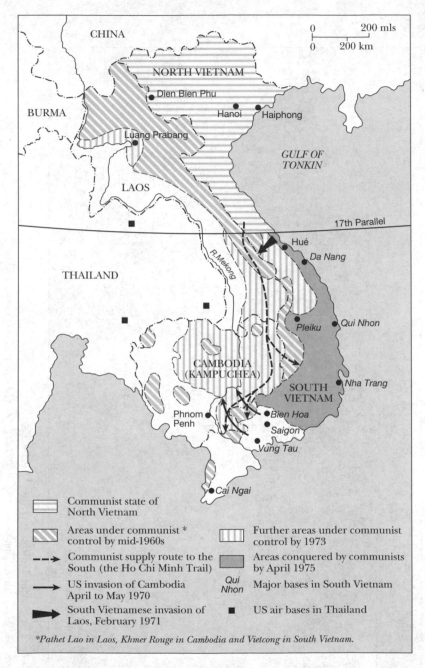

Map 7 War and the advance of communism in Indo-China
Source: M. McCauley, *The Soviet Union 1917–1991* (London, Longman, 1993)

Index

BAKER & TAYLOR